This book examines the life of cardinal Francesco Soderini (1453–1524) from a variety of perspectives and using a range of techniques. It analyses the relationship between Machiavelli, Piero and Francesco Soderini, and reinstates the crucial role played by Rome and contacts with Rome in late fifteenth-century and early sixteenth-century Florentine politics. Soderini's position as one of the chief powerbrokers of papal Rome, in opposition to the Medici, enables a reappraisal of political and ecclesiastical patronage and clientele systems. The cardinal also encouraged cultural, intellectual and building activities. Overall, through its collation of archival sources in and outside Italy, a new vision emerges of the lifestyle and activities of a learned and politically astute Italian cardinal.

CAMBRIDGE STUDIES IN ITALIAN HISTORY AND CULTURE

CHURCH AND POLITICS IN RENAISSANCE ITALY

CHURCH AND POLITICS IN RENAISSANCE ITALY

THE LIFE AND CAREER OF
CARDINAL FRANCESCO SODERINI (1453–1524)

K. J. P. LOWE

Lecturer in Modern History,
University of Birmingham

CAMBRIDGE
UNIVERSITY PRESS

Published by the Press Syndicate of the University of Cambridge
The Pitt Building, Trumpington Street, Cambridge CB2 1RP
40 West 20th Street, New York, NY 10011-4211, USA
10 Stamford Road, Oakleigh, Melbourne 3166, Australia

First published 1993

Printed in Great Britain at the University Press, Cambridge

A catalogue record for this book is available from the British Library

Library of Congress cataloguing in publication data
Lowe, K. J. P.
Church and politics in renaissance Italy: the life and career of cardinal Francesco Soderini,
1453–1524 / K. J. P. Lowe.
p.   cm. (Cambridge Studies in Italian history and culture)
Includes bibliographical references.
ISBN 0 521 42103 9
1. Soderini, Francesco, 1453–1524.   2. Cardinals – Italy – Biography.   3. Florence (Italy) –
Politics and government – 1421–1737.   4. Medici, House of.   I. Title.   II. Series.
BX4705.S66419L69   1993
282.092 – dc20   92-33576 CIP
[B]

ISBN 0 521 42103 9 hardback

BX
4705
.S66419
L69
1993

CONTENTS

ILLUSTRATIONS

ACKNOWLEDGEMENTS

Many, many people have helped me with Soderini over the years, and a significant number have involved themselves beyond the obligations of friendship or duty. Of these, I would particularly like to thank David Chambers and Nicolai Rubinstein. Ian Bavington Jones, Richard Gaskin, Simon Gayford, Maggy Lee, Amanda Lillie and Christine Wong all contributed greatly in one way or another. Conte Luciano Soderini very kindly gave me permission to use his family archive. William Davies and Annie Jackson provided expert editorial advice at Cambridge University Press. My greatest debt of gratitude is to the staff, both past and present, of the libraries and archives in which I have worked.

ABBREVIATIONS

Add MSS	Additional manuscripts
AG	Archivio Gonzaga
Arch.	Archivio
Arch. cap.	Archivio capitolare
Arch. cap. S. P.	Archivio capitolare di S. Pietro in Vaticano
Arch. com.	Archivio comunale
Arch. episc.	Archivio episcopale
Arch. Sod.	Archivio Soderini
AS	Archivio di Stato
ASBo	Archivio di Stato, Bologna
ASF	Archivio di Stato, Florence
ASMa	Archivio di Stato, Mantua
ASMi	Archivio di Stato, Milan
ASMo	Archivio di Stato, Modena
ASPal	Archivio di Stato, Palermo
ASPi	Archivio di Stato, Pisa
ASR	Archivio di Stato, Rome
ASSi	Archivio di Stato, Siena
AV	Archivio Segreto Vaticano
b.	busta
Barb. lat.	MSS Barberini
BL	British Library
BNF	Biblioteca Nazionale, Florence
BV	Biblioteca Apostolica Vaticana
Canc.	Cancelleria
concist.	concistoriale
Cons. e prat.	Consulte e pratiche
C. Strozz.	Carte Strozziane
Delib.	Deliberazioni
fasc.	fascicolo

GC	Ginori Conti
Leg. e com.	Legazioni e commisarie
Lib.	Liber, libro
Magl.	Magliabechiana
MAP	Medici avanti il principato
miscell.	miscellanea
Miss.	Missive
no.	number
Not. antecos.	Notarile antecosimiano
Obl. et sol.	Obligationes et solutiones
Otto di prat.	Otto di pratica
Ottob. lat.	MSS Ottoboniani
pubbl.	pubblici
Reg. sup.	Regesta supplicationum
Reg. vat.	Regesta vaticana
repubblic.	repubblicana
Resp.	Responsive
Sig.	Signori
SPE	Sforzesco, Potenze estere
Vat. lat.	MSS Vaticani latini
vicecanc.	vicecancellarii

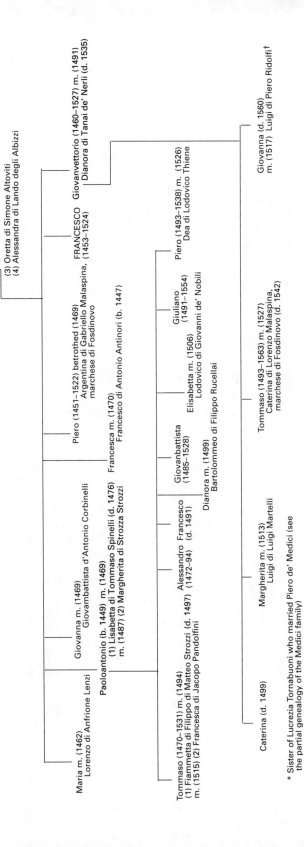

Tommaso di Lorenzo Soderini (1403–85) m. (1) Maria di Giuliano Torrigiani
(2) Dianora di Francesco Tornabuoni (d. 1462)*
(3) Oretta di Simone Altoviti
(4) Alessandra di Lando degli Albizzi

Maria m. (1462)
Lorenzo di Anfrione Lenzi

Giovanna m. (1469)
Giovambattista d'Antonio Corbinelli

Paoloantonio (b. 1449) m. (1469)
(1) Lisabetta di Tommaso Spinelli (d. 1476)
m. (1487) (2) Margherita di Strozza Strozzi

Tommaso (1470–1531) m. (1494)
(1) Fiammetta di Filippo di Matteo Strozzi (d. 1497)
m. (1515) (2) Francesca di Jacopo Pandolfini

Alessandro   Francesco
(1472–94)   (d. 1491)

Giovanbattista
(1485–1528)

Dianora m. (1499)
Bartolommeo di Filippo Rucellai

Giuliano
(1491–1554)

Elisabetta m. (1506)
Lodovico di Giovanni de' Nobili

Piero (1451–1522) betrothed (1469)
Argentina di Gabriello Malaspina,
marchese di Fosdinovo

Francesca m. (1470)
Francesco di Antonio Antinori (b. 1447)

FRANCESCO
(1453–1524)

Giovanvettorio (1460–1527) m. (1491)
Dianora di Tanai de' Nerli (d. 1535)

Piero (1493–1538) m. (1526)
Dea di Lodovico Thiene

Giovanna (d. 1560)
m. (1517) Luigi di Piero Ridolfi†

Tommaso (1493–1563) m. (1527)
Caterina di Lorenzo Malaspina,
marchese di Fosdinovo (d. 1542)

Margherita m. (1513)
Luigi di Luigi Martelli

Caterina (d. 1499)

* Sister of Lucrezia Tornabuoni who married Piero de' Medici (see
the partial genealogy of the Medici family)

† See the partial genealogy of the Medici family

Partial genealogy of the Soderini family based on Litta and
the MSS Passerini.

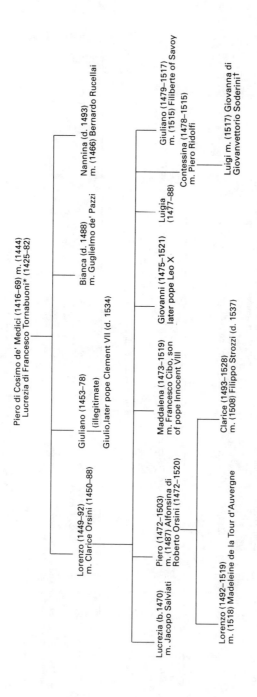

Piero di Cosimo de' Medici (1416–69) m. (1444)
Lucrezia di Francesco Tornabuoni* (1425–82)

Lorenzo (1449–92)
m. Clarice Orsini (1450–88)

Giuliano (1453–78)
(illegitimate)
Giulio, later pope Clement VII (d. 1534)

Bianca (d. 1488)
m. Guglielmo de' Pazzi

Nannina (d. 1493)
m. (1466) Bernardo Rucellai

Lucrezia (b. 1470)
m. Jacopo Salviati

Piero (1472–1503)
m. (1487) Alfonsina di
Roberto Orsini (1472–1520)

Maddalena (1473–1519)
m. Francesco Cibo, son
of pope Innocent VIII

Giovanni (1475–1521)
later pope Leo X

Luigia
(1477–88)

Giuliano (1479–1517)
m. (1515) Filiberte of Savoy

Contessina (1478–1515)
m. Piero Ridolfi

Lorenzo (1492–1519)
m. (1518) Madeleine de la Tour d'Auvergne

Clarice (1493–1528)
m. (1508) Filippo Strozzi (d. 1537)

Luigi m. (1517) Giovanna di
Giovanvettorio Soderini†

* Sister of Dianora Tornabuoni who married Tommaso Soderini
(see the partial genealogy of the Soderini family)

†See the partial genealogy of the Soderini family

Partial genealogy of the Medici family based on Litta,
the MSS Passerini and Pieraccini.

INTRODUCTION

Because of the wealth of records available and the complex structure of the Florentine political system, recent Florentine political history has concentrated upon internal matters; it has concerned itself primarily with microstudies either of relatively short chronological periods or with more and more intensive studies of groupings, areas or families. But although much of the analysis focuses on a period of Florentine history during which the fortunes of the Florentine state cannot be understood outside an international context, the implications of this statement have not been examined. While the purely diplomatic history of the period continues to attract attention, the way in which links between particular individuals, families and regimes, and foreign powers, interacted with and played a large part in shaping the course of Florentine politics, has been largely ignored. In order to study this subject it is necessary, in particular, to reinstate the crucial role played by Rome, and contacts with Rome, in Florentine politics. For if Italy had become the cockpit of European politics, one of the major centres of the European political system was Rome. Its standing as the capital of christendom and the engagement in politics of a succession of popes, taken in conjunction with the considerable wealth and patronage which ecclesiastical office could bestow upon its holders, all ensured that influence at Rome became a political asset of the greatest importance in late fifteenth- and early sixteenth-century Italy.

Despite this, both the nature of the links between Florence and Rome and the lifestyle and activities of the powerbrokers of papal Rome have remained virtually unexplored by historians of the renaissance. This book seeks to throw light on both these basic problems through an analysis of the life of one person – cardinal Francesco Soderini. The critical role played in his career first by his links with the French monarchy and second by his independent status as a curia cardinal, together with his close identification with the regime of his brother

Piero, combine to make him an excellent example of the interplay between Florentine politics, influence at Rome and connections with the wider European political system. Similarly, his conduct after the fall of the Florentine republic shows clearly the way in which Florentine politics cannot be understood outside a context broader than that provided by a concentration on events inside Florence itself. In the long term, an examination of Soderini's circumstances demonstrates how the power disputes of renaissance politics shifted from Florence to Rome, and anticipates, in several senses, the subsequent shift of battlefield from Rome to Paris which can be seen to have taken place later in the sixteenth century after the election of Clement VII.

It is normally assumed that a sequence of well-defined and well-known family rivalries and factions, such as Medici versus Soderini, Guelph versus Ghibelline, Valois versus Hapsburg, and Orsini versus Colonna, dictated political behaviour and groupings in renaissance Italy. While this is true at one level, this book demonstrates that overlapping or partially coinciding interests, or individual antagonisms, often resulted in realignment. These sets of oppositions were more fluid and dynamic than they have traditionally been presented, with pairings and re-pairings constantly evolving. A system of priorities, which themselves were susceptible to change, could subvert the expected and cause very unlikely temporary alliances. In practice, this meant that families did not by any means always function as a collective unit, but individuals arrayed themselves in a more subtle arrangement across the various sides of the dispute or alignment. Sometimes the point of contact between people from opposing family rivalries was that they had an important adversary in common. Relations between these families, factions and groupings were, in consequence, a volatile mixture of tension and accommodation, aggression and rapprochement.

It is therefore essential that an investigation of the life of one Florentine renaissance patrician who became a prince of the church should look at him in the context of his family and city. The Soderini were exceptional in this regard because they seem to have functioned particularly well as a unit; the Medici or the Colonna, by contrast, had renegade members. Francesco's branch of the Soderini was a relatively compact group with few contacts in other branches. Vital to an understanding of his life is an appreciation of Soderini family strategy which, although it promoted rigorous opposition to the Medici after the setting up of the republic, and even more so after 1502, found it necessary at certain vital moments to act in collaboration with the family's most pronounced enemies and sometime cousins from Florence, the Medici. Francesco's most famous brother, Piero, had a career as *gonfaloniere a vita* in Florence which has attracted considerable attention, but Piero's life in Rome has remained obscured. A new emphasis on the nature of fraternal relations in general is paralleled in this book by the consideration that the bond between Francesco and Piero must have been one of unusual closeness based on a convergence of interest and a lack of jealousy. No instance is known when Francesco and Piero publicly took opposite sides in a dispute of any sort. Various of the Soderini nieces and nephews, including those born to Francesco's sisters, also played their part in the furtherance of Soderini family strategy.

The rationale behind the choice of Francesco Soderini as the hinge upon which this study is hung should be clear. Illumination of the mechanics of the Florence/Rome axis necessitated a Florentine with important political connections in his home city who pursued a successful career at the papal court and provoked international regard. Within these structures, the church was the ideal backdrop and a cardinal an exemplary subject. Soderini was the only Florentine elevated to the cardinalate between Giovanni de' Medici in 1489 and a flock of Medici supporters in 1517. His and his family's links to the French monarchy were another crucial determinant in the equation.

The question which is most often asked about a biography of a member of a recognisable group is the extent to which the individual was typical. Whereas a stereotype of a renaissance cardinal is available, it would be unwise to attempt to write of a so-called typical cardinal. Given the restricted number and nature of the cardinalate, these prelates had certain features in common, but these were just as often a result of their office rather than a cause for it. Soderini's circumstances were exceptional even if his red hat was acquired for the conventional renaissance reasons of dynastic clout, influential friends and the availability of large sums of money. He performed his cardinalitial duties, and the lifestyle he adopted conformed to notions of expected largesse and consumption. However, within these confines there was considerable room for choice. Although it would have been slightly unusual, Soderini could have chosen to devote his energies to spiritual matters; instead he channelled them into Florentine politics and ecclesiastical affairs. Some cardinals became great patrons of art or collectors of antiquities; Soderini spent money on building and altering palaces and acquiring real estate. Instead of trying to ascertain what constitutes a typical cardinal, this book attempts to demonstrate that Soderini made choices about his lifestyle in the same way that he took decisions about his political life: on the basis of need, inclination, habit or duty. As a result, it could be argued that, in many important respects, there can be no typical cardinal, although a plurality of certain recognisable types does emerge.

After explaining the selection of topic and person, the matter of format still remains. By presenting a combination of narrative, thematic and case-study approaches, this book offers a model for showing how one life can be used to illuminate the renaissance as a whole. Soderini's longevity was a bonus in this respect for, as an adult in the political sphere, he witnessed the gamut of governments in Florence from Lorenzo de' Medici (1469–92) through the republic to Giulio de' Medici, and his period in the cardinalate spanned the reigns of six pontiffs. The variety of his political life also meant that he met most of the famous people of his time, from the relevant Medici, to Machiavelli, to the Borgia, to the kings and queens of France. Likewise, he met the important begetters of art and culture or at least knew, saw and read their artefacts and works. Living through the renaissance as a member of a series of elites, Soderini was literally surrounded by people whose names are still known to us five hundred years later. While his relations with these famous and talented people will always excite interest, it is the underlying structures and patterns of Soderini's life that are most crucial for an understanding of the renaissance.

One benefit of a not merely political biography is that the constantly shifting focus of this telescopic approach can reveal a blurring of boundaries between different sectors of Soderini's activities. Art, culture and politics were often inextricable one from the other, and the same characters reappeared in diverse roles. The private and the public life are not two separate entities but two parts of the same whole; rigid divisions of this kind often prove to be false and unhelpful. A narrative of sorts of the political life of Soderini is counterbalanced by kaleidoscopic regroupings which concentrate upon ecclesiastical and curial affairs and various other thematic aspects of his non-political life in the hope that a final summation would not be able to separate the parts. This approach does mean, however, that there is no single chronology but instead a weaving of dates and information when and where necessary, and occasionally the reader will have to wait for later chapters to receive a more complete picture of events.

It is perhaps misleading even to have raised the notion of a biography, for in the absence of continuous personal papers, letters and diaries, those wishing to reconstruct the life of a renaissance Italian are dependent for information upon the individual's having led an active public life and a noteworthy or notorious private one. Once again, the particular combination of Florentine patrician and statesman, bishop and cardinal proved remarkably fruitful. The archives of Florence, Rome and the

Vatican, when used to complement each other, yield a richness of documentation which can disguise the fact that Soderini's own records have not survived. This material was especially successful for the reconstruction of the official life of a renaissance cardinal and the maintenance of the Medici–Soderini struggle after 1512.

But it would be foolish to deny that Soderini's life would undoubtedly appear very different if it were possible to have access to his own thoughts and opinions. Dependence on mainly non-personal sources creates fallow periods when little or nothing is recorded, and a bias which is difficult to correct. The letters and records of other people at best can only attribute motive, often on the basis of little understanding. Many plans, strategies and connections must be lost to view. The most obvious points about Soderini as a person are often guessed at through oblique references in out-of-the-way places. The reconstruction of Soderini's life in this book has attempted to make a virtue out of necessity by concentrating upon those aspects about which most can be known, such as church affairs and building; ideally, much fuller sections would have been possible on areas such as Soderini's friends and his literary and scholarly life. In the happy event of more information coming to light in the future, there is plenty of room for it to take its place on the no longer quite so skeletal outline of Soderini's life. But it should never be forgotten that, although an exposition of Soderini's life is an end in itself, it is the wider context of the political and ecclesiastical world of the Italian renaissance which that life illuminates that is the real subject of the book.

PART I

PREPARATION FOR POWER:
SODERINI'S FLORENTINE BACKGROUND
AND EARLY CAREER

CHAPTER I

SODERINI'S EARLY YEARS

FAMILY AND MEDICEAN CONNECTIONS

Francesco di Tommaso Soderini, the subject of this study, was born on 10 June 1453 in the *gonfalone* of Drago, *quartiere* of S. Spirito in Florence.[1] His parents were Tommaso di Lorenzo Soderini and Dianora di Francesco Tornabuoni (d. 16 March 1462), both children of illustrious houses. Dianora was the second and most important of Tommaso's four wives: Maria di Giuliano Torrigiani, Dianora, Oretta di Simone Altoviti and Alessandra di Lando degli Albizzi. She was also the mother of his four most famous sons: Paolantonio (b.1449), Piero (b.1451), Francesco (b.1453)[2] and Giovanvettorio (b.1460).

The genealogist Passerini traces the Soderini back to one Soderino Soderini who was dead by 1268. In 1484 the family were characterised as belonging to the group of 'ancient non-magnate families which run the regime' ('case popolane antiche che hanno il reggimento') in Piero Guicciardini's phrase,[3] one category below the ancient magnate families in a hierarchy of breeding but far more successful than the magnates in terms of voting support.[4] Passerini calculated that from the ranks of the Soderini had come sixteen standard-bearers (*gonfalonieri*) and thirty-four priors, that is, communal officials of the highest rank, and it was for their political activity, rather than for their nobility, that the Soderini were famed.

---

[1] ASF, Tratte 443 bis (Libro dell'età II, secolo XV), 20v.

[2] There had been an earlier child named Francesco who had died; names were often re-used in fifteenth century Florence. See C. Klapisch-Zuber, 'Le nom "refait". La transmission des prénoms à Florence (XIVe–XVIe siècles)', *L'homme*, 20 (1980), pp. 85 and 93.

[3] N. Rubinstein, *The government of Florence under the Medici, 1434–1494* (Oxford, 1966), p. 323, Piero Guicciardini on the scrutiny of 1484.

[4] *Ibid.*, pp. 214–15.

Francesco's great-great-grandfather, Guccio (d.1365), was a great-grandson of Soderino. He seems to have embodied virtues which were to become hallmarks of the Soderini: a respect and ability for public office, a concern for the mechanics of government, a view of Florence's sphere of influence which encompassed not only the countryside around the city (*contado*) and subject towns but also other states such as Milan. The life of his son Tommaso (d.1402) combined other elements which were to be familiar to later Soderini. He passed a significant proportion of his life away from Florence in Avignon where he headed a successful commercial firm. Involved in the political life of the commune in the 1370s, he suffered a reversal of fortune during the Ciompi revolt but returned to Florence in 1381 to resume his political career. His illegitimate and favourite son, Lorenzo, was executed in 1405 when it was discovered that he had forged documents in an attempt to prove that his father had contracted a marriage with his mother, a well-known Avignonese prostitute, Serena de Beraut de Cumengen, in 1361.[5] Lorenzo's two sons, Niccolò and Tommaso (Francesco's father), despite their unpropitious start, also pursued commerce and politics, sharing a business partnership with a member of the Rucellai family and embarking on divergent political careers, relying on the good name of Soderini.

Tommaso went from being an orphan to being the second most important man in Florence.[6] He achieved this by exploiting Medici patronage to the full. Only once did he waver in his allegiance to the Medici, after Lorenzo di Piero's succession,[7] and when he realised that opposition was pointless, he adopted the opposite tack of ingratiating himself and managed to keep his authority intact. As Paula Clarke has shown,[8] one of the crucial points in this ascent came when Tommaso married Dianora Tornabuoni around 1441–2, the marriage having been planned by Cosimo de' Medici whose eldest son Piero was to marry Dianora's sister Lucrezia.[9] Cosimo may have foreseen that Piero's succession would depend upon Tommaso's support and may therefore have sought to bind the two together as closely as possible.[10] Tommaso was important not only to Cosimo, but to Piero and Lorenzo de' Medici, and Lorenzo de' Medici in turn was to reward Tommaso by helping his sons. Tommaso had an extraordinarily successful career in

---

[5] It is possible that Lorenzo's father was not Tommaso but the archbishop of Aix whom he was said to resemble.

[6] For an account of his rise, see P. Clarke, *The Soderini and the Medici* (Oxford, 1991), pp. 16–94.   [7] *Ibid.*, pp. 180–209.   [8] *Ibid.*, pp. 30–2.

[9] D. Silvano Razzi, *Vita di Piero Soderini* (Padua, 1737), p. 167.

[10] *Ibid.*, p. 32.

politics (he was *gonfaloniere* five times: in 1449, 1454, 1460, 1467 and 1479) and diplomacy, and Francesco was brought up in considerable security and comfort in the family palace, which stood in what is now the Via S. Spirito in the *quartiere* of the same name.[11]

Francesco's mother, Dianora, also came from a leading Florentine family, the Tornabuoni, who had been magnates and Tornaquinci until the end of the fourteenth century, but some of whom had then chosen to change their name to Tornabuoni and to be eligible for office rather than keep magnate status and be exempted from political power. Dianora's father, Francesco, was a merchant and minor political figure who was pleased both by Cosimo's exile in 1433 and by his return in 1434. One of her brothers, Giovanni, was head of the Medici bank in Rome and also papal depositor general and so spent much of his life in Rome.[12] Tommaso Soderini created him and his brother, Alfonso, executors of his wills of 10 March 1462 and 9 July 1470.[13] In 1480 and 1484 Giovanni was a member of the same embassies to the pope as Francesco Soderini, and his allegiance to the Medici and their support of him benefited him in almost the same way as they had for Tommaso Soderini.

In the 1446 *catasto* Tommaso declared Dianora's age as twenty-four.[14] There is no information about the education of the Tornabuoni girls[15] but Lucrezia, perhaps as a result of the Medici stimulus, perhaps as a result of childhood schooling, wrote religious lives in Italian and *laude* in Latin.[16] As far as is known, Dianora did not write anything. Seven of the children of Tommaso and Dianora survived into adulthood. They were, in descending order of age: Maria, Paolantonio, Giovanna (Nanna), Francesca, Piero, Francesco and Giovanvettorio.

Very little is known about Francesco's early life. It is likely that, in contrast to their father who had probably been trained for a commercial life, the four boys were educated in the more prestigious humanist style. It is known that Piero and Giovanvettorio went to Giorgio Antonio

---

[11] *Ibid.*, p. 51. It is depicted in the map of Florence of c.1470 by Piero del Massaio, L. Ginori Lisci, *I palazzi di Firenze* (Florence, 1972) I, p. 30. See also Clarke, *The Soderini*, pp. 115–16 and 128.

[12] P. Litta, 'Tornabuoni di Firenze', in P. Litta, L. Passserini Orsini de Rilli, F. Oderici, F. Stefani, *Celebri famiglie italiane* (Milan/Turin, 1819–99), table II, and R. de Roover, *The rise and decline of the Medici bank, 1397–1494* (Cambridge, Mass., 1963), p. 198.

[13] ASF, Not. antecos. M570, 90v (10 March 1461) and M570, 190v (9 July 1470).

[14] ASF, Catasto 655, 167r.

[15] See G. Levantini-Pieroni, *Lucrezia Tornabuoni* (Florence, 1888), p. 25 and B. Felice, 'Donne Medicee avanti il principato', *Rassegna nazionale*, 146 (1905), p. 646.

[16] See F. Pezzarossa, *I poemetti sacri di Lucrezia Tornabuoni* (Florence, 1978).

Vespucci, a friar at S. Marco, to receive lessons in Latin grammar,[17] and so it is probable that Francesco, who was the brother in between, went too. Of the four, the only one who definitely knew Greek was the youngest Giovanvettorio, who is described by Naldo Naldi, in a poem addressed to him, as expert in Latin and knowledgeable in Greek, as are those who have studied Virgil and Quintilian, and read and enjoyed Homer and Hesiod.[18] Piero never showed any sign that he read Greek, but his time with Vespucci allows him to qualify as a student of *litterae humaniores*.[19] It is not known what Paolantonio studied but he certainly knew Latin. Nor is there any evidence to suggest that Francesco knew Greek although he must have known Latin well by the time he went to university. All four, therefore, learnt Latin as children, which in the case of the two older ones, who were politicians and ambassadors, was extremely useful, and in the case of the two younger ones – a teacher of civil law turned ecclesiastic, and an arts student who became a professor of law – was a prerequisite for success in their careers.

Tommaso arranged matches, with the consent of Lorenzo de' Medici, for his and Dianora's children[20] with the offspring of other Florentine patrician families. Paolantonio married a Spinelli and then a Strozzi, and Giovanvettorio married a daughter of Tanai dei Nerli. His three daughters from the marriage married into the Lenzi, the Corbinelli and the Antinori respectively.[21] Only Piero's wife, Argentina, came from a non-Florentine family: the Malaspina counts of Fosdinovo in the Lunigiana.[22]

ACADEMIC LIFE, 1472–8

Francesco Soderini probably first became a student of law in 1472 when he went to the university of Bologna at the beginning of the academic year.[23] He was then nineteen. It was the last year in which students

---

[17] See A. Vespucci, *Lettera a Piero Soderini* (Florence, 1957), p. 5, written from Lisbon in 1504: 'ricordandomi come nel tempo della nostra gioventù vi ero amico, et hora servitore, et andavamo ad udire i principii di gramatica sotto la buona vita e dottrina del venerabile religioso frate di S. Marco, frate Giorgio Antonio Vespucci, mio zio', and A. Verde, *Lo studio fiorentino, 1473–1503* (Florence/Pistoia, 1973–85), III, I, p. 569.   [18] BNF, Magl. VII, 1057, 37r.   [19] Verde, *Lo studio*, III, II, p. 813.

[20] See Clarke, *The Soderini*, pp. 138–42.

[21] See BNF, MSS Passerini 44, table 6 and R. Wedgewood Kennedy, *Alessio Baldovinetti* (New Haven, 1938), p. 133.

[22] On the marriages of the Soderini sons, see L. Passerini, 'Soderini di Firenze', in Litta et al, *Celebri famiglie*, tables V, VI and VII.

[23] BNF, Magl. XXI, 155, 114r. The volume is a miscellany of prose and verse from the fifteenth century, written in the main by two different hands, one in red and one in black ink. In red is written: 'Francesco di messere Tomaso Soderini e compagnia lananioli, è studiante buono e d'assai e vertuoso in sua età', and in black: 'A dì

coming from areas under Florentine jurisdiction were allowed to study at a *studio* other than that of Florence–Pisa. In December 1472 a law was passed, at the instigation of Lorenzo de' Medici, setting out guidelines for the transfer of all faculties of the *studio* except grammar and rhetoric, from Florence to Pisa.[24] This was followed, in July 1473, by a law ordering all those studying away from Florence to return home by September and go on to study at Pisa, or face a fine of 500 *fiorini larghi* and other punitive measures.[25] Bologna had the most famous faculty of law in Italy but Soderini, with many others, obeyed the patriotic if restrictive call, and returned to the fold. The *studio* reopened in Pisa on 1 November 1473 and it is likely that Soderini was present.

It would appear from a series of fulsome comments from his friend, Marsilio Ficino, that Soderini was regarded as an outstanding student. In a letter to one of his teachers, Pier Filippo da Corneo, Ficino complimented Pier Filippo on being the ideal of a man of law and commented that Soderini was well on the way to emulating him.[26] Pier Filippo taught only civil law[27] and there is no evidence that Soderini was studying anything but civil law at this date. Indeed, Ficino specifically praised his achievements as a student of civil law[28] and in a letter of mid-December 1477 hailed him as 'iuriscivilis peritissimus'.

It is now certain that Soderini stayed on at the university of Pisa to teach civil law himself.[29] This is confirmed by a statement of Marco

[lacuna] di novembre 1472 andò allo studio a Bologna'. It is not clear which, if any, of the poems were composed by Soderini. P. Kristeller, *Iter Italicum*, I (London/Leiden, 1963), p.139 assumes that Soderini composed the poem following the statement on Bologna, and suggests that Rosso d'Antonio Giovanni 'might be the real author of the poems'. Verde, *Lo studio*, III, I, p. 319, accepts that Soderini studied at Bologna on this evidence. There is, in addition, an independent source which attests to his having attended the university at Bologna. In ASF, C. Strozz., CXXXVIII, 47r, Marco Strozzi writes of his arrival at the *studio* at Pisa: 'In quo inveni dictum D. Franciscum D. T. de Soderinis qui anno precedenti studuerat in civitate Pisarum et prius in studio Bononiense'.

24 See A. Gherardi, *Statuti dell'università e studio fiorentino dell'anno* MCCCLXXXVII (Florence, 1881), pp. 273–6, where the *provvisione* is published.

25 G. Picotti, 'Lo studio di Pisa dalle origini a Cosimo duca', in Picotti, *Scritti vari di storia pisana e toscana* (Pisa, 1968), p. 26.

26 M. Ficino, *Opera omnia* (Basle, 1576), I, p. 654: 'Sed quid ego verbis iuriconsulti ideam effingo? Petrus Philippus dum pictorum more se ipsam in Francisco Soderino eius discipulo pinget, ideae ipsius re ipsa verum similitudinem assequetur. Nempe talem esse Petrumphilippum etsi adulationis suspitio asserere prohibet, cogit tamen veritas confiteri. Talem quoque Soderinum fore praeceptor studet. Discipuli indoles et initia iudicant.'

27 See Verde, *Lo studio*, II, p. 552 and I, pp. 297, 300, 301.

28 Ficino, *Opera*, I, p. 672.

29 For further details, see K. Lowe, 'Francesco Soderini (1453–1524), Florentine patrician and cardinal' (Ph.D. dissertation, University of London, 1985), p. 6.

Strozzi that he and Soderini left Pisa for Florence on about 19 January 1478 and that on 5 February he, Marco, was sent back to Pisa principally to find someone to teach instead of Soderini.[30] Marco Strozzi was a cleric who first met Soderini at the university, was taken into his employ and was linked to him for many years.[31] Soderini was, therefore, set to become a professor of civil law and it was only due to a decision taken jointly by his father and Lorenzo de' Medici that he changed course and embarked upon an ecclesiastical career.[32] Lorenzo obtained for him the bishopric of Volterra in March 1478. The preferment was almost certainly intended as a reward for Tommaso Soderini's loyalty and was a sufficiently prestigious acquisition to prompt Tommaso to rearrange his provisions for the future of his sons. Francesco, at a relatively late stage of his training, was moved from the law to the church and his younger brother Giovanvettorio was moved from the arts to the law. Thus, Soderini's entry into the church owed everything to opportunism and nothing to vocation.

THE BISHOPRIC OF VOLTERRA

Soderini's appointment to the bishopric in 1478, which was largely due to the support of Lorenzo de' Medici, can thus be seen in two ways. Firstly, it allowed Lorenzo to reward Soderini's father Tommaso by promoting the interests of his son. Secondly, by doing so, he ensured that a position of considerable power in Tuscany was held by a prominent Florentine who was in his debt. For Soderini, his preferment represented a radical change in career; nothing in his life up to that point had prepared him for episcopacy. Indeed, at twenty-four he was too young to take the title of bishop and was not allowed to do so until he reached the age of twenty-seven.[33] Soderini seems to have taken a relaxed attitude to the regulations governing his new vocation as he was only ordained a priest on 27 March 1486.[34]

Soderini's life was never centred on Volterra. By 1481 he had embarked on the career of a curial official which was to occupy the

---

[30] ASF, C. Strozz., cxxxviii, 47r: 'Et anno 1477 circa septuagesimam cum ipso [Soderini] Florentiam accessi et in die cinerum pro quibusdam negociis remisit me Pisas precipue ut alius vices suas in legendo persolveret; quibus peractis redii Florentiam.'   [31] See below, p. 237.

[32] This evidence also comes from Marco Strozzi. See ASF, C. Strozz., cxxxviii, 47r. For a more expanded account, see below p. 171.

[33] AV, Fondo camerale, Obl. et sol. 82, 110r.

[34] Florence, Archivio Arcivescovile, Ser Gabriele da Vacunda, Libro ii di collazione (1484–8), 60r. He was ordained by Rinaldo Orsini, the archbishop of Florence, in the sacristy of S. Lorenzo in Florence.

following thirteen years. However, it is known that he visited the city in May 1478,[35] soon after his appointment. It was not until September 1493 that Soderini said his first mass in the cathedral,[36] assisted by two of his friends from the curia, Jacopo Gherardi and Mario Maffei, who were also office-holders in the diocese of Volterra.

Soderini was, in short, an absentee bishop, and he exercised his ecclesiastical jurisdiction entirely through his diocesan officials. Volterra was guided spiritually by a series of vicars and vicars-general with Soderini as an illustrious but far-away figurehead. In a common move, a more seasoned cleric and relative from a minor branch of the Soderini, Bartolomeo, was appointed as vicar, canon and finally vicar-general to help the inexperienced bishop.[37] The sources are incomplete but it would appear that Soderini took an interest in the affairs of the bishopric primarily when a point of principle was involved or when he wished to influence a nomination. Otherwise, his involvement in ecclesiastical affairs in Volterra seems to have been small. He was, as in all matters, concerned to protect old customs and privileges and to resurrect even older ones if they were advantageous. Soderini featured most prominently in the deliberations of the time in a passive fashion as the proposed recipient of presents and ambassadors.

Despite the fact that he was a Florentine appointed in the wake of the Florentine sack of Volterra in 1472, and that he was in residence[38] very infrequently and irregularly, it appears that Soderini succeeded in gaining the respect of the Volterrans. This was probably due to the assiduousness with which he enriched the resources of the bishopric and with which he patronised various charitable schemes within the city. The rebuilding of the castle of Berignone in the Val di Cecina is an example of his interest in tradition and his concern for grandeur in the form of palaces or castles. This castle had intermittently provided the bishops of Volterra with both a home and a refuge.[39] In a book owned

---

[35] ASF, C. Strozz., CXXXVIII, 47v.

[36] Volterra, Arch. cap., Deliberationes B, Libro 15 antico, 30r, 15 September 1493: 'esset suam primam seu novellam missam pontificalem cantatorus in sua cathedrali ecclesia Volaterrane.'

[37] Volterra, Arch. cap., Deliberationes A, 144v and R. Bizzocchi, *Chiesa e potere nella Toscana del quattrocento* (Bologna, 1987), p. 249.

[38] The house used as the bishop's palace between 1472 and 1618 was the palazzo-torre Toscano, later called the Rapucci and finally the Guarnacci. It is situated on the Piazzetta di S. Michele. See A. Solaini, *Sommario della storia e guida del museo e della città di Volterra* (Volterra, 1927), pp. 56 and 67; L. Consortini, *Il castello antico di Volterra, il palazzo dei vescovi, l'iscrizione di Ranieri II degli Ubertini* (Lucca, 1922), p. 15 and Volterra, Arch. episc., Collazioni 1478–92, 3r.

[39] See E. Repetti, *Dizionario geografico, fisico, storico della Toscana* (Florence, 1833–46), I, p. 304 and Consortini, *Il castello*, pp. 10–13.

and used by Soderini on the laws and privileges of Volterra, the fortunes of the building were described, and it is recorded that he undertook a third rebuilding in 1498.[40] Evidently he was much concerned to maintain and assert, in a literal as well as a figurative sense, the standing and rights of his diocese.

Thus, too, in the 1480s, he can be found enforcing in the strongest possible way his episcopal rights by taking advantage of a disputed election for a new abbot of the abbey of Morrona, in the Colle Pisane, to claim the abbey for his see. The abbey was in the diocese of Volterra and the *contado* of Pisa and had hitherto been a part of the Camaldolese order. Soderini attempted to sequester the revenues of the abbey for the episcopal treasury of Volterra. The attempt was resisted and it took the intervention of Soderini himself, with a band of two hundred armed followers and the backing of the Florentine state, to achieve the desired result.[41]

As bishop and then cardinal, Soderini had considerable local standing to maintain and may have felt obliged to act as patron of the city. The foundation of a *Monte di Pietà* (an offical pawnbroker) in Volterra was the first real expression of Soderini's readiness to involve himself in works for the good of Volterra; his previous acquisition of the abbey at Morrona, although it enriched the revenues of the bishopric, cannot be said to have enriched the town. The two leading organisers of the Volterran *Monte* were said to have been Raffaele Maffei and Soderini,[42] but it is likely that the latter was being used as a figurehead and the inspiration came from his vicar, Marco di Matteo Strozzi.[43] The forty-two clauses of the statutes exist in the Archivio Comunale,[44] dated 18 December 1494. There were to be six presidents, four secular and two

---

[40] See ASF, Capitoli, Appendice 44, 22v: 'Hoc castellum tertio diritum per dominos Florentinos anno domini 1447. Ego F. Soderinus episcopus Vulterranus incepi reparare anno domini 1498 quod faustum felixque: sit mihi et ecclesiae Vulterranae.' This part is written in Soderini's own hand. The manuscript is discussed briefly in G. Volpe, *Volterra* (Florence, 1923), pp. 204–5.

[41] The history of this raid is described by Piero Delfino, the general of the Camaldolese order, in a letter of 13 September 1482. A manuscript copy of this letter survives in Volterra, Biblioteca Guarnacci MS 5706, Documenti istorici e politici spettanti a Volterra, 4.65. It is published in E. Martene and U. Durand, *Veterum scriptorum et monumentorum historicorum dogmaticorum moralium amplissima collectio volumen III* (Paris, 1724), cols. 1119–21. For an Italian translation, see M. Bocci, 'La badia di Morrona e un prepotente vescovo di Volterra', *Volterra*, 3 (1964), pp. 3 and 5.

[42] A. Cinci, 'Il Monte di Pietà in Volterra', in Cinci, *Miscellanea storica volterrana* (Florence/Volterra, 1880), p. 4.

[43] Marco Strozzi was vicar in February 1485, see Volterra, Arch. episc., Collazioni 1478–92, 13r and v.

[44] Volterra, Arch. com., Deliberazioni del magistrato, A 58, 14r ff.

ecclesiastic, one of which had to be either the bishop or his vicar, who on 14 January 1495 was announced to be Giovanni Damiano de Becci of San Gimignano.[45]

The same partnership of Raffaele Maffei and Soderini relaunched an institution known as the *Fraternità*, which had been in existence since at least the fourteenth century.[46] The statutes of its reconstitution also exist in the Archivio Comunale.[47] The statutes themselves are published by the Volterran historian, Cinci,[48] and are a model of their type: four young men between the ages of eighteen and twenty-seven were to be elected and maintained for six years of study in civil or canon law, arts or medicine, and paid fifteen ducats a year in two instalments. If they gave up, they were to pay back to the college the money they had received. Four young women, poor but of good reputation, were to be chosen and given dowries. The rules for election were as follows: Volterrans were to be preferred to outsiders, the poorer to be preferred to the richer, and if all else were equal, those of good habits were to be preferred to those of less good habits. The rest of the money was to be spent on the poor of the area: to keep alive the deserving poor ('poveri vergognosi'), those who had been abandoned during plague and other beggars.[49]

One of the pieces of patronage most obviously beneficial to the city was his request in 1506 for four young Volterrans to go to live with him in Rome.[50] And undisputed gifts from Soderini and from his nephew Giuliano, the subsequent bishop, are kept in the Museo d'Arte Sacra in Volterra.[51] They are six choral books, three dated 1508 and the other three 1510, still in their original bindings of wood, leather and finely wrought metal. The first capital letter of each is illuminated and the surrounding page hedged in by a frieze containing flowers and variations of the Soderini symbol, a pair of antlers. Francesco's three contain miniatures of the Nativity with words appropriate to Christmas (202 pages), the Risen Christ with words appropriate to Easter (190 pages), (see figure 1) and David holding Goliath's head, with words suitable to the period after Pentecost (232 pages). The books contain plainsong and caused the historian Falconcini to remark that Soderini had renovated the choral books with gregorian chant.[52]

---

[45] Cinci, 'Il Monte', p. 8.

[46] A. Cinci, *Storia di Volterra* (Volterra, 1885), La Fraternità, p. 9.

[47] Volterra, Arch. com., G (nera) 33, 1r–9r.

[48] Cinci, *Storia*, La Fraternità, pp. 8–17.   [49] *Ibid.*, pp. 9–10.

[50] See below, p. 243–4.

[51] See M. Cavallini, 'I corali del museo della cattedrale', *Il Corazziere*, 16 July 1933.

[52] B. Falconcini, *Vita del nobil'uomo Raffaello Maffei detto il Volterrano* (Rome, 1722), p. 86.

1. An illumination from the Easter choral book commissioned by Francesco Soderini, now in the Museo d'Arte Sacra in Volterra.

There are signs that Soderini's concern for Volterra exceeded the bounds of mere convention. He was bishop there for thirty-one years and when raised to the purple took the title 'cardinal of Volterra' as his soubriquet. Prompted by his sense of history and tradition, he caused to be copied and then annotated a manuscript on Volterra's ancient laws and privileges[53] and also commissioned a catalogue of the former bishops of the city.[54] Finally, his affection for Volterra can be gauged by his foundation of a chapel in the cathedral dedicated to his namesake S. Francesco, where masses could be said for his soul.[55] It is true that Soderini was largely absent from the diocese, but Volterra was the only one of his bishoprics that he is known to have visited as bishop, and the only one on which he bestowed his patronage. This was doubly striking since, unlike the majority of bishops who became concerned with the interests of their dioceses, Soderini was not a native of Volterra. It would appear that Soderini's regard for the town was reciprocated. Thus, Soderini's unusual solicitude towards Volterra resulted in the perpetuation of his name as a benefactor of the town.

EARLY CAREER AT THE PAPAL CURIA, 1480–94

Soderini's appointment to the bishopric of Volterra in 1478 presented him with several new possibilities: he could live in Volterra and take care of his flock (but he was as yet only administrator and had not taken orders), he could live in Florence but be barred from participation in the political life of the city, or he could go to Rome, to the centre of his new profession, and try his luck in the curial hierarchy. It was the third option which offered the greatest challenge and most excitement, and consequently Soderini used his talents and influence to acquire a post at the curia. His humanist skills, legal training, oratorical gifts and Tuscan background all contributed to make him a promising candidate.

The sources for this period of his life from 1478 to 1494 are unfortunately scarce.[56] The first time that Soderini was recorded as

---

[53] ASF, Capitoli, Appendice 44. See also Volpe, *Volterra*, pp. 204–5.

[54] BNF, Magl. VIII, 80, 56r.

[55] See Lowe, 'Francesco Soderini', appendix 3, pp. 335–6; Volterra, Biblioteca Guarnacci MS 5706, Documenti istorici e politici spettanti a Volterra, 5.29 and Rome, Arch. Sod., XXII, 48r.

[56] One tiny but, in the light of later events, noteworthy item is that the Medici bank in Rome in March 1494 declared that Soderini owed them 46 ducats 7 *soldi*, but Soderini repudiated the debt. See A. Sapori, 'Il "bilancio" della filiale di Roma del banco Medici del 1495', *Archivio storico italiano*, 131 (1973), p. 178.

being present in Rome was when he joined the confraternity of S. Spirito in Sassia on 7 December 1478.[57] The second time was as part of the Florentine embassy of November 1480 to the pope to persuade him to lift the interdict he had placed on Florence after the Pazzi conspiracy.[58] On this occasion Soderini gave a brilliant speech which greatly impressed Sixtus IV[59] and may have led directly to a successful career in the curia. The connection between the two is seen in this light by Marco Strozzi, one of Soderini's most devoted ecclesiastic retainers, who would have been in a position to know the current theories as to what was happening, even if not the real reasons. He believed that the speech generated the offices and titles of *assistente*, referendary and familiar for Soderini.[60] In a similar fashion, when the apostolic protonotary, Ascanio Sforza, delivered a noteworthy oration as head of the Milanese embassy offering obedience to Sixtus IV on his election in 1471, it generated a letter from a fellow protonotary predicting Sforza's later promotion to the cardinalate.[61] An *assistente* was an ecclesiastic who was allowed to assist the pope in certain ceremonial rites at the papal court and it was therefore not a curial post but a mark of high favour.[62] Antonio da Montecatini, the Ferrarese ambassador at Florence, wrote to duke Ercole d'Este on 5 December 1480 that the bishop of Volterra had been honoured with this position.[63] As the speech was only delivered on 27 November, if Soderini had really been made an *assistente* by 5 December, it was almost certainly as a result of his speech.

Soderini was made a referendary at the beginning of May 1481. On 12 May the Florentine government wrote to thank the pope, Girolamo Riario, cardinal Domenico della Rovere and Piero da Rocha, an apostolic protonotary, for Soderini's new position.[64] At this point the *Signatura justitiae* and the *Signatura gratiae* were still one unit,[65] so that the referendaries or legal experts, who worked under the cardinal prefect at the head of the *Signatura*, dealt with supplications addressed to

---

[57] P. de Angelis, *L'ospedale di Santo Spirito in Saxia* (Rome, 1962), II, p. 121.

[58] See below, p. 30.   [59] See below, p. 276.

[60] ASF, C. Strozz., CXXXVIII, 47v: 'Et deinde civitas misit duodecim oratores ad Sixtum Quartum et orationem fecit D. V. R. summe gratam summo pontifici qui deputavit eandem in assistentem et creavit in referendarium et familiarem.'

[61] M. Pellegrini, 'Ascanio Maria Sforza: la creazione di un cardinale "di famiglia"', in *Gli Sforza, la chiesa lombarda, la corte di Roma*, ed. G. Chittolini (Naples, 1989), p. 236.

[62] In October 1513 Soderini's nephew Giuliano was also made an *assistente*.

[63] ASMo, Carteggio degli ambasciatori, Firenze II, 5 December 1480.

[64] See M. Del Piazzo, *Protocolli del carteggio di Lorenzo il Magnifico per gli anni 1473–4, 1477–92* (Florence, 1956), p. 145.

[65] In 1493 Alexander VI separated these offices and Julius II later upheld the separation. See *Dictionnaire du droit canonique* (Paris, 1924–65), VII, 492.

the pope both on judicial matters and on matters connected with the distribution of graces, which did not require papal intervention.[66] In the fifteenth century they were also responsible for deciding upon the fees to be charged for dealing with such supplications. The referendaries, therefore, with the auditors of the *Rota*, which was the court of appeals for canon-law cases initiated at the diocesan level throughout christendom, and the court of first instance for civil cases from the papal states involving sums greater than 500 ducats,[67] were some of the most important legal officials in the curia, and their position presented them with great opportunities for patronage. The reaction of the Florentine government[68] and of humanist friends[69] to the news of Soderini's appointment was correspondingly warm.

Thereafter, Soderini was firmly placed at the centre of a network of people and institutions spreading out from the curia, nearly all of whom would at some stage wish for assistance in pursuit of a claim or favour. For example, Jacopo Gherardi wrote to him on 21 March 1489 from Milan recommending a lawsuit involving Francesco Birago the protonotary,[70] which it was thought that Soderini might judge. Gherardi excuses his interference by saying that he knows that Soderini when judging does not follow the favour of men but only passes judgement on the basis of truth.[71] Francesco Birago's uncle Daniele had been a referendary in the early years of Sixtus's pontificate[72] and so Francesco would have been well aware of how the system worked. This kind of letter must have been written to Soderini with great frequency but very few have survived and there is not a great deal that can be gleaned from the other end, from the supplications which were signed

---

[66] See J. D'Amico, *Renaissance humanism in papal Rome* (Baltimore, 1983), pp. 23–4, and *Dictionnaire du droit canonique*, VII, 492–3.

[67] C. Stinger, *The renaissance in Rome* (Bloomington, 1985), p. 136.

[68] The *Otto di Pratica* wrote to Guidantonio Vespucci, the Florentine ambassador in Rome, on 13 May 1481: 'Con sommo piacere habbiamo inteso el R. do vescovo di Volterra esser facto referendario della Santità del papa. Ringratiarete in nome nostro la Sua Santità et la Excellentia de la S. Hieronimo et chi altri paresse a decto vescovo', ASF, Signori, Minutari 11, 322v.

[69] Sebastiano Salvini wrote to Soderini on 12 May from Florence expressing his delight. See BV, Vat. lat. 5140, 105r–106v.

[70] Jacopo Gherardi arrived in Milan in September 1487 as papal nuncio at the Sforza court where Birago was *consigliere segreto*. See the article on Francesco Birago by P. Bertolini in the *Dizionario biografico degli italiani* (Rome, 1960–), x, p. 583. Soderini kept up his links with this family, for on 12 August 1491 the Florentine government wrote to him 'per monsignore da Birago'. See Del Piazzo, *Protocolli*, p. 469.

[71] *Dispacci e lettere di Giacomo Gherardi*, ed. E. Carusi (Rome, 1909), pp. 295–6.

[72] See P. Bruno Katterbach, *Referendarii utriusque signaturae* (Città del Vaticano, 1931), p. 50 and *Dizionario biografico degli italiani*, x, p. 584.

by the referendaries.[73] Soderini's name is found on many of the
supplications between the dates of 1481 and 1494, and again on a few in
late 1500 and early 1501 when he was on a special embassy to the pope
on behalf of the Florentine government to discuss Cesare Borgia's
successes in the Romagna.[74]

Soderini's superiors and co-referendaries were to be influential in his
career in later life in many ways and several were of help in his
promotion to the cardinalate. His colleagues in this office over three
pontificates included cardinal Giuliano della Rovere, cardinal Giovanni
Arcimboldi, Ardicino della Porta who was made a cardinal by Innocent
VIII on 9 March 1489 and who died on 4 February 1493, Antoniotto
Pallavicino who was made a cardinal in the same promotion of 1489 and
who lived until 10 September 1517, Piero Accolti who was promoted
on 10 March 1511 and who died on 11 December 1532 and Niccolò
Flisco who was promoted at the same time as Soderini and died at
almost the same time, on 14 June 1524.[75] These men must have provided
a solid base of support in Rome for Soderini, and the office was
obviously regarded as a stepping stone to the cardinalate. Thus by being
a referendary he not only became an important political and ecclesiastical patron in his own right, but also acquired all the necessary
contacts to facilitate life as a cardinal. As a referendary, Soderini
obtained the right to eat at the papal table and in this sense became a
member of the pope's *familia*.[76] He is therefore described as a familiar in
contemporary documents,[77] which explains why Marco Strozzi would
have used the term.

Soderini was also made an apostolic secretary by Innocent VIII on 31
December 1487 when the pope increased their number from six to
thirty.[78] The secretaries prepared the pope's letters on diplomatic,
private and political matters.[79] This post was a stronghold of humanists
in the fifteenth century, especially during the pontificates of Pius II and

---

[73] For some examples of supplications, see P. Bruno Katterbach, *Specimina supplicationum* (Rome, 1927), I and II.

[74] See Katterbach, *Referendarii*, pp.53, 59 and 62, and Katterbach, *Inventario dei registri
delle suppliche* (Città del Vaticano, 1932). The earliest of Soderini's signatures that
Katterbach located was in Reg. sup. 806, a volume that runs from 17 December 1481
to January 1482. Soderini's short and voluntary burst of activity in the winter of
1500–1 when he was in Rome, illustrates that the affairs of the curia were still close
to his heart.   [75] Katterbach, *Referendarii*, pp. 42–62.

[76] See D'Amico, *Renaissance humanism*, p. 41 and G. Moroni, *Dizionario di erudizione
storico-ecclesiastico da S. Pietro sino ai nostri giorni* (Venice, 1840–61), XXIII, pp. 147–56.

[77] For example, see AV, Arm. XXXIV, 12, 222r and V, 8 June 1482.

[78] See E. Lee, *Sixtus IV and men of letters* (Rome, 1978), p. 49 and T. Frenz, *Die Kanzlei
der Päpste der Hochrenaissance (1471–1527)* (Tübingen, 1986), p. 333.

[79] D'Amico, *Renaissance humanism*, p. 29.

Sixtus IV,[80] and some of them were still employed in it when Soderini joined. It may have been here that he forged his great friendship with Jacopo Gherardi although it is likely that he had known him before. Sigismondo de' Conti[81] and Giovanpietro Arrivabene were already secretaries upon his arrival, and Lorenzo Cibo, Falco Sinibaldi and Giuliano Cesarini were appointed at the same date. However, the character of the secretariat was changing slightly as eight of the twenty-four new appointees were bishops[82] and none of them was in the front rank of the humanists.

One position that Soderini held in the curia during these years, which Marco Strozzi failed to mention, was that of auditor of contradicted letters. These auditors decided on any ambiguity that may have arisen in the wording of, or any controversy that may have resulted from, the bulls issued in response to supplications.[83] Therefore, Soderini, in his threefold position as referendary, auditor of contradicted letters and apostolic secretary, had responsibility at the beginning and end of the process of writing bulls, and total responsibility for the composition of briefs. He was appointed to the office of auditor of contradicted letters on 1 January 1488[84] upon the resignation of Rinaldo Orsini, the archbishop of Florence. All three curial posts could have been full-time, and yet Soderini only officially gave them up in 1503.[85] In reality, he ceased being a curia official in the summer of 1494[86] when he returned to Florence and embarked on still another career as a diplomat in the service of the Florentine state.

The reasons why he may have left Rome are numerous: he could have been recalled by the family (notably Paolantonio), he could have

---

[80] *Ibid.*, pp. 19, 32–4.

[81] He included this incident in his history. See S. de' Conti, *Le storie de' suoi tempi (1475–1510)* (Rome, 1883), II, p. 40.

[82] See Lee, *Sixtus IV*, p. 49 and W. von Hofmann, *Forschungen zur Geschichte der Kurialen Behörden vom Schisma bis zur Reformation* (Rome, 1914), II, pp. 116–17.

[83] D'Amico, *Renaissance humanism*, p.26. P. Herde, *Audientia litterarum contradictarum* (Tübingen, 1970) contains information about the office. There are no extant registers for this office at this period but a stray record relating to Soderini has survived in BV, Vat. lat. 10966, 176r–184r. On 3 July 1493 Soderini was the auditor of a *causa* between Sinolfo da Castro Oterio, an apostolic protonotary, and Niccolò de Roncionibus (Ronciglione) which concerned the church of S. Maria at Proceno.

[84] Hofmann, *Forschungen*, II, p. 76 and Frenz, *Die Kanzlei*, p. 333.

[85] See Hofmann, *Forschungen*, II, pp. 76 and 119 (Soderini was replaced as secretary by Francesco da Castiglione).

[86] AV, Reg. vat. 870, 179v–180v, safeconduct of Alexander VI to Soderini dated 28 June 1494, giving him permission to take with him up to twenty-five of his personal retinue, and his personal belongings (such as horses, bags, books, clothes and silver) when he leaves Rome on both his own and the pope's business, and goes to Tuscany and certain other parts of Italy.

foreseen the downfall of the Medici, or he may have wanted to be present as the French arrived. Whatever the cause, Soderini left the well-tried and stable environment of the curia for the relatively precarious conditions of Florence.

THE TRANSFORMATION OF THE SODERINI FROM MEDICEANS TO REPUBLICANS

In November 1494 Piero de' Medici was expelled from Florence, and a new republic was initiated. The Soderini family were involved with the new regime from the outset. When Lorenzo de' Medici came to power in 1469, his cousins Paolantonio, Piero and Francesco Soderini were respectively twenty, seventeen and sixteen; they grew to political maturity under his increasingly dictatorial controls. Unlike their father Tommaso, who calculated that his best chance for political power lay in close collaboration with successive members of the main branch of the Medici, his sons, especially after his death in 1485, may have been hankering for a more open and accessible form of government whose participants had more power. The pursuance of this aim became one of the priorities of the new republic, and all the Soderini brothers, now (apart from Giovanvettorio) in their forties, joined others of their station and inclination in occupying the offices of the republic.

One consequence of this was that the Soderini were reclassified as republicans rather than as Mediceans. As far as the Medici were concerned, the sons of Tommaso had reneged on their ancient loyalties as clients and deserved to be treated as traitors. It would be interesting to know what individual members of the Soderini thought of the situation in the first years of the republic, but there is unfortunately little information. Not only was it a question of choosing between the Medici and republicanism; the situation was made more complicated by the necessity of adopting an attitude towards Girolamo Savonarola and his views. Although there may have been a Soderini family strategy, both in relation to the Medici and to Savonarola, no uniformity of views on the friar seems to have been imposed within the family; indeed, it is likely that the strategy itself involved the hedging of bets. Sergio Bertelli, using a few passages from the fragmentary *ricordanze* of Giovanvettorio for the years from 1496 to 1498, points out the association of the family as a whole with a spectrum of pro- and anti-Savonarolian feeling, through choice and family alliances.[87] This

---

[87] S. Bertelli, 'Di due profili mancati e di un bilancino con pesi truccati', *Archivio storico italiano*, 145 (1987), p. 583.

allowed them to take a decision, in December 1498, that the family, for its own good, should adopt a middle position between the supporters and detractors of Savonarola.

From the same source, Bertelli declares that contact with the alternative branch of the Medici, headed by Pierfrancesco and his sons, meant that the Soderini as a family were considering acting in collusion with them to bring about political changes within the city.[88] Thus, individual members of the Soderini clan viewed the situation in Florence after the fall of the Medici in 1494 in a variety of ways. Given the volatility of the republic and the intensity of the factional conflict, this was to be expected, but taken as a whole, the participation of the Soderini family in the offices of the republic ensured that they came to be seen as more or less dependable republicans, even if some of them were ardent Savonarolians.

But whilst the Soderini were active members of the republic, they were just some of many, and were not thought of as the obvious leaders. In fact, it might have been suspected that the death of the eldest brother, Paolantonio, in 1499, would lessen the chances of a pivotal role in the republic for the other brothers by creating a vacuum. On the contrary, by removing the member of the family most tainted by association with Savonarola and his schemes,[89] Paolantonio's death helped to advance the claim of the family to be following a middle course and to pave the way for the election of the next brother, Piero, as *gonfaloniere a vita* three years later in September 1502. The family's identification with the aims and ideals of the republic was sealed by this act.

The ideological transformation of the family from Medicean to republican cannot be traced so simply and may not have followed the same arc. There had been a significant change in conditions in Florence and in the behaviour of the Medici between the start of Tommaso's career and the beginnings of the political careers of his sons. The republicanism of the sons, which became progressively more pronounced, seems to have been genuine from the outset, but an element of opportunism should not be discounted. At the end of Lorenzo de' Medici's life, the Florentine political class was discontented by the diminution of its participation in power. If Paolantonio, Piero, Francesco and Giovanvettorio wanted a greater share in government, it was obvious that the system would have to change and that the Medici would have to be ousted. Ideologically, at this stage, political and family ambition may have operated in tandem with republican values. Equally,

[88] *Ibid.*, pp. 583–4.
[89] See F. Guicciardini, *Storie fiorentine*, ed. R. Palmarocchi (Bari, 1931), p. 147: Paolantonio 'che svisceratamente favoriva el frate'.

in the absence of evidence, it may not, and the Soderini brothers may genuinely have believed in more republican government and its benefits. This view at least has the advantage of taking into account the public service rendered by the four Soderini brothers to the republic before Piero's election transformed their relationship to the city and their reputation outside it.

CHAPTER 2

SODERINI AS A SERVANT OF THE FLORENTINE STATE

Francesco Soderini was sent on nine missions on behalf of Florence between 1480 and 1503,[1] which involved his spending a great deal of time – about five years – away from his home city. The repeated use of him as an ambassador,[2] sometimes on embassies of the highest importance, can be taken as a sign both of his standing and of his political interests. Soderini was well suited for the post of ambassador on many counts. He had a legal training, which was a bonus on embassies involving negotiation. By the end of the fifteenth century, there was a strong case for appointing lawyers as ambassadors to Rome because of the increasing volume of Florentine litigation being conducted at the *Rota*.[3] Churchmen and lawyers would also have been at an advantage as their jobs required them to speak and to understand Latin. In the absence of a shared contemporary language, ambassadors could theoretically have conversed in Latin. There is some evidence that Soderini did learn French during his years in France,[4] and he would presumably not have managed to achieve the relationship that he later did with Louis XII had he been forced to speak through an interpreter.[5] In addition, Soderini was rich enough to cope with the financial setbacks which accompanied diplomatic missions. As a cleric, he was barred from public office-holding within the republic so diplomacy was the main means by which he could satisfy his political ambitions.

Remarkably, Soderini appears never to have refused a mission,

---

[1] For a detailed discussion of these embassies, see Lowe, 'Francesco Soderini', pp. 39–78.

[2] The words for ambassador and orator are used interchangeably at this period.

[3] L. Martines, *Lawyers and statecraft in renaissance Florence* (Princeton, 1968), pp. 270 and 283. [4] See below, p. 265.

[5] See M. de Maulde-la-Clavière, *La diplomatie au temps de Machiavel* (Paris, 1892–3), II, pp. 71–3. The question of interpreters seems to have been overlooked in the literature.

although it is clear on occasion he would have preferred not to go.[6] His repeated compliance in this matter can be taken as evidence of his sense of public obligation to the republic. Testimony of a different kind is to be found in a letter Soderini wrote to Lanfredino Lanfredini in January 1504 upon learning that Lanfredini had been elected ambassador to Rome, but was considering declining the assignment. Soderini accused him of setting a bad example to others, and upbraided him by reminding him that a respectable citizen (*homo da bene*) was not born for himself alone, but to serve others, and in particular, the *patria*.[7] He argued that the principal part of their lives should be pledged to the service of Florence, for which they ought to be prepared to suffer greater exertions than for their fathers or sons.[8] This ideal of patriotic fervour obviously did not find favour with Lanfredini who declined the appointment,[9] but it bears witness to Soderini's commitment to serve Florence through public office. All the Soderini brothers responded to the call of public office under the republic with such consistency that, in February 1499, all four were either elected to or serving on separate diplomatic missions: Francesco was ambassador to the duke of Milan, Piero to the king of France and Paolantonio to Venice. Giovanvettorio was due to leave as ambassador to Rome, but in fact he did not.[10]

Diplomatic activity allowed Soderini to make a series of political acquaintances, contacts and allies who were to be of immense importance in his later career as a cardinal, and who were probably instrumental in the formation of the foreign policy of the Florentine republic. Here Soderini's contacts with France are crucial. The years of his diplomatic activity witnessed a change of staggering proportions in the field of diplomacy, as Italy was invaded in 1494 by a French king, Charles VIII, who wished to press his claim to the kingdom of Naples. The old, internal stability of Italy gave way as new power interests were introduced, and newer and more complex types of diplomatic relation were evolved. It was in this context that Soderini forged his links with the French monarchy. As will be seen (pp. 30–2), he was present at two

---

[6] See a letter of his to Paolo Cortesi of 24 August 1501 in Florence, Biblioteca Marucelliana, B1 10, Part 3, 200r: 'Io son forzato andare né si è potuto più. Multa sunt que offendant et animum et rem bisogna che chi mi ama habbi patientia come ho io.'

[7] Paris, Bibliothèque Nationale, MSS italiens 2033, 43r: 'essendo adunque officio di homo da bene considerare che'l non è nato per se solo, ma per gli altri et maxime per la patria.'

[8] *Ibid.*, 43r: 'la principale parte de la vita nostra è obligata a la patria, per la quale dovemo patire magiori affanni che per li patri e filioli.'

[9] ASF, Sig. e collegi, Deliberaz. di speciale autorità 40, 50v–51v.

[10] P. Parenti, 'Istorie fiorentine', in BNF, II II 131, 129r.

of the most crushing victories of foreign arms in Italy in the final decade of the fifteenth century: the defeat of the kingdom of Naples in 1495 by Charles VIII and the collapse of Milan before the advance of the armies of Louis XII under Giangiacomo Trivulzio in 1499. This must have enabled Soderini to appreciate the vulnerability of Italy to foreign invasion and left him with a respect for the power of France. It also, combined with his and Piero Soderini's contacts with France,[11] must go some way towards explaining the continuing reliance of the Florentine republic on French support, even in the face of strident advocacy in Florence for alternative policies.[12] Public and private interests had merged for the Soderini in their dealings with France to such an extent that it is now unwise to expect to be able to unravel them. In addition, Soderini's exposure to French might in 1495 and 1499 may provide a reason for his unwavering allegiance to the French monarchy after 1512; his attachment to France provided him with allies and a power-base in the political arena of Rome when his connections with Florence could only be of negative value in a Rome dominated by the Medici.

A distinction which may be helpful in discussions of the importance and efficacy of Soderini's diplomatic career is that between negotiating and non-negotiating missions. Of the nine missions, only two, that of 1498 to Milan and that of 1501 to France, were negotiating ones, and the negotiations of the former collapsed with the approach of the French army. Six were clearly non-negotiating, and the embassy to Cesare Borgia falls into a category of its own as the proposals put forward by him could not be accepted as the basis for any negotiation. This concentration on non-negotiating missions was not an impediment to Soderini's success as an ambassador; rather missions of congratulation and explanation led to an identification of Soderini's honour with Florence's honour. There is no evidence to suggest that he was an ineffectual or disinterested negotiator. On the contrary, in the course of the 1501 mission to France, he and Luca degli Albizzi won extremely favourable terms in a friendship treaty signed on 17 April 1502. He seems to have been employed more frequently on non-negotiating missions on account of his episcopal status. This ensured that he

---

[11] Piero Soderini was ambassador to Charles VIII in July 1493 (see G. Canestrini and A. Desjardins, *Négociations diplomatiques de la France avec la Toscane*, I (Paris, 1859), pp. 321–4), to Louis XII in June 1498 (*ibid.*, II (Paris, 1861), pp. 15–21) and to cardinal d'Amboise in Milan in April 1500 (*ibid.*, II, pp. 31–4).

[12] Francesco Guicciardini certainly felt that this was the case, *Storie fiorentine*, pp. 297–300. He wrote (p. 299) that the *gonfaloniere* 'se bene vedessi la ruina della città, non sarebbe per deviare da Francia per la dependenzia che aveva con quello re e lui ed el cardinale suo fratello, che aveva in Francia benefici ed entrata per più migliaia di ducati'.

automatically took precedence over all the others on the embassy, even if they were older and more experienced. One example of this is the 1498 mission to Milan where Soderini took precedence over Francesco Pepi immediately on arrival. Thus, he was never in a subordinate position on an embassy. All the same, his obvious success as an ambassador resulted not solely from his superior rank, but also from his character and aptitude.

Soderini's first embassy, to pope Sixtus IV in Rome in November 1480, has already been mentioned. His oration on behalf of the Florentines was important because it brought Soderini to the eyes of the pope, thus lighting the way to a professional life in Rome. His next mission, in November 1484, was to the same city. He and his five fellow ambassadors were to offer congratulations and obedience to the new pope Innocent VIII who had been elected on 29 August.[13] His third embassy did not take place until 1494, ten years after the previous one. In the intervening years, he had pursued a successful career at the curia. As his return to Florence took place just before the Medici fell from power, it is possible that Soderini may not have wished to be an ambassador again under their regime. But evidence of an estrangement between Soderini and the Medici is lacking, and his cessation of diplomatic activity could have come about from independent and unknown causes, although this may be the point at which Soderini began to have republican leanings.

Soderini first met Charles VIII as the French king approached Florence in November 1494 on his way to reconquer the kingdom of Naples, pressing ancient claims to the kingdom of the house of Anjou. Soderini was one of a number of ambassadors[14] elected to negotiate Florence's retention of her liberty.[15] These negotiations became irrelevant once Charles made a triumphal entry into Florence. But Florence was merely a staging post for Charles on his way south. On 2 December Soderini and Neri Capponi were appointed ambassadors to Charles to accompany him in his conquest of Naples. Throughout the trip access to the king seems to have been easy and was an indication of the friendly state of relations between France and Florence.[16] This was Soderini's first prolonged contact with a French (or indeed any other) monarch. By 13 February it was overwhelmingly obvious that the kingdom of Naples would not fight, and that the victory was Charles's.

[13] ASF, Sig., Leg. e com. 21, 52v-54r.   [14] ASF, Sig., Miss. 1a Canc. 50, 12v.

[15] H. François Delaborde, *L'expédition de Charles VIII en Italie* (Paris, 1888), p. 456 and Y. Labande-Mailfert, *Charles VIII et son milieu (1470–1498)* (Paris, 1975), p. 293.

[16] ASF, Dieci, Resp. 38, 67r, Soderini and Capponi, Rome, 17 January 1495: 'mai è stato giorno non siamo stati col C. re una o due volte'.

Soderini's first-hand experience of the power and of the terror inspired by the king of France were to influence the rest of his political life. Watching a foreign king enter Italy and intervene decisively in her affairs, unopposed, must have been a chilling process.

On 24 December 1495 Soderini received instructions to go as ambassador to Charles VIII in France,[17] and he stayed in France until September 1497. It was his first visit there and the first time that he had left the Italian peninsula. He was to be the leading partner of an embassy comprising him, Neri Capponi and Giovacchino Guasconi. Their main objective was again one of congratulation, reminder and persuasion, rather than of active negotiation, as they were to congratulate the king on his safe return, remind him of Florence's perilous state, and persuade him that he must act to help her. Florence had not joined the Holy League of 31 March 1495 binding the pope, the emperor Maximilian I, Ferdinand and Isabella of Spain, Venice and Lodovico il Moro against the Turks and in defence of christendom (but also against France), and as a consequence felt threatened and isolated. Much of the embassy's time was spent assessing the likelihood of another expedition to Italy by Charles VIII, who in his turn was preoccupied with affairs of succession.

Soderini undoubtedly continued in his friendly relations with the king and must have made an effort to establish a rapport with other important members of the French court, such as the duke of Orléans (the future Louis XII) and Bianca of Montferrat, then regent-duchess of Savoy, both of whom were named by the Florentine *Signoria* as people who should be visited and cherished by Soderini.[18] He may also have encountered there Louise of Savoy,[19] the mother of the next-but-one king of France, Francis I. The inability of the French kings in this period to produce male children who lived to adulthood meant that the succession took two sideways steps through consecutive princely lines of the royal house. It was to Soderini's credit that by the time Louis XII ascended the throne in April 1498, Soderini–French relations were potent enough to survive the new circumstances. Other important contacts were the French cardinals André d'Epinay and Guillaume Briçonnet and two disaffected cardinals who were waiting for pope Alexander VI to die: Giuliano della Rovere and Paolo da Campo Fregoso.

[17] These were published by Canestrini, *Négociations*, I, pp. 640–8. The originals are in ASF, Sig., Leg. e com. 21, 146r-149r.

[18] ASF, Sig., Leg. e com. 21, 145v-146r.

[19] Unfortunately, nothing further is known about Soderini's relations with Louise of Savoy at this point, but Francis I did not settle permanently at the French court until 1508 when he was still only thirteen, five years after Soderini left France. See R. Knecht, *Francis I* (Cambridge, 1982), p. 9.

This embassy was a vital one for Soderini as it made his reputation as an ambassador. The estimation by the *Signoria* and *Dieci* of Soderini's worth in their letters, and the respect shown him by other rulers, are signs of his success. Another reason for the high regard in which he was held may be the report (*rapporto*)[20] he delivered on his return.[21] The central section describes a series of conversations with Giangiacomo Trivulzio,[22] Giuliano della Rovere[23] and Battista da Campo Fregoso.[24] Just as all three of these people wished to exploit Charles VIII's return to Italy to their own advantage (Trivulzio wanted to seize power in Milan, cardinal della Rovere wanted to take over Savona and Fregoso wished to retain his power in Genoa), so all three were necessary agents in Charles's invasion plans. Soderini also discusses the meetings he had on his way home: with Ludovico Sforza in Milan, Ercole d'Este in Ferrara and Caterina Sforza in Imola. He ends with an assessment of the character of the king of France and the chances of his coming to Italy, saying that the king was very well-disposed towards the venture.[25]

Soderini had occasion once again to witness the might of the French on his fifth embassy, to Milan in 1499. His instructions are dated 28 December 1498;[26] he was to join Francesco Pepi who was already resident ambassador in Milan. His object was to obtain advice and support about Pisa, Venice and the state of Italy from Ludovico Sforza, the duke of Milan. The duke himself fled from the city on 2 September 1499 just in advance of the arrival of Louis XII's armies, led by Giangiacomo Trivulzio. Soderini and Pepi left on 4 September, as soon as the safe-conduct promised by Trivulzio materialised.[27] The powerlessness of Milan in the face of French strength must have been both depressing and exhilarating for Soderini, because he cannot have avoided making comparisons between Milan and Florence, but on the other hand he may have been able to console himself with the knowledge that France was Florence's ally.

Soderini's sixth embassy was as a special envoy to the pope. His

[20] On these reports, see Maulde-la-Clavière, *La diplomatie*, III, pp. 385–6.
[21] ASF, Lettere varie 14, 18r-19r, 20r-22v and 23v and Lowe, 'Francesco Soderini', appendix 1, pp. 317–25.
[22] On Trivulzio, see C. Rosmini, *Dell'istoria intorno alle militari imprese e alla vita di Gian Jacopo Trivulzio detto il Magno* (Milan, 1815) and Litta, 'Trivulzi di Milano', *Celebri famiglie italiane*, table 3.
[23] For his French years and connections, see Labande-Mailfert, *Charles VIII*, p. 382.
[24] See P. Luigi Levati, *Dogi perpetui di Genova an.1339–1528* (Genoa, 1930) and Litta, 'Fregosi di Genova', *Celebri famiglie italiane*. [25] ASF, Lettere varie 14, 22r.
[26] ASF, Sig., Leg. e com. 23, 26v. [27] ASF, Sig., Resp. 12, 522v and 525r.

commission is dated 21 October 1500,[28] that is, over a year after he returned from Milan. The aim of the mission was to respond in person to requests voiced on behalf of Alexander VI by Agostino de Sroto, one of the pope's cubiculars, in relation to Cesare Borgia's exploits in the Romagna. This was the only embassy that Soderini was sent on by himself and was the least important of the post-1484 ones. He was in Rome for under four months, and much of his time was spent on minor or routine matters, or on his own private affairs. During his stay, a rumour circulated that the pope wished Cesare Borgia to be king of the Romagna and to re-establish Piero de' Medici in Florence.

Soderini's two embassies to France from September 1501 to May 1502, and from November 1502 until the announcement of his elevation reached France in June 1503,[29] allowed a flowering of the professional and personal bond between him and the French monarch. The seventh embassy enabled Soderini to meet Louis XII for the first time, although he had witnessed his strength in Milan two years before. He was sent with Luca degli Albizzi, in effect to be resident ambassador at the French court.[30] They had been elected on 31 August,[31] principally to formalise the relationship between France and Florence and to congratulate the king on his acquisition of the kingdom of Naples. It took until 17 April 1502 for the friendship treaty to be drawn up and signed at Blois. Soderini and degli Albizzi signed on behalf of Florence, and cardinal Georges d'Amboise and marshal de Gié on behalf of the king of France.[32] Louis and the Florentines swore to observe a pact of friendship, lasting for three years, and they agreed to have friends and enemies in common. In return for financial payment from Florence, Louis gave a guarantee that he would protect and defend the city against any molestation, even to the extent of going to war.

Arriving back in Florence on 18 June, a mere four days later, on 22 June, Soderini left on his eighth and best-known embassy, accompanied by Niccolò Machiavelli, to Cesare Borgia. The mandate for this embassy is not extant,[33] although there is a short notice that Soderini

[28] There are four copies of this commission: in ASF, Miscell. republl., busta VI, 206; ASF, Sig., Leg. e com. 26, 43r-44v; BNF, II IV 309, 58r-60v; and BNF, II IV 295, 112r-115r.   [29] BNF, GC, 21, 28r-28v and ASF, Dieci, Resp. 72, 248r.

[30] There is some controversy over the date of Florence's first resident ambassador in France. See G. Mattingly, 'The first resident embassies: mediaeval Italian origins of modern diplomacy', *Speculum*, 12 (1937), pp. 427 and 438-9.

[31] ASF, Sig., Leg. e com. 23, 53v. These instructions are published by Canestrini, *Négociations*, II, pp. 63-9.

[32] A copy of this treaty is in Rome, Biblioteca Angelica, MS 2110, 55v-57r.

[33] See *Le legazioni e commissarie di Niccolò Machiavelli*, ed. L. Passerini and G. Milanesi (Florence/Rome, 1875), II, p. 6.

was being sent.[34] Cesare had been a constant threat to Florence since the spring of 1501. In June 1502 a rebellion broke out in Arezzo and the surrounding Valdichiana, fostered by Vitellozzo Vitelli and Piero de' Medici and, it was suspected, Cesare Borgia. Cesare, in response, asked to see some Florentine representatives.[35] No meeting between Soderini and Machiavelli is recorded before this date, and yet after a few days, a firm bond seems to have been forged, based on a mutual interest in politics.

Given Machiavelli's fame, it is hardly surprising that their respective roles on the embassy have been discussed, as has the authorship of the letters sent back to Florence. In both areas, just as on the later mission of Francesco Vettori and Machiavelli to Maximilian I, Machiavelli took a subordinate role to that of the 'chief of the mission and primary negotiator'.[36] Machiavelli left Urbino after two days to report in person to the *Signoria*, as Cesare Borgia was so threatening. Soderini struggled on alone until the second half of July, attempting to persuade Cesare that the Florentines were interested in his friendship (whereas in fact they were firmly in the French camp), and that a treaty would soon be reached; and eventually Cesare and Soderini parted on bad terms. Acquaintance with Machiavelli and Cesare may have been thought-provoking, but at the time, the embassy was unpleasant and confusing.

Soderini's ninth and final embassy was yet again as resident ambassador to France. Finding ambassadors who were prepared to go on this mission had proved well-nigh impossible. Refusals to serve the republic as ambassador were commonplace at this time and were rightly construed by contemporaries as a sign of disaffection with the way in which the republic's affairs were being conducted. The appointment of a permanent *gonfaloniere*, on 22 September 1502, was designed in part to meet these objections by providing a consistent central element in the political system and in the formulation of policy.[37] The election of Piero Soderini to this position changed the course of Soderini family history, catapulting its members into the political limelight. From being active, but ordinary, participants in the political affairs of the republic in their various ways, they suddenly became the ruling family. The implication of this for their relationship with the Medici should be obvious, for they were now perceived as the main opponents to the Medici and the

---

[34] ASF, Sig., Leg. e com. 26, 88v.

[35] *Dispacci di Antonio Giustinian, ambasciatore veneto a Roma dal 1502 al 1505*, ed. P. Villari (Florence, 1876), I, p. 36.

[36] R. Devonshire Jones, 'Some observations on the relations between Francesco Vettori and Niccolò Machiavelli during the embassy to Maximilian I', *Italian studies*, 23 (1968), pp. 102 and 110.

[37] Guicciardini, *Storie fiorentine*, pp. 239–40.

primary obstacle to be removed before the Medici could return to power in Florence. Suddenly it became the fault of the Soderini in particular, rather than the republican government as a whole, that the Medici had been ousted. To what extent this opposition was forced upon the Soderini and to what extent it was welcomed as a fair representation of opposing belief systems is still not clear. Both Piero and Francesco had always supported the republic and it would not be fair at this point, that is eight years after the implementation of the republic, to describe this advocacy as opportunistic.

The first major consequence for the family of Piero's election as *gonfaloniere a vita* was that, on 3 November, Francesco was chosen for the unpopular task of ambassador to France, in conjunction with Alessandro Nasi. Refusal would have been inadvisable. In reality, this was a continuation of Soderini's previous mission to France which had ended only three months before. As residents, the ambassadors would pass on all the Italian news and glean as much as possible of French policy towards the peninsula and Florence.[38] Just as Piero's election was greeted joyously by the French king, so too Francesco, as his brother and as an old French hand, was welcomed warmly on his arrival on 10 December.[39]

Nearly seven months later, news of a second and momentous consequence reached the French court: Soderini had been promoted to the cardinalate.[40] It was the end of his diplomatic career and the beginning of his cardinalitial career, but the former had led to the latter. Soderini's diplomatic activity is of crucial importance because it enabled him to broaden his political outlook away from the home base of Florence and the religious base of Rome, and it introduced him to important political contacts who were to be essential in later life. Many of the political figures that he mentioned in his diplomatic letters became friends, acquaintances or patrons, as did some of the heads of state to whom he was sent as ambassador. The most obvious examples of this are the kings of France but he also met figures such as cardinal Giuliano della Rovere (the future Julius II), cardinal Georges d'Amboise and the marquis of Mantua. The experience of living and working abroad made him aware of different types of behaviour and of what could be expected from whom. It was an ideal apprenticeship for a curia cardinal.

[38] The instructions are in ASF, Sig., Leg. e com., 23, 59r–60v.
[39] N. Machiavelli, *Lettere*, ed. F. Gaeta (Milan, 1961), p. 111, Buonaccorsi to Machiavelli, 21 December 1502: 'C'è hoggi lettere in privato dallo corte proprio, et danno nuove della adrivare suo là, et dicono esserli stato facto honore grandissimo, et visto tanto volentieri quanto huomo che vi andassi mai.'
[40] BNF, GC, 21, 28r–28v and ASF, Dieci, Resp. 72, 248r.

PART II

THE CARDINAL AS A POLITICAL FORCE, 1503–1513

CHAPTER 3

SODERINI'S ELEVATION TO THE CARDINALATE

Francesco Soderini was elevated to the cardinalate in Alexander VI's ninth and final promotion on 31 May 1503.[1] Five of the new cardinals were Spanish, some of them barely known, even by contemporaries at court,[2] three were Italian and one Austrian; all were bishops except Jacopo Casanova who was a steward to the pope. An interesting description of the new cardinals is given by Giovanvettorio Soderini, the Florentine orator in Rome; it illustrates well fundamental aspects of the honours system, such as the great importance of family ties and the desirability of having held a high post in the curia.[3] In it, two of the new cardinals were described as the nephews of important men (one was a papal nephew), and three others as members of the papal bureaucracy.[4] Like renaissance bishops, fifteenth- and early sixteenth-century cardinals were not, in the main, chosen for their devotion to the religious life; rather, their ability to join these elites depended upon their capacity to muster the patronage of some of the most influential men in Europe.

The internal politics of Soderini's appointment were not altogether straightforward; on their own, Florence and the Soderini regime did not carry enough weight to obtain a red hat for the city.[5] It was, in any case, families and dynasties in conjunction with their cities, rather than cities alone, which were able to manipulate the patronage networks to their advantage; sometimes, the acquisition of a cardinalate for a member of the family signalled, as was true for the Soderini, the

---

[1] C. Eubel, *Hierarchia catholica medii aevi*, II (Münster, 1901), p. 26.
[2] ASMa, AG, b.855, 340r, Rome, 31 May 1503, Giovanni Lucido Cattanei to marquis Francesco Gonzaga.
[3] For information on clerks of the apostolic chamber and on secretaries who became cardinals, P. Partner, *The pope's men: the papal civil service in the renaissance* (Oxford, 1990), p. 75.   [4] See ASF, Sig., Dieci, Otto, Leg. e com. 68, 119v.
[5] For a comparison with the negotiations leading to Ascanio Sforza's promotion to the cardinalate in 1484, see Pellegrini, 'Ascanio Maria Sforza', pp. 268–87.

consecration of a new power.[6] The last Florentine cardinal before Soderini had been Giovanni de' Medici, whose promotion in 1489 was, after all, out of the ordinary as he was a boy of thirteen.[7] His father Lorenzo de' Medici had married a daughter, Maddalena, to Franceschetto Cibo, Innocent VIII's son, in 1487, and had thereby placed himself in position to ask for a red hat for Florence. He was given the choice of his son Giovanni or Gentile Becchi, the bishop of Arezzo – although Francesco Soderini was mentioned as a possible candidate at one point – and naturally he chose his son.[8] The only other Florentine promoted to the cardinalate in the fifteenth century was Alberto Alberti in 1439.[9]

This prompts the question of who had helped in the elevation of Soderini to the purple. The Florentine government sent five letters of thanks, one to the pope on 6 June, followed by others to Cesare Borgia, the college of cardinals, cardinal Antoniotto Pallavicino[10] and cardinal Adriano Castellesi on 7 June. The pope and the college are expected addressees, but the links to the pope's son and the two cardinals require further investigation. Soderini of course knew Cesare Borgia, and from the letter it is quite clear that the son had prevailed upon his father in support of Soderini's candidacy,[11] but the extent to which this had been a decisive factor in Soderini's appointment is not known. Antoniotto Pallavicino was one of the more senior cardinals, having been elevated on 9 March 1489, a leading canon lawyer and one of Soderini's superiors when a referendary.[12] Adriano Castellesi was promoted at the same time as Soderini. He had an interesting career in the curia, ranging from papal *nuncio* in England to papal cubicular, to treasurer general, to secretary, and in March 1498 he had offered Alexander 20,000 ducats to be promoted, but without success.[13] He was a great intimate of

---

[6] See Bizzocchi, *Chiesa e potere*, p. 351.

[7] See G. Picotti, *La giovinezza di Leone X* (Milan, 1928), p. 191.

[8] *Ibid.*, pp. 170, 181–2.

[9] Moroni, *Dizionario*, xxv, p. 24 and Eubel, *Hierarchia*, ii, p. 8.

[10] He was also cited by Jacopo Gherardi as one of the people to thank. As Gherardi was present in Rome at the time, presumably he knew what he was saying. See Volterra, Biblioteca Guarnacci, MS 6204, 33v, 3 June 1503, Gherardi to Soderini.

[11] ASF, Sig., Miss. 1a Canc. 54, 159v: 'La Excellentia vostra ha monstrò in omni sua actione amare et desiderare tanto accrescere alla città nostra honore et utile che la ha voluto che habbiamo, oltre a molti altri obligo ancora seco, della dignità et honore del cardinalato conferito al R.mo M. di Volterra, cittadino nostro, il che riconosciamo da quella sappiendo la opera ne ha facta con la Sanctità di Nostro Signore' and later in the same letter 'la voluntà è caldissima et quando ne sarà la occasione, la Excellentia vostra conoscerà essersi affaticata et havere conferito il benficio in una città la quale non stima cosa alcuna avanti la gratitudine de beneficii ricevuti'.   [12] See above, p. 22.

[13] See the entry on Adriano Castellesi by G. Gragnito in the *Dizionario biografico degli italiani*.

Alexander, one of the few high-ranking Italians in a papal household otherwise dominated by Catalans.[14] He had reason to know Soderini who, when a referendary, had signed the brief of Innocent VIII authorising the annulment of Castellesi's marriage with a certain Brigida di Bartolomeo of Volterra on the grounds of ill health and consequent non-consummation.[15]

Another possible patron, although unacknowledged in this first series of letters, was Louis XII. It was generally believed by, for example, the Mantuan ambassador in Rome,[16] that the combination of the French king and Piero Soderini had brought about this elevation. Guicciardini thought that Francesco Soderini was a suitable candidate but that the reason for his acquisition of this honour was not the backing of France and Florence, which was only a front, but the large sum of money that he paid for it,[17] which Cambi suggested could have been as much as 20,000 *scudi*.[18] Parenti too considered that Soderini was worthy of the honour although it had cost him dearly.[19] There is no surviving evidence that Louis agitated on behalf of Soderini although he evinced great pleasure on hearing of his election. Soderini's fellow ambassador, Nasi, described the reactions of both the legate, cardinal Georges d'Amboise, and the king, who showed himself 'to be as happy and well satisfied as if a French cardinal had been elected'. Nasi took this as proof that the pope must be francophile as he had elevated such a good friend of the king's to this rank.[20]

From this exchange it seems unlikely that Louis had involved himself practically in the matter of Soderini's candidacy, but it was true that Soderini's appointment found favour with France. The letter of congratulation addressed by Louis to the *Dieci* makes this quite clear and

[14] M. Mallett, *The Borgias* (London, 1969), p. 233.

[15] The brief is published by A. Ferrajoli, 'Il matrimonio di Adriano Castellesi poi cardinale e il suo annullamento', *Archivio della reale società romana di storia patria*, 42 (1919), pp. 302–4 and discussed by P. Paschini, 'Tre illustri prelati del rinascimento', *Lateranum*, 23 (1957), pp. 48–50.

[16] ASMa, AG, b.855, 340r, 31 May 1503, Giovanni Lucido Cattanei.

[17] Guicciardini, *Storie fiorentine*, p. 261: 'si gli conveniva quello grado. Nondimeno non gliene dettono questi meriti, ma lo acquistò con qualche favore di Francia e della città, in nome; in fatto, lo comperò buona somma di danari, sendo così allora la consuetudine del papa.'

[18] G. Cambi, 'Istorie', in *Delizie degli eruditi toscani*, Ildefonso di S. Luigi, 24 vols., xx–xxiii (Florence, 1785–6), ii, p. 191.

[19] Parenti, 'Istorie', BNF, ii ii 133, 103v.

[20] ASF, Dieci, Resp. 72, 248v: 'Sua Maestà ne mostrò essere benissimo contenta et satisfacta non altrimenti che se fussi electo uno cardinale franzese, et ripigliando il legato le parole aumentò le commendationi, et de questo si persuadeva il papa dovere essere buono franzese, havendo assumpto a questa dignità uno si buono amicho della Maestà del re.'

shows that Louis was preparing to employ Soderini as an advocate of French interests in Florence, even inviting the *Dieci* to believe Soderini as they would believe the king in person.[21] From Louis' point of view, he had gained a valuable French protégé and ally in the college of cardinals at no financial cost to the crown.

On 10 June Soderini received formal permission from Louis to resign his post and at dawn on 12 June he set out for Florence with the good wishes of the whole court.[22] On 10 June he had written a letter to the *Dieci* in which he described that morning's audience with the king, in the course of which Louis had proposed writing to the pope and Cesare Borgia to thank them for Soderini's promotion.[23] This announces fairly clearly the persons whom Louis considered were responsible for Soderini's red hat. The interesting one is Cesare Borgia. His support, combined with Alexander VI's willingness to accommodate Piero Soderini's demands for his brother[24] in order to gain the favour of Florence, and Louis' esteem for Soderini, provides a sufficient explanation for Soderini's promotion. It should not be forgotten that backing from the unlikely partnership of Louis XII and Cesare Borgia had already helped to dictate the choice of Piero Soderini as *gonfaloniere a vita* less than a year before.[25]

There was widespread rejoicing in Florence at the news, which reached the city almost immediately on 1 June and provoked a great party with bonfires and illuminations.[26] Soderini wrote to the *Signoria* on 6 June a characteristically patriotic letter in which he expressed his thanks and devotion to Florence. He claimed that his preferment was an honour not so much to him as to his birthplace, stated his willingness to sacrifice everything in the service of the republic if need be, and ended by commending himself, his brother and his family to the city.[27] In a similar letter to the *Dieci*, Soderini expressed his loyalty to Florence. He said that he had always placed his talents at the disposal of his fatherland and that his election to the cardinalate would put him in a position where his services would be even more valuable.[28] It was, he claimed,

[21] Canestrini, *Négociations*, II, p. 77, Lyon, 12 June 1503.
[22] BNF, GC, 21, 31v and 32r.   [23] ASF, Dieci, Resp. 72, 272r.
[24] Immediately after his election as *gonfaloniere* in 1502, Piero Soderini was openly expressing his ambition for Francesco to be made a cardinal. See Giustinian, *Dispacci*, I, p. 207.
[25] S. Bertelli, '"Uno magistrato per a tempo lungho o uno dogie"', in *Studi di storia medievale e moderna per Ernesto Sestan*, II (Florence, 1980), pp. 481–4.
[26] L. Landucci, *Diario fiorentino dal 1450 al 1516*, ed. I. del Badia (Florence, 1883), p. 256 and P. Vaglienti, *Storia dei suoi tempi, 1492–1514*, ed. G. Berti, M. Luzzati and E. Tongiorgi (Pisa, 1982), p. 178.   [27] ASF, Sig., Resp. 26, 125r.
[28] ASF, Dieci, Resp. 72, 252r: 'fin qui ogni mio studio è stato in ornando et augenda patria, così habbi a essere tanto per lo advenire, quanto io lo potrò meglio

a signal honour to Florence that so many of her sons should feel these sentiments.

Soderini made a triumphal journey from Lyons to Florence with a stay of over a week in Piacenza. He reached the Badia Fiesolana on 15 July, and according to contemporary diarists he was greeted by a large troop of possibly five hundred horsemen and young men who had carried his cardinal's hat up there.[29] One of the graffiti in the kitchen of the Palazzo Davanzati also attests to his arrival: 'A dì 15 di luglio 1503 / vene a Fiorenz il Gardenal / de Pietro Sodarino' but the name Pietro has quite rightly been crossed out.[30] Soderini entered Florence by the Porta S. Gallo on 16 July, a Sunday, and was met by some of the richest men in the city, both old and young, and twenty-two doctors[31] from the university of Pisa.[32] He rode to S. Maria del Fiore and dismounted at the steps. The whole cathedral had been marvellously decorated. Present at the mass were the *Signoria* and Piero Soderini, although, in the absence of the archbishop of Florence, Rinaldo Orsini, who had been imprisoned by Alexander VI and Cesare Borgia,[33] the mass had to be led by a substitute. When it was over, Cosimo Pazzi, the bishop of Arezzo, read out the brief that had created Soderini cardinal, said some words in Latin, placed the hat (*cappello*)[34] on his head and sang the

dimostrare, acciochè cotesta inclita città conosca di quanto benefitio li sia havere del suo nido cavato tali figliuoli che voglino essere grati verso la patria loro et per la dignità habbino molte commodità di potere.'

[29] Landucci, *Diario*, p. 257 and Vaglienti, *Storia*, p. 180.

[30] E. Cecchi, 'Le scritte murali', in *Palazzo Davanzati*, ed. M. Fossi Todorow (Florence, 1979), p. 40.   [31] Cambi, 'Istorie', II, p. 193.

[32] A. Fabroni, *Historia academiae Pisanae volumen I–III*, 3 vols., I (Pisa, 1791), p. 149.

[33] L. von Pastor, *A history of the popes*, ed. F. Antrobus, VI (London, 1898), p. 125. Rinaldo was one of several Orsini upon whom the pope exacted retribution after Orsini involvement in the conspiracy of October 1502, at La Magione, against Cesare Borgia.

[34] There seems to have been a certain amount of flexibility in the arrangements for giving cardinalitial insignia, and the various types of cardinals' hats. For example, when Giovanni de' Medici was made cardinal *in petto* in February 1489, his *cappelli* and *napponi* were sent to Florence, but he had to wait until March 1493 to receive the dress and insignia from the abbot of the Badia Fiesolana. See Picotti, *La giovinezza*, pp. 191 and 687. Pompeo Colonna, on the other hand, received the insignia in Flanders in July 1517 from cardinal Luigi d'Aragona and the *cappello* from the pope in Rome in October. See A. Consorti, *Il cardinale Pompeo Colonna* (Rome, 1902), pp. 59–60. Paris de Grassis described the series of consistories at which the newly created cardinals of March 1511 were initiated into the college. On 10 March they received the red *biretta*, on 14 March they were given their red hats, on 17 March they were allocated their titular churches and received their cardinalitial rings, and on 19 March the ceremony of the opening of the mouths took place. See L. Frati, *Le due spedizioni militari di Giulio II* (Bologna, 1886), pp. 244, 246, 249 and 253.

'Te Deum'.[35] The canons of the cathedral gave him a second red hat (perhaps a *biretta*) in a silver bowl. Then Soderini left and went to visit the *Signoria* and his brother in the Palazzo Vecchio where he was given a richly decorated and beautiful silver object worth 1,500 florins,[36] which was the custom of the city when one of its sons visited Florence for the first time since his elevation to the cardinalate. Finally, he rode through the Mercato Nuovo and the Porta Rossa and across the Ponte S. Trinita to his father's house at the foot of Ponte alla Carraia.[37]

He stayed in Tuscany until he heard of Alexander VI's death on 18 August, when he hurried to Rome for the conclave, arriving on 30 August.[38] The next pope, Pius III, was elected on 22 September[39] but was dead by 18 October, so Soderini attended two conclaves within six months of his creation. Cardinal Giuliano della Rovere was elected pope Julius II on 1 November 1503 and reigned until 20 February 1513; thus his pontifical reign formed the background to Soderini's first, formative ten years as a cardinal. Della Rovere had arrived back in Rome for the first conclave of 1503 from France, having been an exile for almost ten years. Unable to secure election in September 1503, the tide of opinion had turned in his favour by October, and in addition to the Spanish votes, he also managed to secure those of the French party. After the shortest conclave in the history of the papacy, lasting only one day, della Rovere was elected pope after a few hours on 31 October and a formal announcement was made on 1 November.[40]

Soderini's promotion provided the opportunity for contemporaries to evaluate his character. The most famous of these assessments is that by Guicciardini. He wrote that Soderini deserved to be a cardinal because he was about fifty years old, had spent a long time at court, was cultured and clever in worldly matters and was quite well bred according to the standards of other priests. He continued that Soderini, who was in many ways virtuous, was, however, in cases where avarice and ambition were involved, extremely immoderate and without respect, without faith and entirely without conscience.[41] Nardi wrote that Soderini was

---

[35] Of the contemporary and near-contemporary Florentine historians, Cambi gives by far the fullest description of this event, revelling in all the details. See Cambi, 'Istorie', II, p. 193.

[36] Parenti, 'Istorie', BNF, II II 133, 115r and *Ricordanze di Bartolomeo Masi*, ed. G. Odoardo Corazzini (Florence, 1906), p. 59.

[37] All this information comes from Cambi, 'Istorie', II, p. 194.

[38] Pastor, *History of the popes*, VI, p. 189.   [39] See below, pp. 80–1.

[40] Pastor, *History of the popes*, VI, pp. 208–10.

[41] Guicciardini, *Storie fiorentine*, p. 261: 'Soderini...uomo che per la età che era di circa a cinquant'anni, per essere stato lungo tempo in corte, per essere litterato e di gran cervello nelle cose del mondo ed assai costumato, secondo lo uso degli altri preti, si gli conveniva questo grado...el Soderino, uomo in molte cose virtuoso,

worthy because he was both modest in his style of life and very experienced in the management of affairs of state.[42]

Soderini's preferment was also the occasion for letters of advice on how he should conduct himself in his new life. Of these, the most interesting was from Bartolomeo Fonti, who counselled how a cardinal should behave and cautioned against the dangers awaiting him. First of all, he explained that a much greater range of people would be interested in him now he was a cardinal and not just a bishop; now the eyes of kings and princes, towns and nations would all be on him.[43] He warned that Soderini would never experience any difficulty as great as that of reconciling the requirements of the cardinalate with those of God and man. In an extended metaphor, he explained that what was necessary for clear sailing in the ship of the church through stormy seas was not golden ornamentation, silken ropes, purple sails, silver oars and clothes woven with gold, but virtue and talent.[44] Finally, Soderini was told to guard against the wrong sort of friend. The gap between rhetoric and reality is here at its most blatant, as it was precisely this wrong sort of friend who had caused Soderini to be elevated to the cardinalate.

pure, dove lo menava la avarizia e la ambizione, immoderatissimo e sanza rispetto, sanza fede e sanza conscienzia alcuna.'

[42] J. Nardi, *Istorie della città di Firenze*, ed. L. Arbib, 1 (Florence, 1838–41), p. 267: 'uomo certamente degno di così fatto grado e per la modestia della vita, e per esser molto esercitato nel maneggio delle cose degli stati.'

[43] B. Fonti, *Epistolarum libri III*, ed. L. Juhasz (Budapest, 1931), p. 42.

[44] *Ibid.*, p. 43: 'Veruntamen tibi cum sit adnavigandum tempestuosum hoc pelagus et agitatae ecclesiae sapienter et fortiter consulendum, etiam atque etiam te adhortor, non aurata corymba, non Sericos rudentes, non purpurea vela, non remos argenteos, non Attalicas vestes, sed ingentes illas animi tui virtutes et singulares ingenii dotes spectandas admirandasque cunctis in ecclesiae nave explices.'

CHAPTER 4

THE RENAISSANCE CARDINALATE AND THE CONCEPT OF THE POLITICAL CARDINAL

It is not clear how far Bartolomeo Fonti's maxims would have been in the forefront of Soderini's mind as he donned his red hat, for his activities as a cardinal remained centred on the essentially political concerns which had characterised his career thus far. In contrast to his brother Piero who was openly devout, Soderini appears not to have made a special show of his religious feelings although he complied with and was attached to all the exterior trappings necessary to a high-ranking religious life, and seems never to have questioned the basic tenets of his christian faith. This should not be interpreted to mean that religious concerns were not important for Soderini, merely that he took for granted their place in his life. However, the precarious balance between the demands of God and man which Fonti envisaged each cardinal having to maintain was easily struck for Soderini in favour of the latter. It is possible that Soderini himself had no very positive or personal sense of what the demands of God were. As for the demands of men, they seemed to entail the continuation of his lifelong and consuming interest in politics.

What kind of an elite was Soderini to join? He and the other eight newly elected cardinals of 31 May 1503 joined a college already containing thirty-six cardinals, thus bringing the total to forty-four. Alexander had created forty-three cardinals, the largest number created by a single pope in the history of the college, but the advanced age of some of the cardinals ensured a high turnover. Since Sixtus IV, the renaissance popes had tended to increase the number of cardinals in the college. The majority of cardinals lived in Rome, but a minority always chose to be non-resident. This minority was normally composed of a few non-Italians who preferred to remain in their country of origin, Italians who for reasons of state or family resided within their own city or territory, and politically disaffected cardinals who were at odds with the reigning pope or his family and stayed outside the curia, agitating in their own power bases. These potential troublemakers often came back to Rome when a new pope was elected. Non-resident cardinals were like the country members of a club; with residence came full membership, for it was residence in Rome which enabled them to take advantage of the rich pickings to be had at the papal court.

The college of cardinals, as an institution, was in a state of flux during this period. Paolo Prodi and Wolfgang Reinhard have described the process whereby the equivalent of the pope's international senate was transformed into a mainly Italian nobility, whose function was to dance attendance on the papal monarchy.[1] The papacy had developed princely or monarchical functions because it had in effect acquired a principality – the revamped papal states. Once the cardinals' role as decision-makers and policy-formers had been taken from them and replaced with the ineffectual role as nobles, they forfeited their power as a college to influence the pope's actions. It is not clear how apparent this process was to the renaissance cardinals themselves. Perhaps Soderini did understand that he had influence with individual popes because he was a cardinal, but that possibilities for group action and group pressure by the cardinals were increasingly curtailed or rendered ineffective.

All attempts at cardinalitial breakaway or collective action during his lifetime ended in failure. For example, participation in the French-sponsored Council of Pisa of 1511 caused certain cardinals to be stripped of their benefices and deprived of their hats, against the representations of the rest of the college. Equally, Soderini's attempt to muster support for his brother Piero and the republican regime in Florence at the end of August 1512, when he headed a delegation of seven cardinals to Julius II, asking him to intervene against the Spanish, produced no positive results.[2] A delegation to Adrian VI of between eleven and thirteen cardinals, in February 1523, complained of Adrian's treatment of the college.[3] The cardinals claimed that only the pope's confidants were consulted and that the college was bypassed and its privileges ignored; Adrian apologised. However, of the renaissance popes of the sixteenth century, possibly only Adrian retained a vestigial belief that the opinion of the cardinals – as individuals, and not as a group – could matter or carry weight.[4] Papal, princely government became more and more personal. Increasingly, the pope chose as advisors his friends and relatives, rather than either the corporate body of the college or individual cardinals.

[1] P. Prodi, The papal prince (Cambridge, 1987), pp. 80–3 and W. Reinhard, 'Struttura e significato del Sacro Collegio tra la fine del xv e la fine del xvi secolo', in Città italiane del '500 tra riforma e controriforma (Lucca, 1988), p. 257–8.
[2] See below, p. 66.   [3] See below, pp. 157–8.   [4] See below, pp. 138–9.

The conventional explanation for the marginalisation of the cardinals' advisory role is that, by the end of the fifteenth century, the college was composed mainly of Italians, and thus was not representative of the universal church. Too much, however, may have been made of this as, despite the increase in the Italian core, many non-Italian cardinals remained. David Chambers has calculated that of the 162 cardinals created during the period 1480–1534, 93 were Italian, but 29 were Spanish and 22 were French.[5] Others, such as Barbara McClung Hallman and Peter Partner, reach slightly different conclusions using slightly different criteria,[6] but the proportion of Italian to non-Italian is approximately the same. How much this was a result of deliberate policy by successive popes and how much it has been rationalised as such after the event is unknown. At the same time as the proportion of Italians was rising, cardinals were being appointed exclusively by the pope, without having been proposed or approved by the college. The national composition of the college affected the popes even more directly: the last non-Italian pope before the latter part of the twentieth century, Adrian VI, was elected in 1522 and died in 1523.

Hand-in-glove with the Italian complexion of the college and the cardinals' loss of autonomous corporate power went the politicisation of the papacy, bringing it into line with other influential secular governments. Nepotism and political appointments abounded, and brought in their wake the development of factions.[7] Outside rivalries and factions replicated themselves in mirror images within the college: for instance, the Colonna cardinal was set in opposition to the Orsini cardinal. Nepotism had been a visible factor since the pontificate of Calixtus III, but Sixtus IV, Alexander VI and Julius II carried it to new lengths.[8] Explanations for nepotism also abound: an unadorned attempt to create new papal and princely dynasties; an expression of piety (*pietas*) towards one's relatives and fellow citizens; a pre-industrial system of consensual government involving elites and clients.[9] What is

---

[5] D. Chambers, *Cardinal Bainbridge in the court of Rome* (Oxford, 1965), p. 6.

[6] See B. McClung Hallman, *Italian cardinals, reform and the church as property* (Berkeley, 1985), p. 4 and Partner, *The pope's men*, p. 209.

[7] Reinhard, 'Struttura', p. 258.

[8] See P. de Roo, *Material for a history of pope Alexander VI*, v (Bruges, 1924), pp. 111–15.

[9] See W. Reinhard, 'Nepotismus. Der Funktionswandel einer papstgeschichtlichen Konstante', *Zeitschrift für Kirchengeschichte*, 86 (1975), pp. 145–85; Reinhard, 'Papa Pius: Prolegomena zu einer Sozialgeschichte des Papsttums', *Von Konstanz nach Trient: Festgabe für August Franzen*, ed. R. Bäumer (Paderborn, 1972), pp. 261–99; and Reinhard, *Freunde und Kreaturen. "Verflechtung" als Konzept zur Erforschung historischer Führungsgruppen. Römische Oligarchie um 1600* (Munich, 1979).

certain is that the loyalty of each cardinal became a matter of concern, and cardinals were classified both according to which pope had promoted them, and according to their political affiliation. Thus, at conclaves, cardinals' cells were covered in coloured cloth to indicate their papal allegiance; those cardinals created by the deceased pope sported violet, whereas the rest displayed green.[10]

This notion of being the creation (or the *creatura*) of a particular pope to whom one owed especial loyalty was important, and by the end of the fifteenth century there were many cardinals who owed loyalty to the dynasty of one of the ex-popes. Moreover, most cardinals arrived in Rome with their political loyalties and bases of support already spoken for: they came from one of the fairly large stock of great Italian families, or they had been recommended by foreign powers, or they belonged to one of the major religious orders.[11] The question of allegiances thus shows the multi-faceted complexity of the networks of patronage and obligation in the college. Soderini was judged to be a Borgia political appointment, owing his loyalty to Florence as his place of birth and *patria*, the republican regime as his family's power base and the kings of France as his extra-Florentine backers.

The issue of divided or fragmented loyalties is complicated but crucial. A system of priorities, taking into account the context of each individual action, meant that there were primary and secondary interests, which could be more or less important at different times. As well as the division of the cardinals into various national and regional groups, they also divided into age groups and, as has been seen, into clusters determined by the pope under whom they had been promoted. The older cardinals ('i cardinali vecchi') behaved at times as a separate entity, whose views did not coincide with those of their younger colleagues, as in September 1523 over the question of whether Soderini should be released from prison.[12] The split was made very obvious in this instance because the older cardinals had all been promoted before Leo X's pontificate. In addition, the cardinals regrouped along lines of common interests and pursuits: those who went hunting, those who were lawyers or theologians, those who were interested in music. These groups could of course overlap; politics and fishing,[13] for example, were not mutually exclusive. Individual popes could decide upon the

---

[10] D. Chambers, 'Papal conclaves and prophetic mystery in the Sistine chapel', *Journal of the Warburg and Courtauld Institutes*, 41 (1978), p. 323.

[11] K. Lowe, 'Questions of income and expenditure in renaissance Rome: a case study of cardinal Francesco Armellini', *Studies in church history*, 24 (1987), p. 183.

[12] See below, p. 139.

[13] For a description of a fishing trip which Soderini went on, see M. Sanuto, *I diarii* (Venice, 1879–1903), VIII, 23, 13 March 1509.

exact recipe which resulted in the college – for instance, they could appoint more political cardinals, or make more religious appointments, or French ones, or promote their relatives – but a mix of cardinals still remained.

That there was a group of cardinals at court at any one time who were more interested in politics than in theology or an ostentatious and splendid life is testified to in a letter from Soderini to the *Dieci* of 15 October 1503. Soderini had heard an interesting piece of information about events in the Romagna which he communicated first to one of the pope's brothers and then he also told cardinal d'Amboise and other cardinals 'interested in affairs of state'.[14] No other 'political' cardinals are named but there is obviously a select group known to be interested in affairs of a political nature. Cardinal Georges d'Amboise was a political cardinal *par excellence*, a Frenchman, promoted on 17 September 1498, who was already known to Soderini on account of the latter's trips to France.

During his career in the curia, Soderini rose from being a junior member of this circle to being its most important protagonist. Marino da Pozzo, secretary to cardinal Pisani, wrote to Francesco Spinelli following Soderini's death in 1524 that a great cardinal had died: 'In political matters there was no one else like him in the college of cardinals.'[15] Natural ability in political matters was not granted to every cardinal, but Soderini was constantly complimented on this gift. Nardi, for example, wrote that at Rome, 'both on account of his nature, and because of his long experience of worldly affairs, he was very wise and shrewd.'[16] Another cardinal might be dismissed for not being a political animal.[17]

The main political division in Europe was that between the Hapsburgs and the Valois, between the forces of the empire (and Spain) and those of France. The two French kings whose reigns overlapped Soderini's career as a cardinal were Louis XII, who ruled from 1498 to 1515, and Francis I, who succeeded in 1515 and stayed on the throne until his death in 1547. The two contemporary emperors were Maximilian I (1493–1519) and Charles V (1519–56). Both the Hapsburgs and the Valois were urged by broad strategic considerations to intervene in the affairs of the Italian peninsula, and both ruling houses had claims to the duchy of Milan and the kingdom of Naples which could only be effectively pressed by their presence in Italy. Given the political clout of

[14] ASF, Dieci, Resp. 75, 218r.   [15] Reported in Sanuto, *I diarii*, XXXVI, 368.
[16] Nardi, *Istorie*, II, p. 69.
[17] See a letter of Francesco to Piero of 18 November 1503 in ASF, Sig., Dieci, Otto, Leg. e com. 35, 15r.

the cardinals, it is hardly surprising that these two super-powers, who held the balance of power in Europe, created their own coteries of supporters in the college, who formed the two main parties. As Soderini's francophile tendencies were well known throughout his career in the curia, relations with the Hapsburgs appear to have been kept to a minimum except in time of emergency, and he was viewed for twenty years as an imperial enemy. But, as will be seen, Soderini was not so politically naive as to refuse to deal with the imperial party when it suited his interests. Because of the system whereby various cardinals were promoted by foreign powers, naturally they were labelled according to their foreign backers. But although this labelling had meaning and sometimes even reflected ideological beliefs, it should not be forgotten that desire for advancement in one form or another often made this process more fluid and less rigid than might have been thought.

The college was, it should be remembered, a very small and privileged body of between thirty and fifty men. Within the smaller, political group there were many different factions grouping and regrouping around the main parties, such as anti-emperor, anti-Medici, pro-emperor, pro-French. In the last analysis the whole college could be divided in this fashion, although some of them paid little attention to political allegiances except when forced to, for example at the time of a conclave. Some could not even manage this. The Venetian diarist, Sanuto, has a list of the cardinals who entered the conclave of November 1523 which elected Clement VII and notes to which party they belonged. Sixteen, including cardinal Medici himself, were Medicean, thirteen were pro-French, four imperial and six were neutral.[18] Given the compactness of the college, its balance was easily upset and a large influx of new creations, as in 1517, meant a shift in relative patterns of allegiance. In Sanuto's list one might have expected those who had been raised to the purple by Leo to vote for the next Medici cardinal, but, in confirmation of the view that allegiances were not clear-cut, of those still alive, ten were Medicean and eight French supporters, with three cardinals each being registered as neutral and imperial.

Soderini's political views as a cardinal were fixed by the attitudes and allegiances which he had acquired as a Florentine patrician. These involved a very close identification of his own and his family's interests with those of the Florentine republic, and as a consequence of this, a feeling of rivalry with, and later hatred of, the Medici. Another vitally important political reality for Soderini was that the future safety of the

---

[18] Sanuto, *I diarii*, xxxv, 223–4.

republic lay in a strong alliance with France. The following account of Soderini's political career up to 1513 is therefore organised around these three themes.

CHAPTER 5

A PRINCIPAL OR A SUPPORTING ROLE IN FLORENTINE POLITICS?

Having a Florentine cardinal at the curia who was not a Medici was of obvious diplomatic and political use to the republic. Soderini was useful to Florence in minor political and religious matters, in that he had much more influence with and greater access to the pope than had the Florentine ambassador who would normally have carried out these tasks. The affairs that he dealt with were essentially local issues, not ones of great importance. For example, year after year, he was asked to help expedite the indulgence for the feast day of the cathedral of Santa Maria del Fiore on 25 March. He and the Florentine ambassador usually applied for this together and the report sent by Roberto Acciaiuoli on 9 March 1508 is typical: 'with the help and work of cardinal Volterra it was arranged according to your wishes'.[1] The intervention of a cardinal made the application more likely to succeed. On this point the Florentine ambassadors all co-operated equally happily with Soderini. He also regularly introduced the new Florentine orator to the pope on his arrival.[2] From Florence, the *Signoria*, the *Dieci* and the First Chancery all wrote to him, from time to time, asking him to use his influence with the pope, the college or a particular cardinal in the interests of Florence or her *contado*. The matters could be diverse: some ran on for years, others were short-term even if part of a larger movement, and still others were small affairs of the moment.

At the end of August 1507 he was asked to help untangle the muddle over the dowry of Piero de' Medici's widow, Alfonsina Orsini. This was merely one stage in the long-drawn-out business, and the affair itself was one small prong of the counter-attack launched against Florence by the Medici after their expulsion. Alfonsina claimed that the republic had confiscated possessions or goods which had formed part of her dowry

[1] ASF, Sig., Resp. 30, 49r.
[2] ASF, Dieci, Resp. 84, 178r, Rome, Alessandro Nasi, 26 November 1505.

and that it must repay her, and she took the government to court over it. The situation was complicated because she was a member of the Orsini family who were the greatest enemies of the Colonna. Therefore, the factional struggle in Rome between Orsini and Colonna could be seen to be mirrored by the opposition of the Florentine Medici to the Soderini, and as the Orsini were linked to the Medici, not only by Alfonsina's marriage to Piero but also by Clarice's marriage earlier to Piero's father, Lorenzo, the Soderini had little choice but to ally themselves, in a general way, to the Colonna. Soderini was thus an enemy twice over to Alfonsina.

At the same time, he was asked to help the community of S. Gimignano which wanted to reform certain Franciscan convents.[3] This matter was part of the much larger monastic reform movement of the fifteenth century, when many monasteries changed from being conventual to observant.[4] Other Florentine or Tuscan subjects requiring Francesco Soderini's attention in the early years were the clerical tax imposed by Piero Soderini and the government, and the university at Pisa. The pope became involved with the former when the general of the Vallombrosan order refused to pay and so many of his goods were confiscated, and Vallombrosa and other monasteries in the order were ransacked. The pope responded by summoning both Soderini and the Florentine ambassador and threatening to put Florentine merchants in Rome in prison in Castel Sant'Angelo if the damage were not made good.[5]

Soderini was also asked to intercede to help people with quarrels with Florence; these could be cardinals or curia officials or Florentine merchants living away from the city. Some of these grievances, as usual, were linked to the Medici. The financial collapse of the Medici bank had created enormous debts and many felt that Florence, which had been so identified with the family, ought to take on the obligation to discharge them. Soderini wrote to the *Signoria* about one such case on 1 July 1504. Two brothers, Bonifaccio and Giovanstefano de Ferrero, respectively the bishop of Ivrea and the cardinal of Bologna, had complained that they had not been able to obtain satisfaction from Florence in respect of some credits which the bishop of Ivrea claimed that his predecessor had been owed by the Medici, and that he was now owed in his turn. Soderini advised the *Signoria* that since the bishop had right on his side,

---

[3] ASF, Sig., Miss. 1a Canc. 56, 29v, 30 August 1507.

[4] For general points, see N. Rubinstein, '"Reformation" und Ordensreform in italienischen Stadtrepubliken und Signorien', *Reformbemühungen und Observanzbestrebungen im spätmittelalterlichen Ordenswesen*, ed. K. Elm (Berlin, 1989), pp. 521–38.

[5] E. Loccatelli, *Vita del glorioso padre San Giovangualberto* (Florence, 1583), pp. 296–7.

it was better to administer justice with a good grace. Otherwise, he considered shame and damage would result and in the end the government would be forced to fulfil its obligations.[6] This letter and one of 3 July from the cardinal of Bologna prompted immediate action in the form of letters despatched by the chancery to both Giovanni Acciaiuoli, the ambassador at that time, and Soderini on 9 July.[7]

Soderini's standing in Rome could also be used to further the patronage links of the Soderini family and their dependants and associates. Piero and Francesco Soderini took up much of their correspondence recommending people to each other. Some were straightforwardly friends and acquaintances of Francesco, such as Antonio Segni,[8] Giovanni Vanulio, Baccio del Vantagio,[9] ser Marco da Marradi[10] and ser Bastiano da Casina.[11] These covered the whole social spectrum: Segni was a servant, Vanulio, an auditor of the *Rota*, ser Marco was a notary and ser Bastiano was described as a priest. In the early days under Julius, Francesco sometimes recommended friends of the pope to Piero. For example, on 23 November 1504 he recommended the marquis of Finale to Piero: 'Your Excellency knows how much he is worth in his own person, because he has the backing of the pope and because of going to France, but above all because of his very close ties to you and me.'[12] This was quite a gallery of reasons. On 16 October 1505 he wrote in favour of messer Baldo da Prato who was then castellan of the fortified castle at Ostia: 'he is very much in the favour of the pope and an old friend of our family and altogether a man and client who deserves every success.' This part of the letter was written by Francesco himself,[13] and was a family courtesy. Francesco recommended these people in the same spirit that he recommended his brother Giovanvettorio to cardinal Ippolito d'Este on 1 September 1509 when Giovanvettorio was going as ambassador to the emperor.[14] Here he

---

[6] ASF, Sig., Resp. 27, 96r.   [7] ASF, Sig., Miss. 1a Canc. 55, 31v-32r.

[8] BNF, GC, 29 (109), 3422782, Francesco to Piero, Rome, 31 October 1505. Segni was later to die for his service to the Soderini.

[9] *Ibid.*, 3422786, Francesco to Piero, Rome, 15 November 1505. Francesco recommended Vanuli and Vantagio in the same letter.

[10] BNF, Magl. VIII, 1392, letter no. 91, Francesco to Piero, Bologna, 23 January 1507.

[11] BNF, GC, 29 (109), 3422760, Rome, 31 October 1504. Francesco had written in his own hand 'amicus est'.

[12] *Ibid.*, 3422772: 'V. Ex. cognosce quello che merita per la persona sua et per essere huomo di N. S. et per andare in Francia, ma sopra tutto per essere amicissimo vostro et mio.'

[13] *Ibid.*, 3422777: 'è acceptissimo alla S.tà del N. S. et antiquo amico di casa nostra et tucto amico et homo che merita ogni bene.'

[14] ASMo, Arch. Estense, Cancelleria ducale, Carteggio dei principi esteri (cardinali) b.1427/178, Soderini to cardinal Ippolito d'Este from Empoli.

could expect Ippolito to respond well because he was a fellow-cardinal. Usually, a recommendation was a way of alerting a friend or contact to the presence of a third friend or contact. Unless a job or position or favour were specified, recommendations were not worth much in terms of patronage, especially as so many were busy recommending.[15]

However, Soderini's position at Rome offered him greater prospects than that of a mere dealer in low-grade patronage. His status as a cardinal and his links with both France and the pope, all equipped him for a leading role in the affairs of the republic. Whether he used these opportunities simply to act as the servant of policies made in Florence, or whether his contribution was of a more active nature, is perhaps the most important issue raised in the discussion of his political career prior to 1512.

Soderini was certainly capable of playing a more active part. Although he was a junior cardinal, his brother was the constitutional head of the Florentine republic for life, and Julius II, at the beginning of his pontificate at least, looked favourably upon his new Florentine advisor. Perhaps Julius was pleased by Francesco Soderini's and Francesco Remolino's expedition to Cesare Borgia in November 1503, when Cesare had been rumoured to be leaving Ostia and going first to La Spezia by sea and thence to Ferrara and Imola. He was detained at Ostia and taken to Magliana and held there.[16] Ambassadors' letters through 1504 and 1505 continually report on the close relationship between Soderini and Julius. In February 1504 Soderini is described as never leaving the ear of the pope and being with him every day;[17] in September he was privileged, either alone or with cardinal Riario, to accompany Julius on a short trip to Frascati and other places around Rome.[18] On 13 September Giustinian confessed his worries about Soderini's intimacy with Julius and invited the Venetian government to consider how much dissension Soderini could be sowing in a mind already well enough disposed to receive the bad impressions being fed into it.[19] In 1505 Soderini was reported to be the sole cardinal

---

[15] V. Illardi, 'Crosses and carets: renaissance patronage and coded letters of recommendation', *American historical review*, 92 (1987), p. 1133 states that in fifteenth-century Milan, letters of recommendation were coded and divided into three categories according to how much support was being given; some letters of recommendation were therefore disingenuous.

[16] See F. Guicciardini, *Storia d'Italia*, ed. S. Seidel Menchi (Turin, 1971), I, pp. 572–3 and J. Burchard, 'Liber notarum', ed. E. Celani, in *Rerum italicarum scriptores*, ed. L. Muratori, XXXII, II (Città di Castello, 1913), p. 413.

[17] Sanuto, *I diarii*, v, 838 and 805.

[18] See ASF, Dieci, Resp. 79, 364r, and ASF, Sig., Otto, Dieci, Miss. 7, 25r.

[19] Giustinian, *Dispacci*, III, p. 229.

accompanying Julius both around Rome and on a visit to Nepi,[20] and he went in convoy with the pope on his triumphal journeys to Perugia and Bologna in the autumn of 1506.[21]

This intimacy with the pope often prompted Julius to consult Soderini in conjunction with the Florentine ambassador. It was presumed that he could listen in to any of the conversations between pope and ambassador, even though cardinal de' Medici was never treated in this fashion. The more serious the discussion, the more likely it was that Soderini would be summoned. For example, Julius sent for him and Matteo Niccolini, the Florentine ambassador, in December 1509 when the sons of Giovanni Bentivoglio had conspired to return to Bologna and had been found out.[22] A confession had been extracted from one of the servants and a copy of it was shown to Soderini. In it the servant confessed that Giuliano de' Medici had, with the protonotary Bentivoglio, been one of the ringleaders of the plot to retake Bologna.[23]

For his part, Soderini co-operated closely with the ambassadors in Rome wherever possible. Six orators had been elected to offer Florence's congratulations to Julius II on 4 and 6 November 1503: Guglielmo Capponi, Antonio Malegonelle, Tommaso di Paolantonio Soderini, Matteo Strozzi, Cosimo Pazzi and Francesco Girolami,[24] and their commission was dated 29 November. The resident orator, Giovanni Acciaiuoli, was not elected until 21 March 1504 and returned to Florence eighteen months later on 18 October 1505.[25] From then until the fall of the republic in September 1512 there was on average one ambassador a year. Acciaiuoli was followed by Alessandro Nasi (commission 13 November 1505), Francesco Pepi (10 October 1506), Roberto Acciaiuoli, Giovanni's cousin (4 May 1507), Matteo Niccolini (27 July 1509), Pierfrancesco Tosinghi (24 July 1510) and Antonio Strozzi (23 December 1511).[26] It has been suggested that 'although [Piero] Soderini's supporters were no more prominent in the *Dieci* than his opponents, they were conspicuous as ambassadors',[27] but this was no guarantee that they would see eye to eye with Francesco. From 1502 to 1512 the role of Florentine ambassador in Rome was absolutely crucial, and although all the men on the above list were good republicans, they differed in both their attitudes to Piero and their relationships with Francesco. For example, Francesco got on well with Giovanni

[20] *Ibid.*, III, p. 354 and ASF, Dieci, Resp. 84, 3v.
[21] Pastor, *History of the popes*, VI, pp. 270 and 282.
[22] ASF, Dieci, Resp. 98, 297r.   [23] *Ibid.*, 308r.
[24] ASF, Sig. e collegi, Delib. di speciale autorità 40, 49r.   [25] *Ibid.*, 51v.
[26] ASF, Sig., Leg. e com. 23, 63r–88v.
[27] R. Cooper, 'Pier Soderini: aspiring prince or civic leader?', *Studies in medieval and renaissance history*, I (1978), p. 99.

Acciaiuoli, far better than with his two successors, Nasi and Pepi, both of whom Francesco had been with as co-ambassador on diplomatic missions. With Nasi, in particular, the relationship was conducted along strictly professional lines. This could have been the result of jealousy but could also be in response to the increased power of the whole family; Nasi may have felt that the republic had become too identified yet again with the fortunes of just one family, the Soderini.

Soderini's position was not without its ambiguities. It would appear that the Florentine government did not fully appreciate the circumstances under which he worked in Rome. On one occasion, in June 1506, he wrote asking the *Signoria*, both in a particular case relating to cardinal Jacopo Serra, the legate in Perugia, and in general, to accord more respect to the cardinals because they were in a position to be very useful to the city. He also asked that the *Signoria* proceed in a different fashion with cardinals (and most especially with those who were known to look favourably on Florence) than with men who were not senators of the church.[28] Most Florentines only seemed to understand the importance of cardinals in a Florentine context, and not what they stood for in Rome. Although Florence was practised enough at receiving them as guests to the city, there had been remarkably few Florentine cardinals in living memory, and most Florentines, although aware of the increase in status injected by such promotion, had no real idea what this involved. Consequently, cardinals' complaints were treated as casually as complaints from Florentine ruling families, with no thought as to what loss of patronage or favour this might entail.

The relative autonomy which Soderini enjoyed as a cardinal, together with the closeness of his relationship with his brother Piero, caused many in Florence to question his alleged involvement in the formulation of policy. He was suspected most often of interference in foreign policy. A blatant example of this involved Soderini's engagement of Giovanpaolo Baglioni as a *condottiere* for Florence in October 1503. On 13 October Soderini wrote to the priors and the *gonfaloniere* explaining that on his own initiative he had issued a *condotta* to Giovanpaolo and Gentile Baglioni; there had been insufficient time to seek authorisation. He added that he felt sure the French king and cardinal d'Amboise would be pleased by this.[29] The notarial document, also of 13 October, authorising a *condotta* of 23,000 gold ducats to Baglioni, was drawn up by Raimondo Raimondi, a member of Soderini's household; Soderini was doing it 'on behalf of the Florentine republic'.[30] This incident shows clearly how Soderini, freshly arrived from France, could exploit

[28] ASF, Sig., Resp. 29, 94r.   [29] ASF, Dieci, Resp. 76, 129r.
[30] *Ibid.*, 127r–128r.

his position of favour with the French monarchy to sanction his dealings with Florence. Niccolò Machiavelli was sent to Rome by the *Dieci*, with instructions dated 23 October, to observe the election of a good pope, to help enlist Baglioni as a *condottiere* (subject to certain conditions) and to take his cue from Soderini.[31] It seems likely that Machiavelli was therefore sent after the event to regularise a decision already taken by Soderini.

Were the Soderini brothers acting independently of the usual republican channels of government decision-making? Roslyn Pesman Cooper has considered this in some detail.[32] It appears that the Florentine government did not immediately ratify Baglioni's *condotta* because, in February 1504, there were discussions about the appointment of a captain and *condottieri*, with all the old arguments. Piero Soderini was in favour of the Colonna and Savelli, and his opponents in favour of the Orsini and Baglioni. Pesman Cooper states that 'the *condottieri* finally engaged included Marcantonio Colonna, Jacopo and Luca Savelli and Giovanpaolo Baglioni'.[33] On 4 April 1504 Francesco Soderini again supervised the drawing up of a *condotta*, this time for Marcantonio Colonna, written out in Francesco Cappello's hand.[34] Cappello was a Florentine public servant in Rome. This *condotta*, too, was not acceptable to the government and Marcantonio was not engaged until later. It is quite clear that Soderini had set up this contract without the authority to do so, and that the contract was known about, because Manfredo Manfredi wrote to Alfonso d'Este in April that he had been told by an agent of the Colonna in Florence that Soderini had concluded an agreement in Rome.[35] As usual, the *condotta* seems to have been a vehicle for a piece of Soderini–Medici rivalry. Cerretani wrote that it was fixed in such a way that cardinal de' Medici with his supporters, and cardinal Soderini with his, each had their part in it.[36] Cardinal de' Medici's part must have been an opposing one.

By the end of 1504 Francesco and Piero's joint ventures were annoying the Florentines and notes circulating in the city called for the removal of both brothers, 'il Dogie e il cappello'.[37] It is important here to note that these nicknames had been chosen because they refer to positions of power emanating from sources outside Florence, that is,

---

[31] Machiavelli, *Le legazioni*, ed. Passerini and Milanesi, II, pp. 299–301.

[32] See R. L. Cooper, 'Piero Soderini: *gonfaloniere a vita* of Florence, 1502–1512'(Ph.D. dissertation, University of London, 1965), pp. 236–63 and R. Cooper, 'Machiavelli, Francesco Soderini and Don Michelotto', *Nuova rivista storica*, 66 (1982), pp. 342–57.   [33] Cooper, 'Piero Soderini', p. 160.

[34] ASF, Dieci, Resp. 78, 18r–21r.   [35] Cooper, 'Piero Soderini', p. 195.

[36] B. Cerretani, 'Istoria fiorentina' in BNF, II III 74, 322v.

[37] Parenti, 'Istorie' in BNF, II II 134, 45r.

from Venice and the papacy; they were, in essence, a protest against interference in the city's affairs by non-Florentine forces. But the joint ventures of the Soderini brothers did not always succeed. Marcantonio Colonna left the services of Florence, probably piqued because he wanted to be captain and the role had gone instead to Ercole Bentivoglio. Parenti believed that Francesco Soderini had promised the title to Marcantonio on Piero's behalf but that Piero had then been unable to acquire it for him, which certainly seems plausible.[38] Soderini does not seem to have learnt his lesson, or perhaps he merely thought that he had been unlucky, for in May 1505 he arranged for the possibility of Florence hiring 1500 German infantry; but the offer was declined. In August the question of the appointment of Don Miguel de Corella came up.[39] Francesco wrote to Piero at least twice on his behalf,[40] but there was stiff opposition to his appointment, and Parenti thought that this was due to the belief that the initiative for engaging him had come yet again from Francesco Soderini. When the fuss had died down, Piero wrote to Francesco that Don Miguel had been hired to guard over the district and countryside, which would be very worthwhile and honourable if he performed his duty.[41]

It does seem as if there were two systems in operation: one going between the *Dieci* (or some other part of the Florentine government) and the Florentine ambassador in Rome, and the other, sometimes on a parallel, sometimes on a divergent course, between Piero and Francesco Soderini. In addition, Piero did correspond personally with the Florentine ambassadors, and they with him,[42] and Francesco corresponded with the *Dieci* and vice versa. A private, family channel of communication as opposed to a public, republican one was what was feared most by opponents of the regime in Florence. Years of Medicean rule, which had used precisely this strategy, had made many wary of family members acting in accord with one another, whatever their motive. It is undoubtedly the case that Piero and Francesco were very close personally as well as politically, and there is no record of their ever having had an argument or disagreement. Francesco is generally regarded as the stronger character of the two. Scipione Ammirato's remark that if Piero had been the cardinal in the family, he would have become pope, and if Francesco had been the *gonfaloniere*, he would have

---

[38] *Ibid.*, 76r and v, and see also Cooper, 'Piero Soderini', p. 313.

[39] G. Sasso, 'Machiavelli, Cesare Borgia, Don Micheletto e la questione della milizia', in Sasso, *Machiavelli e gli antichi e altri saggi*, II (Milan/Naples, 1988), pp. 57–117.

[40] See Razzi, *Vita*, p. 91, Francesco to Piero, Rome, 26 August 1505, asking for a safe-conduct for Don Miguel de Corella.   [41] ASF, Sig., Minutari 19, 19r.

[42] See Cooper, 'Pier Soderini', p. 99 and ASF, Signori, Minutari 19 and 20.

made himself 'signor di Firenze' shows how their attributes have been historically perceived.[43] Francesco followed the wishes of his brother and tried, it appears, when he had the initiative, to make his brother follow his, but lack of the complete correspondence between the two renders this sort of statement suspect. It could be that Piero had asked Francesco to draw up these *condotte* but had then failed to convince the members of the government in Florence of their desirability; it is not necessarily true that Francesco had the idea and then tried to persuade Piero to adopt it. This second view was the generally accepted reading at the time but it is not necessarily the correct one.

The role of Machiavelli as a go-between for the transaction of business by the Soderini brothers highlights the difficulties involved. Machiavelli was clearly a confidant of Francesco; they shared a common political outlook and used the same vocabulary for the discussion of political affairs and policy.[44] Machiavelli was sent to Rome in 1503 and 1506, and in 1503 his closeness to Francesco was already receiving criticism in Florence. In December of that year one of the members of the *Signoria* complained about Machiavelli, and Buonaccorsi reported that he would tell Machiavelli about these things when he returned to Florence as he did not want to write them down: 'let it suffice to say that there are troublemakers and those to whom it is displeasing that you write praising Francesco Soderini.'[45] The issue of the ordinance establishing a militia (*ordinanza*) further illustrates the point. Roberto Ridolfi hypothesised that Machiavelli and Soderini discussed the matter during Machiavelli's stay in Rome in the autumn and winter of 1503,[46] and the ordinance was first mentioned in a letter of 29 May 1504 from Soderini. Credit is certainly due to Machiavelli for the inspiration behind the scheme to set up a national militia in Florence, and the fact that it was implemented in December 1506 is due, in some measure, to the close relationship that Machiavelli had achieved with Soderini. For in March 1506 Francesco wrote to Piero, on Machiavelli's behalf, praising the initial stages of the project and urging him to appoint a suitably disciplinarian commander.[47] The whole affair shows the impossibility of distinguishing between Machiavelli's public role as a

---

[43] S. Ammirato, *Delle famiglie nobili fiorentine* (Florence, 1615), p. 131.

[44] See, for example, two letters from Soderini to Machiavelli of 29 May and 26 October 1504, Machiavelli, *Lettere*, pp. 126–7 and p. 135, which discuss *bene pubblico* and *bene privato*. In the first letter Soderini writes 'chi vole venire a la extremità se inzegna a nettare tutto il camino di mezo'.

[45] Machiavelli, *Lettere*, pp. 122–3.

[46] R. Ridolfi, *Vita di Niccolò Machiavelli*, (Florence, 1972), I, p. 128.

[47] See on this N. Rubinstein, 'Machiavelli and the world of Florentine politics', in *Studies on Machiavelli*, ed. M. Gilmore (Florence, 1972), pp. 14–16.

servant of the Florentine state and his private role as a protégé of the Soderini.

Whatever the truth of the matter, given the ingrained tendency of the Florentines to search for and excoriate clashes between the public interests of the state, and the private interests of leading office-holders and patrician families, such unofficial activities could not but attract adverse comment. For instance, Guicciardini cited three occasions on which he claimed that Francesco Soderini played an independent role in the formulation of foreign policy. In one example, Guicciardini showed how independent action by the *gonfaloniere* and his brother left the official servants of the state in ignorance of so-called Florentine policy with consequently embarrassing results.[48] In the other two examples, Guicciardini attributed Soderini's actions firstly to the pursuit of his feud with the Medici,[49] and then to the furtherance of private rather than public interest.[50] These later disagreements over Florentine *condottieri* (for Guicciardini's examples all concerned the hire of soldiers) were probably displaced from the row over Soderini's engagement of Baglioni on his own initiative in October 1503. In each of the cases mentioned by Guicciardini, there is a perfectly ordinary explanation for Soderini's behaviour. Guicciardini had written that Marcantonio and Muzio Colonna had been hired in 1505 'through the influence of Piero Soderini who trusted them because they were enemies of the Orsini and also because this was the wish of Francesco, who wanted the support of the Colonna in order to be able to stand comparison with cardinal de' Medici, the relative and favourite of the Orsini'.[51] At this point personal competition between the two cardinals can be said to have forced Francesco Soderini's hand. The Colonna–Soderini alliance was a direct result of the Orsini–Medici one as obviously the Soderini and Medici cardinals could not ally themselves with the same Roman family. As the Colonna had their power base in and around Rome, Francesco Soderini, who was resident in the city, would deal with them, rather than Piero who was two hundred miles away. Marcantonio Colonna was one of the foremost *condottieri* of his day, and a natural choice. However, the fact remains that Soderini had no constitutional right to make such arrangements and in the context of the republic, such actions would always occasion criticism. The resulting confusion over what policy was being pursued and the attendant backbiting represented real weaknesses which the Soderini's attachment to the forms and procedures of republican government rendered them unable to remove.

Despite these difficulties, the first period of Francesco Soderini's

[48] Guicciardini, *Storie fiorentine*, p. 280.   [49] *Ibid.*, p. 277.   [50] *Ibid.*, p. 290.
[51] *Ibid.*, p. 277.

career as a cardinal went relatively smoothly, with his links with France and his close relations with the pope underlining the value of having a Florentine cardinal at the curia. Problems only arose when, during the aftermath of the defeat of Venice at Agnadello on 14 May 1509, and the disintegration of the League of Cambrai, the pope and the king of France fell out. Soderini's position as a client of the French king, and Florence's position as an ally, ensured that relations between Soderini and Julius were soured. Thus in late May or June 1509, after Soderini had been ill and had been visited by two of his nephews, Tommaso and Giuliano di Paolantonio, and had wanted to accompany Tommaso back to Florence when he was better, the pope, significantly, had not granted him permission.[52] Soderini may have obediently accompanied the pope on his expedition against Bologna in 1510, but with the victory of French arms before Bologna in 1511, Florence provided the meeting place for the council of reforming cardinals with which Louis XII hoped to challenge Julius' spiritual authority. As the brother of the *gonfaloniere*, Soderini could hardly hope not to be implicated in this move. It seems likely that the deterioration in relations between Soderini and Julius was not prompted by the Council of Pisa but predated it. Soderini himself appears to have avoided any trace of personal involvement in the council, and indeed in October 1511 he was given the cardinal bishopric of Sabina when it was taken from Bernardo Carvajal for his part in the proceedings at Pisa.[53] If Soderini retained some sort of relationship with Julius, it is still the case that the collapse of the papal–French alliance caused Soderini's hitherto simple political circumstances to become more complex.

When Soderini's relationship with Julius became more strained, his visits to Florence attracted more comment. Because of his links with the French and supposed involvement in the Council of Pisa, these visits were undertaken in the teeth of increasing papal opposition. In May 1509, as has been seen, the pope refused Soderini permission to go to Florence. But by August of that year he must have been induced to change his mind as there was a gathering of the Soderini clan in Florence to celebrate the feast of the Assumption,[54] and in September Soderini and one of his nephews, Giuliano, visited Paolo Cortesi in S. Gimignano. They were accompanied, for at least part of the time, by Geremia Contugi, one of Soderini's satellites, the bishop of Krania in Thessaly.[55]

---

[52] ASF, C. Strozz., III, 134, 160r and v, Marco to Giovanni Strozzi, undated but circa May 1509 as Giuliano was made bishop on 23 May 1509.

[53] See below, p. 183.

[54] Volterra, Arch. com., Deliberazioni, A 68, 126r and v.

[55] See P. Guicciardini, *Cusona* (Florence, 1939), p. 142, and below, p. 162.

During this visit Soderini also went to meet two unnamed French cardinals who were at the house of Giovanfrancesco di Poggio Bracciolini at Strozzavolpe, which could secretly have been one of his reasons for going to Tuscany and also one of the pope's reasons for trying to stop him.[56] In October he was in Pisa on a visit[57] but knew that he ought to hurry back to Rome.[58] In the summer of 1510 he again went to Florence.[59] From Vallombrosa he wrote to Bramante on 1 July 1510 of the ominous times which were making life difficult for him.[60] He stayed away the whole summer, ignoring first the wishes and finally the commands of the pope to return, but eventually he did return and tried to make his peace with Julius. In August 1510 Julius had finally dispatched one of his familiars, Girolamo della Mirandola, to Florence on an ordinary mission to discuss the excommunication of the duke and cardinal of Ferrara and to order Soderini back to Rome, and at the end of September Soderini complied.[61]

As the relationship between Julius and the Soderini had deteriorated so badly, patching it up was no easy matter. In the summer of 1511 Soderini was again to be found in Florence. He was ill and the pope wrote him a sympathetic letter.[62] He did not return to Rome until 21 December. This was no ordinary summer break; Soderini stayed away because of the breakdown in relations between France and the papacy. In November he was somewhere in the *contado*, probably at S. Miniato or S. Gimignano.[63] By early December the pope was furious, claiming that Soderini wanted to be anti-pope (this was a frequent charge levelled at the participants in the Council of Pisa but Soderini was not a participant). The pope and the bishop of Pistoia, Niccolò Pandolfini, were overheard saying such appalling things about Piero and Francesco Soderini that it was impossible to imagine worse.[64] All this time Soderini was using his illness as his excuse for not going back to Rome. In mid-December 1511 the French decided to abandon Bologna on account of the great numbers of Swiss in the pay of the Holy League

---

[56] *Ibid.*, p. 115.   [57] Sanuto, *I diarii*, IX, 252, Rome, 7 October 1509.

[58] See a letter from Soderini to Cortesi of 13 September 1509 from S. Gimignano, in Florence, Biblioteca Marucelliana, BI 10, Part 3, 229v–230r.

[59] There is no record of his being there before August (see for example, Machiavelli, *Le legazioni*, ed. Passerini and Milanesi, IV, p. 77, letter of the *Dieci* to Machiavelli of 22 August) but he must have been there in July also for the pope to have sent after him in August.

[60] See A. Rossi, 'Nuovi documenti su Bramante', *Archivio storico dell'arte*, I (1888), p. 136.   [61] Sanuto, *I diarii*, XI, 20.

[62] Sanuto, *I diarii*, XII, 370 and XII, 538, from conte Hironimo di Porzil, Rome, 7 and 10 August.

[63] *Epistolario di Bernardo Dovizi da Bibbiena*, ed. G. Moncallero, I (Florence, 1955), p. 334.   [64] *Ibid.*, I, p. 389, 6 December and I, p. 418, 17 December.

(which comprised the pope, Venice, Spain and England, all now ranged against France). The pope twice made a joke at Soderini's expense, saying that the Swiss must be good doctors of venereal disease, because they had been able to cure cardinal Volterra so that in a trice he could hurry back to Rome, when previously he had been unable to move.[65] There were other references to Soderini's having syphilis[66] which is why Julius was able to jest in this fashion. Soderini arrived in Rome just before Christmas to try to mend relations between Florence, Julius and France.[67]

In March 1512 Soderini was once again granted permission to leave Rome, this time to go to the kingdom of Naples,[68] but it was easier for him to obtain this than permission to go to Florence. The pope was uneasy about his straying very far. In fact, Soderini was again ill 'with his usual complaint', and he was probably given leave to go to the baths at Bagni di Pozzuoli, secured for him through the intercession of cardinal del Monte.[69] As the situation in Florence became more critical, and the date for the summer recess of the curia came closer, in mid-June Soderini again asked permission to go to Florence. The pope refused but gave him permission to go wherever he wanted within the papal states. He immediately rushed to the northern borders. Julius sent orders to cardinal Cornaro, who was legate in Viterbo, that if Soderini passed into Florentine territory, he should be apprehended. Soderini gave up at this point and wrote saying that he would not cross the border.[70]

Soderini returned from the *patrimonio* to Rome after 20 August, when things looked extremely bleak for Florence. There were two reasons for this: he wanted to persuade the pope to intervene and save his brother, and he was afraid for his own safety.[71] This was to become an increasingly frequent worry. The *Dieci* wrote to Soderini on 20 August requesting that he intervene with Julius to try to halt the advancing Spanish army of the Holy League, egged on by the Medici.[72] By the 28th, Soderini had an interview with the pope, expostulating that it would be disastrous if the Spanish should obtain a toehold in Florence, but the pope merely replied that everything had been determined by the League and that he could do nothing by himself.[73] This was, in effect,

---

[65] *Ibid.*, I, p. 424, 20 December.
[66] See, for example, Paris de Grassis' entry for 8 May 1510 in BL, Add. MSS 8443, 44r and v, and below, p. 166.   [67] *Epistolario di Bernardo Dovizi*, I, p. 432.
[68] *Ibid.*, I, p. 486, Dovizi to Giovanni de' Medici, Rome, 19 March 1512.
[69] *Ibid.*, I, p. 479, 17 March 1512.
[70] Sanuto, *I diarii*, XIV, 404, Rome, 14 June 1512 from frate Anzolo Lucido.
[71] Sanuto, *I diarii*, XIV, 635, Rome, 21, 22 or 24 August, from the orator Foscari.
[72] Cooper, 'Machiavelli, Francesco Soderini and Don Michelotto', pp. 355–6.
[73] Sanuto, *I diarii*, XV, 9, probably 28 August, from Foscari.

a washing of hands, as Soderini explained in a letter to the *Dieci* of 29 August.[74] Another source records that Soderini took six cardinals with him to plead for help for Florence against the Medici but was unable to obtain any.[75] Unfortunately, the names of these six are not known, but together they made up perhaps twenty-five per cent of the cardinals resident in Rome, a sizeable proportion to be there in the summer months and to be willing to lodge a complaint. The only possible Florentine or Florentine subject present can have been Piero Accolti from Arezzo. All the others must have been motivated by either pro-French or anti-Spanish feelings, or by sentiments of loyalty towards Soderini or by some vague notion that Italy possessed some separate identity with which foreign powers should not interfere.[76]

The fall of the Florentine republic in 1512 was brought about through Spanish force of arms. Soderini had long realised that the key to political stability lay with strong foreign allies and he had come to identify the interests of France very closely with those of the Florentine republic. The breakdown in relations between the pope and France represented a serious threat to this stability. Julius's development of a rabidly anti-French policy ensured that, given the alliance between France and Florence, the expulsion of the French from Italy would have unpleasant consequences for the republic. When Julius, by joining the Holy League in October 1511, acquired a Spanish army with which to expel the French, it was almost inevitable that the Medici would return to Florence in its wake. Soderini's position as a cardinal, by offering an extra-Florentine power base, gave his family the possibility of pursuing its dynastic interests by other means.[77] At this juncture, however, although he could ensure that his complaints were heard by the pope, he proved unable to muster sufficient support to shore up the precarious situation in his home territory.

---

[74] Cooper, 'Machiavelli, Francesco Soderini and Don Michelotto', p. 356.
[75] Sanuto, *I diarii*, xv, 10, 28 August, from an unknown author.
[76] That this was a sentiment at the time was illustrated in a discussion of October 1504 between Giustinian and Soderini on the then current league and the coming to Italy of the Holy Roman Emperor. Soderini at one point said: 'Io vi parlo adesso non come cardinale né come cittadino fiorentino, ma come bono amico et italiano.' See Giustinian, *Dispacci*, III, p. 273, 24 October 1504.
[77] See Pellegrini, 'Ascanio Maria Sforza', p. 217.

CHAPTER 6

RELATIONS AND RIVALRY BETWEEN THE SODERINI AND THE MEDICI

Soderini influence at Rome and representation at the curia were also crucial because Rome was where the Medici were. In exile from the republic, the Medici had shifted the centre of their activities to Rome. This was no doubt partly due to Piero de' Medici's wife being an Orsini, and partly due to the fact that cardinal Giovanni de' Medici had already been living in Rome in the *rione* of Sant'Eustachio some of the time since 1489, and as a cardinal was firmly established at the papal court. Many of the Florentine bankers in Rome had helped finance cardinal de' Medici and Piero after 1494 when they had been short of ready money and living precariously in the city.[1] After Piero's death in 1503, the most important members of the Medici family living in Rome were his brothers, cardinal Giovanni and Giuliano, his widow, Alfonsina, and his son, Lorenzo.

Thereafter, the Medici acted as a focus for the considerable Florentine community in Rome. For example, cardinal de' Medici and his relatives gave a party in celebration of their patron saints Cosmas and Damian in Rome on their feast day, 27 September 1504. According to Parenti, there were echoes of former glory, with Giuliano being addressed as *Magnifico*, and many disparaging words were spoken about Soderini rule in Florence.[2] Giovanni Acciaiuoli, the Florentine ambassador, sent home a report of this feast, commenting that all sorts of people from the Florentine community (*natione*) were present, perhaps seven-eighths of the total number.[3] Acciaiuoli took some of them to task for their

---

[1] M. Bullard, '"Mercatores florentini romanum curiam sequentes" in the early sixteenth century', *Journal of medieval and renaissance studies*, 6 (1976), p. 67. The contemporary diarists all remark on the Medici links with the Florentines in Rome.

[2] Parenti, 'Istorie', BNF, II II 134, 33r.

[3] *Miscellanea fiorentina di erudizione e storia*, ed. I. del Badia, I (Florence, 1902), p. 93. The Florentine nation was given official recognition in June 1515, but had been in existence since the late fifteenth century. See J. Delumeau, *Vie économique et sociale de Rome dans la seconde moitié du XVIe siècle*, I (Paris, 1957), p. 209.

attendance but only succeeded in quarrelling with them. This famous Medici hospitality so worried the Florentine government that they summoned a *pratica* to discuss what could be done.[4] In 1495 a provision had been passed which prohibited any Florentines in Rome from associating with the exiled Medici, but patently this was ignored.[5] The *pratica* resulted in no new action being taken although, when things became more critical in 1510, the provision was renewed.

In many ways the position of the Soderini with Piero as *gonfaloniere* and Francesco in Rome, parallelled that of the Medici during their later years in power. It might be expected that Francesco Soderini would try to rival the social activities and public displays of the Medici cardinal. Contemporaries were obviously worried about the consequences for Florentine political stability of too overt a rivalry between the cardinals. One venerable citizen of Florence, according to Nardi, voiced a possible drawback to Soderini's promotion when he said that he hoped that the two Florentine cardinals would not harm their native city by pursuing their own ends, with Soderini acting as a secret, and Medici an open, enemy.[6] However, Soderini was not ideally suited to counter the public magnificence of the Medici; he was not by nature open-handed and he lacked their financial resources.

In 1504, Parenti described their differences in style: 'Medici with great enthusiasm dispensed favours to and helped any who asked him; he lived generously and showed munificence towards no matter whom. Soderini's style was quite the opposite; he was careful, restrained, cautious, ponderous and stern when helping whoever asked him.'[7] By 1508 the contrast was stark enough for Guicciardini to comment that cardinal de' Medici's help for Florentines in Rome put Soderini in a bad light, 'for being by nature very miserly and closefisted, and by not helping or favouring any Florentines, he provided a contrast which showed up to great advantage the munificence and kindness of cardinal de' Medici.'[8] It was almost as though cardinal de' Medici adopted a more princely, and cardinal Soderini a more republican, style of patronage to mirror their contrasting political attitudes.

Other vital differences between the two cardinals lay in the incomes

---

[4] ASF, Cons. e prat. 67, 258v–260r and Cooper, 'Piero Soderini', p. 228.

[5] M. Bullard, *Filippo Strozzi and the Medici: favor and finance in sixteenth-century Florence and Rome* (Cambridge, 1980), p. 62.   [6] Nardi, *Istorie*, I, p. 267.

[7] Parenti, 'Istorie', BNF, II II 134, 33v: 'El Medico favoriva et serviva svisceratamente qualunche il richiedesse, teneva larghissima vita e mostrava liberalità grandissima verso qualunche; el Soderino teneva opposito stilo, assegnato, rattenuto, cauto, pesato et grave, nel servire chi lo richiedeva; pareva che il pontefice inclinasse più al Medico che quest'altro.'   [8] Guicciardini, *Storie fiorentine*, p. 323.

at their disposal[9] and their financial contacts; at times, the two became indistinguishable. Even before Giovanni de' Medici became pope, the Medici were an infinitely richer family than the Soderini. In 1472 Tommaso Soderini, the father of Piero and Francesco, had been included on a list of Florence's wealthier citizens, and he and his sons proceeded to add to their assets after this date.[10] In the Florentine tax known as the *ventina* of 1498, Piero Soderini received the highest assessment of his *gonfalone* of Drago, S. Spirito, followed by his brothers Paolantonio and Giovanvettorio.[11] Francesco must have had his share of this family wealth, but it was not on the same scale as the Medici riches. Although the Medici bank collapsed at the same time as the family's Florentine political fortunes in the 1490s,[12] credit and prestige were vouchsafed by their international friends and contacts. Consequently, cardinal Giovanni had been able to run up large debts which he carried with him to the papacy, and one of his main considerations in the allocation of papal patronage to banks and bankers was the extent of their wealth.[13] As the Medici already occupied the favoured position of friends of the ancient banking families in Rome, Soderini had to look elsewhere for his credit and his cash, and he appears to have availed himself of the services of Bernardo da Verrazzano, obviously not a member of the old Florentine banking aristocracy, but a newcomer from the Chianti, without a family name.[14] This may be taken as an illustration of the way in which the established position of the Medici in Rome must have limited the range of options open to Soderini, who had been absent from Rome for the preceding ten years. In the same way, as has been seen in chapter 5, since the Medici were connected by marriage to the Orsini, if Soderini wanted to obtain political allies amongst the Roman barons, he was almost forced to turn to the Orsini's great rivals, the Colonna.

However, in the period before 1512, the Medici–Soderini rivalry expressed itself most obviously in a series of rancorous personal exchanges between the two cardinals. Soderini was twenty years older than cardinal Giovanni, was of a different temperament and had different tastes. But the personal rivalry was forced upon them as a result of the political differences between the two Florentine families, rather than necessarily being of their own making. For example, in a consistory of 5 July 1508, Cosimo de' Pazzi was proposed for the archbishopric of Pisa. Soderini commented to the other cardinals that he was an honest

---

[9] See below, pp. 245–8. [10] Clarke, *The Soderini*, p. 119.
[11] Cooper, 'Piero Soderini', p. 85. [12] De Roover, *The rise*, p. 370.
[13] Bullard, '"Mercatores"', p. 68.
[14] See Lowe, 'Francesco Soderini', appendix 4, pp. 347–50.

man and that his family had always been opposed to tyrants. The insult and implication was clear to all: the Pazzi had been responsible for the murder of Giuliano de' Medici in 1478, thirty years before. When business was over, cardinal de' Medici and his friends went to demand an explanation from Soderini.[15] In the extant reports it is nearly always Soderini who initiates these verbal battles. He seems to have had a much sharper tongue than cardinal Giovanni de' Medici and even when Soderini affairs were doing well and Medici ones badly (as in 1508), he appears to have been unable to resist a jibe. Contemporaries certainly saw the rivalry in personal as well as political terms. Friends of the Medici became almost automatically enemies of the Soderini and vice versa, resulting in a polarization of loyalties which had consequences for Italian and international relations. Thus, in April 1510 the Venetian ambassador wrote home that of the two Florentine cardinals Soderini was a great enemy of Venice and Medici a great friend.[16] In practice, of course, allegiances were never as clear-cut as this.

The Soderini therefore found themselves impaled on the horns of a dilemma. The obvious parallels between the situation of the two families and the personal rivalry of the two cardinals were impossible to conceal. They led to fears and accusations that the Soderini were trying, in Florence, to replace the dominance of the Medici with that of their own. Furthermore, many believed that it was Francesco Soderini who was the real villain. Jacopo Pitti put the following words about Piero Soderini into the mouth of the character Tito (supposedly a portrait of Agnolo Guicciardini): 'The greatest stumbling block he always had to keeping his respectability was the goading he received from certain citizens intent on evil, and from his brother the cardinal, who would have been happy to take over the empty places left by the Medici with a faction of unpleasant minor despots.'[17]

This replacement theory is hard to disprove, but if Francesco Soderini were making genuine efforts to push his family towards Medicean status in Florence, they must have failed. Certainly at the level of display, the Medici continued to outflank the Soderini at every move. For example, after 1503 Francesco may have felt that he needed a grand country house in Tuscany. One of the easiest ways of purchasing such property during these years was to buy up estates that had been confiscated from the Medici when they were declared rebels in 1494.[18] On 8 August 1509,

[15] Sanuto, *I diarii*, VII, 581, 10 July 1508.   [16] *Ibid.*, X, 74.

[17] J. Pitti, 'Apologia de' Cappucci', *Archivio storico italiano*, series I, 4, part 2 (1853), p. 316.

[18] See A. Anzilotti, *La crisi costituzionale della repubblica fiorentina* (Florence, 1912), p. 11.

Soderini and his nephew Tommaso di Paolantonio were named as the buyers of Colle Salvetti and Vicarello and their estates which lay eight to ten miles to the south-east of Pisa, for the sum of 3,030 gold florins.[19] In his will of 10 February 1511 Soderini left Colle Salvetti to Tommaso and there is no mention of Vicarello.[20] In making this purchase, Soderini was acquiring a material interest in the continued exclusion of the Medici from Florence and perhaps establishing a claim, along with other leading families, to succeed to the position of prominence vacated by the Medici. Unfortunately, this attempt failed because the Medici returned to power in Florence in 1512, and on 28 September of that year they were given a limit of fifteen years to reacquire all their moveable and immoveable goods (*beni mobili ed immobili*).[21] As a result, Soderini was forced to resell these two possessions to Lorenzo de' Medici, duke of Urbino, on 16 December 1517 for the same sum of 3,030 gold florins.[22]

It is extremely unlikely that Piero Soderini hoped to step into the shoes of the Medici or to replace the Medici in the minds of the Florentine people, but evidence has recently come to light that he was prepared to engage in a contest at a territorial level and attempt to obliterate their memory with images and spaces of his own. For instance, he chose to replace an *ex voto* of Lorenzo de' Medici, situated in the church of the convent of Le Murate, with a painting of the Virgin Mary, and he paid for the erection of a chapel to San Salvatore at the convent of San Gallo which had been rebuilt by Lorenzo de' Medici.[23] These acts can be interpreted in several ways, but as yet remain random and minor examples of Soderini engagement in a heavily weighted struggle. More generally, although the Soderini as a family continued to concentrate their resources in the *quartiere* of S. Frediano, they never approached the expansionist tactics employed by the Medici in their *quartiere* of S. Lorenzo.

As for Francesco, whatever his private ambitions may have been, the extent to which the fortunes of his family were implicated with those of the republic, and his residence in Rome, made Soderini replacement in Florence impractical for him, and would have made any attempt on his part, in Rome, to mirror the political style of the Medici counter-productive. The result was that the Soderini were impeded, either

---

[19] ASF, C. Strozz., I, 10, 39v and 40r. See Repetti, *Dizionario*, I, p. 770 and v, p. 747. See also ASF, Not. antecos. M 239 (1512–19), 1511r.

[20] See ASBo, Notarile, Tommaso Grengoli, busta 18, filza 13, under date and Lowe, 'Francesco Soderini', appendix 3, p. 338.   [21] ASF, C. Strozz., I, 10, 38r.

[22] *Ibid.*, 18r.

[23] ASF, Il minutario di Goro Gheri, I, 173v and Razzi, *Vita*, pp. 149–50.

willingly or unwillingly, from shows of tyrannical force or possession, and did not gain whatever advantages might have accrued from a policy of personal aggrandisement. Nor did their efforts to avoid such appearances meet with the approval of their countrymen, who had grown accustomed to hearing their rulers protest one political ideology whilst pursuing another, and who therefore disbelieved their protestations as a matter of course.

With the fall of the republic, family circumstances changed considerably. Piero Soderini fled into exile in Ragusa (Dubrovnik) where, because of the substantial Italian community and because of the favourable relations maintained between Florence and Ragusa under the republic,[24] he was sheltered at a castle a little way up the coast at Valdinoce.[25] Here he passed his time praying and gardening.[26] When men from Julius came to apprehend him, they were told that he had taken ship to Turkish waters and a priest, Marino Benchi, was despatched under cover to tell Francesco what had really happened.[27] Leadership of the family passed to Francesco who, as a cardinal, retained a freedom of manoeuvre denied to his brother. At first Julius' enmity prevented Francesco from exploiting his position to help Piero, but on Julius' death in February 1513 he was able to strike a bargain with the Medici.

During the ensuing conclave,[28] Soderini effected a deal with cardinal de' Medici, possibly through the agency of one of Giovanni's *conclaviste*, Bernardo Dovizi,[29] whereby, in return for his vote and influence with other cardinals (probably some of the French faction), Soderini was able to obtain the rehabilitation of the exiled members of his family and the

---

[24] Cooper, 'Piero Soderini', p. 487, wrote that Piero had property in Ragusa which had been made over as a gift to his wife in November 1507 by a Florentine merchant, Gregorio Draghi di Cozi, who was living there. This must have been the result of some deal.

[25] See G. Gelcich, *Piero Soderini profugo a Ragusa: memorie e documenti* (Dubrovnik, 1894), p. 15.

[26] See one of Elio Lampridio Cervino's elegies to Piero Soderini in Dubrovnik, Biblioteka Male Brače, MS 68, p. 303 and MS 195, p. 147, which are both later copies. The notation for this used to be MSS 280 and 309, lib. VII, eleg. XX and lib. VII, eleg. VIII. On Cervino, see S. Škunca, *Aelius Lampridius Cervinus poeta ragusinus (saec. XV)* (Rome, 1971), esp. pp. 145–6. See also Donato Sanminiatelli's review of G. Gelcich, *Piero Soderini profugo a Ragusa: memorie e documenti* (Dubrovnik, 1894) in *Archivio storico italiano*, series V, 15 (1895), p. 170.

[27] Gelcich, *Piero Soderini*, p. 20.

[28] F. Vettori, *Sommario della storia d'Italia dal 1511 al 1527*, ed. A. Reumont, in *Archivio storico italiano*, appendice VI (1848), p. 338.

[29] A. Bandini, *Il Bibbiena o sia il ministro di stato delineato nella vita del cardinale Bernardo Dovizi da Bibbiena* (Livorno, 1758), p. 14.

promise of a Soderini–Medici marriage alliance.[30] Soderini and Medici were both ill during this conclave. Perhaps unsurprisingly, Soderini renounced a cell in the most auspicious position in the Sistine chapel, under Perugino's painting of the *Donation of the keys* (by Christ to St Peter), in favour of a more convenient one close to the *Cantoria*, proving that he was not unduly influenced by superstition.[31] Initially, the favourite candidates for the papacy were Raffaele Riario, the Hungarian Thomas Bacócz, the Venetian Domenico Grimani and Niccolò Flisco, but each of these had factions or individuals opposed to their election.

In the first round of voting, cardinal Medici secured only one vote,[32] but the second round announced his election, which took place on 9 March. It appears that the younger cardinals voted *en bloc* for Medici, whereas the older cardinals were divided.[33] Cardinal Giovanni took the name of pope Leo X and duly fulfilled his first obligation to his fellow Florentine, obtaining a pardon for the five Soderini who had been exiled from Florence: Piero and Giovanvettorio di Tommaso, and Tommaso, Giovanbattista and Piero di Paolantonio.[34] On 21 March, Leo wrote to Piero, inviting him to go to Rome and addressing him as his relative;[35] Leo's father, Lorenzo de' Medici, was in fact Piero's first cousin. It must have seemed a good solution to a thorny problem, as it would have been impossible for Piero to return to Florence and live as a private citizen without evoking some kind of anti-Medicean display, but nor was it convenient to leave him forever, a slightly pitiful figure, in exile on the Dalmatian coast. Rome was cosmopolitan enough to absorb ex-heads of state and Piero Soderini was a quiet and rather timid one who showed no signs of wanting to continue or reactivate the struggle.[36] He claimed that he wanted to lie low and that he loved his country more than anything else,[37] the implication being that if

---

[30] Mario Equicola thought that the marriage was to be between Lorenzo di Piero de' Medici and a (non-existent) daughter of Piero Soderini. See A. Luzio, 'Isabella d'Este ne' primordi del papato di Leone X e il suo viaggio a Roma nel 1514–1515', *Archivio storico lombardo*, 6 (1906), p. 457, letter from Equicola to Isabella of 21 March 1513.   [31] Chambers, 'Papal conclaves', pp. 323 and 325.

[32] Sanuto, *I diarii*, XVI, 82–3.

[33] For further details of the conclave, see Pastor, *History of the popes*, VII, pp. 15–25.

[34] ASF, Repubblica, Balìe 43, 136r and v.   [35] Razzi, *Vita*, pp. 127–8.

[36] Dubrovnik, Historijski Archiv, Miscellanea, saec. XVI, F. III, I, f.30, Piero to Marino de Bona, Rome, 31 May 1516: 'Noi per la gratia de Dio stiamo bene et passiamoci el tempo quietamente et dolcemente.'

[37] See Parenti, 'Istorie', BNF, II IV 171, 94v, 1513. Piero Soderini 'mostrò volere pocho travaglare di chose di stato, non etiam volere tornare nella città di Firenze, ma starsi a Roma et attendere a sue mercatantie et quietamente vivere'. See also an undated letter from Piero to Francesco Maria della Rovere, duke of Urbino: 'Et

Florence appeared content with her present government then he would not interfere.

There followed a period of limbo. In Florence the full extent of Medici power remained unclear; at first they returned merely to the place of eminence that they had enjoyed under Lorenzo, and only gradually extended their powers and position beyond that.[38] In Rome the nature of the relations between the Soderini and the Medici was equally unclear. The ambiguity of the situation is best exemplified by Machiavelli's famous anxiety over the extent of his obligation to the Soderini and the possible consequences in Florence of his overt recognition of it in Rome. Ousted from employment in Florence because of his republican past, Machiavelli decided to try to obtain a post in the curia, which generated an exchange between him and Francesco Vettori, the new Florentine ambassador to the pope. Unfortunately an unknown number of letters in this series is lost, so sometimes they seem out of sequence and questions which have not apparently been asked are being answered at length.

On 9 April 1513 Machiavelli wrote to Vettori saying he understood that Soderini was trying hard to be reconciled with the pope, and asking whether Vettori thought that he should write to Soderini asking him for a recommendation to the pope or whether it would be better if Vettori spoke to Soderini about this, or whether he should do nothing.[39] On the 9th, too, Vettori wrote to Machiavelli that he had been considering deeply whether he should speak to Soderini about him and had decided against it because he was unsure exactly how Soderini stood in the eyes of the pope: 'Nor am I certain that he would do it willingly because you know how cautiously he proceeds. On top of this, I do not feel convinced that I am the best intermediary between you and him, because although he has shown me adequate signs of fondness, he has not shown me as much as I would have thought.'[40] The difficulty was that Vettori had been instrumental in Piero Soderini's downfall and was now serving the Medici, and the question of how to respond to Piero's changed circumstances still remained sensitive. Vettori's sense of patriotism, friendship and honour were all intact in regard to Francesco but he suggested that Machiavelli try another route to obtain his goal.

sopra tucto li racchomando la mia patria, la quale io amo quanto la propria vita.' He goes on to warn the duke to beware of traitors, ASF, Urbino I, G, CCXXXVI, II, 98or. Francesco Maria was duke from 11 April 1508 to 31 May 1516 and again from December 1521 to his death on 21 October 1538. It is likely that this letter dates from the period 1513–16.
[38] See J. Stephens, *The fall of the Florentine republic, 1512–1530* (Oxford, 1983), pp. 65–72.   [39] Machiavelli, *Lettere*, p. 240.   [40] *Ibid.*, p. 241.

Paolo Vettori was about to become a member of the *Otto* and would be able to dispense permission for Machiavelli to go to Rome.[41] Machiavelli wrote back to Vettori on the 16th in an optimistic frame of mind, reporting that both Giuliano de' Medici and Francesco Soderini were so sympathetic that he could not believe, were his cause to be handled with some dexterity, that he would fail to find a job, if not in Florence, then certainly in Rome or the papal states.

Between April and December 1513 something happened to change Machiavelli's attitude to the Soderini family, presumably the collapse of France's power in Italy coming close on the heels of the election of Leo X. The Boscoli conspiracy in Florence, and Machiavelli's torture because of possible involvement in it, were already past by April. This means that anti-Soderini attitudes did not definitively harden until this date and that for a few months after Piero Soderini's deposition there was still room for manoeuvre. By December Machiavelli spoke of 'those Soderini' whom he would be forced to visit and speak to when he was in Rome. What has happened to the mutual affection and even admiration? Is this another example of Machiavelli's writing without restraint and impulsively criticising his ex-patrons because they had not immediately rushed to help him? He had often criticised Piero and his form of republican government in the past,[42] although at a personal level the two of them were friends, but there was no one whom Machiavelli did not criticise. Machiavelli's fear that he would be imprisoned in the Bargello on his return to Florence if he visited the Soderini was an extreme reaction to the political uncertainty. Admittedly the regime was young and suspicious[43] but not absurdly so.

Machiavelli realised that the charge of ingratitude could be levelled against him, and Vettori's reply deals at some length with the question. He says that the problem of Francesco Soderini is easily dealt with by going to see him only once. Piero is a different matter and Vettori counsels that no visit at all be made: 'Piero has closed off his mind nor do I think that he cares to be visited, and especially not by you. If you do not visit him I do not think that ingratitude will be imputed to you, because on investigation I do not find that he or his supporters gave you such benefits that you are obliged to them in an extraordinary manner. You did not owe your official position to them for you were appointed three years before he became *gonfaloniere*; and in subsequent positions that he gave you, you served him faithfully and did not receive other

---

[41] *Ibid.*, p. 242.

[42] See J. Najemy, 'The controversy surrounding Machiavelli's service to the republic', in *Machiavelli and republicanism*, ed. G. Bock, Q. Skinner and M. Viroli (Cambridge, 1990), pp. 110–11, 114 and 116–17.   [43] Machiavelli, *Lettere*, p. 305.

than ordinary rewards.'[44] It is not clear why Piero should have been particularly anxious not to see Machiavelli although it would be extremely interesting to know. It surely could not be merely a fear of old memories, as Nardi writes that Piero was visited by many old Florentine friends and relatives.[45] It is not even that Nardi could have based his picture on Piero's later years in Rome, because immediately on his arrival Piero went to see the Florentine ambassadors at the house of the most senior of them, Jacopo Salviati,[46] and spoke quite openly of his plans.[47] He showed no intention of going underground or becoming a recluse except in a political sense.

Most telling of all is the detailed way in which Vettori examines the nature of the relationship between Machiavelli and Piero Soderini (and, as an extension, Piero's family). He tries to assure Machiavelli that there has been nothing out of the usual in it, that it was a perfectly ordinary working relationship, following well-tested patterns. He says that the Soderini were not his patrons, did not benefit him in such a way as to make his obligation towards them extraordinary, that they had not acquired his position for him, that under Piero's aegis he had not received supplementary rewards for his service. Vettori cannot have picked these points at random. He must have been replying to criticisms that Machiavelli himself felt to be at least plausible and probably more. Others must have considered that Machiavelli was a creature of the Soderini and that his fortunes were inextricably linked with theirs. In August 1512, as his final act as *gonfaloniere*, Piero Soderini, fearing for his life, had chosen to send his protégé Machiavelli to Francesco Vettori, who then took an oath from the men deposing Piero that they would not harm him.[48] At this moment of crisis, Machiavelli was the person whom Piero Soderini felt he could trust the most; but Machiavelli was once again performing a private service for his patron and not a public service for the republic.

By December 1513 it would appear that continuing links with the Soderini were recognised openly as grave political disadvantages for anyone wishing to remain in Florence. It may have been simply this fact which made Machiavelli wary of his old patrons. However, although it

---

[44] *Ibid.*, pp. 311–12, 24 December 1513.   [45] Nardi, *Istorie*, II, p. 29.

[46] There were two Florentine ambassadors in Rome at this time, Jacopo Salviati and Francesco Vettori. See R. Devonshire Jones, *Francesco Vettori, Florentine citizen and Medici servant* (London, 1976), pp. 86–7.

[47] ASF, C. Strozz., I, 136, 218v, 13 May 1513, Francesco Vettori to his brother Paolo, Rome. Piero had arrived in Rome on 9 May. 'Venne a vicitarci charo in chasa Jacopo e dice volere finire e' dì sua qui, et havere mandato per la mogle lasser venuto qui. Credo li tegga chostì reputatione assai.'

[48] Devonshire Jones, *Francesco Vettori*, p. 64.

is possible to assert, on the basis of evidence from Piero Soderini's period in office, that Machiavelli's political involvement with the Soderini was not partisan,[49] the nature of the personal bond between them later acquired partisan overtones. After 1512, Machiavelli still wanted a job in the government of Florence and was prepared to work for whoever was in charge. A clearer indication of Machiavelli's position is provided by traces of Piero Soderini's concern for Machiavelli's future after the downfall of the republican regime. It has usually been assumed that Machiavelli's relationship with the Soderini effectively ceased at this point. It did not. Piero Soderini had always acknowledged his duty to, and his affection for, his protégé. He was a responsible man and in his will of 16 May 1512 he left sums to many of the employees in the Palazzo Vecchio, including those in the First and Second Chancery, where Machiavelli worked.[50]

During his years in Rome, Piero Soderini probably kept up a fairly frequent correspondence with Machiavelli, to judge by the extant letter of 13 April 1521. The tone of the letter is one of affectionate familiarity: Piero greets his correspondent as 'Niccolò carissimo'. He writes that since Machiavelli was not satisfied with the job in Ragusa (for Soderini to suggest the job of chancellor, and for Machiavelli to refuse it, must have necessitated at least two letters), he has found him another one, managing the affairs of Prospero Colonna. Soderini jokes that this job and its salary – 200 gold ducats and expenses – are to be preferred to his present task of writing histories for *fiorini di suggello*.[51] This is presumably a reference to a commission Machiavelli received on 8 November 1520 from the Florentine *studio* to write the history of Florence at a salary of 100 florins a year.[52] Machiavelli rejected the Colonna job too.

What is evident from this exchange is that Piero and Machiavelli were still close to each other, and Piero was still accepting responsibility for Machiavelli, eight and a half years after they had ceased to work together for the Florentine republic. It seems likely that the overall view of Machiavelli's relationship with Piero Soderini would be substantially different if the correspondence between the two of them after 1512 were still extant. As it is, the 1521 letter shows up the inadequacy of the view that Machiavelli and Piero had the usual ties linking men in their positions, and nothing more. Similarly, were the correspondence between Machiavelli and Francesco Soderini to come to light, it is

---

[49] R. Black, 'Machiavelli, servant of the Florentine republic', in *Machiavelli and republicanism*, ed. G. Bock, Q. Skinner and M. Viroli (Cambridge, 1990), p. 95.

[50] Razzi, *Vita*, pp. 153–4.   [51] BNF, Autografi Palatini v, 40r.

[52] See Ridolfi, *Vita*, I, p. 285 and N. Machiavelli, *Le opere*, ed. P. Fanfani and L. Passerini (Florence, 1873–7), I, p. lxxxix.

arguable that they too would be found to have had more enduring bonds of friendship – Soderini had been a godparent to one of Machiavelli's children[53] – than has previously been thought. Machiavelli's intercourse with the Soderini during this period was curtailed, but not broken. But it was a time of readjustment for everyone connected with the Medici, especially their ancient opponents, and much of that readjustment, if it was not to be covert, had to take place on more neutral or open ground. In so far as relations between the Medici and Machiavelli's old patrons, the Soderini, were to be normalised, that process would have to take place in Rome. For Machiavelli, who insisted upon remaining in Florence, normal relations and open fraternising with the Soderini were not an option because he was not in Rome.

The election of a Medici pope in 1513 had implications for many other families and individuals, in addition to the Soderini and Machiavelli. For example, the della Rovere clan who, under the auspices of Julius, had smoothed the way to Medicean ascendancy in Rome by restoring the Medici to control in Florence, now were swept aside by the new broom of Leo. Whereas the duke of Urbino, Francesco Maria della Rovere, who was Julius' nephew, had welcomed cardinal Giovanni de' Medici and his relatives to his court at Urbino when they were exiled from Florence, now Giovanni, in his pontifical garb, looked on the duchy of Urbino as a parcel of land to be given to an ambitious family member as part of a kingdom in the Romagna, and viewed the duke as an annoyance. Thus the followers and families of the old della Rovere pope and the new Medici pope found that instead of standing side by side in the winners' enclosure, they were facing each other across the track. Yet another division on the basis of family loyalty took its place at the papal court.

---

[53] Ridolfi, *Vita*, I, p. 131.

CHAPTER 7

THE SODERINI AND THE KINGS OF FRANCE

It has been seen that Soderini owed his appointment in part to the approval of the French king. Nor had Louis XII sought to conceal his delight when news had reached him of the election of Piero Soderini as *gonfaloniere a vita* in Florence in September 1502. According to the Florentine ambassador to France, Luigi della Stufa, Louis had 'raised his hands to heaven, as though thanking Almighty God'.[1] In his congratulatory letter to the *Signoria*, Louis praised the choice of Piero Soderini, commenting in particular upon his 'great experience of French as well as Italian affairs'. Undoubtedly, the Soderini brothers had forged important personal links with Louis, which flourished in the Soderinian Florence of the first decade of the sixteenth century, but, more remarkably, these bonds between the Soderini family and the French monarchy survived alterations in the political fortunes and circumstances of the Soderini and a new king on the French throne.

The key to an understanding of this lies in the history of relations between Florence and France.[2] Between 1455 and 1469 France's authority in Italy grew, especially in relation to Milan and Florence. Increasingly, Florence and Lorenzo de' Medici placed themselves under French protection, and increasingly this came to be seen as a natural alliance whose existence was not in question. France was turned to in time of need. For example, Louis XI arranged for Lorenzo's son, Giovanni de' Medici, to obtain the first benefices of his career in France in 1483.[3] But the bond which was originally made between Lorenzo de' Medici, the head of the ruling family, on behalf of Florence, and the French kings Louis XI and Charles VIII, developed an independent

---

[1] A. Gherardi, 'Come si accogliesse in corte di Francia la nuova dell'elezione del gonfaloniere Soderini', *Archivio storico italiano*, series V, I (1888), p. 132.

[2] For fuller background, see B. Buser, *Die Beziehungen der Mediceer zu Frankreich während der Jahre 1434–1494* (Leipzig, 1879).

[3] G. Picotti, *La giovinezza di Leone X* (Milan, 1928), pp. 71–2.

existence. The relationship became quasi-constitutional as well as personal. Lorenzo's son, Piero, may have lost French support and have had to flee before the approaching army of Charles VIII in 1494; however, the resultant newly established republic, following well-worn precedent, continued to ally the city with the kingdom of France. It was during this republican period that the Soderini, in their turn, proceeded to enhance their personal relationship with Louis XII.

Thus both the Medici and the Soderini, as heads of government, ambassadors and cardinals, developed enduring links at a private and a public level with individual French kings, which led on to familial ties to the French monarchy as an institution. Successive French kings then chose to continue the relationship with successive members of the Medici and Soderini families. This is perhaps the most surprising aspect of Soderini's French favour. He had first met Charles VIII in November 1494, and then again at the beginning of 1496 when he was sent to France as Florentine ambassador. In the autumn of 1501, he met the next French monarch, Louis XII.

Once re-established in Rome, Soderini continued to betray his allegiance by acting as part of a French group in the curia. The system of official cardinal 'protectors' of foreign powers was in its infancy, and France may or may not already have had one.[4] When the position later became vacant on the death of cardinal Federico Sanseverino in August 1516, Soderini might have seemed an obvious choice, but instead the honour was given to cardinal Giulio de' Medici, whose cousin Giuliano had just concluded a marriage with a relative of Francis I. Throughout his curial career, Soderini fulfilled the function of a supernumerary cardinal protector of France, even if he lacked the title. Upon arrival in Rome in 1503, he attached himself to cardinal Georges d'Amboise, known as cardinal Rouen, the French king's mentor, whom he had come to know in France. On 23 September 1503 he wrote to the *Dieci* about the election of cardinal Francesco Todeschini Piccolomini as the new pope Pius III, claiming that 'everything had come from God, and after him from Rouen'.[5] On 21 September Soderini had been one of thirteen cardinals to vote for cardinal Rouen in the conclave (the others included Flisco, Medici, Aragon and Sforza), but this was not enough. D'Amboise, Sforza, Soderini and various others then hit upon the plan

---

[4] Compare A. Degert, 'Les origines de l'ambassade française permanente à Rome', *Bulletin de littérature ecclésiastique*, 22 (1921), p. 44 who states that cardinal Jean Balue was made protector of France in 1485, and J. Wodka, 'Zur Geschichte der nationalen Protektorate der Kardinäle an der römischen Kurie', *Publikationen des Österreichischen Historischen Instituts in Rom*, IV, 1 (Innsbruck, 1938), p. 98 who claims that the first cardinal protector of France was Federico Sanseverino, who was promoted in 1489 and died in 1516.   [5] ASF, Dieci, Resp. 75, 319r.

of electing cardinal Piccolomini, in return demanding that d'Amboise and Sforza have rooms in the palace. On the 22nd Soderini voted for d'Amboise and then Piccolomini and the latter was elected with the name Pius III.[6] This bid for a French pope left Soderini firmly in the middle of the French camp, a position he was to occupy until his death, and from then on there are frequent references to his association with a French group.[7] He kept up with French news, writing to his own agent, to the Florentine ambassador at court[8] (at least until 1512) and to the king when the need arose.[9] Soderini, in both Florence and Rome, was regarded as an expert on France, and he was consulted on French matters[10] whether urgent or otherwise.

How did loyalty to France affect Soderini's perceptions and pursuit of Florentine interests? From the very outset of his career, Soderini saw himself as the servant of two masters: the Florentine republic and the French monarchy,[11] and there were good reasons for him to see the interests of Florence and France as complementary and perhaps even congruent. As a curia cardinal, French backing must have seemed to verge on a necessity. As will be seen, rich benefices were essential for the maintenance of a cardinal's position in Rome and the patronage of the king of France must have appeared worth cultivating on that score alone. On 10 June 1503 Soderini informed the *Dieci* that the king of France had written to Alexander VI and Cesare Borgia, both to thank them for Soderini's promotion and to ask them to give him benefices in France and the kingdom of Naples.[12] How successful this intervention was at this point is not clear, but the later acquisition of the bishopric of Saintes was a considerable feat and Soderini did amass many smaller French benefices.

More intangible but more important was the political backing which Soderini gained from France. This was most obvious in the period after 1512 when the Soderini had lost their political base in Florence, but were able to maintain room for manoeuvre in Rome in part through the

[6] See Burchard, 'Liber notarum', II, pp. 384–7.

[7] See, for example, Burchard, 'Liber notarum', II, p. 421, 8 December 1503.

[8] The letters to the orators were frequent and full of homely sayings and advice: 'Questi tempi ... non lasciano riuscire alcuna cosa secondo la ragione' and 'in questi tempi e casi, chi perde el tempo perde l'ochasione', ASF, Sig., Otto, Dieci, Miss. 6, 168r and 185r, 11 July and 19 August 1508. Piero Soderini also wrote to the Florentine orators at court giving news of Francesco.

[9] For example, he wrote to Louis XII on 13 March 1513 recommending the bishop of Nice, Paris, Bibliothèque Nationale, Collection Dupuy 262, 14 (old 16). I would like to thank Nicolai Rubinstein for this reference.

[10] Giustinian, *Dispacci*, III, p. 344, 21 December 1504.

[11] See the letter from Soderini to the *Dieci*, from Piacenza, 5 July 1503, in ASF, Dieci, Resp. 73, 17r. [12] ASF, Dieci, Resp. 72, 272r.

patronage of the kings of France. It was however present also in the period from 1503 to 1512, but in a different form. Before 1512, French support for Soderini had gone hand in glove with wider French backing for the Florentine republic. In February 1507, on his way back from Bologna, Soderini arrived in the city with three other cardinals: Antoniotto Pallavicino, Raffaele Riario and Guillaume Briçonnet. They were fêted during their stay and treated, amongst other things, to a feast at the Soderini family palace.[13] The presence of four cardinals, one of them French, must have emphasised the status which had accrued to the city with the acquisition of Soderini's red hat, and allowed the Florentines a glimpse of the opportunities presented by his privileged relationship with France. After 1512, the support was channelled into a much more personal and active protection of Soderini and his family whose interests and activities had shifted to Rome. What this meant in practice was that Soderini, who had throughout been viewed as a member of the French party, increasingly came to be viewed as being under the personal protection of the French monarch and as such was beyond the reach of his enemies.

If French support was important for the exploitation of Soderini's role as a cardinal, it was even more important (at least in his eyes) for the fortunes of the Florentine republic. This was not a view shared by all his contemporaries. Machiavelli for one wrote rather bitterly in the *Decennale primo*: 'E per esser di Francia buon figliuoli, / Non vi curasti, in seguitar sua stella, / Sostener mille affanni e mille duoli.' ('And because you are the obedient children of France, in following her star you do not mind putting up with a thousand troubles and a thousand sorrows') and 'Voi vi posavi qui col becco aperto / Per attender di Francia un che venisse / A portarvi la manna nel deserto.' ('You stand here with your mouth open waiting for one coming from France to bring you manna in the desert').[14] Certainly Machiavelli was well placed to see the extent of Soderini dependence. In June 1510 he received an instruction from Piero Soderini to go to the king of France which opened: 'When you have carried out all the commissions given to you by the *Dieci*, say to the king on my behalf that I only desire three things in this world – the honour of God, the good of Florence, and the good and honour of the king of France. And because I am not able to believe

[13] Parenti, 'Istorie', BNF, II II 134, 130r and v.
[14] N. Machiavelli, 'Decennale primo', in *Il teatro e gli scritti letterari*, ed. F. Gaeta (Milan, 1965), p. 240. For an interesting analysis of other Florentine attitudes towards France during this period, see C. Bec, 'Les Florentins et la France ou la rupture d'un mythe (1494–1540)', *Il pensiero politico*, 14 (1981), especially pp. 382–6.

that Florence can achieve any good without the honour and good of the crown of France, I do not esteem one without the other. In addition, I can assure the king that my brother the cardinal is of the same opinion and frame of mind.'[15]

It has to be remembered that these words were intended for the king of France, and there is reason to believe that Francesco Soderini was capable of a more clear-sighted analysis of French intentions than such rhetoric implies. For instance, in his report (*rapporto*) on France of 1497,[16] Soderini showed real insight into the character of Charles VIII and his estimate of the chances of a French invasion can hardly be accused of groundless optimism. He described Charles VIII as someone who often deferred the execution of acts, even those that he desired, and declared that the intercession of God would be necessary to bring him to Italy.[17] The subsequent French invasion of Milan in 1499 can have done nothing but confirm Soderini's sense of the power of France, and convince him that so long as French military presence was evident in the peninsula, the favour of the French king brought with it more benefits than dangers.

Unfortunately, no further visit to Italy was forthcoming from the French during the span of republican rule in Florence. However, it cannot be denied that in a period when Italy was the unwilling host of the great European powers, the continued stability of any Italian regime depended to a greater or lesser degree upon the active support of one of the non-Italian countries. Just as the return of the Medici to Florence was made possible in 1512 by the presence of Spanish troops, so in order to anticipate and prevent such moves, the republic also had to have the backing of a foreign power. The choice of France was not a foolish one; France was still the most powerful country in Europe and had been a successful invader of the peninsula in the recent past.

This dependence on France worked well enough while Soderini was able to combine French backing with the favour of the pope. The situation only started to deteriorate when relations between Julius and Louis XII were soured by the aftermath of the League of Cambrai. Committed to their French alliance, the Florentines watched this process of polarisation with alarm. As Julius came definitely to oppose Louis and to plot his expulsion from Italy, Soderini's position became all but impossible. He had lost favour with the pope and could not regain it except by repudiating France, which he was not willing to do. Instead,

[15] Machiavelli, *Le legazioni*, ed. Passerini and Milanesi, IV, pp. 2–3.
[16] ASF, Lettere varie 14, 18r–19r, 20r–22v, and 23v. This is published as appendix 1 in Lowe, 'Francesco Soderini', pp. 317–25.
[17] Lowe, 'Francesco Soderini', appendix 1, p. 324.

the Soderini attempted to close the gap between the two powers by once again exploiting their special relationship with the French crown. This would have been accomplished most effectively by a visit to France from Francesco. However, as Piero wanted Machiavelli to explain to Louis XII in June 1510, despite Francesco's pressing personal and political obligations to the most christian king, a cardinal's first master ('primo signore') was always the pope, and Julius' rooted determination to keep Francesco under surveillance in Italy had, therefore, to be respected.[18]

Since Francesco could not go himself, the next best option was to send Machiavelli, who was by this time probably the Soderini's most trusted diplomatic agent. It seems likely that Machiavelli was sent as a personal messenger of the Soderini rather than as an official representative of the Florentine republic. There is no extant official instruction, but instead Machiavelli received a letter from Piero Soderini underlining the importance of the French alliance and the maintenance of peace between Julius II and Louis XII,[19] and a shorter letter from Francesco which emphasised again the significance of the mission for the family and his confidence in Machiavelli's ability to undertake it.[20] He placed at Machiavelli's disposal Giovanni Girolami who appears to have been his agent at the French court.[21] Machiavelli was perceived by contemporaries to be an envoy from the Soderini, not from Florence. For example, the bishop of Tivoli, Camillo Leonini, wrote on 3 August of a messenger of the *gonfaloniere* and his brother at the French court who was doing good service for the pope.[22] It seems clear, therefore, that the initiative for healing the breach between the pope and the French king came not from the French treasurer, Robertet, as was claimed, but from the Soderini,[23] who had more to lose from open hostility than almost anyone else.

As has been seen, these attempts at mediation failed, with fatal results for the Soderini regime in Florence. After the collapse of the republic, some commentators saw the Soderini's francophilia as a mistake and attributed it to the pursuit of private rather than public advantage. Guicciardini in particular saw Francesco Soderini's French connections, and especially his possession of French benefices, as the crucial factor in attaching the republic to France.[24] While there is clearly some truth in Guicciardini's emphasis on Francesco's French allegiance as a potent

---

[18] Machiavelli, *Le legazioni*, ed. Passerini and Milanesi, IV, p. 3.
[19] *Ibid.*, pp. 2–4.   [20] Machiavelli, *Lettere*, pp. 209–210.   [21] *Ibid.*, p. 10.
[22] See Sanuto, *I diarii*, XI, 190, and Cooper, 'Pier Soderini: aspiring prince', p. 101.
[23] Cooper, 'Pier Soderini: aspiring prince', p. 101.
[24] Guicciardini, *Storie fiorentine*, p. 299.

influence on the policy of his brother and, therefore, on the policy of the republic, it is not necessary to accept Guicciardini's explanation of this in terms of personal interest. The constant comparison of the public and private spheres was a common, even commonplace, trope in fifteenth- and sixteenth-century comments on affairs of state, but, as has been seen, there were excellent political reasons for the maintenance of links with France which had nothing to do with private interest. While Soderini's first-hand knowledge of France and her kings, together with his direct experience of the brute force of French power, undoubtedly led him to place more faith in France than some of his compatriots, the fact remains that Soderini's attachment to France was always mediated through his perception of the interests of Florence. Hence, the only time that he counselled the abandonment of the French alliance was when the armies of Cesare Borgia threatened the republic in 1502 and French help was too far away to provide any hope of effective protection.[25]

[25] Machiavelli, *Le legazioni*, ed. Passerini and Milanesi, II, p. 57.

PART III

NEW TIMES AND CHALLENGING
CIRCUMSTANCES, 1513–1524

THE FORTUNES OF THE SODERINI AND FAMILY STRATEGY IN RELATION TO FLORENCE, THE MEDICI AND FRANCE, 1513–17

It is important to remember that although Soderini's elevation to the cardinalate obviously entailed a change in the focus of his activities from Florence to Rome, this did not mark a definite break. Rather his standing as a cardinal must be seen as part of the Soderini family's attempt to establish a position of security for themselves and the republic with which they were to become increasingly identified. Just as the Medici sought to set up a power base in Rome by gaining high ecclesiastical office for members of the family, so the presence of a Soderini cardinal greatly strengthened that family's hand in a power struggle which nevertheless remained centred on Florence. In the period after 1512–13, Soderini family standing was effectively reliant upon the prestige and efforts of Francesco.

When his brother was *gonfaloniere* (1502–12), Francesco Soderini often returned to Florence or Tuscany for the summer months.[1] He may have continued to return to Tuscany after the fall of the Florentine republic. However, on one occasion, in 1515, Leo X chose to appoint Soderini as cardinal-governor in charge of Rome rather than allow him to pass through Florence with the pope and the rest of the papal court who were on their way to Bologna for a meeting with Francis I.[2] After 1512 the normal links of patronage between a great ecclesiastical statesman and his birthplace are not discernible in Soderini's relationship with Florence. One instance of his acting in such a role is his involvement in the foundation, in 1514, of S. Giuseppe in the *popolo* of S. Frediano, a convent for lay sisters (*pinzochere*) and later for Augustinian nuns – and even here the real incentive may have come from ser Marco da Favilla, one of Soderini's vicars-general at Volterra and an enthusiastic cleric who had adopted Florence as his home.[3] In the written

---

[1] See above, pp. 63–50.　　[2] See below, pp. 162–3.

[3] See G. Richa, *Notizie istoriche delle chiese fiorentine*, IX (Florence, 1761), p. 174, C. Calzolai, *S. Frediano in Cestello* (Florence, 1972), p. 132 and ASF, MAP, LXXXV,

constitution of S. Giuseppe, Marco Favilla and Lionardo and Lisabetta del Chiaro are described as its founders, and the Soderini as its patrons.[4] The only other example of Soderini's Florentine patronage comes from a list of the subscribers to the church of S. Giovanni dei Fiorentini in Rome in 1518.[5] His name appears immediately after that of pope Leo and is followed by those of prominent Mediceans as well as those of some of his own relations.[6]

If Soderini's politics excluded him from a patronage role in Florence after 1512, in Rome he could not be dissociated from his Florentine origins. The change in Soderini's own attitude to Florence can also be gauged from a comparison of his two extant wills of 1511 and 1524. In the first there is a clause allowing for the eventuality of his death in Florence, whereas in the second there is no such arrangement.[7] In short, the whole centre of Soderini's activities shifted decisively to Rome only after 1512. From that date onwards, Rome became the home of most of the prominent members of the Soderini family. Soderini's status as a cardinal, and Piero's enforced retirement, now meant that he was the effective head of the family. Whether he was going to use that position to continue the struggle against Medici domination of Florence or to effect a lasting settlement between the two families was an open question in 1513.

Certainly, Soderini had taken the first steps towards reconciliation in the bargain he had struck with Leo X. Goro Gheri, in a letter of 14 January 1517, claimed that Soderini had only agreed to support the election of Giovanni de' Medici in order to save his family, which he feared would be ruined were he to refuse. Indeed, he went so far as to claim that Soderini's proposal for a secret ballot in the 1513 conclave had been prompted by his desire to play the Medici false, or in Gheri's words 'he wanted to be able to say one thing and to do another'.[8] Admittedly, Gheri was a devoted Medicean who was obsessed by the threat to

---

421. In 1527 Marco Favilla was the governor of two convents of nuns in or near S. Frediano, BNF, Nuovi acquisti 987, 30v and 31r.

[4] BNF, Palat. 153, 18v and 19r, Costituzioni delle monache di S. Giuseppe in S. Frediano.

[5] Rome, Archivio di S. Giovanni dei Fiorentini, vol. 431. See also R. Olitsky, 'San Giovanni dei Fiorentini: the sixteenth-century building history and plans' (M.A. dissertation, New York Institute of Fine Arts, 1951), pp. 10, 91.

[6] Rome, Archivio di S. Giovanni dei Fiorentini, vol. 431, 2r.

[7] See ASBo, Notarile, Tommaso Grengoli, busta 18, filza 13 (1506–18), under date, unpaginated, and Lowe, 'Francesco Soderini', appendix 3, p. 340.

[8] ASF, Il minutario di Goro Gheri, I, 231r. Soderini also tried to introduce a secret ballot during the 1521 conclave. See Sanuto, *I diarii*, XXXII, 260 and G. Gattico, *Acta selecta caeremonialia S. R. E.* (Rome, 1753), I, pp. 318, 320.

Medici power posed by the Soderini. He was the official substitute in charge of Florence for Lorenzo, duke of Urbino, through the latter part of 1516 and much of 1517.[9] In the same letter, he argued that the Soderini only allowed themselves to benefit the Medici for one of three reasons, ceremony, fear or error, and counselled that his masters behave in such a fashion that the Soderini and others who would not acquiesce voluntarily were, quite simply, forced to comply with the wishes of the Medici.[10]

Soderini family stategy changed course in the aftermath of the events of 1512 and 1513, once more reacting to alterations in the fortunes of the Medici, for as a consequence, the circumstances of the Soderini family as a whole, as well as of individual members, had shifted irrevocably.[11] The senior, career politician in the family had lost his life-tenure as *gonfaloniere*. Piero could, therefore, no longer manoeuvre and cajole foreign potentates and the pope in order to obtain a bishopric or a red hat for his younger brother; he was out of power. Now the Soderini as a family, and Francesco as its most active member, had to rely upon their direct connections with the French kings and the popes. Piero retired from politics with a good grace and perhaps with a sigh of relief, but he did not altogether retreat from the demands of Roman life. He had social cachet for three reasons: he was the ex-*gonfaloniere* of Florence, the brother of a cardinal and a Florentine blood relation of the pope. As such, he attended, for example, the wedding feast of one of Leo's nieces, Emilia Ridolfi, with Jacopo d'Appiano V, the ruler of Piombino, in August 1514.[12] Francesco Soderini was not among the guests, although seven other cardinals were; he may have been in Tuscany for the summer months. Piero and his wife, Argentina Malaspina, lived rather anomalous lives in Rome, with Piero insisting that he had no further interest in politics and that he merely wished to live quietly, as a private person. As far as is known, he never returned to Florence although he did express a desire to travel to Vicenza to visit Francesco's bishopric.

It was recognised that Piero's position represented a new twist on an old theme. Rulers ousted from power were numerous in early sixteenth-century Italy, but those who, having once been in positions of the highest authority and having been overthrown, chose to renounce the struggle, were not. It was to Piero's credit that he managed to create and

---

[9] Stephens, *The fall*, p. 103.   [10] ASF, Il minutario di Goro Gheri, I, 231r.

[11] For evidence that contemporary observers tended to assess the Soderini chances in family as well as individual terms, see A. Bardi, 'Filippo Strozzi (da nuovi documenti)', *Archivio storico italiano*, series v, 14 (1894), p. 33.

[12] Sanuto, *I diarii*, XVIII, p. 470.

carry off this original role for himself. His situation could not fail to cause comment. On the *festa di Agone* of 1514,[13] in Rome, there was a procession of eighteen chariots, each on the theme of a virtue; the sixteenth chariot depicted fortune in the form of a wheel. On top of the wheel was the Florentine lion, the *marzocco*, and a man driving in a nail; under the wheel was a man dressed in a cloak and hood. The former was said to be a Medici, and the latter Piero Soderini.[14] Piero's decision not to attempt to climb back up the wheel of fortune but to enjoy his private life did not entirely deflect attention away from him. In part, this was because he was still a member of a family which was prominent in political and ecclesiastical affairs, and which was still viewed as the main opposition to the Medici in Florence. Although the centre of the Soderini world after 1512 was Rome, they were all still considered Florentines and not Romans.

In Rome, altered family circumstances forced an intensification of Francesco's activities as a prelate rather than a change of personal policy. His success as a cardinal and manipulator of benefices had already allowed him to bestow the bishopric of Volterra upon one of his nephews, Giuliano di Paolantonio, thus starting an episcopal dynasty. At this date, although neither Piero nor Francesco had sons, they still enjoyed a sufficiency of nephews through the male line. But the political calibre of the nephews seems to have been rather poor, and the role played by the next generation in both Florentine and Roman affairs was consequently limited. Four of Paolantonio's sons were alive: Tommaso, Giovanbattista, Giuliano and Piero, and Giovanvettorio only had one son, also called Tommaso.[15] Of these, only Giovanbattista and the two Tommasos even attempted to lead political lives. Giovanbattista had stayed with Piero in Florence until 1512, where his behaviour had occasioned talk from Machiavelli,[16] and after 1512 he probably lived in Rome with Piero or Francesco. Giuliano too stayed close to his uncle Francesco, but played no overt political role.

Additionally, the Soderini were at a disadvantage because they lacked marriageable daughters and nieces with the Soderini name. Overall, the four Soderini brothers had in 1512–13 only two nubile females in their

---

[13] For further information on this *festa*, see Stinger, *The renaissance*, pp. 58–9.

[14] See Sanuto, *I diarii*, XVIII, 14–15 and F. Cruciani, *Teatro nel rinascimento: Roma, 1450–1550* (Rome, 1983), p. 438.

[15] See Passerini, 'Soderini', tables VI and VII. Tommaso di Giovanvettorio later copied his uncle Piero by marrying into the Malaspina family.

[16] H. Butters and J. Stephens, 'New light on Machiavelli', *English historical review*, 97 (1982), p. 67. Giovanbattista was also the nephew whom it was rumoured at some point between 1506 and 1508 that Clarice de' Medici would marry. See Bullard, *Filippo Strozzi*, p. 50.

families, Margherita and Giovanna (known as Anna) di Giovanvettorio. According to the family historian, Passerini, the former married Luigi Martelli in 1513.[17] Family strategy encompassed not only the acquisition of a red hat and rich benefices for a male member of the family, but the forging of advantageous marriage alliances by female members. Lorenzo de' Medici's spectacular success with his children in this respect – one son a cardinal and one daughter married to the son of the pope – illustrates how these kinds of tactics could ensure the survival of a family as a political force across two generations. Anna Soderini was the sole female whose marriage alliance could be used to help her family, and consequently her marriage to a Medici or Medici relation was part of the exchange transacted between the two families as the price of Piero Soderini's return to Rome in 1513.

Finally, beyond the barter in benefices and dowries, property as a form of joint asset was also an important element in family strategy. This had been made clear after 1478 when Francesco changed career to become a cleric. His father Tommaso authorised an exchange between the portion of Tuscan property allocated to Francesco, which was mainly around Pisa and Pistoia, and that earmarked for Giovanvettorio, as Giovanvettorio, not Francesco, was to be the academic lawyer at Pisa.[18] It will also become apparent later, in the history of Soderini's housing complex in the Borgo in Rome (see pp. 193–209).

The Soderini family were most in need of strategies and policies because of their position *vis-à-vis* their relations, the Medici. The rivalry between the two families was displaced from Florence to Rome. In his book on the fall of the Florentine republic, John Stephens has shown how minor the role of the Soderini was in anti-Medicean activity in Florence after 1512. In part, of course, this was because the most important Soderini lived in Rome and not in Florence, and therefore the principal anti-Medicean activity by the Soderini took place in the capital of christendom rather than on Medici home territory. Nor did those desirous of political change in Florence after 1512 speculate, in the main, about the return of the Soderini in the way that malcontents under the republic looked to the Medici. All the same, whenever trouble arose in Florence, the name of the Soderini was invoked like that of a bogeyman or a spectre from the past. For example, in April 1516, a contemporary diarist Parenti reported a prophecy which spread around the city that the king of France wanted to restore Piero Soderini

---

[17] Passerini, 'Soderini', table VII.
[18] ASF, Not. antecos. B726, 198r and v, and 292v, and ASF, Capitani di Parte Guelfa, Numeri rossi 75, 7v.

and his form of government.[19] Similarly, when Lorenzo, duke of Urbino, died in 1519, a spy in Florence reported that the Soderini, 'who were the opposing party to the Medici', had risen up.[20]

Other reasons for this lack of focus in Florence around the Soderini, in opposition to the Medici, are manifest: the Soderini had never aspired to the dominance achieved by the Medici although political observers refused to credit this, conditioned as they were by years of Medicean false republicanism. Also, Piero ruled more or less as *primus inter pares* with other patricians, often failing to have his schemes approved through the normal channels of government and yet refusing, in the main, to resort to non-constitutional action. In part, this may have been due more to circumstance than to design. Francesco, not Piero, was characterised as the ambitious one – in Bernardo Dovizi's words, Francesco was dynamic (*gajardo*) while Piero was reserved (*fredo*)[21] – but, as a cleric, Francesco was ineligible for office in Florence. In addition, no particular nephew emerged as a leader around whom support could crystallise. However, the real constraint on Soderini dynasticism may have been Soderini inclination: Piero did not believe in such behaviour. Instead, he wrote to Francesco on 14 January 1511 saying that, after the Prinzivalle della Stufa conspiracy had been revealed, he was taking steps to ensure that if he were to be assassinated, 'the city would not suffer but would always keep the same form of government as at present.'[22] The result of this republican reticence was that, while the fortunes of the Soderini family in Florence had become ineluctably linked with those of the republic, the fortunes of the republic were not similarly bound up with the return of the Soderini.

The situation looked different in Rome. There Francesco's status as a cardinal and his links with the French meant that he could continue to be a source of considerable anxiety and irritation to the Medici. From a Roman perspective, the Soderini were the natural, indeed obvious, opponents of the Medici because of their Florentine background. Thus Goro Gheri, who knew both places, participated in the Roman view of Soderini as a great danger and the Soderini as an alternative to Medici rule. For Gheri, who habitually saw politics in terms of the Florence–Rome axis, the removal of Soderini was the key to political stability in both places. Thus he observed in June 1517: 'The question of Soderini

---

[19] BNF, II IV 171, 127r. See also H. Butters, *Governors and government in early sixteenth-century Florence, 1502–1519* (Oxford, 1985), p. 298.

[20] Sanuto, *I diarii*, XXVII, 266.   [21] *Ibid.*, V, 695.

[22] BNF, GC, 29 (10a), January 1510 (i.e. 1511). The point is made in Cooper, 'Pier Soderini: aspiring Prince', p. 119.

should be settled, because once he was sorted out, Rome and Florence would be put in order.'[23]

Later in 1524, Niccolò Martelli wrote a treatise on how to run a state, with special reference to Florence. Martelli had been named as a participant in the 1522 conspiracy against cardinal de' Medici in Florence, and the treatise was an attempt to win his way back into the favour of the Medici. In it he described Soderini's career as precisely the sort of unwelcome phenomenon which the Medici should cut short if they wished to maintain their power. He singled out the threat posed by ambassadors who could use their embassies as a means of establishing links with foreign powers and also of gaining a knowledge of the policy of the governing group.[24] He isolated as dangerous the authority which accrued to high ecclesiastical office.[25] Here he even cited the example of Soderini whose death in 1524 had, he claimed, marked the end of the Soderini family's active opposition to the Medici since, lacking the support and leadership of the cardinal, they no longer felt themselves capable of influencing events. When, in 1526, Martelli fell into the hands of Clement VII, he supplemented these remarks by emphasising the role of Soderini's relationship with the French king in his resistance to Leo and Clement.[26] While these remarks come from a tainted source – on both occasions Martelli was telling the Medici what they wanted to hear – and cannot be accepted as straightforward evidence for Soderini's intentions, they can be used as examples of the Medici view of Soderini and the ways in which he exploited his opportunities in order to challenge and resist Medici ascendancy.

Just as conditions in Rome changed significantly for Soderini when cardinal Giovanni de' Medici was elected pope in March 1513, so they shifted again when, in Leo's first promotion of 23 September 1513, four new cardinals were created. Two of them, Giulio de' Medici and Innocenzo Cibo, were Leo's relatives and the other two, Lorenzo Pucci and Bernardo Dovizi da Bibbiena, were Florentine citizens or subjects.[27] There was a new rival Medici cardinal for Soderini but this time one who had the whole-hearted backing of the pope. The greater opportunities provided by his relative's high position meant that the new Medici cardinal was a more important figure at the papal court than cardinal Giovanni had been. When Hanno, the Indian elephant

---

[23] Quoted in F. Winspeare, *La congiura dei cardinali contro Leone X* (Florence, 1957), pp. 145–6.

[24] See C. Guasti, 'Documenti della congiura fatta contro il cardinale Giulio de' Medici', *Giornale storico degli archivi toscani*, 3 (1859), p. 226.

[25] *Ibid.*, p. 227.   [26] *Ibid.*, p. 239.   [27] Eubel, *Hierarchia*, III, pp. 14–15.

who had been presented to Leo X by the king of Portugal,[28] died in
Rome at the beginning of June 1516, someone, possibly Aretino,
composed an extremely clever pastiche of his will in which he left
different parts of his body and different attributes to various cardinals.
Cardinal de' Medici was bequeathed Hanno's ears 'so that he would be
equipped to hear the affairs of the whole world'.[29] The satirist knew the
idiosyncracies of his subjects, and this was no idle jibe. On the other
hand, Hanno left his common sense to Soderini, 'so that he can keep in
check his extraordinary munificence',[30] which was an attack on his
meanness and caution, a usual butt for the pasquinades of these years.
Cardinal de' Medici's fault was the greater, but being satirised for a vice
as petty as parsimony was far more shaming and made Soderini appear
the lesser character.

On the other hand, the extent to which the relations between the
Medici and the Soderini were shaded, sometimes good and sometimes
bad, rather than constantly oppositional, should not be underestimated.
They were not only rivals, but also on occasion accomplices, for their
common geographical and cultural framework resulted in their both
adopting viewpoints and allegiances that could be categorised as
Florentine in a broader context. Their relationship encompassed a range
of nuanced behaviour, from tension and rivalry to cooperation and
coexistence. Thus, sometimes, as in the conclave of September 1503, the
Medici and Soderini cardinals voted together (at this point, with the
French party)[31] or appeared on the same side in projected breakdowns
of the college of cardinals according to international groupings. There
is no evidence to suggest that either of the Medici popes punished
Soderini by blocking his access to appointments or benefices; on the
contrary, as will be seen later, Soderini continued to prosper (apart from
the period of the conspiracies) under their pontificates. Twice, in 1513
and in 1523, Soderini made a deal with individual Medici cardinals
chasing the pontifical tiara, offering to give them his support in return
for some concession(s) to his family.

Clearly, to see Medici/Soderini relations wholly in oppositional
terms oversimplifies and distorts the real complexities of the matter. But
what exactly were the Soderini, as a family, trying to achieve in Rome?
At times, their aim appears to have been mere survival; at others, it was
more aggressively to provide support in Florence for alternatives to

---

[28] For further information on Hanno, see R. Cimino, 'Un elefante alla corte dei papi',
    Atti dell'accademia delle scienze di Torino, 118 (1984), pp. 72–93.
[29] V. Rossi, 'Un elefante famoso', in *Scritti di critica letteraria (3). Dal rinascimento al
    risorgimento* (Florence, 1930), p. 236.   [30] *Ibid.*, p. 234.
[31] Pastor, *History of the popes*, VI, p. 192.

Medici rule. Soderini choice was conditioned by the fact that they had less money than their Medici opponents, fewer important extra-Florentine contacts, and no longer had a family member holding political office of a critical nature. As a consequence, their objectives in both Florence and Rome were limited, with corporate subsistence taking precedence over opposition and intervention. Only during periods of Soderini ascendancy and Medici crisis or complacency did they attempt to dispute power with their rivals, although antagonism and criticism undoubtedly formed the major constituent of the relationship.

Initially, the agreements fixed between the two families went well and it appears that Soderini was consulted, along with other Florentine and Tuscan cardinals, on matters of importance. On 24 November 1513, for instance, Francesco Vettori, the Florentine orator in Rome, wrote that the pope was consulting Lang, Soderini, del Monte, Pucci, Medici and Dovizi about the affairs of the Venetians and the emperor.[32] After this auspicious beginning, their relationship rather fades from view – indeed the years from 1513 to 1516 are among the least well documented of any of Soderini's adult life.

In the period between 1513 and 1517 the marriage alliance which had been part of Soderini's deal with Leo X had gone badly awry. The first suggested match was to have been between Anna di Giovanvettorio, and Lorenzo di Piero de' Medici,[33] the son of Alfonsina Orsini. A marriage to a Medici of such standing, who was in political terms the heir to power in Florence, would obviously have represented a major coup for the Soderini. Nothing came of this proposal because it was blocked immediately by Alfonsina,[34] whose plans for her progeny were vastly more ambitious. The next suggestion was that Anna should marry Luigi di Piero Ridolfi, Leo's nephew from the marriage of his sister, Contessina. This was a far inferior deal for the Soderini as the man himself was less important and did not even carry the name of Medici. Nevertheless, they accepted. Nerli wrote that 'although at the time cardinal Soderini showed himself to be satisfied by the exchange, one saw later, when circumstances allowed, and when the cardinal was able to demonstrate his feelings, how unwillingly he was forced to appear content at such an arrangement'.[35]

Even this substitute transaction did not go smoothly. It appears that the suggestion for this match may have come from the Soderini, not from Leo as a peace offering, and it seems that both sides had managed

---

[32] ASF, Dieci, Resp. 118, 317r.   [33] See Nardi, *Istorie*, II, p. 71.
[34] See F. Nerli, *Commentari de' fatti civili occorsi dentro la città di Firenze dall'anno 1215 al 1537* (Augusta, 1728), p. 124.   [35] *Ibid.*, p. 124.

to get themselves into the unenviable position of being dissatisfied with what was on offer and of feeling that they had been treated badly. No more is heard about the match until 1516, when, on 17 October, Goro Gheri wrote to Baldassare Turini that the pope had agreed to Anna di Giovanvettorio as a prospective bride, but that the Ridolfi relatives were only agreeing on condition that she brought with her a dowry of extraordinary magnitude. The figure of 4,000 ducats was proposed, 2,000 from Giovanvettorio and 2,000 from Francesco Soderini.[36] By January 1517 it was agreed that the pope would decide the amount of the dowry, which he duly declared should be 10,000 ducats. Francesco had already promised to pay, and Piero stood surety for him.[37]

This huge dowry excited comment at the time, and although the Medici and Ridolfi were extracting money because they were in the stronger position, to outsiders the arrangement appeared to be one of great splendour and of almost regal proportions. Marco Strozzi wrote from Rome to his uncle, Giovanni Strozzi, in Ferrara that the dowry was rumoured to be larger than that paid to the duke of Urbino.[38] The wedding finally took place on 25 January. Soderini provided the wedding feast with an array of cardinals; unfortunately, only the Florentine Mediceans, Giulio de' Medici, Lorenzo Pucci and Bernardo Dovizi, as well as the Medicean nephew Cibo, are named. All these had been promoted in Leo's first promotion of 23 September 1513. Also present was another papal nephew, Luigi de' Rossi, an apostolic protonotary, who acquired his red hat at Leo's massive promotion of 1 July later the same year, and whose star was obviously rising. Interestingly, Alfonsina, as one of the most important Medici in Rome, had been invited even though it was due to her that the first marriage had not taken place, and she had never demonstrated any love for the Soderini; but she declined.[39] Soderini later defaulted on his payments for the dowry so even this elementary arrangement between the two families collapsed in disarray.

Soderini's role as main provider for the family can be seen at its clearest in the arrangements for this dowry. In his will of February 1511, he had bequeathed his main residence in the Borgo in Rome[40] to his ecclesiastical nephew, Giuliano, with the proviso that other members of the family should have access to a room in it whenever they needed

[36] ASF, Il minutario di Goro Gheri, I, 108r and v.
[37] ASF, Manoscritti Torrigiani, busta III, fasc. 20, folders I and II. See also C. Guasti, *I manoscritti Torrigiani* (Florence, 1878), p. 417.
[38] ASF, C. Strozz., III, 134, 102r and v, 31 January 1517.
[39] ASF, C. Strozz., index, series I, VII, p. 27, postscript of secretary Ser Bernardo di Piero Fiamminghi to a letter from Alfonsina Orsini to Goro Gheri, secretary of Lorenzo, duke of Urbino, 25 January 1517.   [40] See below, pp. 193–209.

one.[41] In addition, Tommaso di Paolantonio was to receive the seven shops with houses on Borgo Alessandrina.[42] By January 1518, Soderini was using these houses to discharge his debt to Luigi Ridolfi for Anna's dowry.[43] Although both Piero and Giovanvettorio had played a part in financing the marriage, it was Francesco who had to sort out the resultant mess.

It might be argued that a perfectly genuine attempt on Soderini's part to reach agreement with the Medici had been undermined, first by the latter's pride and then by their avarice. This was not Goro Gheri's view, and there is surely enough evidence of animus against the Medici in Soderini's career, both before and after 1513, to make the chances of a permanent settlement emerging from the ruins of the republic extremely slim. It seems almost certain that Gheri was right, and that in striking a bargain with cardinal de' Medici, Soderini was using his family's last asset, his independent standing as a cardinal, as a means of staving off ruin. This having been achieved, he surely intended to take up the struggle once again.

By late 1516 Soderini had become a major preoccupation for Goro Gheri, and on account of the survival of Gheri's letterbook, the general tenor of Medici feeling for and against Soderini can be gauged. Gheri and his friends, hardline Medici supporters, certainly did not under-estimate the extent of the rivalry between Soderini and the Medici; rather it might be supposed that they overestimated it. But the letters stand as documents that chart what the Medici themselves might have felt. It is doubtful if the Medici themselves would have expended so much effort to find out minor details of Soderini's movements, but as Gheri and his associates continued to do so, it is probable that they were doing it on Medici directive. A good indication of the depth of feeling is that Gheri considered the Soderini ungrateful beasts and thought that they had betrayed the trust placed in them by Lorenzo de' Medici. He described them in December 1516 as 'those accursed Soderini', going on to say that 'had Lorenzo of happy memory believed that such ingratitude could reign in them, he would never have made messer Tommaso Soderini as rich as he did and the first man in the city'.[44] Gheri was apparently unaware of the irony of these words, which can be taken as an indication of the extent of his distorted extremism,

---

[41] ASBo, Notarile, Tommaso Grengoli, busta 18, filza 13 (1506–18), under date, and Lowe, 'Francesco Soderini', appendix 3, pp. 333–5.

[42] ASBo, Notarile, Tommaso Grengoli, busta 18, filza 13, and Lowe, 'Francesco Soderini', appendix 3, pp. 336–7.   [43] See below, p. 204.

[44] ASF, Il minutario di Goro Gheri, I, 187v, Gheri to Baldassare Turini, 15 December 1516.

because in a literal sense it had been Tommaso who had made Lorenzo the 'first man', by ensuring a smooth take-over of leadership on Piero de' Medici's death in 1469.

In another letter, of 14 January 1517, Gheri sets out this argument even more fully. He here assumes that the rivalry is not curable or stoppable, but to the death, and he also assumes that the usual techniques of large-scale bribery with honours or money or responsibilities which the Medici used to quell dissatisfaction, will not work with Soderini. The reference to the Medici adversity and the Soderini response to it is particularly telling. Gheri wrote

> And then if you think that by favouring the Soderini you will ever succeed in making them Medicean or quietening them down, for my part I confess I find this impossible to believe. For when I think that our patrons Piero di Cosimo and Lorenzo gave them their standing and their powers (I want you to know that there was a time when messer Tommaso Soderini could not cross the Ponte Vecchio for fear of the constables), to tell the truth it failed, and by the Medici family Tommaso was made the first man in the city in terms of standing and power. Then the Soderini showed such ingratitude at every point towards the Medici, and at the time of their adversity they were aware of what severity and strange behaviour they used with them. Think, therefore, of what one could expect from them both on account of what happened and on account of the standing in which they now find themselves.[45]

It is not clear what it was that prompted these outbursts, as Gheri seemed suddenly to pick up interest in the Soderini at about this time, but it could have been some local Tuscan dispute, possibly a minor row between Volterra and Florence in 1516. These subject towns had always presented difficulties to Florence, but with the rather muddled Medici government of these years, the problems must have magnified. Soderini was always thought of in connection with Volterra which, with S. Gimignano and Colle Val d'Elsa, was a stronghold of low-level Soderini support.[46] Therefore, any independence on the part of the town would probably have been seen by the Medici as being Soderini-inspired. Earlier in the same letter of 14 January, Gheri fretted over the high standing and reputation of 'those who have always been enemies of the regime' and who had the possibility of taking action, and said that he worried much more when such people as, for example, the Soderini, could be heads of state by themselves, have a cardinal in the family, and be rich and highly esteemed inside Florence.[47]

[45] Ibid., I, 231v and 232r, Gheri to Turini, 14 January 1516 (i.e. 1517).
[46] Ibid., I, 216r, Gheri to Turini, 1 January 1516 (i.e. 1517): 'Volterra ha una trecca de amici in Volterra, in San Giumignano et in Colle.'   [47] Ibid., I, 230v.

So even Gheri is not sure what attitude to adopt towards the Soderini; at one point they are creations of the Medici, raised to their present height by Piero di Cosimo and Lorenzo; at another they are the longstanding enemies of the Medici. Another discrepancy concerns Florentine public opinion on the Soderini. Here Gheri reckons that the citizens are favourably inclined. In another letter of 8 December 1516 to Baldassare Turini, he explains that, in general, the citizens of Florence are pleased when friends of the Soderini encounter adverse circumstances, but that they are still more pleased when misfortunes befall the Soderini themselves.[48] These differences show up Gheri's passion. He was so concerned to make the Soderini seem a serious threat that he was prepared to use any argument to back up his case. On the other hand, he was well informed about the relevant aspects of Soderini's life, and seems to have had a good understanding of Soderini's machinations against the Medici.

If Medici–Soderini relations had returned to an uneasy amity in 1513, Gheri's remarks of 1516–17 show that the period of pseudo-accommodation had not lasted for long. By 1517 relations were definitively soured. In January 1517, in what must have seemed to Soderini an act of gratuitous aggression, Leo repossessed the palace attached to the church of SS. Apostoli which Soderini had renovated.[49] This was followed, in June 1517, either by Soderini's involvement in a conspiracy against Leo or, as will be argued below, by Soderini's being falsely accused by Leo of involvement in a fictitious conspiracy.

Just as the return of the Medici to Florence in 1512 and the advent of a Medici pope in 1513 forced a change in relations between the Soderini and Florence, and between the Soderini and the Medici, so too an increase in Medici power and status effected a gradual rapprochement between the Medici and France, especially after 1515, which had ramifications for the Soderini. Traditionally, it was the city of Florence which had evolved links with France, and both Florence's ruling families developed these links at a personal level. But France's favour was not an exclusive gift; nor did individual members of the Medici family always share the same allegiances. A consideration of Franco-Medicean relations in the year 1515 illustrates this well. On 1 January Louis XII died and was succeeded by his cousin and son-in-law, Francis, the count of Angoulême. Yet another Valois had failed to produce an heir. In February of this year, Giuliano de' Medici, the brother of Leo X, celebrated his marriage to Filiberte of Savoy who was the younger half-sister of Francis I's mother. The *Otto di Pratica* in Florence wrote

---

[48] *Ibid.*, I, 176r.   [49] See below, p. 213.

to Jacopo Salviati in Livorno instructing him to greet the bridal couple on their behalf, and to stress to the bride the ancient friendship between the Florentines and 'her house' which it was to be hoped would grow, especially after this marriage.[50] In September Francis I achieved an important victory at Marignano where he defeated the Swiss cantons. The pope decided that his best course of action was to come to terms with the French king, and Leo made a papal entry into Florence before going on to meet Francis I in Bologna. An accord was signed at Viterbo whereby Francis agreed to protect Florence and the Medici family, and to maintain Giuliano and Lorenzo in their present situations.[51]

In January 1516 Ferdinand of Aragon died. This affected Medici–French relations because France and Spain were the two most powerful kingdoms in Europe, and if the Medici wished to achieve international renown, they had to ally themselves with one or the other. By signing the Concordat of Bologna, in addition to conceding to the French king the power to nominate to all higher church offices in France, Leo had put himself under the obligation to support Francis I were he to attack Naples. Now was Francis's moment to proceed. However, the attack never came, as the emperor Charles V arrived in northern Italy and Francis was put on the defensive over Milan.[52] In March 1516 Giuliano de' Medici died, leaving Lorenzo to carry on the crucial family ties with France. Lorenzo had earlier considered a Spanish match with a daughter of the king of Navarre, but decided instead to find a French bride. In April 1518 he married Madeleine de la Tour d'Auvergne, whose mother was a Bourbon cousin of Francis I. The two Medici marriage alliances of 1515 and 1518 brought increased honour and prestige to the Medici and kinship to the pope for Francis; they were mutually profitable moves. The titles and honours which Francis gave to the Medici – Lorenzo was awarded the order of St. Michael and Giuliano was given the duchy of Nemours and the county of Lavaur – were part of the same strategy.

One might have thought that, in consequence, French backing for the Soderini would have lessened, but this was not the case. As will be seen, when Soderini needed Francis I, the king offered his help willingly. But it must have sobered the Soderini considerably to realise that, just as Rome was no longer so open an international arena for them as previously, because there was a Medici pope, so too the Medici rapprochement with France meant that yet another of their spheres of

[50] C. Lupi, 'Delle relazioni fra la repubblica di Firenze e i conti e duchi di Savoia', *Giornale storico degli archivi toscani*, 7 (1863), p. 302.

[51] Parenti, 'Storia', BNF, II iv 171, 120v and J. Thomas, *Le concordat de 1516* (Paris, 1910), I, pp. 305–6.   [52] Devonshire Jones, *Francesco Vettori*, pp. 124–5.

influence had been neutralised. Medici influence extended in a chrono-logical sequence from Florence to Rome to France; the Soderini had already taken exactly the same route in an attempt to escape from Medici control, but with the arrival of the Medici, very little territory remained available to them. On the other hand, it was only French support which enabled Soderini to remain buoyant enough to attempt to challenge the Medici, either in Rome or Florence. It is intriguing to see the finer points of a system which could allow these two Florentine families, riven at this point by institutionalised antagonism, to be clients of the same patron and to take their separate places in the orbit of the French monarch, thereby gaining increased stature which then enabled them to play out their rivalry on a different footing.

CHAPTER 9

THE 'CONSPIRACY' OF 1517

The story of the first conspiracy, according to the Medici, and taken from the confessions extracted under torture,[1] went as follows. In March 1516 Leo X had expelled from Siena its ruler, Borghese Petrucci, and had substituted in his place the vice-castellan of Sant'Angelo, Raffaele Petrucci, bishop of Grossetto. Borghese's brother, cardinal Alfonso,[2] agitated against this rearrangement of his family's affairs, and on 15 April 1517 his majordomo, Marcantonio Nini, was arrested. Interrogation began the next day. Nini at first only disclosed that in the previous August there had been discussions amongst three cardinals about the very serious illness of the pope. But by 27 April a letter that Nini had written to cardinal Petrucci on 11 August 1516[3] was produced as evidence, and he was asked to explain about the surgeon Battista da Vercelli who was mentioned in it. More and more confessions were literally wrung out of Nini, and cardinals calling themselves Carcioffo, Paritas, Palea, Exiguus and Rubeus were named as being part of a conspiracy against the pope.

Cardinal Petrucci, backed up by the sacred college, with an understanding that he would be returned to power in Siena, and ignorant of the confessions, came to Rome, met his friend cardinal

---

[1] The most important trial for which records are extant is that of Marcantonio Nini which began on 16 April 1517 and ended on 23 June 1517. It is published by A. Ferrajoli, *La congiura dei cardinali contro Leone X*, in Miscellanea della reale società romana di storia patria, VII (Rome, 1920), document no. 1, pp. 219–70. There are trials of lesser personages also in this volume. The enormous volume of 634 *fogli* of the trial which was in the possession of Lorenzo Pucci has never been found. The trial against Adriano was with it, as is known from the notarial act of its consignment, which was found by Ferrajoli. See *La congiura*, p. 137.

[2] Alfonso Petrucci had been promoted to the cardinalate by Julius II on 10 March 1511, Eubel, *Hierarchia*, III, p. 13. Bandinelli Sauli was promoted at the same time.

[3] This letter has always been dated 11 August 1515 but to have internal coherence, it must be of the following year.

Bandinelli Sauli,[4] rode with him to the Vatican and the two of them were then imprisoned on 19 May. The pope declared in consistory that they, with others, had tried to poison him, and three cardinal judges were appointed to deal with their case: Remolino, Accolti and Farnese. Alessandro Farnese had been made a cardinal in 1493, Francesco Remolino in 1503 and Piero Accolti in 1513. Therefore, Accolti was the only cardinal with strong reasons for loyalty to Leo. However, their loyalties were never put to the test as they played no part in the subsequent trial and judgement. On 29 May cardinal Riario[5] was arrested, implicated by the confessions of the other two, and he was interrogated by cardinal de' Medici. On 1 June the pope declared his intention of pardoning the guilty. On the 3rd, notes in the hands of the accused cardinals were read out, in which they confessed their errors. On the 4th, Riario too was sent to Castel Sant' Angelo and on the 8th the pope announced that there were two other guilty cardinals,[6] who, if they came forward and confessed, would be pardoned, but if they did not would be dealt with by the judges.

No one confessed until Francesco Soderini was publicly accused, whereupon he and Adriano Castellesi implored mercy and were punished with a fine of 12,500 ducats each.[7] On the 20th, Lorenzo de' Medici, duke of Urbino, arrived unexpectedly in Rome, and Soderini and Castellesi fled. On the 22nd, in consistory, the other three cardinals were stripped of their benefices. On the 27th Nini and Battista da Vercelli were killed, and on 4 July cardinal Petrucci was strangled in his cell. On 17 July a pact was finalised with Riario who promised to pay the vast fine of 150,000 ducats;[8] on the 24th he left prison and by

---

[4] For information on Sauli, see M. Hirst, *Sebastiano del Piombo* (Oxford, 1981), especially p. 99, where he also discusses Sauli's relationship with Paolo Giovio.

[5] Raffaele Riario was the dean of the college of cardinals. He had been made a cardinal on 10 December 1477. See Eubel, *Hierarchia*, III, p. 3.

[6] In Nini's trial, it is made clear by Nini that Soderini was involved in many discussions with, and knew of decisions taken by, cardinal Petrucci. Palea is the name used by the conspirators for Soderini, see Ferrajoli, *La congiura*, pp. 250–1, and 253. Why this name was chosen for Soderini is unclear, as he was not a man of straw.

[7] There is a certain amount of controversy over this figure, which is discussed by Ferrajoli, *La congiura*, pp. 74–6. Cornelius de Fine in his diary in BV, Ottob. lat. 2137, f.33, stated that Soderini had to pay 12,500 ducats. Paris de Grassis, BL, Add. MSS 8444, 14v–16r, related how the price was originally fixed at 12,500 ducats each but was subsequently raised to 25,000 ducats each. Parenti, 'Istorie', BNF, II IV 171, 135r, stated that Soderini paid 20,000 ducats. I think it probable that the pope had either set the fine at 25,000 each in the beginning as suggested in the conspirators' account, of which only 12,500 was to be paid immediately, or he doubled it, thus giving the two cardinals yet another reason to leave Rome.

[8] In ASF, Sig., Otto, Dieci, Miss. 9, 64r, there is a letter from Antonio Pucci to the captain of Monte Pulciano, of 1 July 1517. The three cardinals have been stripped

Christmas 1518 he had been restored to the cardinalate. Sauli was less fortunate; he received a fine of 25,000 ducats, was forced to make humiliating public confessions, and was never properly pardoned. Adriano Castellesi, who went to Venice, was formally deprived of his red hat and his benefices on 5 July 1518. Soderini stayed in exile until Leo X's death.

This narrative illustrates clearly the limits of a cardinal's powers in the face of papal hostility. A prince of the church was only a prince while he had the favour of the pope. The renaissance period is full of examples of popes threatening and enforcing the incarceration of cardinals in the papal prison in Castel Sant'Angelo,[9] stripping them of their cardinalitial garb and depriving them of their rank. The legal justification behind these moves would have been that the cardinals had committed treason by, for example, taking part in a rebellion or merely by opposing papal policy too strenuously. Formal trials appear in the main not to have taken place, although discussion of the act in consistory could have been a substitute. The precedent may have been set by pope Sixtus IV's use of cardinals Giovanni Colonna and Giovanni Battista Savelli as hostages in June 1482. They had been accused of treason in connection with the struggle taking place between the pope and king Ferrante in the kingdom of Naples, and they were held in Castel Sant'Angelo.[10] Fresher in the college of cardinals' collective memory must have been the incident of June 1510, when cardinal François Guillaume de Clermont was denied his cardinal's dress and imprisoned in Castel Sant'Angelo by Julius II because he attempted to escape to France, against the pope's wishes, at a time when Julius was planning to go to war with France.[11] Attempts to intervene by other cardinals and remonstrations from foreign governments and rulers were usually ignored. The pope created cardinals, within limits, and he could also choose to strip them of their red hats, within reason; they remained his subjects, even if he had created them princes.

The Medici side of the story seemed simple enough. But from the start some contemporaries were unwilling to believe it. Goro Gheri reported the experience of Francesco Maria della Rovere of Urbino who found himself in the presence of six or eight people, all of whom believed that cardinal Soderini had not erred in any respect, and he added that if Francesco Maria was a relative of Francesco Soderini, he

---

of their benefices, and Pucci continues: 'credo faranno mala fine, dico etiam della vita'. Riario also lost the palazzo della Cancelleria to the Medici.

[9] R. Ingersoll, *The ritual use of public space in renaissance Rome* (New York, 1986), p. 418.

[10] Pastor, *History of the popes*, IV, pp. 355–6.   [11] *Ibid.*, VI, p. 326.

was also a relative of the Medici.[12] Marco Minio wrote back to Venice on 9 June 1517 giving the names of the two cardinals cited in consistory and adding that the misdemeanour of one of them especially was of the slightest possible description.[13] Even Paris de Grassis suspected that in attacking cardinal Riario the pope was pursuing a vendetta which had originated in the Pazzi conspiracy, and he described Riario as an 'unfortunate old man' (*infelix senex*).[14]

For their part, leading Mediceans never doubted the conspirators' guilt. Gheri wrote to cardinal Dovizi on 20 June 1517 about Soderini's request to leave Rome, saying that he understood well Soderini's desire to take a little air, but to cure the humour that he currently felt, it would be necessary to give Soderini a room with only a little air in it.[15] If the charges were often not taken seriously, the dangers to the named cardinals were real enough. Cornelius de Fine tells the tale of Soderini's fleeing from Rome, sending his sumptuous litter ostentatiously out along the Via Tiburtina, whilst he and a few companions took a different road. The litter was followed and apprehended by Leo's guards, but was found to be empty.[16] Soderini's caution in his dealings with Leo was obviously necessary. The consistorial records for that day stated that Soderini was leaving with the pope's permission.[17]

All this evidence has been discussed before in various ways. In addition, there is an anonymous undated sixteenth-century history of the conspiracy written from the point of view of the conspirators.[18] It is probably all that remains from the proposed revision of the trial.[19] It presents another side to the story, and starts with a discussion of the pope's motives in behaving as he did. There is an indication at the end that it was written by the supporters or followers of the cardinals (*i fautori dei cardinali*). Its bias is unmistakable, but it is useful to have the cardinals speaking in their own defence. In both the way in which the events are described and in the additional details that it provides, this is an invaluable source. After a description of the pope's manoeuvres in Urbino and Siena, the history gives a clear exposition of Leo's motives:

---

[12] ASF, Il minutario di Goro Gheri, II, 421v, Gheri to Turini, 1 August 1517.
[13] *Calendar of state papers and manuscripts relating to English affairs existing in the archives and collections of Venice*, ed. Rawdon Brown, II (London, 1867), no. 902.
[14] Paris de Grassis, BL, Add. MSS 8444, 12r and v.
[15] ASF, Il minutario di Goro Gheri, II, 305r.
[16] BV, Ottob. lat. 2137, f.34, and Paris, Bibliothèque Nationale, Fonds latins 12552, 103v.   [17] AV, Fondo concist., Acta miscell. 70, 38r.
[18] AV, AA. Arm. I–XVIII, 5042, 1r–13r. I would like to thank Nelson Minnich for drawing my attention to this document. It has no title and is the only document in the *busta*. It is in a mid-sixteenth-century hand and must be a copy as there are no corrections.   [19] See Ferrajoli, *La congiura*, pp. 134–41.

he needed money, but had difficulty moving the college of cardinals who had been created by other pontiffs, and were more authoritative and older than he was. He decided, therefore, to resolve the situation in two ways: first, by destroying the way of life, the position and the reputation of the old cardinals, and second, by creating so many new cardinals who depended on him, 'that not only would he be able to obtain anything he wanted with the help of their votes as long as he lived, but he also calculated that after his death they would be able to be of great advantage to his family and supporters'.[20]

This was a clever move of Leo's, and there had never before been so large a creation. Although membership of the college increased throughout the sixteenth century, repeated attempts to put a ceiling on the number of cardinals finally resulted in a limit of seventy in 1586.[21] To set the process in motion, Leo began publicly to complain of Petrucci, secretly locked up one of his secretaries, Marcantonio da Siena, and arranged for Petrucci to come to Rome on the pretext of signing some chapters agreeing to an alliance 'in favour of and for the benefit of the Medici family and Florence and also in obedience to the papacy', and for Siena to pay 25,000 *scudi* to the papacy.[22] Full of hope, Petrucci returned to Rome from Genzano, and the next day, on his way to see the pope, he met Sauli and Cornaro on the Borgo Nuovo and the three of them went on together. On arrival, Petrucci and Sauli were led away to Castel Sant'Angelo and the pope called the college to congregation to tell them that these two had plotted against his person. The pope's evidence came from the confession of Marcantonio, who had been tortured until he admitted that Petrucci, dissatisfied with the pope, had plotted to poison him by means of the doctor, Battista da Vercelli, and that Riario, Soderini, Castellesi and Sauli knew of this. The pope kept this part secret and only divulged the part which related to Petrucci and Sauli. He immediately appointed three judges and spoke with so much artifice that the initiative was taken away from the college of cardinals who could only praise his clemency.[23] Four people were involved in the interrogation of the two cardinals: Mario Perusci, procurator fiscal; Giovanni Giacomo Gambarana, the auditor of the criminal court of the governor of Rome; the chaplain to Raffaele Petrucci, the vice-castellan Domenico Coletta; and the notary, a Piedmontese boy of eighteen called Giampietro Perracci who was a copyist in Gambarana's court.[24]

Neither cardinal had said anything incriminating at the end of four

---

[20] AV, AA. Arm. I–XVIII, 5042, 2r and v.

[21] McClung Hallman, *Italian cardinals*, p. 4.

[22] AV, AA. Arm. I–XVIII, 5042, 3r. This illustrates well the family element in the conspiracy.   [23] *Ibid.*, 4v and 5r.   [24] *Ibid.*, 5r.

days. In the next consistory Riario was detained and sent to Castel Sant'Angelo. He was told that if he did not confess he would be subjected to the same treatment as a lay person, that is, torture, which would cause horrible physical damage. If he did confess, however, the pope promised that they would all be pardoned. He was only required to confirm that Marcantonio's story was true. Weak in mind and body he complied. Torture was then used on the other two (there was great discussion in Rome about this at the time) and eventually Petrucci gave in, and also confirmed Marcantonio's story. Sauli was the most resilient, but after twenty-four hours of examination without food or sleep, and then the rope, he too gave in and confessed to whatever they wanted. Vercelli was brought to Rome especially to join in the confession.

The three cardinals were then requested to make 'a handwritten confession in which they admitted their guilt and asked for pardon from the pope'.[25] All this was carried out in secret and not even the relatives of the cardinals knew what was taking place. The pope called a congregation and, with tears in his eyes, thanked God that he had been able to get to the root of the matter, told them about the confessions of Marcantonio and Vercelli, and showed them the handwritten statements of the cardinals.

He said that he was going to free them after giving them some form of punishment as an example.[26] The supporters and relatives of the three cardinals, while deploring the strange behaviour of the pope in not using the judges he had appointed, and in choosing an uneducated boy as a notary, were delighted by his forgiveness.[27] Sauli came to his senses after the torture and demanded to be allowed to recant, realising that 'false methods of persuasion had induced him to confess to a lie of huge proportions, not only in contravention of his own honour, but also to the slander of the other people named'.[28] He decided he would prefer to die than live in this false position. The interrogators told him that if he retracted this would 'ruin the substance of all their trial and at the same time ruin the pope's plans'.[29] One of his brothers, Stefano, came

---

[25] *Ibid.*, 6r.   [26] *Ibid.*, 6r.   [27] *Ibid.*, 6v.

[28] *Ibid.*, 6v and 7r. Throughout the account Sauli is described as brave, strong and honourable which adds fuel to the theory that the revised version was commissioned by his brother Stefano. See C. Longolius, *Orationes duae pro defensione sua. Oratio una ad Luterianos. Eiusdem epistolarum libri quatuor, etc.* (Florence, 1524), 135r and v, letter to Stefano Sauli of 14 May 1522. Pastor, *History of the popes*, VII, p. 198 stated that a report of the cardinals' conspiracy had been written by Ziegler, avowedly under the influence of those who wanted a revised account. See Jacopo Ziegler, 'Clementis Septimi episcopi romani vita', in *Amoenitates historiae ecclesiasticae et literariae*, ed. J. Schellhorn, II (Frankfurt/Leipzig, 1738), pp. 315–28. Ziegler wrote this circa 1526 but it contains no new information.   [29] AV, AA. Arm. I–XVIII, 5042, 7r.

to see him in prison, but when cardinal Sauli wanted to tell him what had happened, Stefano praised the pope's clemency and told him that he would be released, and that he should dedicate the rest of his life to serving the pope and his family, and in particular cardinal de' Medici, 'from whose work all this good had proceeded'.[30] When told he had been pardoned and would be released as soon as possible, 'recognizing that the opinion of those outside was different from his own', he made up his mind to say nothing more about retracting.

Riario's fine was set at 150,000 *scudi* and Sauli's at 50,000 and while his brothers, who were unable to pay tried to negotiate a reduction, the cardinals were deprived of their hats and benefices. Cardinal Petrucci was strangled by 'a moor',[31] but not before he told his confessor, Ugolino da Orvieto, that he had wrongly incriminated the other cardinals. Sauli was transferred to a worse prison and his brothers agreed to pay 25,000 *scudi* to try to get him out quickly. As a condition of his release, he had to agree not to retract or change anything that had been said in the trial. Nini and Vercelli were taken to Tor di Nona, where they screamed all night that they had been wrongly condemned. The next day, when they were put in a cart and driven through Rome to their execution, a man was placed next to each of them 'who under pretence of comforting them, impeded them from speaking, pressing a pious image (*tavoletta*)[32] up against their mouths every time they tried to open them'.[33] Their names were Leonardo Bartolini and Filippo de Carolis, 'both of them satellites of pope Leo'. Nini and Vercelli still managed to protest their innocence once or twice.

The affair, however, was not allowed to rest there. One morning, in consistory, the pope said that although he wished it were all over, there was more to come. Two more cardinals were implicated. The pope asked them to come forward, assuring them of a pardon. All filed past one by one, but no one spoke. The pope then retired to a room with the three judges and cardinal Pucci[34] and made them look at that part of the

---

[30] *Ibid.*, 8r.

[31] *Ibid.*, 8r. See too D. Gnoli, 'Le cacce di Leon X', *Nuova antologia*, 2 (1893), p. 620 on Petrucci.

[32] See S. Edgerton, 'A little known "purpose of art" in the Italian renaissance', *Art history*, 2 (1979), who discusses some late sixteenth- and early seventeenth-century *tavolette* remaining in the possession of the church of S. Giovanni Decollato in Rome. [33] AV, AA, Arm. I–XVIII, 5042, 8v.

[34] Cardinal Pucci's role has not been adequately assessed. It seems likely that he was in charge of the trial although he did not join in the questioning of the lowly suspects. As the main volume is missing, we do not know whether he conducted some of the inquisitions of the cardinals. It must be remembered that he was in possession of the volume containing the trial records, and in this account he had knowledge of its contents. He was a Florentine and a close friend of Leo, who had been responsible

trial which had named Francesco Soderini and Adriano Castellesi. Pucci returned and said in a loud voice that Soderini and Castellesi were guilty and again assured them of a pardon if they confessed. They, 'not knowing what to do', knelt and told the pope that they had sinned (*peccavimus Beatissime Pater*). The pope demanded to hear what they really felt about the conspiracy against him. 'To escape from their dilemma, they had felt compelled to say that they were guilty, thinking that this would suffice to quench his rage. On hearing him add this other demand, they were mute and stayed kneeling for quite some time without knowing what else to say. Finally, cardinal Pucci approached and repeating to them the words of the trial which he knew by heart, he made such a fuss that Soderini said I know not what.'[35] The pope pardoned them but imposed a fine of 25,000 *scudi* each, of which they agreed to pay half immediately and half within a month. Having paid the first half they fled. Soderini went to Fondi and reached an arrangement whereby he agreed not to appeal against what had taken place, or to start any actions against the pope, and the pope in return agreed not to harm Soderini in any way nor to recall him from Fondi against his will.[36] Sauli was released but confined to Monterotondo where, shortly afterwards, he fell ill, and was carried back to Rome. Before he died he told his confessor, Fratre Silvestro di Prierio, that his confession had not been true and that he had only agreed to it through weakness of spirit. He asked him to tell the truth to a new pope and Silvestro did, according to this account, tell Adrian VI.

The history lists the rewards and benefices gained by those who carried out Leo's orders. A son of Perusci was given the bishopric of Massa with an annual pension of 500 *scudi*, which had been Sauli's.[37] Perusci himself was made a conservator of Rome. Gambarana was made bishop of Albenga, which had been another of Sauli's benefices,[38] and afterwards governor of Rome. The vice-castellan was made bishop of Sovana.[39] The notary was given benefices worth 400 *scudi* which had belonged to Marcantonio, and later offices worth 2,500 *scudi*.

---

for his elevation. I have no independent information about his attitude towards, or his relationship with, Soderini.

[35] AV, AA, Arm. I–XVIII, 5042, 10r. This 'non so che' could be taken as an indication that there was only one narrator in the account.   [36] *Ibid.*, 10v.

[37] See Eubel, *Hierarchia*, III, p. 254. He was bishop from 16 July 1517 to 1524.

[38] The succession of bishops in this bishopric is telling. Sauli held the bishopric from 5 August 1513, cardinal Giulio de' Medici from 19 November 1517 and Gambarana from 5 May 1518.

[39] The bishopric of Sovana was held by Alfonso Petrucci from 1 October 1510, by Lactantio Petrucci from 27 July 1513, and by Domenico Coletta from 2 December 1517.

The account finishes with a summing up of the two sides of the case. For Leo, there are the trial and the handwritten confessions. Against him, there are fairly convincing arguments: his ambition for Urbino, Florence and Siena, his desire to diminish the authority of the old cardinals, so that he could change the world after his own fashion,[40] an acute lack of money which he needed for his relatives, for war and for his own entertainment. His actions point to his duplicity: he did not keep his promise to the sacred college, he used ordinary people in the case instead of the judges appointed, he allowed an unlettered boy to write up the trial, he gave the prisoners no time to prepare a defence and he ordered the strangulation of cardinal Petrucci. As for the guilt of the accused, Riario had time to leave Rome after the first two had been taken prisoner. If he had been guilty, surely he would have done so. Even stranger was the behaviour of Soderini and Castellesi. Both were men of considerable political experience, both had plenty of warning that the conspiracy had been discovered and yet neither attempted to leave the city. The chronicler, Parenti, also made this point.[41] According to the history, Soderini's continued presence in Rome proves his innocence, since, as a member of a faction opposed to Leo, he was automatically suspect and at risk. On the other side, cardinal Pucci's conduct was especially damning, particularly the way in which he prompted the confessions as though they had been ordered by Leo himself. The rewards for the good services by the torturers were also suspicious. But the pope had achieved his first objective, and moved on to the second, promoting thirty-one cardinals on 1 July 1517, from whom he obtained substantial sums of money. The history ends by saying that the supporters of the accused cardinals leave the business of reaching a verdict on this case to those 'who are able to weigh up the arguments of both sides with sound judgement and without personal involvement'(senza passione).[42]

It would be difficult for anyone charting the lives of the Soderini to be 'without passion' in this affair but this account does shed light on several questions of importance. It is very concerned with motive, and indeed the question of why Leo might have wanted to fake a conspiracy needs a relatively convincing answer. Lack of money and a desire to rid himself of a variety of enemies are good reasons. The history contains only one date which is at the beginning: 'in the year 1517'; otherwise the many consistories and congregations mentioned are never dated,

---

[40] AV, AA, Arm. I–XVIII, 5042, 12r.

[41] Parenti, 'Istorie', BNF, II IV 171, 135r.

[42] AV, AA. Arm. I–XVIII, 5042, 13r. Again the verb is in the singular, pointing to a single author.

and the account is full of phrases such as 'later', 'one morning', 'next day'. On the other hand, it is very precise in the matter of names, as though its author wanted to put the guilty on record. It is especially surprising that the names of those keeping Nini and Vercelli quiet, and the names of Petrucci's and Sauli's confessors, are written down. The history must have been based on first-hand information and on some research. The account is virulently anti-papal, but also of necessity anti-Medici, and the author never misses a chance to point out how Leo manoeuvred to obtain pro-Medici decisions at the expense of other considerations. By the death of Leo X, three of the five cardinals were dead, and Adriano Castellesi disappeared soon afterwards on his way to the conclave in 1521. Soderini was the sole survivor. If he had been guilty, would he and Stefano Sauli have expended so much effort to secure a revision of the trial?

CHAPTER 10

SODERINI AS A DISAFFECTED CARDINAL IN EXILE, 1517–21

Soderini fled to Fondi which was just over the border from the papal states in the kingdom of Naples. It was a Colonna fief and Soderini was able to go and stay there because of his friendship with Pompeo Colonna.[1] In Fondi he was formally outside the pope's political jurisdiction and he took immediate steps to protect himself further. On 4 July 1517 Francis I wrote to the *gonfaloniere* and *comune* of Florence, taking the whole Soderini family under his protection and warning in no uncertain terms of the dire consequences for any who should attempt to molest his 'dear and beloved Soderini ... who have always been good and loyal servants of the crown of France'.[2] He also offered, on condition that he was provided with a safe-conduct, to go to Florence and appear before the judges in defence of the Soderini. By the end of July, Soderini had reached an extraordinary agreement whereby the orators of the most powerful countries and states in Europe guaranteed that he would stay in Fondi and certain other specified places, and stated that he was not obliged to return to Rome, even if summoned by the pope.[3] Originally the orators of the kings of France and England were

---

[1] Prospero Colonna was involved in negotiations on behalf of Soderini on 25 July 1517 and 6 February 1519. See Guasti, *I manoscritti*, pp. 465–7. The first is mislaid, but was published in Ferrajoli, *La congiura*, pp. 338–40. The second is in ASF, Manoscritti Torrigiani, pergamene, under date. See also Sanuto, *I diarii*, XXIV, 420.

[2] See ASF, Diplomatico, Riformagioni, Atti pubbl., under date. The document is published by Canestrini and Desjardins, *Négociations*, II, pp. 778–9.

[3] Copies of these agreements, which seemed to take place simultaneously in Rome and Fondi, and which were notarised by Pietro Ardinghelli and Enrico Umbstat respectively, exist in ASF, Manoscritti Torrigiani, *busta* III, fasc. 20, folders 3 and 4. See also Guasti, *I manoscritti*, pp. 418 and 465. In a separate *pergamena* of 28 July 1517 (in Manoscritti Torrigiani etc. folder 3), Soderini names as his special procurators Geremia Contugi and Alfonso Paragrano. On 25 July 1517 Leo had addressed a brief to Soderini imparting this information, which is published by Ferrajoli, *La congiura*, pp. 338–40, but the notarised documents had the full force of law.

to be included, but, rather inexplicably, they fell by the wayside, leaving those of the emperor, the king of Spain, the king of Portugal and the doge. It may be that Francis thought that his other manoeuvres to protect Soderini were more important.

The question can surely be posed: why did these orators agree to involve themselves and their rulers in the affairs of this stray cardinal? A partial explanation can be found by investigating Leo's international relations at this juncture. In August 1516 Francis I of France and king Charles I of Spain signed the treaty of Noyon and had not yet embarked upon the sustained competitive rivalry which was to take up much of their energy.[4] Leo was isolated, fighting for control of Siena and Urbino, and desirous of exhibiting his strength, at least *vis-à-vis* his own cardinals. Therefore, this unique agreement was to a certain extent a response, on the part of the rest of Europe, to Leo's plans to enhance and exalt the standing of the pope and the role of the papacy in Italian and international affairs. Whether the legal rights of the pope could be overridden in this fashion is unclear, but as an international display of solidarity for a particular individual this agreement is unparalleled in the renaissance, and Soderini was the catalyst for it.

In September 1518 the matter flared up again when Soderini sent one of his servants to the pope at Viterbo to ask permission to live anywhere in the kingdom of Naples and in Naples itself, 'without arousing suspicion or jealousy'.[5] This the pope granted on condition that the orators renewed their guarantee. Soderini had apparently asked to be allowed to stay in one of four places: the kingdom of Naples, France, Piedmont or Vicenza.[6] The kingdom of Naples, whilst more acceptable to Soderini than just Fondi and its immediate surroundings, must have been the least satisfactory outcome for him. France would presumably have been the best, and Vicenza and Piedmont at least had the merit of being further away from Rome and Florence and the nets of the Medici (although, as has been seen, the Medici had just married into the house of Savoy). Benedetto Buondelmonti,[7] who supplies this information, was extremely agitated by the mere suggestion that Soderini be allowed to wander through the kingdom of Naples and consult and hobnob with any powers that he wished, and at one point he described him as

---

[4] On this subject, see M. Mignet, *Rivalité de François I et de Charles-Quint* (Paris, 1875).

[5] See ASF, MAP, cxliii, 154 and Lowe, 'Francesco Soderini', appendix 2, p. 326.

[6] ASF, MAP, cxliii, 156, Buondelmonti to Gheri, Viterbo, 28 September 1518.

[7] For information on Buondelmonti, see R. Bizzocchi, 'Forme e techniche del potere nella città (secoli xiv–xvii)', *Annali della facoltà di scienze politiche, università di Perugia*, 16 (1979–80), especially pp. 89–97, and Bizzocchi, 'La dissoluzione di un clan familiare: Buondelmonti di Firenze nei secoli xv e xvi', *Archivio storico italiano*, 140 (1982), especially pp. 34–43.

having a 'restless mind' (*cervello inquieto*).[8] For confirmed Mediceans like Buondelmonti and Gheri, Soderini's political skill and experience combined with his standing as a cardinal and his international contacts made him one of their most dangerous enemies.[9] Even when his fortunes were at their lowest ebb, as they surely were during his period at Fondi, Soderini remained an object of concern and fear for the Medici.

Having acquired permission to move around within the kingdom of Naples, Soderini tried hard to receive permission to go to Vicenza for eighteen months, saying that he wanted to set the church there in order (he had obtained the bishopric of Vicenza in a threefold exchange in June 1514).[10] Buondelmonti saw this as a provocative move; Vicenza was a place where Soderini could say what he wanted and see who he wanted in such a way that

> we, the Mediceans, would not be able, or only with difficulty would we be able, to know a small part of the truth, and I think we would do well to consider that this man is trying to go to an area where he knows that we are without supporters, in a place where all those for two hundred miles around are very opposed to us ... he will be close to Mantua and Ferrara, and will be able to hold talks with them at will and similarly with the Venetians. In addition, he will be able to do the same in Germany, and using the searoute, the kingdom of Naples and anywhere else he goes, so that in that location with great ease and without a worry in the world, he will be able to carry on to his heart's content.[11]

He then accuses Soderini of going to live 'in the lap and breast of our chief enemies and of those who most desire our downfall' ('nel grembo et seno delli inimici nostri capitali et di quelli che più desideron la ruina nostra'). This letter displays all the Medici fears about Soderini and about enemies and contrary alliances.

Soderini did indeed have good friends in Mantua and Ferrara. He had been on good terms with marquis Gianfrancesco Gonzaga of Mantua even before his elevation to the cardinalate.[12] He developed a close

---

[8] See ASF, MAP, CXLIII, 154 and Lowe, 'Francesco Soderini', appendix 2, p. 328.

[9] Lowe, 'Francesco Soderini', appendix 2, p. 327.   [10] See below, p. 178.

[11] ASF, MAP, CXLIII, 155, Buondelmonti to Gheri, Viterbo, 27 September 1518: 'noi non potremo mai o con difficultà sapere una pichola parte del vero, et mi pare molto bene da considerare che questo homo cerca di potere stare dove lui sa che noi non habbiamo un amico, ma in un paese che tutti quelli che vi sono presso a 200 miglio ci sono inimicissimi ... lui sarà vicino ad Mantova, ad Ferrara et con lloro potrà tenere quelle pratiche vorrà et il simile con Venetiani. Ulterius in Alamagnia anchora ochorrendoli potrà fare il medesimo et per lla via di mare, nel reame et in ogni locho che più li verrà con modo in tal locho facilissimamente et sanza uno sospetto al mondo, lo potrà fare ad suo beneplacito.'

[12] ASMa, AG, b.2911, lib. 177, 73v–74r.

relationship, and entered into a lively correspondence, with the marquis's wife, Isabella d'Este, and introduced her to Sigismondo and Margherita Cantelmo.[13] He had known Mario Equicola, probably since the 1480s, and remained close to him throughout his life.[14] Through the Mantuan link, Soderini came to know Alessandro Gabbioneta[15] and Giovanni Giacomo Calandra.[16] Soderini later tried to cultivate the next marquis, Federico.[17] He also corresponded with other members of the Este house of Ferrara[18] and wrote copiously to Caterina Sforza of Imola (if a sample of his letters to her between 1505 and 1508, preserved in the Medici letter collection in Florence, are to be used as a guide).[19] Soderini had met Ercole d'Este and Caterina Sforza in the autumn of 1497 on his way home from an embassy to the king of France, and had been impressed with their protestations of affection for Florence.[20]

In 1473 Caterina Sforza had married Girolamo Riario of Forlì, a papal nephew, receiving Imola as her dowry, much to the annoyance of Lorenzo de' Medici, who had wanted to gain possession of Imola for himself. In 1488 Girolamo was murdered in a conspiracy, and with the help of Florence and Milan, Caterina was made regent for her son, Ottaviano Riario. In 1497 she married Giovanni di Pierfrancesco de' Medici, a member of an estranged, cadet branch of the family.[21] The Florentines took Ottaviano into their pay in 1498 as protection against the Venetians' expanding into the Romagna. Subsequently, pope Alexander VI, in an attempt to find a state for his son Cesare Borgia, declared that the Signore of Imola and Forlì had forfeited his state because of non-payment of dues. Cesare began his first campaign in November 1499 and had conquered the two towns by January; Caterina was taken to Rome. Upon Cesare Borgia's death in 1503, the towns reverted to the papal states. As will be understood, Caterina Sforza's relations with both the Medici and the Borgia were rather complex, and it is interesting that she maintained an independent relationship with Francesco Soderini during the first decade of the sixteenth century. During his exile, he kept up with his Mantuan

---

[13] ASMa, AG, b.858, 1 December 1509.
[14] See S. Kolsky, *Mario Equicola: the real courtier* (Geneva, 1991), pp. 38, 62, 134.
[15] See, for example, ASMa, AG, b.2921, lib. 231, 96r, 25 March 1514.
[16] ASMa, AG, b.862, 27 August 1514.   [17] ASMa, AG, b.809, 5 April 1519.
[18] See, for example, ASMo, Arch. Estense, Cancelleria ducale, Carteggio dei principi esteri (cardinali), b.1427/178, 12 January 1507, letter to cardinal Ippolito d'Este.
[19] See, for example, ASF, MAP, cxxv, 143.
[20] ASF, Lettere varie 14, 21v. He described Caterina Sforza as a 'donna di ingegno, di prudentia et di animo'.
[21] E. Breisach, *Caterina Sforza* (Chicago, 1967), pp. 174–5.

contacts in particular, and even wrote to Equicola from Fondi on 5 April 1519, reproving him for not coming to see him as he had promised, and for not writing.[22] These potential allies in Northern Italy would certainly have been one reason why Soderini tried so hard to go to Vicenza.

Soderini appears to have profited from the ambivalent attitude of the Gonzaga and Este towards the re-emergence of the Medici as rulers of Florence at the beginning of the sixteenth century. The Gonzaga had no great political interest in Florence at this time, and seemed unconcerned about who was in power. The Este, on the other hand, had traditionally been anti-Medicean and were associated with exile groups. In both cases, therefore, these families were not politically embarrassed by continuing contact with Soderini during the period 1517 to 1521. Unfortunately, very few letters have survived from Soderini's stay at Fondi – only a couple to the Gonzaga and their friends in Mantua and the Este in Ferrara – and there is hardly any indication of the volume of mail going to Soderini.[23]

Earlier, on 30 August 1518, Buondelmonti had written to Lorenzo, duke of Urbino, telling him that Soderini was at Fondi, that many of Soderini's servants had died, many others were ill, and that two of his nephews, Tommaso di Giovanvettorio Soderini, and Pierfrancesco di Lorenzo Lenzi, were both on the point of dying.[24] This provided Soderini with his excuse to move, and this is the reason given in the notarial document drawn up by Eliseo da Colle at Fondi on 6 February 1519,[25] and guaranteed by the orators of the same powers as previously. Fondi was notoriously unhealthy and infamous for its malaria so the reason was probably genuine enough. The Medici faction was worried in a general way by the number of disenchanted cardinals living away from the curia. At one point Buondelmonti lists them: Domenico Grimani, Ippolito d'Este, Sigismondo Gonzaga, Matthias Schinner, Matthias Lang, Adriano Castellesi.[26] It should be noted that Gonzaga and Este cardinals were on this list. The only comforting feature for the Medici was that this gang of malcontents was not united by any

---

[22] ASMa, AG, b.809.

[23] Very occasionally there are instances of surviving minutes of letters to Soderini which hint at a considerable correspondence. See, for example, one of 20 May 1520 from Ferrara, in which Soderini is thanked for his letter of 25 April, in ASMo, Arch. Estense, Cancelleria ducale, Carteggio dei principi esteri (cardinali), b.1427/178.

[24] ASF, MAP, cxliii, 141, Buondelmonti to the duke of Urbino, Rome, 30 August 1518.

[25] ASF, Manoscritti Torrigiani, pergamene, under date. On 9 April 1519 the doge Leonardo Loredan renewed his obligation and included the new concession, *ibid.*, under date. [26] ASF, MAP, cxliii, 155.

common feeling except dislike of the pope, but their presence in foreign lands, territories and courts must have accentuated the Medici unease because they were also acutely aware that many other *signori* and cities in Italy were their enemies.[27]

With Soderini's transformation from a neighbourly rival to a real enemy in exile, the Medici stepped up their terrorist methods. Soderini servants had always been at risk from the Medici – for example, Antonio Segni was killed acting as a go-between for Francesco and Piero in November 1512[28] – and many of Soderini's familiars, including two notaries, Enrico Umbstat and Eliseo da Colle, went with him into exile. It was his servants who enabled him to continue his links with other powers and thus kept him as a force to be reckoned with. In return, some of them were seized by the Medici and tortured. This befell one of Geremia Contugi's brothers, Piero, in January 1518 and by his confession he implicated another brother, Lodovico,[29] who was then placed on the hit list.[30] He in turn was intercepted and examined about a trip he had made earlier, on Soderini's behalf, to Francesco Maria della Rovere.[31] At the same time, the Medici also declared an interest in speaking to Giovanni Girolami, another of Soderini's agents, but as far as is known, he escaped apprehension. In December 1518 one of Soderini's secretaries, unfortunately unnamed, was intercepted by Medici supporters in Lucca and some writings were confiscated, because the Medici were worried by his frequent trips both to Lucca and to Mantua (possibly in connection with the Urbino question) on Soderini's behalf.[32]

Vague hints about other political ties sometimes come from later letters when Soderini wrote to thank those who had helped him during this time, for example Raimondo Cardona, the viceroy of Naples on the nomination of the emperor Charles V in his role as king of Naples. He would have been a very necessary ally. On 10 January 1522 Soderini wrote in recognition of his obligation to Cardona for all the favours shown to him in his house, and to signify that in Rome he was totally at the service of the emperor, willing even to shed his blood for him, and should be viewed by both Cardona and the emperor as the most faithful

---

[27] ASF, Il minutario di Goro Gheri, III, 368v, Gheri to Buondelmonti, 10 March 1518 (i.e. 1519).

[28] See *Carteggi di Francesco Guicciardini*, ed. R. Palmarocchi, I (Bologna, 1938), p. 122, Pandolfo de' Conti to Guicciardini, Florence, 13 November 1512.

[29] ASF, Il minutario di Goro Gheri, IV, 86r.

[30] ASF, MAP, CXLIV, 12, Turini to Gheri, 1 February 1517 (i.e. 1518) and ASF, Il minutario di Goro Gheri, IV, 91v, Gheri to Turini, 3 February 1517 (i.e. 1518).

[31] ASF, MAP, CXLIV, 25, Turini to Gheri, 12 February 1518.

[32] ASF, Il minutario di Goro Gheri, III, 281v and 282r.

of brothers.[33] This hyperbolic letter, whilst it may be just a form of politeness, could also be of some political consequence. Soderini must have negotiated with the emperor or his viceroy while at Fondi, and the Medici interceptions of Soderini servants should be seen in this light. Soderini's French connections did not preclude friendly ties with individual members of the Spanish or Hapsburg camp.

Throughout his period of exile, the Medici were anxious to monitor Soderini's political contacts. At one point Buondelmonti revealed considerable anxiety about the possibility that Soderini might come to an arrangement with Cardona behind the backs of the Medici.[34] It was for this sort of reason that Buondelmonti was so keen to prevent Soderini from leaving Fondi. Away from the centre of Rome, and contained at Fondi, the threat which Soderini posed to Medicean hegemony was controlled. At Fondi, too, Soderini was an easier target for would-be assassins. There is no direct evidence of an attempt on Soderini's life; however, Soderini considered assassination more than a possibility and kept himself constantly guarded,[35] a fact which Buondelmonti reported rather dolefully to Gheri in July 1518.[36] The Medici had not shrunk in the past from murdering a cardinal and Buondelmonti's interest in the security precautions taken by Soderini indicate his awareness that the problem of Soderini was susceptible to a violent solution. Indeed, in a letter to Gheri of September 1518, he may even have expressed a wish that Soderini could be dealt with in a summary fashion.[37] But maybe Soderini, with patrons such as the king of France, was regarded as too important a character to be assassinated in this manner.

Therefore, although Leo probably did not interfere directly with Soderini, he did attempt to isolate him as much as he could. This is illustrated by an incident in November 1520, when cardinal Riario, for fear of arousing the pope's suspicion against himself, journeyed to Naples partly by sea, to avoid passing through Fondi.[38]

[33] BNF, Magl. VIII, 1392, letter no. 94.
[34] ASF, MAP, CXLIII, 154 and Lowe, 'Francesco Soderini', appendix 2, pp. 327–8.
[35] In January 1518 Soderini was reputed to have twenty-five guards, ASF, Il minutario di Goro Gheri, IV, 72v.   [36] ASF, MAP, CXLIII, 92.
[37] ASF, MAP, CXLIII, 154 and Lowe, 'Francesco Soderini', appendix 2, p. 328.
[38] Sanuto, I diarii, XXIX, 405 and 406.

CHAPTER II

SODERINI OPPOSITION TO THE MEDICI IN FLORENCE AND ROME, 1521–3

In December 1521 conditions changed yet again when Leo died and Francesco Soderini hurried to Rome for the conclave, arriving on the night of the 5th.[1] At congregation on the 6th he delivered a most elegant speech in which he thanked God for the death of the Medici pope Leo, yet grossly attacked both the dead pope and the whole house of Medici, exhorting the cardinals to elect a good pope and not one who kept the world at war. He then announced, rather dramatically, that he would not be able to attend congregation in future as he was not safe.[2] According to Francesco Tornabuoni in Florence, who admitted that his news was not particularly accurate, and who assessed which cardinals were likely to be made pope (*papabile*) and to what degree, Soderini had arrived in Rome with reasonable favour but had alienated the whole college (but especially the Medicean cardinals such as Cesarini) by speaking so disparagingly and without any cause (*senza alcuna ragione*) of Leo. After this, he lost his reputation for caution and with it his supporters.[3]

It was probably this congregation that is described in a letter of 21 December sent by messer Zorzi, conte del Zaffo, to a friend, but as the theme of all Soderini's speeches at this time was the same – the undesirability of the Medici – it is hard to tell them apart. According to Zorzi, Soderini condemned the tyranny of the Medici. Cesarini replied that he knew of no tyranny connected with Leo, and that although the late pope had created many cardinals for money it was still a good thing because they were all better than Soderini, and that Soderini might live to repent of his words: 'Soderini did not reply to this, but he visibly hardened in his attitude towards the Medici so that he said he would like

---

[1] ASF, Otto di prat., Resp. 19, 135v.
[2] Sanuto, *I diarii*, XXXII, 230 and XXXII, 252 from Gradenigo.
[3] ASF, Sig., Otto, Dieci, Miss. 10, 211v, Tornabuoni to Luigi Guicciardini, 17 December 1521.

any cardinal other than Medici as pope. It was thought that this very public arrogance of cardinal Volterra aided rather than harmed cardinal de' Medici.'[4]

On the 15th the Venetian orator reported that Soderini had again spoken out loudly against the Medici in congregation (there was one every day during a *sede vacante* and Soderini was obviously still attending them) and had urged the cardinals to observe Julius's bull and not to elect a pope for reasons of simony.[5] But the assessments of candidates' chances depended so much upon the point of view of the assessor. Francesco Tornabuoni had written from Florence at the beginning of the month that both the Orsini and Colonna were united in favouring cardinal de' Medici and that the majority of the college was also 'more or less inclined to do this'.[6] This shows that when the need arose, even families and factions as opposed as the Colonna and the Orsini could unite in a common cause. In his letter of the 17th, Tornabuoni wrote that cardinal de' Medici had seventeen certain votes in the college, and that cardinal Colonna supported him with all the Ghibelline faction and the backing of the imperial orator.

Divisions along long-standing Guelph-Ghibelline lines undoubtedly took place, due to the persistence of already established groupings of friends and foe, although the labels had become detached from their original meanings. Guelph families, and individual members within them, no longer necessarily supported the pope; in any case, antagonisms between popes and emperors took different forms in the early sixteenth century from those of the twelfth and thirteenth. Nor were Ghibellines necessarily imperial partisans. Already by the fourteenth century the names had lost their former significance, and in Florence, for example, which was traditionally a Guelph city, the designation of Ghibelline was attached to political opponents who were considered to deviate from the views of the ruling party. Thus in 1364 the absurd pronouncement was made by the government in Florence that 'anyone who appeals to the pope or his legate or the cardinals shall be declared a Ghibelline'.[7] A hundred years later, in 1461, Luigi Guicciardini declared that Guelph and Ghibelline factions were absent from the city because everyone was now a Guelph.[8]

Nevertheless, Soderini, as a political deviant, was pronounced a

[4] Sanuto, *I diarii*, XXXII, 288.

[5] *Ibid.*, XXXII, 260. A speech of this kind was also recorded by Bernardo Rutha, an apostolic protonotary, in a letter of 19 December 1521 to Isabella d'Este, ASMa, AG, b.865, 463r. [6] ASF, Sig., Otto, Dieci, Miss. 10, 194r.

[7] *The catholic encyclopedia* (New York, 1913), VII, p. 58.

[8] This is quoted in A. Brown, 'The Guelph party in fifteenth-century Florence: the transition from communal to Medicean state', *Rinascimento*, 20 (1980), p. 41.

Ghibelline, and the label stuck to him outside Florence. He was also forced to be a Ghibelline on another count, because the Medici, being Guelphs, naturally formed connections with other Guelphs, leaving the Soderini to ally with Ghibellines. This can be seen most easily in the alliances forged by the two Florentine families with the Guelph Orsini and the Ghibelline Colonna. Under normal circumstances, therefore, the Colonna would not join forces with the Medici, but in the extraordinary surroundings of a conclave, strange partnerships coalesced. The Guelph/Ghibelline factor, even if operating with changed criteria, was a critical but sometimes opaque element in the divisions between dynasties, families and factions.

Other, less likely, candidates in the 1521 conclave were the Venetian Domenico Grimani and the adopted Roman Alessandro Farnese[9] on account of their politics, and Niccolò Flisco and Giovanni Piccolomini because of their blameless lives.[10] One of the pasquinades written during the conclave and addressed to Soderini referred to cardinal de' Medici's popularity and advised Soderini to ally his fortunes with those of the emperor and not those of the French, in case Medici won the papal tiara.[11] Soderini's preferences were so well known at court that this suggestion amounted to little more than a joke. Nardi, writing after the dust of combat had long settled, recorded a contrary view about cardinal Colonna, that he had continually spoken out during the conclave to the effect that there was no one in the college worthier of being pope than Soderini.[12] Filippo Strozzi wrote, on 21 December,

---

[9] Sanuto, *I diarii*, XXXII, 282 and 284.

[10] ASF, Sig., Otto, Dieci, Miss., 10, 211r.

[11]
        BV, Ottob. lat. 2817, 27r: Ad Cardinalem Soderinum
        E' ti bisogna Soderin star forte,
        Poi che tu hai fatto così bel sermone
        In el collegio contra di Leone
        Ch'à posto sottosopra questa corte;
        Che se per caso o per tua mala sorte
        Medici havessi questa electione,
        Salvar non ti potria falce o falcione
        Perché sol Dio te camparia da morte.
        Donque non ti ritrar dal ghibellino,
        L'aquila sequi e non guardar al giglio
        Se voi dar scaccomatto al medicino
        Perché mutar al tempo el suo consiglio
        Vien da prudente. Onde el mio Soderino
        Opra il tuo ingegno con ogni tuo artiglio
        Che mai cade im periglio
        Il bon nocchiero con li suoi sergenti
        Che navigare sa secondo i venti.

See also V. Marucci, A. Marzo and A. Romano (eds.), *Pasquinate romane del cinquecento* (Rome, 1983), I, p. 233.   [12] Nardi, *Istorie*, II, pp. 70 and 371.

that Soderini had been heard to say that he did not want the papal crown at any price, because he wanted to live safely in Rome for the few years that were left to him.[13]

All the venom and name-calling between cardinal de' Medici and Soderini came to nothing when a compromise candidate, the Netherlandish bishop of Tortosa, was unexpectedly elected pope in his absence. His loyalties lay firmly in the imperial Hapsburg camp as he had been the tutor of the young Charles V and a counsellor of Margaret of Austria in the Netherlands. The pasquinades composed for the conclave leading to the election of Adrian reflect Soderini's reputation at the time. In only one of them is there an open reference to the conspiracy: 'Per scisma tocca il papa' a Bernardino / per eresia se nel porta Grimano / per casa illustre dassi al Mantovano / per coniurazioni al Soderino' ('In terms of schism, it is Bernardino's turn, if it is heresy that counts, Grimani will be chosen as pope, if an illustrious family is a prerequisite, it will be given to Gonzaga, if conspiracies are the criteria for office, Soderini will claim it').[14] But in the others his characterisation was, if anything, slightly worse: only scoundrels would want his election as pope, there was no one 'more murderous, evil and treacherous' than Soderini; he was compared to Judas Iscariot, and allotted the tarot card of the devil.[15] His struggle with the Medici was also recorded, for example, in a dialogue between Pasquino and Rome. Rome asks whether, if the papal crown falls to Soderini, she will have peace. Pasquino says that he does not know, but that he hopes that at least the Medici will be crushed.[16] In another dialogue two Florentines argue over the misfortunes that will befall Florence if Medici or Soderini is elected pope. They end by deciding that it is a waste of breath to talk about it as both alternatives are unattractive.[17] The medals made after Leo's death also chart the same course; one had Medici and Soderini with the papal kingdom between them and these words around them 'nec mihi nec tibi' ('neither for me nor for you');[18] another has Medici

---

[13] ASF, C. Strozz., III, 108, 51v, Filippo Strozzi to his brother Lorenzo.

[14] V. Rossi, *Pasquinate di Pietro Aretino ed anonime per il conclave e l'elezione di Adriano VI* (Palermo/Turin, 1891), p. 27 and Marucci et al, *Pasquinate*, I, p. 163. But G. Cesareo, *Pasquino e pasquinate nella Roma di Leone X* (Rome, 1938), p. 1 cites one that picks out Soderini's 'tradimenti'.

[15] Rossi, *Pasquinate*, pp. 4, 18, 19, 23, 46 and Marucci et al, *Pasquinate*, I, pp. 141, 152, 153 and 178.

[16] Rossi, *Pasquinate*, p. 9 and Marucci et al, *Pasquinate*, I, p. 145.

ROMA: Se toccassi a Volterra, arò mai pace?
PASQUINO: Non so, ma spera di veder almeno
Medici spenti, onde Fiorenza iace.

[17] Rossi, *Pasquinate*, pp. 24–5 and Marucci et al, *Pasquinate*, I, p. 159.

[18] BV, Ottob. lat. 2817, 87v.

being crowned pope and Soderini putting on spurs, with the legend 'I'll wait for you at Fondi'.[19]

Soderini's priorities, as revealed by his actions on his return to Rome in 1521, were precisely those of 1513 – Florence and the Medici – but this time there was no new Medici pope. Indeed, for seven months there was no pope at all. As has been seen, Soderini immediately launched a propaganda campaign against the Medici and especially against the memory of Leo X. Even if the frequency and intensity of his anti-Medicean out-bursts had alienated moderate opinion, at the beginning of February he succeeded in persuading the college of cardinals to imprison the governor of Rome's notary who had been in charge of the trial in the 'conspiracy' of 1517.[20] Soderini argued that Leo had persecuted him for no reason at all and that he wanted to clear his name. Three cardinals – Flisco, Jacobazzi and Cesi – were assigned to the case.[21] Soderini showed his power in other ways too. In April 1522 he held up, and could have blocked, the signing of a licence by the whole college of cardinals, giving the duke of Urbino charge of the Florentine forces.[22] This appointment later created a small social embarrassment for della Porta, the duke of Urbino's ambassador in Rome. On 20 September he wrote that he had visited all the cardinals except Cibo and Soderini: the former because he was a public enemy and the latter because the duke was captain of the Florentine forces in charge of the preservation of the present regime in Florence, and della Porta had not known how to carry out this public office, 'because Soderini was so opposed to the present government of Florence'.[23] Yet again Soderini was being defined in relation to his opposition to the Medici.

Soderini had returned to the struggle with renewed passion. The situation of the Medici, on the other hand, was not without its difficulties. As ever, the political situation in Italy was dependent on the alignments of the great powers with native factions and interests, and the election of a new pope could cause fundamental shifts in these patterns of alliance. In an interesting postscript to a letter to Robertet, the chancellor of France, de Abbatis wrote from Cambrai on 7 February 1522 that at present cardinal de' Medici found himself in the most desperate straits of his life because the imperial ambassador had written

---

[19] *Ibid.*, 91v.   [20] Sanuto, *I diarii*, XXXII, 442, 2 February 1522, from Gradenigo.

[21] ASMo, Arch. Estense, Cancelleria estero, ambasciatori (Roma), b.27 (fasc. 182-II), P. Antonio Taurello to duke Alfonso, 1 February 1522.

[22] ASF, Urbino I, G, CXXXIV, 60r, Girolamo Staccoli to duke of Urbino, Rome, 21 April 1522.

[23] ASF, Urbino I, G, CCLXV, 9r and v, della Porta to duke of Urbino, Rome, 20 September 1522.

to the emperor that Adrian had been elected pope through the efforts of cardinal Colonna. Cardinal de' Medici was worried that, because of cardinal Colonna and Prospero Colonna, he would not have much favour with the pope. Finally, cardinal de' Medici was in an unfortunate position, according to de Abbatis, as cardinal Soderini was allied with the Colonna, and Prospero Colonna was in charge of an army that might help the Soderini return to power in Florence, as the Soderini belonged to the Ghibelline faction.[24] (As has been explained, the designation Ghibelline in this context only implied opposition to the Medici.) In fact, of course, the split at this point was not between so-called Guelphs and so-called Ghibellines but between supporters of France and supporters of the emperor, and although Soderini was putting on a good show of being a friend of the emperor, his loyalties lay with the king of France.

A comparison between de Abbatis' views and those of Juan Manuel, who, although he was Spanish, represented Charles V as the imperial ambassador, shows the variety of opinion. Here we have an eyewitness in Rome, in the service of the emperor, writing to the emperor himself. In a letter of 4 February he considers the emperor's enemies, writes that they would be most formidable but for their lack of money, and states that Soderini is one of the principal leaders of this hostile party.[25] The emperor was equally hostile to Soderini. On 21 March 1523, as a rather delayed response to the 1522 conspiracy against cardinal de' Medici, he placed the Soderini and all their clients under the ban of the empire and declared them rebels.[26] The personal relationship formed with Cardona, ostensibly an imperial servant, did not guarantee any degree of closeness to the emperor, and although Soderini's friends and patrons, the Colonna, were pro-imperial, most of his other friends and acquaintances were not.

Thus, although contemporary perceptions varied, it was clear to all that the Italian political scene was in a state of flux, and it was likely that the change would favour the Soderini, not the Medici. Such expectations were consistent with tendencies to see Soderini and Medici on opposite ends of a seesaw of political fortune; all events contributed to the rise of one and consequent fall of the other. If such widespread speculation can be seen as giving Soderini a psychological advantage, it

---

[24] Paris, Bibliothèque Nationale, Fonds français 2962, 157v and G. Molini, *Documenti di storia italiana copiati su gli originali autentici e per lo più autografi esistenti in Parigi* (Florence, 1836), pp. 156–7.

[25] *Calendar of letters, despatches, and state papers relating to the negotiations between England and Spain*, ed. G. Bergenroth, II (London, 1866), p. 401.

[26] ASF, Diplomatico, Riformagioni, Atti pubbl., 21 March 1523.

would appear that he attempted to use this to the full, even before the arrival of the new pope.

Firstly, Soderini's hand can be detected in the attempt by Renzo da Ceri to expel the Medici from Florence and depose the Petrucci in Siena. According to Guicciardini, the expedition had been initially proposed by Soderini with the intention of installing his family back in power in Florence.[27] Soderini was assuredly involved and the affair provides yet another illustration of the importance of his links with France. According to Galeotto de' Medici, a cousin of the main branch of the Medici family,[28] who at this point was the Florentine orator in Rome, on 23 February 1522 Renzo arrived in Rome to find his men-at-arms. Rumour had it that he was promised 6,000 *scudi* for himself and 6,000 for his brother in benefices in France for the enterprise.[29] Bernardo da Verrazzano, a Florentine banker who worked in Canale di Ponte and who had links with Soderini, was to arrange the financial transactions.[30] By 11 March there had been little progress and no sign of the money, although the stated intention was still the same; the group was to march on Siena and then to Florence where they wanted to 'change the regime'.[31]

Eventually a force set off but it failed completely because troops were sent from Florence to guard Siena. Baldassare Castiglione wrote that Renzo had gone with 8,000 or 10,000 men-at-arms and a good number of light horse and had approached Siena, but had been able to do nothing.[32] After ten days without bread and precious little other food, most of the troops deserted and returned to Rome. Many died from hunger, and those who survived would not move an inch away from the bakeries, so that as many were in danger of death from over-eating as before had been threatened by starvation.[33] On 16 June, Renzo was back in Rome, in discussion with Soderini, the French ambassador, Nicholas Raince, and a special messenger from the king of France, who told the others that the king wanted to come to Italy and that the king's mother, Louise of Savoy, would provide the money. The king made the duke of Ferrara his captain and wanted to hire Renzo again, but he refused. Soderini said that he could give no more money until he was reimbursed for the sums he had already spent.[34]

This attempt was foiled, but Soderini may have been involved in the

[27] Guicciardini, *Storia d'Italia*, III, p. 1482.

[28] Litta, 'Medici di Firenze', in *Famiglie celebri italiane*, table XVIII. Galeotto's and Lorenzo il Magnifico's respective great-great-grandfathers were brothers.

[29] ASF, Otto di prat., Resp. 22, 46v.   [30] See Bullard, *Filippo Strozzi*, p. 99.

[31] ASF, Otto di prat., Resp. 22, 77r.

[32] *Lettere di Baldassare Castiglione*, ed. P. Serassi (Padua, 1769), I, p. 24.

[33] *Ibid.*, p. 24.   [34] ASF, Otto di prat., Resp. 25, 261r.

almost simultaneous conspiracy of May, this time inside Florence and against cardinal Giulio de' Medici. Events followed a familiar pattern; a French courier was captured by the Medici, he was tortured and a confession was extracted.[35] Two young men, Jacopo da Diaccetto and Luigi Alamanni, were executed. Many others were named but managed to escape, including the Soderini nephews Tommaso, Giovanbattista and Piero di Paolantonio and Tommaso di Giovanvettorio Soderini.[36] Francesco Soderini's part in this is hard to ascertain. After the 1523 conspiracy, he was blamed for playing an active role in the earlier attempt of 1522. But, at the time, public opinion appears to have recognised that Medici rivalry was the main motive for the decision to outlaw the Soderini.[37] Also named were Zanobi Buondelmonti and another Luigi Alamanni, Antonio Brucioli, Battista della Palla and Niccolò di Lorenzo Martelli. According to the last named, who was however writing especially for the Medici, Soderini's role in this conspiracy was of great importance. Martelli stated that the conspirators' political aim was to get rid of the Medici and to reinstate Piero Soderini to his office as *gonfaloniere a vita*, to have eight *Signori*, who were to change every two months, and an office of eight, without whom the *gonfaloniere* and the *Signori* could not act. The eight would be in office for three years: 'and thus bit by bit they wanted to convert the Florentine government into that of the Venetians'.[38]

The protagonists of this conspiracy were members of the circle of the Orti Orucellari, young men from influential families who wanted an aristocratic regime and a glorious enterprise. While the extent of Soderini's involvement is not clear, obviously the Medici would have used the allegation to justify further moves against him, and once again it was the intervention of the French king, Francis I, that protected him. In July 1522 Francis gave a safe conduct and personal guarantee to the goods and persons of the Soderini family, Zanobi Buondelmonti, Luigi Alamanni, Bernardo da Verrazzano and Battista della Palla.[39] The letters patent for the safe conduct state, in the preamble, that the Soderini family had also served Charles VIII and Louis XII, thus

---

[35] Guasti, 'Documenti', p. 122.   [36] *Ibid.*, p. 124.

[37] See *Calendar of letters ... between England and Spain*, II, p. 425 and Cambi, 'Istorie', III, p. 211. The latter wrote that the Soderini had been declared rebels and their goods confiscated as they did not obey the command of the *Signoria* to appear before them, 'che fu tenuta chosa inumana, per non avere loro machinato niente contro allo stato, ma solo perché il cardinale de' Soderini, che era in Roma, non era amicho del nostro arcivescovo cardinale de' Medici'.

[38] Guasti, 'Documenti' p. 245. For the background to this idea, see F. Gilbert, 'The Venetian constitution in Florentine political thought', in *Florentine studies*, ed. N. Rubinstein (London, 1968), pp. 463–500.   [39] ASF, Sig., Resp. 37, 251r.

stressing the continuous relationship between this Florentine house and the French monarchy.[40] On 15 August, Galeotto de' Medici reported from Rome that the Soderini had caused this letter of protection to be printed and pinned up in all the churches and on all the corners of Rome 'which was held to be an ineffectual and frivolous act'.[41] In the immediate aftermath of the conspiracy, most of the remaining non-clerical members of the Soderini family were declared rebels in Florence on 3 and 14 June.[42] Coincidentally Piero Soderini (who had been listed as a conspirator) died in Rome on 14 June,[43] and Soderini lost the support of his closest brother.

These two attempts to undermine the Medici hold on Florence having failed, Soderini continued the struggle in Rome. Here he had two main aims: the first to clear his name (and embarrass his opponents) over the alleged conspiracy of 1517; the second to protect his family's property in Florence from the depredations of the Medici. In July there was a congregation on what should happen to the governor of Rome's notary, but Soderini persuaded the cardinals to postpone taking a decision until the new pope reached Rome.[44]

After Adrian's arrival, Soderini began to weary him with complaints, so that initially he asked cardinal Cesi to produce the transcripts of the trials in order to look at them,[45] and then almost immediately took the affair out of the hands of Cesi, whom Soderini thought impartial, and promised to give it to two others.[46] Unfortunately for Soderini, two weeks later the notary was freed, to the great delight of cardinal de' Medici (whose relative was thereby temporarily cleared of scandal) and to the chagrin of Soderini, Sauli and the rest.[47] This case had precipitated a fresh onslaught of slander between the two cardinals, as a major revision of the trial would have meant acknowledging the possibility of Leo's guilt. Adrian tried, on several occasions, to defuse the enmity but was not successful. On 29 September he told them that they could elect lawyers to fight on their behalf, as cardinal de' Medici wanted to stop

[40] ASF, Capitani di Parte Guelfa, Numeri rossi 75, 75v.

[41] ASF, Otto di prat., Resp. 25, 478v.

[42] ASF, Otto di guardia (epoca repubblicana) 182, 59r, 67v and 68r.

[43] See, for example, *Lettere di Baldassare Castiglione*, I, p. 45, Castiglione to marquis Federico Gonzaga.

[44] It is possible that Soderini, in his capacity as cardinal governor of Rome, had been able to suggest the notary be imprisoned, rather than its being the result of agitation as a mere cardinal. See Sanuto, *I diarii*, XXXIII, 367, 13 July 1522.

[45] ASF, Urbino I, G, CCLXV, 147r, Giovanni Tommaso Manfredi to duke of Urbino, Rome, 10 September 1522.

[46] ASF, Urbino I, G, CXXXII, 302v, della Porta, Rome, 13 September 1522.

[47] ASF, Urbino I, G, CCLXV, 151v, Giovanni Tommaso Manfredi, Rome, 29 September 1522.

Soderini's slandering of Leo's name; Soderini chose Marchione Bardassino and cardinal de' Medici, Agnolo da Cesi.[48]

Also in July 1522 another prolonged dispute had started, this time connected with Soderini's fight to maintain possessions that the Office of Rebels in Florence had confiscated and were treating in the same way as the possessions of other members of the Soderini family who had been declared rebels.[49] Soderini's clerical status meant that he could not be classified as a rebel, nor could his possessions be confiscated. He made a spirited defence through his procurator, ser Gaspare da Gambassi, listing his properties and their state of repair, but the appeal was not allowed and Soderini must have known that it would not be. Soderini then handed in a supplication to cardinal Campeggio who was in charge of the *Signatura* of justice, claiming that the Florentines were behaving illegally, which was a first step towards having the case heard in Rome in front of the *Rota*.[50] On 21 July Galeotto de' Medici posted a copy of Soderini's supplication to Florence.[51] On 23 July he tried to persuade Campeggio not to sign the supplication but Campeggio replied that he had to. The foundation of the Soderini defence was that the Soderini were Roman citizens, courtiers and members of the household of cardinals, and that on these grounds, therefore, they wanted to prohibit Florentine proceedings against them.[52] However, on the following day, the 24th, cardinals Aragon and della Valle had queried the supplication and withheld their signatures, and cardinal del Monte had not made up his mind but was not keen to sign (were these the three cardinal governors of Rome[53] for this period?). So a decision was postponed until the congregation on the following Saturday, when a further decision would be taken whether to concede the appellation or to wait for Adrian's arrival which was imminent.[54]

By December there was a Soderini lawsuit in front of the auditor of the *camera*. The summons for the case was directed to the government of Florence (or was it to the Medici?) – certainly to Galeotto de' Medici's master or masters, or so he wrote in a letter of 22 December: 'You are cited to appear in front of the auditor within ten days to reply to a case brought by cardinal Soderini'.[55] Hope must have risen again for Soderini. The commune of Florence had behaved ruthlessly. They

[48] ASF, Otto di prat., Resp. 27, 75r, Galeotto de' Medici, Rome, 29 September 1522.
[49] See Stephens, *The fall*, p. 121.
[50] ASF, Otto di prat., Resp. 25, 323r, Galeotto de' Medici, Rome, 14 July 1522.
[51] *Ibid.*, 364r. The copy of the supplication is in the same volume, 371r–372r.
[52] *Ibid.*, 369v, Galeotto de' Medici, Rome, 23 July 1522.
[53] See below, pp. 160–1.
[54] ASF, Otto di prat., Resp. 25, 347r, Galeotto de' Medici, Rome, 24 July 1522.
[55] ASF, Otto di prat., Resp. 27, 305r and v.

had confiscated the possessions in execution of the sentences and had then proceeded further. Unable to find the account books which the Soderini had deposited with certain friends, they had unjustly invoked the power of ecclesiastical censure through the medium of the archbishop of Florence (cardinal Giulio de' Medici), and had excommunicated Soderini's friends, telling them to hand over the books immediately. It appears that the friends did not comply and that new forms of Medici intimidation were employed: the sacking and laying waste of fruit trees, farms, meadows and other possessions of the Soderini.[56] These malpractices resulted in the Soderini turning to Adrian and the *Rota* for help. However, the Medici also had influence at the papal court and won over Adrian. He promised to suspend the suit and to try again to effect peace between Soderini and cardinal de' Medici out of the courts, although Galeotto de' Medici wrote that as all the malignity stemmed from Soderini, he thought that it was 'a cure for the incurable'.[57]

There is no record that further action was taken by the pope. It is very unlikely that Adrian would have countenanced a suspension of all special papal privileges to the city or commune of Florence which is what the Soderini were requesting,[58] much as he would have disapproved of cardinal de' Medici's abuse of ecclesiastical power, and his use of it for his own political ends. This example perfectly illustrates the extent to which the Soderini had shifted their activities to Rome, and how they fought out what were essentially Florentine battles on Roman soil. As they had failed to achieve satisfaction using Florentine channels, they transferred the dispute to Rome, claiming that they were Romans and not subject to Florentine jurisdiction. The old cry that they were Roman citizens adds an antique touch. Piero Soderini, had he still been alive, would have had the strongest claim to this title. The four of Francesco Soderini's nephews who were named could have claimed that they were part of Soderini's household which may have given them special exemption from Florentine secular courts, but not all of them were living with him, and it would have been difficult for those who were not to present a coherent case. But the minutiae of the claim are not important. The fact that Soderini thought that he could control or fight Florentine issues using Roman courts is.

[56] There are two drafts of what appears initially to have been a letter to the pope from the Soderini setting out this tale of woe, in ASF, Otto di prat., Resp. 27, 276r–278r (Italian) and 272r–274r (Latin).

[57] ASF, Otto di prat., Resp. 27, 352r, 31 December 1522.   [58] *Ibid.*, 278r.

CHAPTER 12

THE 'CONSPIRACY' OF 1523 AND ITS AFTERMATH

The roots of the so-called conspiracy of 1523 went back several years. The Imperatore brothers in Sicily had been contemplating an uprising since 1517[1] in conjunction with the treasurer, Niccolò Leofante, the count of Cammarata,[2] the marquis of Cefalù and others. They wanted to make Marcantonio Colonna king of Sicily under a French protectorate. When Colonna died in March 1522,[3] they decided to deal directly with Francis I.[4] In April 1523 Francesco Imperatore left a second time for France and passed through Rome to see his brother Cesare, who was then in the service of cardinal Pompeo Colonna. Different members of the Colonna family had links to both the kings of France and the Hapsburgs. In Rome, Imperatore met Francesco Soderini, a protégé of the king of France, with whom Soderini kept in frequent contact. Earlier in 1522, a French courier had been stopped and among the papers found on him were letters from Soderini and other cardinals to the king of France. The letters were not written in cipher but such expressions were used in them that it was difficult to understand them.[5] Soderini now wrote on behalf of the Imperatore brothers to his nephew, Giuliano, in France and possibly also to his nephew, Tommaso, in Venice[6] (the Tommaso mentioned could be either Tommaso di

[1] Francesco Imperatore had been in trouble before this. See an edict of 30 May 1516 warning him to behave on pain of fines etc. in Palermo, Arch. comunale, Sala diplomatica, Atti, bandi e provviste (1516–17), Ind. v (no. 39), 15v.
[2] He was later killed and all his possessions seized for his part in the conspiracy. See letters of 10 July, 12 September and 16 October 1523 in ASPal, Tribunale del real patrimonio, Lettere viceregie e dispacci patrimoniali 256, 85r and v, and 261, 8r and 57r and v, which discuss his financial affairs and the sale of his goods.
[3] See the *Dizionario biografico degli italiani*, XXVII, pp. 365–8.
[4] V. Epifanio, 'Il cardinale Soderini e la congiura dei fratelli Imperatore', in *Atti del congresso internazionale di scienze storiche 1903*, 3 (Rome, 1906), p. 386.
[5] *Calendar of letters ... between England and Spain*, II, p. 415, 21 April 1522, Juan Manuel to the emperor.
[6] The imperial ambassador recorded that he wrote to Piero Soderini in France but it is much more likely that the letter was to Giuliano not Piero. See *Calendar of*

Paolantonio or Tommaso di Giovanvettorio). On 26 April 1523 Francesco Soderini was summoned to the Vatican by the pope, and confronted by the letters. He could not deny that he had written them and was consigned to Castel Sant'Angelo.[7] Francesco Imperatore had been intercepted by Medici agents on 6 April, at the earliest, and had been tortured by the 13th. Cardinal de' Medici had come rejoicing to Rome.

Extracts from the letters are recorded in Bergenroth's *Calendar of letters ... between England and Spain* and more fully in the Urbino Fondo in the State Archives in Florence and in the Gonzaga Archives in the State Archives in Mantua.[8] In none of these sources is the invasion of Sicily specifically mentioned; Bergenroth writes that, in the extracts, the cardinal exhorted the French to invade Italy very soon and recommended to them Francesco Imperatore, a Sicilian nobleman from Palermo.[9] The Urbino and Gonzaga extracts contain transcriptions, but the sections transcribed contain only possible arguments that Giuliano Soderini could use to persuade the French king to invade. There is mention of Milan but none of Sicily. Soderini prophetically tells Giuliano that if the king has something he wishes to communicate, it would be better to commit it to someone's mouth than to a letter. He is hopeful about the French king's prospects.[10] It is just possible that these extracts constitute the whole letter. They are written in rather unnatural language which presumably accounts for some other ambassadors' recording that they were written in code. Brewer records information obtained from the imperial ambassador that the Sicilian nobleman was carrying letters from Francesco Soderini showing that he had organised a rebellion in Sicily and that Francis had sent a fleet there. This move was designed to force the withdrawal of the imperial army from Lombardy, thus leaving Milan at the mercy of the French king, to the ruin of Italy, so it was claimed, particularly after the recent victory of the Turk.[11] The consistorial records of 27 April 1523 note that Soderini was detained in Castel Sant'Angelo because of the coded letters

---

letters...between England and Spain, II, p. 537, 6 April 1523. The report of Galeotto de' Medici in ASF, Otto di prat., Resp. 24, 203r, 10 April, states that Francesco Imperatore was going to France via Venice and that he was carrying, amongst other letters, one from Soderini to his nephew the bishop (i.e. Giuliano). Angelo Germanello wrote to the marquis on 11 April that Imperatore was carrying letters from Soderini to a nephew in France and from Soderini to the king of France, ASMa, AG, b.867, 316r.

[7] The route he took is described in another letter by Germanello of 27 April, ASMa, AG, b.867, 322r.

[8] See ASF, Urbino I, G, CXXXII, 347r and v and ASMa, AG, b.867, 347r and v.

[9] *Calendar of letters ... between England and Spain*, II, p. 537.

[10] ASF, Urbino I, G, CXXXII, 347r and v.

[11] *Letters and papers, foreign and domestic, of the reign of Henry VIII*, ed. J. Brewer, III, II (London, 1867), p. 1267, 1 May 1523.

which had been intercepted calling the king of France to Italy so that the whole of Italy would be vexed by war.[12]

This conspiracy is difficult to categorise. On one hand, it can be seen as a continuation of the efforts of 1522, as it had, as its starting point, French help. After all, Soderini at this point was declaring his French partiality rather than appearing to maintain a neutral position, but this declaration should have been far less newsworthy or controversial than the 1522 Renzo da Ceri episode. Sicily was further away from Rome, out of the limelight of Tuscany. On the other hand, Adrian clearly saw this affair in a different light, as it was always called a conspiracy whereas Renzo da Ceri's venture was labelled an enterprise or undertaking (*impresa*). In essence, the charge against Soderini, everywhere described as conspiracy, was that of external treason (*proditio*) of Roman law: Soderini stood accused of contact and collusion with a foreign enemy, in this case, France.

As usual it had been a Medici initiative that had led to Soderini's downfall. Cardinal de' Medici and Luis de Cordoba, count of Cabra, known as the duke of Sessa, who was Charles V's Spanish ambassador,[13] had plotted against him and for the time being they had the ear of the pope.[14] On 25 and 26 April there had been discussions in consistory about the possibility of a league in Italy and elsewhere to lead a crusade against the Turk. Soderini, representing French interests, had said that the French king would not join such a venture unless Milan were returned to him.[15] Initially, it was thought by many that Soderini had been imprisoned because of these views. For example, the Venetian ambassador, Foscari, wrote home on 29 April that this was the reason Soderini had been taken to Castel Sant'Angelo, but he later said that this was not the cause and that it was at the request of cardinal de' Medici, because Soderini had asked the king of France to come to Italy.[16] The Bolognese orator Albergati managed to combine the two explanations; according to his account, Soderini had been imprisoned for many reasons, but the main one was because he had been delegated by the pope to secure peace between christian princes but instead of sowing harmony and peace, he had sown discord and war, advising the king of France of all the secrets of Rome.[17] The Mantuan L'Abbadino wrote almost identical words to marquis Francesco Gonzaga; Soderini is described as acting against the christian religion, in which case, it was

[12] AV, Fondo concist., Acta miscell. 70, 69r.
[13] E. Rodocanachi, *Les pontificats d'Adrien VI et Clément VII* (Paris, 1933), p. 288.
[14] See, for example, Cambi, 'Istorie', III, p. 244.
[15] Sanuto, *I diarii*, XXXIV, 122.   [16] *Ibid.*
[17] ASBo, Lettere dell'ambasciatore al Senato 6 (1523), unpaginated, 30 April 1523.

explained, he would also be acting against the pope.[18] L'Abbadino was in the pope's guardroom when Soderini was led out to Sant'Angelo and he described him as 'very lifeless and pale'.[19] Angelo Germanello, also writing to the marquis, described him as half dead and said that he went without uttering a word.[20]

Reactions to the news were varied. Cardinal Trivulzio, admittedly one of the French party, remarked that the pope had not been elected to lock up his cardinals.[21] The Ferrarese orator expressed quite a popular opinion when he wrote of Soderini as a poor old man and said that he thought the whole thing was a plot by the Spanish to force Adrian to exhibit more publicly his imperial bias, so that he could no longer say he wished to remain neutral, and to discourage those of the French party by launching an attack on a man of such authority.[22] Castiglione commented that poor Soderini had certainly been left the bitterest of pills to the end.[23] Paolo Giovio[24] and John Clerk,[25] the English ambassador in Rome, had other opinions and news to voice: the former claimed that the pope should be congratulated upon imprisoning the crafty, francophile Soderini while the latter stated 'All men are glad that the pope has got rid of so pestiferous a counsellor'.

Bernardo da Verrazzano, a close friend of Soderini, and Soderini's secretary Eliseo da Colle, were also taken prisoner.[26] Giovanbattista Soderini, who was with Francesco at the time, escaped.[27] Mario Maffei wrote to his son Paolo that, as the pope was such a just man, he felt sure there must be good reasons for his treatment of Soderini. He also thought that Soderini would be treated humanely but added that others had already been tortured.[28] It appears that Soderini was treated well, especially by the castellan Enrico Cardona. Cardona was the archbishop of Monreale, one of the prelates whom Adrian had brought with him from Spain.[29] Soderini was in his charge,[30] and the Spaniard took pity

[18] ASMa, AG, b.867, 76v. [19] ASMa, AG, b.867, 56r.

[20] ASMa, AG, b.867, 322r. [21] Sanuto, *I diarii*, XXXIV, 149.

[22] ASMo, Arch. Estense, Cancelleria estero, ambasciatori (Roma), b. 28, Lodovico Cato, Rome, 29 April. The despatch is in code but there is contemporary deciphering. [23] *Lettere di Baldassare Castiglione*, I, p. 107.

[24] P. Giovio, *Lettere*, ed. G. Ferrero, I (Rome, 1956), p. 102, 8 June, Giovio to Federico Gonzaga: 'Diro ben ch'el papa è stato un omo da benissimo a ficare in prigione quello segnalato versipelle infranciosato del Volterra, quale eri ne lo essamine sudoe sudore frigido e sincopizo, non sapendo rispondere a quelle interrogazione, quale gli sono siropi, per dargli presto la cassia del capello.'

[25] *Letters and papers*, III, II, p. 1298, Clerk to Wolsey, 11 June.

[26] See, for example, Bardi, 'Filippo Strozzi', p. 39.

[27] *Ibid.*, and ASF, Otto di prat., Resp. 24, 231r and v.

[28] Volterra, Biblioteca Guarnacci, MS 5376, 2 May.

[29] In 1527 he was created a cardinal by Clement and appointed viceroy of Sicily. For further information, see P. Pagliucchi, *I castellani del Castel Sant'Angelo*, (Rome, 1906), I, part II, pp. 76–7. [30] ASF, Urbino I, G, CCXXXVI, II, 1031r, 23 May.

on the old man and to reassure him that his food was not poisoned, ate it with him.[31] Then the pope softened slightly towards Soderini and allowed two and then three of his servants to wait on him in the castle. Later the pope sent a groom to Soderini's palace to collect a silver vase that held holy water, a red velvet chair, an inkwell and a purple gown lined with fur, which were all carried back to Soderini in Castel Sant'Angelo.[32] Soderini's case was assigned to del Monte, Accolti and Cesi.[33] Accolti had been one of the judges in the 1517 'conspiracy' as well. Soderini complained at this and two other judges were added, his friend Enrico Cardona, and Ghinucci, the bishop of Ascoli Piceno and Worcester.[34] From 30 April to 2 May an inventory was made of the contents of Soderini's palace by the criminal judge Rossello Rosselli.[35]

The two sides drew up battle lines almost immediately. The Medici and imperial party pressed for Soderini's execution. Sessa wrote to the emperor telling him to ask the pope for Soderini's execution, adding that if strict justice were to be done he should take the case into his own hands. He said that if the emperor destroyed Soderini, he would have destroyed his most dangerous enemy. Cesare de Grassis, who betrayed the cardinal, asked for 1,000 ducats from the emperor as reward.[36] The French king moved to help his friend and the defender of French interests at Rome, and wrote demanding the release of Soderini.[37] On 4 July he wrote again, saying that he was convinced that Soderini, a man of flawless integrity and common sense, had been put in prison solely because cardinal de' Medici had denounced him as favouring the French. He added that, if the pope wished to be fair and impartial, he should mete out the same penalty to those who manifestly defended the affairs of the French king's enemies.[38] This last is a telling point. Soderini had, after all, done nothing more than was being done by many other cardinals at the same time. Cardinal de' Medici's power and desire for revenge after the 1522 conspiracy were far more the causes of Soderini's plight than any alleged act of treason on his part.

Adrian was placed in a difficult position both by his temperament and

---

[31] See Sanuto, *I diarii*, XXXIV, 222.

[32] ASR, Notari dell'AC 410, 128v and Lowe, 'Francesco Soderini', appendix 5, p. 372.

[33] AV, Fondo concist., Acta miscell. 6, 420r, 29 April 1523.

[34] ASF, Otto di prat., Resp. 24, 235r.

[35] ASR, Notari dell'AC 410 (Jacopo Apocello), 122r–128v. This is transcribed in Lowe, 'Francesco Soderini', appendix 5, pp. 358–73.

[36] *Calendar of letters ... between England and Spain*, II, p. 552.

[37] ASF, Urbino I, G, CXXXII, 416r, 26 June 1523, della Porta to the duke of Urbino: 'è stato vero che'l re di Franza ha scritto al papa ferventemente sopra la liberatione di Vulterra'. See also *Letters and papers*, III, II, p. 1319.

[38] See Sanuto, *I diarii*, XXXIV, 342.

by the political situation. He was probably genuinely shocked that Soderini, beneath his conciliatory façade, was so blatantly pro-French. He was innocent of the ways of the curia, had no understanding of the Medici–Soderini rivalry and was naturally inclined to stop French expansion.

Once he had imprisoned Soderini he had an opportunity to reflect upon what would be the correct course of action, what his exact relationship to his cardinals ought to be, and what the dignity of the cardinalate involved. Other people, especially other cardinals, were also concerned about this. As Filippo Strozzi wrote to his brother, on 28 April, when the pope told the cardinals about Soderini in consistory that morning, there were those who criticised Soderini and those who defended him, according to taste, 'however, it was the prestige of the cardinalate which was closest to the hearts of most of them'.[39] Even lay people thought that the pope was in a tight corner. L'Abbadino, the Mantuan ambassador, wrote home about the imprisonment, commenting that it showed little respect for the rank of cardinal.[40] An unknown man wrote to Bernardo Spina from Florence, on 15 May, expressing quite a common view when he argued that it was not seemly (chonveniente) for the pope to jail such a man only to release him without some great display, and he reckoned that Soderini would lose his hat at the least and be exiled from Rome.[41] This view again came into vogue in July when it was increasingly obvious that the pope was not going to harm Soderini physically and wanted to behave correctly towards him. It was suggested that he return to his haunts in the kingdom of Naples.[42] Of course, this commonsensical point of view was not the one expressed by the imperialists or Mediceans who pursued their case to its logical conclusion.

Soderini, for his part, refused to be cowed by his latest misfortune, and this probably saved his life. He insisted that his case be dragged through the courts and that he be defended.[43] Since his only crime had been to conceal his true allegiance, his tenacity on this point is not surprising. As a letter of 20 May to his brother Giovanvettorio showed, he took this latest reverse with the stoicism to be expected of so experienced a political hand: 'It is displeasing to me to hear of the fear in which you are forced to live, but nonetheless I praise every provision you make, because in matters of politics one can never live too cautiously.'[44] It probably also explains why, according to della Porta,

[39] Bardi, 'Filippo Strozzi', p. 39.
[40] Letter of 6 May in ASMa, AG, b.867, quoted in Pastor, History of the popes, IX, p. 195.   [41] ASF, C. Strozz., CVI, 20, 84r.
[42] ASF, Urbino I, G, CXXXII, 451v, della Porta to duke of Urbino, Rome, 17 July.
[43] ASF, Urbino I, G, CXXXII, 414v, 24 June.   [44] Published in Razzi, Vita, p. 123.

when in mid-July he was offered an escape route (the possibility of buying himself out of prison), he chose not to do so.[45] He must have known that, by then, there had been a change in the relationship between himself and the pope: rather than Soderini's being worried about his life or his benefices, it was the pope who was worried about what to do with him. The malice of the Medici had landed the problem of Soderini squarely on Adrian's shoulders.

Since no one dared to defend Soderini, the pope had to order someone to do it. The man chosen was a consistorial advocate, Tarquinio di Santa Croce, and messer Gaspare was found to be his procurator.[46] Soderini was even given a copy of the charges against him and fifteen days to prepare a case.[47] All this took time and delayed proceedings. On 4 July Soderini was examined about the conspiracy against cardinal de' Medici and he denied everything, saying, however, that if it had succeeded he would have been delighted, because tyranny would have been ended and Florence liberated. These were 'the scurrilous words of an impassioned man'[48] but why was Soderini being examined on this question? It would seem to be because of cardinal de' Medici's influence, proof again that the ostensible charge was not the whole truth. Ambassadors in Rome wrote that the pope passed his days with cardinal de' Medici and the duke of Sessa.[49] But as the summer came and went, it seemed more and more likely that Soderini would lose his hat and not his head. The cardinals had been asked for their opinion of the case[50] and three of these opinions have survived.[51] All state that because of the confusion of the times, Luther's heresies, the threatened invasion of the Turks, the struggle between France and the emperor, it would be wiser not to proceed harshly against Soderini, because he was only a little spark and it would be foolish, in seeking to extinguish the spark, to fan a great fire (a clear reference to the dire consequences of alienating permanently the French king).[52] All thought that Soderini had written the letters, but none thought it of any great

[45] ASF, Urbino I, G, cxxxII, 443r.
[46] Ibid., 451v and ASMa, AG, b.867, 346r. This may be the ser Gaspare da Gambassi who was his procurator in the 1522 dispute with the Office of Rebels in Florence.
[47] See ASF, Otto di prat., Resp. 24, 358r and Sanuto, I diarii, xxxIV, 302.
[48] ASF, Urbino I, G, cxxxII, 425v.
[49] See, for example, ibid., 443r. Medici and Sessa had been waiting in the antechamber when the judges reported on Soderini on 11 June, and had been hovering while Soderini's house had been ransacked and inventoried on 30 April: 'Mons. R.mo Medici, accompagnato dal duca di Sessa, è ritornato a casa tutto iocundo', ASMa, AG, b.867, 56r and v. [50] Sanuto, I diarii, xxxIV, 359.
[51] BV, Vat. lat. 3920, 60r–61r, 137r and v, 140r and v.
[52] Ibid., 140r: 'ne dum scintillam extinguere cupimus, incendium maximum excitemus'.

significance. Precedents were quoted of other occasions when the pope had pardoned indiscretions of a similar nature. In all this, the reputation of the French king and Soderini's standing with him were the deciding factors. There was no condemnation of Soderini, only regret for the turbulent times. The opinions are undated, but in August the Venetian ambassador wrote that he thought things would go badly because cardinal de' Medici wanted them to.[53]

On 14 September the pope died, but left an unsealed papal bull (*motu proprio*) instructing the cardinals not to release Soderini.[54] Galeotto de' Medici saw the significance of this, and condemned it as a terrible thing that a dying pope should have the authority to deprive of their votes those who might oppose his views. The implication, of course, was that a dying pope could influence the choice of his successor.[55] It was a slightly naive command as the cardinals were sovereign during a papal vacancy (*sede vacante*)[56] and they were unlikely to allow one of their own number to be penalised in this fashion. Papal vacancies were also occasions for granting amnesties to prisoners in the jails.[57] At congregation the day after Adrian's death, Soderini's procurator and Giovanvettorio demanded his release, and the cardinals agreed to put the matter on the agenda for the following day.[58] It was finally agreed that Soderini should be released as some of the older cardinals refused to enter the conclave without him and were unwilling to attend congregation or even commence the papal funeral masses.[59] Fear of a schism forced a decision in favour of the cardinals who had been created before Leo's pontificate and brought defeat for Leo's *creature*.[60] Soderini stayed in prison until the start of the conclave and was visited there by many of the other cardinals.[61] The nascent revolt in Sicily was snuffed out with surprising vigour and harshness.[62]

---

[53] Sanuto, *I diarii*, XXXIV, 359.

[54] See *Calendar of letters ... between England and Spain*, II, p. 589 and Sanuto, *I diarii*, XXXIV, 438.   [55] ASF, Otto di prat., Resp. 30, 94r.

[56] Bullard, *Filippo Strozzi*, p. 128. See below, p. 161.

[57] L. Spinelli, *La vacanza della sede apostolica dalle origini al concilio tridentino* (Milan, 1955), p. 153 states that this was the reason for the release of Soderini from jail at this point.

[58] ASBo, Lettere dell'ambasciatore al Senato 6 (1523), unpaginated, Vianesius Albergatus to the *Quaranta* in Bologna, Rome, 15 September.

[59] *Ibid.*, 18 September.   [60] Rodocanachi, *Les pontificats*, p. 88.

[61] See ASF, Sig., Otto, Dieci, Miss. 11, 41v, Roberto Acciaiuoli to Luigi Guicciardini, 25 September and also BV, Barb. lat. 2799, 32v.

[62] For background, see G. Salvo Cozzo, 'Transunto del processo contro i fratelli Imperatori', *Archivio storico siciliano*, N. S. 7 (1882), pp. 341–53. The original document is in Palermo, Biblioteca comunale, 4Qq D.47, 169r–177v.

CHAPTER 13

SODERINI'S LAST DAYS

After a protracted and difficult conclave lasting fifty days,[1] cardinal Giulio de' Medici emerged as pope on 19 November, and took the name of Clement VII. A list of the cardinals (with their political leanings) entering the conclave makes it seem as though the battle was straightforwardly between the Medicean and the French factions, with very few cardinals supporting the emperor.[2] But this is an illusion because most of the imperialists came into line in support of the election of cardinal de' Medici, whose candidature was backed by the emperor. Medicean family links to France and the Valois belonged to the sphere of Florence, rather than Rome, and cardinal de' Medici had invested much effort in his friendship with the Hapsburg clients and servants, the duke of Sessa and Adrian. The French supported Niccolò Flisco, and one independent cardinal – Alessandro Farnese – had a chance. However, in the ensuing stalemates between the French and Mediceans, the balance was held by the die-hard imperialists and their candidate Jacobazzi, who were implacably opposed to Medici. When Colonna finally agreed to vote for Medici, the outcome was certain. Yet again Soderini made a deal for his family and agreed to vote for another Medici. He was in no position to do anything else. He was nearing seventy, had been a prisoner for six months and had not been released in time to renew any of his contacts. The best that he could hope for was the re-establishment of his family both in Florence and Rome, and a trouble-free remainder of his life.

The election of Clement was held up in order to settle these details.[3] Nardi later wrote that Soderini had not opposed this election but rather joined in with it because he knew that it was not possible to stop it.[4] In

---

[1] On this conclave, see Pastor, *History of the popes*, IX, pp. 231–43.
[2] Sanuto, *I diarii*, XXXV, 223–4.
[3] *Ibid.*, XXXV, 207, the secretary of the Venetian orator to his brother, Rome, 18 November. [4] Nardi, *Istorie*, II, p. 83.

140

one sense Soderini succeeded in his plan with Clement because Clement kept his word and, on 2 December, sent a brief to the priors and the *gonfaloniere* in Florence asking them to restore the possessions of the Soderini, to recall the family from exile and generally to allow them to take up again their position in the city.[5] Florence had no choice but to comply as the order came from the centre of Medici power. On 18 December Tommaso, Giovanbattista and Piero di Paolantonio, and Tommaso di Giovanvettorio, who had been punished for their part in the conspiracy of 1522 against cardinal de' Medici, now Clement VII, were offered a pardon as thanks for Clement's election, and Piero's good name was rehabilitated.[6] On 23 February Filippo Strozzi, always an interested observer of these permutations, wrote from Rome to his brother that the restitution of the Soderini was a good thing, and that henceforth Francesco Soderini would be committed to more social behaviour as Clement had made it clear that nothing less would be acceptable.[7] Both of them initially made an obvious effort to get on with each other and even the habitually sceptical Galeotto de' Medici wrote that Soderini spoke with such affection about Clement that he (Galeotto) truly believed that he had resolved to live quietly and contentedly.[8] Clement, in line with the jokes engendered by his choice of papal name, did seem to have more forgiveness in him than other members of his clan. The character of the individual Medici should not be discounted. The Venetian orator, Marco Foscari, wrote on 27 November that the pope had pardoned everybody and that often he and Soderini, who had been such enemies, now ate together.[9]

Both for this reason and because Soderini was ill and bedridden from February until his death in May 1524, the last six months of his life were amongst his least active politically. Soderini had often been ill in the past and had spent months during which he was incapacitated but this time he was in his seventieth year and, as the Venetian orator wrote in January 1524, 'he is in danger of dying because he is old'.[10] The fact that he continued to function as a force in ecclesiastical affairs indicates that his non-involvement in political affairs could have been the result of a conscious decision, or perhaps it was merely that his physical resources were dwindling, and politics were more tiring and time-consuming than church affairs. He had never stopped working when he had been

[5] ASF, Diplomatico, Riformagioni, Atti pubbl., 2 December 1523.
[6] ASF, Repubblica, Balìe 43, 207v and see Stephens, *The fall*, p. 167.
[7] ASF, C. Strozz., III, 108, 58r.
[8] ASF, Otto di prat., Resp. 32, 157v, 24 November.
[9] Sanuto, *I diarii*, XXXV, 242, 27 November.
[10] *Ibid.*, XXXV, 376, 24 January 1524.

ill in previous years, and the few pieces of information about him from this period all attest to the soundness of his mind. In March and April 1524 there were cases of plague in his household, according to Venetian and Mantuan reports,[11] but Soderini did not die of plague although it was reported in England that he had done so. He finally died on 17 May from his illness of several months and was buried quickly.

With him went the last vestige of a personal Medici–Soderini rivalry. Those who commented on his death in letters, often ambassadors at the papal court, paid tribute to his intelligence and his flair for politics. Were there to exist letters from Mediceans recording their feeling at this date, no doubt other sentiments would have been voiced; Gheri, for example, must have been delighted. To outsiders the Medici issue was almost a dead one since Clement had been elected pope and had carried on the Medici succession, and only a few Florentines had looked to the Soderini for government after 1512. Francesco Soderini had outlived most of his contemporaries, and had to deal with several successive generations of rulers in almost every country, state or town, often managing the transitions with great skill. His most important connection had always been with France, and after mentioning Florence, politics and the Medici, most observers would have adverted to the French link.

When Soderini was released from prison, Francis I must have been pleased but his mind was on other things. Soderini's death coincided with the news of spectacular French defeat at the hands of the imperialists who, according to one Venetian correspondent, had driven the French out of Italy.[12] Those Mediceans and imperialists who wished to celebrate the end of the Soderini had cause for double celebration in the defeat of the French. The Medici–imperial alliance had triumphed completely over the Soderini–French one, in such a way that the huge fire of France and the tiny spark of Soderini had gone out together.

The Medici pursued Soderini even beyond the grave. In 1526 there was a court case to assert the falsity of his final will of 22 February 1524. The clue to the reason for this case may lie in one of the examiner's questions: 'Has the witness ever heard that Soderini had not made a will during his last illness but that it had been done by his brothers and next of kin in an attempt to salvage his goods and heredity from the clutches of the pope and the apostolic see?'[13] However, Clement VII's papal

---

[11] *Ibid.*, xxxvi, 150 and 186, and ASMa, AG, b.868, 541r.

[12] Sanuto, *I diarii*, xxxvi, 367, Ser Hironimo Lippomano, 21 May 1524. See also Pastor, *History of the popes*, ix, pp. 259–60.

[13] Rome, Arch. Sod., iii, 243v–244r, testimony of Staglia de Actis of 5 February 1526.

brief, giving Soderini permission to make this will, is not a forgery[14] and there is no reason to suppose that his will is not in order. In fact, it is much more likely that the case was, in some fashion, prompted by a Medici desire to keep the Soderini and their possessions under their control. In the 1524 will there is a clause allowing for the foundation of a college in Paris for Italian students of canon law and theology. Members of the Soderini family were to have first refusal at the college, followed by any other Florentines, and then by anyone of Italian birth.[15] The choice of Paris can be easily explained: the Medici were in power in both Florence and Rome which ruled out endowments to either university. Soderini's links with France, and the fact that Paris was well away from the Medici sphere of influence, must have made Paris an attractive alternative. For the Medici, on the other hand, the projected foundation must have looked ominous. Therefore, it is very likely that Soderini's attempt to provide a base in Paris for disenchanted or outlawed members of his family and possibly other anti-Mediceans by founding a college at the university, was thwarted at a preliminary stage by direct or indirect interference from Clement VII, a Medici pope.[16]

[14] See AV, Arm. XXIX, 72, 243r–244r.
[15] See Rome, Arch. Sod., III, 186r–189v and Lowe, 'Francesco Soderini', appendix 4, pp. 346–7.
[16] For an expanded version of this argument, see K. Lowe, 'Cardinal Francesco Soderini's proposal for an Italian college at Paris in 1524', *History of universities*, 4 (1984), pp. 167–78.

PART IV

THE LIFESTYLE OF A RENAISSANCE CARDINAL

CHAPTER 14

OFFICIAL DUTIES IN THE CURIA: THE CONSILIAR, THE CEREMONIAL, THE SOCIAL

The rhythms and style of Soderini's life changed considerably as soon as he became a curia cardinal. From a life arranged around the gathering and weighing-up of information he was thrust into one of cyclical ritual, advice-giving and decision-making. There had been much ceremony as a diplomat but the nature and degree of it at the papal court was different. Soderini attended his first congregation on 31 August 1503,[1] pronounced his first absolution after mass on 6 September, celebrated his first mass as cardinal on 10 September, the seventh in the series of funeral masses (*novinae*) for Alexander VI.[2] His initiation had been remarkably fast. On the evening of 10 September he and three other curia cardinals, Ferrero, Sanseverino and d'Albret, were sent to meet three more cardinals, d'Amboise, Sforza and Aragon, who were coming to Rome for the conclave.[3] Soderini had had a taste in his first two weeks at Rome of each of the three main activities of a cardinal: the consiliar, the liturgical and ceremonial, and the social.

The consiliar function was extremely time-consuming and ranged from the almost daily consistories and congregations, to the smaller select committees delegated to discuss specific issues, to quasi-informal discussions with the pope about affairs of church and state. A lessening in the autonomous power of the college was not matched by a corresponding fall in business to be transacted; indeed, the rise in importance of the revamped papal states meant that there was an increase, at least in temporal business. The difference between a consistory and a congregation was that at the former the pope was present while at the latter he was not. Exceptionally, extraordinary congregations of cardinals may have been summoned by the cardinals themselves to address specific problems relating to their office as a

---

[1] Burchard, 'Liber notarum', II, p. 362.   [2] *Ibid.*, p. 368.
[3] *Ibid.*, p. 369.

whole; more generally, they formed a regular part of the curial diary decided upon by the pope. How arduous these consiliar duties became depended upon the degree of seriousness with which individual popes took their custody of the church, as well as upon the current state of christendom. Soderini, having held a post at the curia prior to being a cardinal, must have known about this aspect of life. With his legal background he was to be greatly in demand during the following years but unfortunately the material is patchy, especially for the earlier part of this period under Julius II. This could be because Soderini did less as he was a junior cardinal or it could be that the records have not survived. A related subject is his other involvement in the administration of the catholic church and the running of the curia, as shown by the offices that he held such as legate, governor or protector. These are all activities which made possible or facilitated the pope's business.

Matters dealt with in consistory ranged over a wide spectrum from politics to affairs of faith and doctrine, from the reception of ambassadors to possible candidates for canonisation, from administration of the papal states to appointments to benefices, from decisions on heresy to the crusades.[4] A secret consistory was only open to cardinals whereas a public one could include bishops and other members of the curia. They were also held in different places, secret ones taking place in the *sala del papagallo* or *dei palafrenieri*, and public ones in the *sala del concistoro* or the *sala ducale*.[5] Reaction to many of the major dramas of the period was registered in consistory. For example, after the Pax Romana of 1511, in a secret consistory of nine cardinals including Soderini, Pompeo Colonna was stripped of his bishopric of Rieti, the monasteries of Grottaferrata and Subiaco and all his other benefices and church possessions, for his crime against the person of the pope and the honour and status of the Roman church.[6] The major ecclesiastical business was also carried out in consistory but it was forced to give way to the year's liturgical requirements. Soderini had to write explaining this to the *Dieci* in December 1503.[7] In addition, consistory provided regular, if not private, access to the pope for every cardinal. The need to maintain favour with the pope in order to be able to operate as an ecclesiastical patron was one reason why a cardinal would want to remain in Rome, and consistories provided the setting for frequent meetings.

Theoretically, the cardinals in consistory were advising the pope on

---

[4]   P. van Lierde and A. Giraud, *What is a cardinal?* (London, 1964), p. 95.
[5]   See J. Shearman, 'The Vatican *stanze*: functions and decorations', *Proceedings of the British Academy*, 57 (1971), pp. 5, 8 and 9 and P. Partner, *Renaissance Rome, 1500–1559* (Berkeley, 1976), p. 134.   [6]   BL, Add. MSS 8442, 245v–246r.
[7]   ASF, Dieci, Resp. 76, 320v.

all these matters; even when proposing clergy for benefices they were supposedly counselling the pope on who was the best candidate. But the situation was not as simple as that; other forces were at work. In the eleven recorded cases of Soderini's acting as proposer between 8 November 1504 and 22 May 1505, all were to benefices in France, from Besançon to Rheims, and from Chartres to Clermont and Sarlat, and on 18 May 1517 Soderini proposed candidates to Lecce and Alessano, both suffragan bishoprics of Otranto.[8] The reason Soderini was cardinal proposer on these occasions was not because he knew the candidates but because he knew or had strong ties with the areas and their rulers. These links were forged between a plurality of cardinals and many different states. France, for example, would have had a relatively large pool of cardinals who could have been called upon to propose candidates for French benefices either from French nationals or from friends and allies. Soderini is also supposed to have helped Giovanni di Domenico da Prato obtain the bishopric of Aquila on 6 March 1504, and Pietro Dandolo obtain the bishopric of Vicenza on 20 October 1507.[9] This level of influence and cooperation with the pope and with foreign rulers was a necessary part of the indirect patronage required of a successful cardinal, for favours of this sort had to be repaid in kind. Support by a cardinal for aspirants to vacant bishoprics and their patrons necessitated support of a similar nature for the cardinal when he subsequently wished to acquire a benefice for himself or one of his clients.

Almost all the information about the commissions on which Soderini sat comes from the years 1522–4. But commissions varied so much in the object of inquiry and in their level of importance, that the subjects need investigation as well as the frequency. These commissions usually contained either one or two members from each order of the cardinalate: deacon, priest, bishop. Normally cardinals commenced their career attached to a Roman church that carried with it the title of cardinal deacon or cardinal priest, and progressed through the ranks as and when more senior cardinals died and their churches and titles became vacant. The exact hierarchy of these Roman church appointments is not yet known, but obviously some had financial advantages and others priorities of ceremonial precedent. Cardinals were initially assigned to their Roman churches by the pope, shortly after their

---

[8] See AV, Fondo concist., Acta miscell. 6, between 111r and 135v and AV, Fondo concist., Acta vicecanc. 2, 30r and v.

[9] For Giovanni da Prato, see A. Ferrajoli, 'Il ruolo della corte di Leone X', *Archivio della reale società romana di storia patria*, 36 (1913), p. 196; for Dandolo, see D. Delcorno Branca, 'Un discepolo del Poliziano: Michele Acciari', *Lettere italiane*, 28 (1976), p. 468.

promotion to the cardinalate had been announced, and lobbying for these positions was not uncommon. In a similar manner to other ecclesiastical assets, these churches and titles could be, and were, exchanged.

Soderini had entered the college as the cardinal priest of S. Susanna. There were only six or seven possible cardinal bishoprics in use during this period as opposed to a possible forty-one cardinal priesthoods and a possible nineteen cardinal deaconships, so that (if this system of representative selection by the orders was followed) the chances of being one of the cardinal priests on any particular commission were less than those of the cardinal deacons, and much less than those of the cardinal bishops, who must have been on an irritatingly large number of committees. Soderini's first known commission was to review and put in order the electoral capitulations drawn up during the conclave before Pius III's election and to refer them to the college. The commission was deputed to do this in a congregation of 27 October 1503 after Pius III's seventh funeral mass, and the committee consisted of six cardinals: Bernardo Carvajal, Ludovico Podocataro, Soderini, Flisco, Castellesi and Sanseverino.[10] As with most commissions, the sources which so painstakingly note the participants have here omitted to reveal the outcome. Often, too, essential details such as what the cardinals would actually be discussing in connection with a particular problem, are either omitted or left vague. This is an occasion on which Soderini's legal training would have been an asset.

On 18 December 1504, the bishop of Acqui, Ludovico Bruno, who had been the emperor's ambassador at the papal court, arrived in consistory and asked the pope, on behalf of the emperor, to take action against and excommunicate the rebels in Bohemia and Austria. The request seemed of such importance to the pope, the Venetian ambassador Giustinian wrote, that it should not be conceded hastily. He wanted advice on it so he delegated the task of discussing it to cardinals Antoniotto Pallavicini (a lawyer), Giovanni di San Giorgio (an auditor of the *Rota*), Bernardino Carvajal, Soderini, Colonna and Medici.[11] On 25 March 1509 Soderini was appointed to the least well documented of his commissions. According to the Venetian ambassador in Rome, six cardinals were chosen by the pope 'to consult': two bishops, Carafa and Carvajal, two priests, Soderini and Isvalies, and two deacons, Medici and Farnese.[12] This was at a very tense and crucial time in Veneto-papal relations when the League of Cambrai had been signed and Venice was

---

[10] Burchard, 'Liber notarum', II, p. 397.   [11] Giustinian, *Dispacci*, III, p. 342.

[12] Sanuto, *I diarii*, VIII, 38–9.

under papal censure. By July there was a peace of sorts between Julius and Venice. On 26 October the same six cardinals were described by Ser Paolo Capello, yet another Venetian orator in Rome, as being deputed to hear the Venetian ambassadors.[13] Perhaps they had the more general portfolio of Venetian affairs during this period of crisis and change.

No more committees emerge until that of August 1513 when, in the wake of the Council of Pisa, Leo X set up a commission to inquire into the restoration of peace and the healing of the schism, and to examine the spiritual condition in France. This was no easy matter since the council had given out many benefices and made many dispensations which would cause great havoc were they to be rescinded, but the French would in any case not have agreed to this. On the other hand, papal approval of what had taken place would not do either since the participants and followers had been declared schismatic.[14] Three cardinals – Soderini, Accolti and Farnese – were deputed to work in conjunction with the French orators to find a solution.[15] When Soderini was unable or unwilling to return to Rome for this – probably he was at his villa of Colle Salvetti in Tuscany – Antonio del Monte and Marco Vigerio were chosen to replace him.[16] This was an extremely important commission and vital issues would have been touched upon. Soderini was probably chosen on account of his French connections and sympathies.

In June 1517 there was a consistory about Franciscan observance and the appointment of a general. Seven cardinals, one of whom was Soderini, were deputed to do this.[17] Then came exile. Finally, after his return to Rome in December 1521, he received a flood of commissions. One of these was to investigate the legality of the new venal offices instigated by Leo X during his pontificate, and to seek the best way of declaring them invalid. At Leo's death, according to the Venetian ambassador Gradenigo, the number of venal offices had risen to 2,150.[18]

---

[13] *Ibid.*, IX, 297. Some of the cardinals are assigned to the wrong order. See also R. Cessi, *Dispacci degli ambasciatori veneziani alla corte di Roma presso Giulio II* (Venice, 1932), pp. 145–6, 148 for further information on Soderini and the pope and Venice during the autumn of 1509.

[14] See W. Ullmann, 'Julius II and the schismatic cardinals', in *Schism, heresy and religious protest*, ed. D. Baker, Studies in church history, 9 (Cambridge, 1972), p. 189. The cardinals involved in the Council of Pisa only became schismatic when the Fifth Lateran Council had been announced, and their proposed aim was thereby rendered totally invalid.

[15] ASF, Dieci, Resp. 117, 68r, Francesco Vettori, the orator in Rome, 20 August 1513.

[16] *Ibid.*, 90v, 25 August.   [17] Sanuto, *I diarii*, XXIV, 321.

[18] Pastor, *History of the popes*, VIII, p. 97.

The commission was a part of Adrian's attempt at curial reform.[19] In particular, concern was expressed over the college of knights (*cavalieri*) of St Peter which had been set up by Leo in 1520. Four hundred and one knights each paid 1,000 ducats for such privileges as enrolment in the Roman nobility and the title of count palatine, in addition to the material advantage of reaping interest on the down payment.[20]

Leo's great increase in venal offices noticeably intensified a trend that had existed previously, which Adrian VI sought to reverse. There was a movement among the cardinals to try to obtain confirmation of the capitulations of the conclave, thereby confirming the validity of Leo's actions and, more specifically, the validity of the venal offices that he had instituted. On the investigating committee were cardinals Campeggio, Flisco, del Monte, Jacobazzi, Accolti and Soderini, five of them (all except Flisco) distinguished lawyers.[21] On 21 December 1521 Filippo Strozzi wrote from Rome to his brother, Lorenzo, in Florence saying that the offices that mattered most to them were those of the knights of St Peter, of which they had about thirty, and that their value was decreasing so that they were now worth only about 500 or 600 ducats.[22] Strozzi considered that the offices were being rescinded for two reasons: papal necessity, and 'the natural inclination to damn the memory of Leo', and he also commented that Grimani and Soderini and some others had already condemned the excessive number of offices.

By early February 1523 the commission of cardinals had been set up, and on 10 February the six of them congregated at Soderini's house. The palace of a particular cardinal would appear to be an unusual venue for this type of papal business. The congregation is described in a letter of 11 February written by Galeotto de' Medici, the Florentine ambassador in Rome. First the conservators (*conservatori*) arrived and stated that in their opinion the wish to revoke the offices could only be part of a greater desire to ruin the world and all the papal court. After them came the advocates who argued vociferously in favour of the preservation of the offices. 'Then the Roman noblemen (*gentilhomini*), trying to persuade the cardinals not to ruin the city, court and inhabitants, turned to Soderini and told him that they were suspicious both of his motives and of the motives of some of the other judges, and that even if he had been offended by Leo or hated cardinal de' Medici, he should not seek

---

[19] For a discussion of the reasons for the failure of curial reform in connection with church money and property in the 1530s, see McClung Hallman, *Italian cardinals*, pp. 164–8.   [20] Pastor, *History of the popes*, VIII, pp. 96–7.

[21] *Ibid.*, IX, p. 107 who cites a letter of A. Germanello of 13 February 1523 in ASMa, AG.   [22] ASF, C. Strozz., III, 108, 50r.

revenge by attempting to remove goods from them, the noblemen.'[23] Finally, the knights and other officials entered, making the same lament but with less restraint. Among them was a Spaniard who said: '"Signori cardinali, one can see every day men who will kill for thirty pieces of silver, and we are in the same position. Do not think that we will submit to this thievery and injury." Soderini replied to everybody in one sentence, that he had been many years at court and had never displeased anyone and although it was true that he had been harmed by Leo, he was not trying to exact revenge by taking away their possessions, but on the contrary had been given the job by the pope and had not sought it out.'[24] The rivalry between the Soderini and the Medici was understood to permeate and disrupt even appointments such as this.

Del Monte spoke next and defended Soderini, reminding those present that he, del Monte, was protector of the Romans, and that the commission would examine everything very carefully. Possibly del Monte's office was a reason for his inclusion on this commission. Protectors of individual cities and their peoples had been part of the general move which commenced in the thirteenth century towards appointing a particular cardinal to safeguard the interests of various institutions, such as religious orders or kingdoms, at the Roman curia.[25] The Roman people were often in need of such a spokesperson as many papal decisions affected their city. Accolti spoke more sharply, telling them to refer to the pope. Rome was full of rumour, most of which had a basis in fact. In a Venetian ambassador's letter of the same date, it was claimed that the whole of Rome was afraid because only a few people (*pochi*) did not have one of these offices, and that in addition to wanting to cancel all the offices created by Leo, Adrian wished to cut the number of remaining offices substantially so that there were, for example, 25 instead of 105 archivists.[26]

By 14 February three auditors of the *Rota* had been seconded to the commission – Simonetta, Cassiodoro and Staffileo – and instructions were given to debate whether or not Leo had been legally entitled to alienate the goods of the church by creating the offices, and a deadline

---

[23] ASF, Otto di prat., Resp. 24, 28r and v: 'Dapoi entrorono li gentilhomini romani, persuadendoli ad non volere ruinare la ciptà, la corte et le persone loro, voltandosi a Volterra et dicendoli che l'haveano, insieme con qualcunaltro iudici, a suspecto. Et che se lui si tenea offeso dalla S.ta M. o havea odio con Monsignor de' Medici, non se havea a vendicare col fare opera di torre a loro et altri la roba.'

[24] *Ibid.*, 28v: 'Volterra rispose a tutti in una sententia, che era stato tanti anni in questa corte nè havea mai dispiacuto ad alcuno et che era ben vero era suto iniuriato da Leone, ma non era per vendicarsene, maxime per verso, che levassi loro la roba, et che questa cura li era suta data da N. S. et non ricercòla.'

[25] *The catholic encyclopedia*, III, p. 341.   [26] Sanuto, *I diarii*, XXXIII, 620.

of eight days was announced for those who wanted to present their case in writing.[27] The judicial review dragged on, however, and on 25 February Galeotto wrote that a distinction was being drawn between those who had paid for their offices, who were still to receive dividends, and those who had not paid and who could have no such expectation.[28] On 1 March he wrote that both categories were to be paid at least until December.[29] On 6 March he wrote that 136 knights and 28 cubiculars (*cubiculari*) had proved unable to show payment for their offices, and that, in any case, Adrian was still anxious to ascertain whether or not Leo had possessed the right to sell these offices. This was a commission of the greatest contemporary importance, and one that produced violent reactions and counter-reactions amongst all the curia officials of the time. It also helped to define the notion of office-holding by focusing attention upon the right of the papacy to sell or expand the number of offices. Great resentment was occasioned against Soderini who was the most senior cardinal; he became a target for attack and a figurehead to hate. Consequently, many were delighted when he was imprisoned in May 1523, because apparently he had told Adrian that Leo legally had not been in a position to sell the offices. Many of the offices had been cancelled on his advice, and many more were due to be.[30] This commission brought Soderini more notoriety than any other.

There is far less information about his other commissions, mainly a sentence or two in ambassadors' letters. The commissions could be of great political or doctrinal significance but were often merely a way of resolving a quarrel and not always connected with church affairs in the strictest sense. Soderini was involved in all types. A commission of September 1522 was instituted to make provision against the infidel and it consisted of nine cardinals, including Soderini, three from each order.[31] In January 1523 four cardinals (again including Soderini) were chosen to undertake a review of the restitution of Modena and Reggio to duke Alfonso of Ferrara, which was a part of Adrian's attempts to reorganise the papal states.[32] The cardinals opposed the motion.[33] This commission continued through March and April.[34] A distinction can

---

[27] ASF, Otto di prat., Resp. 24, 26v, Galeotto de' Medici.   [28] *Ibid.*, 42r and v.

[29] *Ibid.*, 48v.

[30] See Sanuto, *I diarii*, xxxiv, 222, a summary from the Venetian orators sent to render obedience to Adrian.

[31] ASF, Otto di prat., Resp. 27, 3r, Galeotto de' Medici, 4 September 1522.

[32] *Ibid.*, 497r, 23 January 1522 (i.e. 1523).

[33] See Pastor, *History of the popes*, ix, p. 161.

[34] See *Letters and papers*, iii, ii, p. 1208 for 3 March 1523 and ASBo, Lettere dell'ambasciatore al Senato 6 (1523), unpaginated, Vianesius Albergati to the Quaranta.

thus be made between a commission proper where a group of cardinals was elected to pass corporate judgement, and a matter which involved only one cardinal, or one cardinal on each side, where no joint decision was reached and which was essentially a question of cardinals' being employed in the settlement of disputes. All three were taking decisions in a particular case, but the route to the verdict differed. Therefore, cardinals could be deputed either to a commission or to a specific lawsuit.

In February 1523 three cardinals were selected to talk about 'the things pertinent to peace between the christian princes so that a crusade against the Turks could be arranged': they were Soderini, Colonna and Cornaro, and perhaps in this case they represented the cities of Florence, Rome and Venice.[35] In the consistorial records for 11 February there is a note of the election of these three prelates but the purpose for which they were elected is not clear.[36] In March 1523 Soderini had an interesting doctrinal issue upon which to decide. The Greek patriarch of Jerusalem wanted to uphold the union, forged at the Council of Florence in 1439 under Eugenius IV, between the Greek and Latin churches, and he offered full obedience to the Roman church in return for a confirmation of the union. Accolti and Soderini were deputed to work out what should happen.[37] Soderini's level of activity in this sphere rose in April when he was on two other committees, one of which was concerned with unspecified Bolognese affairs[38] and the other of which was on papal alliances. Soderini and Flisco advised the pope to remain neutral and to show favour to no one, although the other cardinals proposed other courses of action.[39]

Soderini's final commission was to investigate the influence of Martin Luther, given to him, Accolti and Cornaro on 9 December 1523 by Clement VII.[40] On 14 December Soderini spoke about Luther; the great Augustinian reformer, cardinal Giles of Viterbo, and cardinal Cristoforo de Numai, general of the Franciscan order, had been added to the committee. They all recommended that a papal nuncio be dispatched to the parts where Luther had gained a following to see what

---

[35] Sanuto, *I diarii*, XXXIII, 617, 12 February 1523: 'a tratar le cose pertinenti a la pace di principi christiani, per poter atender contra il turcho'.

[36] See AV, Fondo concist., Acta miscell. 70, 51v and 52r. Topics discussed in this consistory ranged from Rhodes to sending a legate to Hungary. It is published by A. Mercati, *Dall'Archivio Vaticano* (Città del Vaticano, 1951), II, Diarii di concistori del pontificato di Adriano VI, p. 101.

[37] AV, Fondo concist., Acta miscell. 6, 417r.

[38] ASBo, Lettere dell'ambasciatore al Senato 6, 10 April 1523.

[39] *Calendar of letters ... between England and* Spain, II, p. 538, 11 April 1523.

[40] AV, Fondo concist., Acta vicecanc. 3, 14r and Sanuto, *I diarii*, XXXV, 278.

action or remedies would be appropriate. Five candidates were proposed: the archbishop of Cosenza, Giovanni Ruffo de Theodolis; the bishop of Chieti, Giovanpietro Carafa; the bishop of Capo d'Istria, Bartolomeo de Asonia; the bishop of Pola in Istria, Altobello Averoldi and the Franciscan bishop-elect of Skara in Sweden, Giovanfrancesco of Potenza. However, as Soderini remarked, the Lutherans were most incensed against the Franciscan order so the last-named was perhaps unsuitable.[41] In general, Luther's doctrines were seen as some sort of disease and the towns and areas that held them were seen as 'infected'.[42] But, as his last remark implies, Soderini remained able to see the situation in more pragmatic terms.

Soderini also played an individual part in giving advice, both in taking decisions in legal cases, in a formal setting, and therefore advising the pope in an indirect fashion, and in giving his opinion informally to the pope when it was asked of him. Cardinals were often employed in this formal way to settle arguments, especially between members of the same family or between the local church organisation and the central bureaucracy. It may be that Soderini was saddled with this task slightly more frequently than were those cardinals who did not have a legal training, but there is not enough evidence to support a view either way. A typical example dates from 1504 when he was deputed to decide on a matter between Giovanni da Vesc, the resigning bishop of Agde in France, and cardinal Flisco, the incoming one;[43] it was a minor matter presumably connected with the terms of provision. It should be noted, however, that once again Soderini had been chosen to adjudicate upon a French dispute. An instance of his involvement in a cardinalitial capacity in a Malaspina family quarrel occurred in 1513. Two brothers, Lorenzo and Galeotto, were in severe disagreement, and they were each given a cardinal to speak on their behalf to try to find a satisfactory arrangement. Lorenzo was given Soderini and Galeotto, cardinal Grimani.[44] In fact, Soderini was related to the Malaspina (as Piero Soderini had married Argentina Malaspina, who was the sister of Lorenzo and Galeotto) and this may have been a reason for his selection, but as he was out of Rome Lorenzo had to find a substitute.[45]

Soderini became involved additionally in affairs which were more

[41] AV, Fondo consist., Acta vicecanc. 3, 15v.
[42] Ibid., 22r, 15 January 1524: 'Fuit postmodum factam verbum de rebus Lutherianis et dictum fuit Latislaviam civitatem nobilissimam infectam esse Lutheriana peste cum multis aliis locis nobilissimis.'   [43] See Eubel, Hierarchia, III, 110.
[44] AV, Arm. XL, 2, 22r, 13 June 1513, letter to Lorenzo Malaspina.
[45] See P. Paschini, Domenico Grimani, cardinale di S. Marco (m. 1523) (Rome, 1943), p. 77.

closely linked to the church, and especially in disputes between the religious orders and the bishops over jurisdiction. An example is the case of the important Benedictine monastery of SS. Trinità di Terra and the redistribution of its possessions to endow the new bishopric of Cava. In 1513 Cava was constituted an independent diocese having, since 1396, been under the control of the bishop-abbot of SS. Trinità. The new bishopric was in dire need of money and the monastery was supposed to provide a dowry. The transfer of power and money away from the monastery pleased neither the abbot and monks nor the order as a whole, and the process was obstructed. An independent assessor, Giovanbattista de Angelis of Naples, abbot of S. Benedetto de Capua, had valued the possessions at 1,400 ducats and Soderini was called in to pass sentence, which he did on 17 March 1516, ordering a long list of former possessions of SS. Trinità to be handed over to the town of Cava.[46]

Examples of the informal giving of advice to the pope are more difficult to detect because there is often no record of the conversations between the pope and Soderini, although the settling of papal business in this way would have been frequent. For example, in December 1522 Soderini advised Adrian VI to incorporate Siena within the papal states, but the pope apparently thought it better for Siena to preserve its independent government and to pay annually a certain sum of money to him in recognition of his suzerainty, in defiance of the fact that, strictly speaking, the emperor was the feudal overlord.[47] Perhaps Soderini saw himself as a Tuscan expert, or possibly it was Adrian, a foreign pope, who saw him in that light. Certainly, this advice to destroy Sienese independence represented a very Florentine point of view.

There is piecemeal evidence that Soderini occasionally gave advice when it was not wanted. Galeotto de' Medici reports that on 3 February 1523 there was a congregation in the *sala del concistoro* in the Vatican which consisted of Carvajal, Soderini, del Monte, Accolti, Colonna, Jacobazzi, Cornaro, Trivulzio, Campeggio, Valle and Cesi.[48] During the congregation the cardinals' grievances against the new pope Adrian were aired. The major complaint was that he was forsaking old traditions and old patterns of behaviour, not out of wilfulness but out of ignorance. Even though Carvajal was the senior cardinal, it was Soderini who spoke. He said that it was necessary to make the pope

---

[46] Rome, Arch. Sod., II, 276r–278r.

[47] *Calendar of letters ... between England and Spain*, II, p. 517.

[48] The Mantuan ambassador, Angelo Germanello, reported that there were thirteen cardinals. See Pastor, *History of the popes*, IX, p. 482.

understand the accusation of the college that he did not pay enough attention to the cardinals in whatever he did. He complained that the pope neglected to give them audiences and excluded them from a say in the management of the *stato ecclesiastico*. Adrian had cancelled previous papal concessions and ignored precedent, using new regulations in the chancery to their detriment. Not only the cardinals' dignity but the dignity of the subjects of the church had suffered. The cardinals had been accustomed, both in consistory and in other particulars, to have a great many commissions from their friends and protectors who had looked to them and who were served in their turn, whereas at present, under the new regime, they did not have anyone who sought them out. This is a very clear statement about the patronage system at work in the college of cardinals. The relationship was symbiotic; the cardinals needed their clients as much as the clients required their patrons. Cardinals relied on their acknowledged access to the pope in order to attract clients to their entourage, and the upper echelons of this clientele, in their turn, relied on this aspect of their patron's reputation to bring clients at a lower level into their own patronage networks.

Soderini's complaints continued. He wanted to lecture the pope about the damage done by confiscating the belongings of the newly dead, having not allowed them to make a will, as this was the reason why members of the papal court were leaving Rome.[49] He also suggested remonstrating with Adrian that the cardinals did not like or approve of his counsellors, nor of the advice they gave him. The cardinals were all in agreement over these complaints, and after the congregation, they went in a body to see him and to air their grievances. Adrian was reasonable and agreed either to change or, at the least, to consider the cardinals' charges. Finally, Soderini overran his brief by suggesting that those cardinals who had held legations for some years should resign them so that the offices could be redistributed, and more of the cardinals could have a share in the office-holding. The pope declined to reply. Nor were Soderini's fellow cardinals pleased as Soderini had not said beforehand that he was going to propose this.[50] It would have produced a fairer system and anticipated later schemes for reform, but was too novel to be adopted at this point. After all, the main complaint was that Adrian had introduced changes because of bad advice, and that matters should revert to their original state; advocacy of innovatory reforms had not been an issue.

---

[49] Incomes from benefices formed part of the belongings of prelates and could legitimately be bequeathed. See McClung Hallman, *Italian cardinals*, p. 80.

[50] This whole description is taken from a letter of Galeotto in ASF, Otto di prat., Resp. 24, 20r and v.

Soderini also played his part as a cardinal by governing part of the lands under control of the papacy. Here he acted in the place of the pope, who did not have time to supervise personally all his territory. It is not known exactly when Soderini was made a governor of the Campagna and Marittima, but it was probably early in the reign of Leo X. He already had the title by 17 September 1514 when the pope wrote to three cardinals, Riario, Carvajal and Soderini, encouraging them to set up a confraternity or institution in the province, similar to those set up by Ferdinand and Isabella in Spain, to get rid of assassins, thieves and malefactors.[51] Soderini was addressed as the governor of the province and said to have the power of a legate *a latere*. The concern expressed for travellers, and the desire to emulate Spain, are both interesting features. Security was a constant problem and Campagna and Marittima were very important for communications with Rome and stability in the neighbourhood of the city.

Almost exactly a year later, on 18 September 1515, the pope wrote again to the governor or his lieutenant, instructing him to order all dukes, barons and lords in the province not to admit or harbour killers, rebels or criminals in their lands or dominions on pain of having all their privileges and immunities revoked.[52] The letter then catalogued some of the horrors that these people had perpetrated. Perhaps the timing of these letters in mid-September suggests that the crime rate rose in the hot summer months and that a report of it was sitting in the Vatican when the pope and cardinals returned from their summer retreat. From a letter of Goro Gheri to Lorenzo de' Medici, duke of Urbino, of 27 November 1516, it emerges that the governorship of the Campagna should not really have been given to a cardinal but to a lesser prelate or to a nobleman.[53] The office must have been bestowed in this case as a special mark of favour. A couple of years later, after Soderini had fled to Fondi, Leo X was obviously considering giving the governorship to Simone Tornabuoni – a member of the Florentine ruling class, a nobleman and a relation of the pope – as a mark of disfavour to Soderini. The latter had protested at this, saying that if Tornabuoni were given the office, he would be an absentee governor and that the province would go to ruin.[54] As Soderini was in enforced exile just

---

[51] AV, Arm. xl, 2, 285r. For more information on the province see P. Partner, *The lands of St Peter* (London, 1972), pp. 136, 274, 426.

[52] AV, Arm. xxxix, 31, 130v–131r.

[53] ASF, Il minutario di Goro Gheri, I, 148r and v. The exact differences in function, rank and status between cardinal legates, nuncios and governors are not clear at this stage.

[54] ASF, MAP, xliii, 25, 16 January 1518, Rome, Benedetto Buondelmonti to Gheri.

outside the province, over the boundary at Fondi, in the kingdom of Naples (it had been suggested at the time of his flight that he went initially to Campagna because he had a legation there),[55] he was the very opposite of absentee. It is interesting that Soderini should have opposed the appointment on practical, rather than juridical, grounds. The supplier of the information, Benedetto Buondelmonti, wrote that the pope was determined to deprive Soderini, after which no more is heard of the affair.

The only other occasion on which Soderini acquired the title of governor was also in circumstances out of the ordinary. Adrian VI was elected pope in January 1522 and took seven months to arrive in Rome. During this unusually long popeless period in Rome, a series of stand-ins, called cardinal governors of the city, was arranged, according to ancient law, one from each of the three orders, every month. Soderini must have been appointed to this office at once as he, Accolti and Gonzaga were the three governors at the beginning of February 1522 and he was then re-appointed for a further term,[56] perhaps because two of the three governors appointed in February, Grimani and Cibo, were ill.[57] In March Grimani, de Grassis and Cesi were in office.[58] Soderini was in this position again at the beginning of May, having presumably been re-elected in April for another period. The three governors from 13 May onwards were Farnese, Vendôme and Salviati.[59] It is probable that during their term of office these cardinals were expected to live in the Vatican which might be a reason for reports from Juan Manuel, the imperial ambassador in Rome, that they were plundering the palace.[60] They must, too, have had access to the papal treasury which might provide yet another explanation for Adrian's remark that he had found the church exhausted and poor whereas other pontiffs had found it rich.[61] Juan Manuel seemed to have difficulty distinguishing between the French party and the ruling party, but this might have been a common difficulty as Rome during these seven months, but especially at the beginning, was united by anti-imperial and anti-papal feelings. Most people dreaded the possibility that Adrian might stay in Spain and start another schism on the pattern of Avignon, and analysed his every move for possible indications of this. For example, concern was expressed

[55] *Il diario di Leone X di Paride de Grassi*, ed. M. Armellini (Rome, 1884), p. 50.
[56] Sanuto, *I diarii*, XXXII, 443.   [57] *Ibid.*, XXXII, 475.   [58] *Ibid.*, XXXIII, 57.
[59] *Lettere di Baldassare Castiglione*, I, p. 31, Castiglione to marquis Federico Gonzaga on 13 May 1522.
[60] *Calendar of letters … between England and Spain*, II, p. 401, 4 February 1522.
[61] See R. McNally, 'Pope Adrian VI (1522–1523) and church reform', *Archivum historiae pontificiae*, 7 (1969), p. 284.

because he did not immediately adopt a papal name.[62] The French would have been the alternative party or papacy had Adrian remained in Spain.

On 23 February Juan Manuel reported that the cardinal of Volterra, who was ill in bed, commanded cardinal Colonna, and Colonna commanded the cardinals Accolti and Jacobazzi.[63] On 12 March he reported that the cardinal governors of Rome had done their best to plunder the pope. The 'captain' of them all was cardinal Accolti, who was always of the same mind as cardinal Colonna. The other governors were cardinals Flisco and Orsini. But, the ambassador insisted, the cardinal of Volterra was the master of them all, and, as he was ill, he governed the church from his bed.[64] Exactly what the position of cardinal governor entailed is not clear, although it probably related more to temporal than to church affairs;[65] but the governors lacked juridical and legislative powers. On the other hand, they must have exercised considerable influence in the matter of minor curial appointments and the day-to-day running of the bureaucracy. How the cardinal governors were chosen is also not known, although yet again one representative was picked from each of the three orders of the cardinalate.[66] Nor is it plain whether Soderini's appointment as the first cardinal governor to represent the cardinal bishops (he had been appointed to the cardinal bishopric of Sabina in October 1511)[67] was a real indication of his status, but it does seem likely. Carvajal, who was his senior, seems to have faded out at this point although it ought to have been his moment of glory. The title of 'dean' (that is, senior member) of the Sacred College did not, however, carry with it increased power, only enhanced prestige and a greater ceremonial role. When Carvajal died on 16 December 1523, Soderini assumed the title in consistory[68] and kept it only for the few months until his death, but his office was always recorded both in official records and in private documents.[69]

Soderini was but little employed as a legate, perhaps because, having served so much as a diplomat, he preferred to stay near the centre of power. Alternatively, he may have been passed over as untrustworthy. He was nearly sent as legate to Ferrara in December 1504 when duke Ercole was very ill, because the pope feared Venetian interference. The Ferrarese ambassador was opposed to the appointment but the duke

[62] Pastor, History of the popes, IX, pp. 53–4.
[63] Calendar of letters … between England and Spain, II, p. 404. [64] Ibid., II, p. 408.
[65] See Prodi, The papal prince, p. 90. [66] The catholic encyclopedia, III, p. 338.
[67] See below, p. 183. [68] Moroni, Dizionario, LXVII, p. 149.
[69] See, for example, BV, Barb. lat. 3552, 43r.

recovered and no legate was sent.[70] In June 1504 there was a rumour that Soderini and cardinal Francesco Alidosi had been sent as legates to the king of France but it proved to be false.[71] Although it was only a ploy to stop him visiting Florence[72] (and possibly to stop him seeing the French king), he was appointed legate in Rome on 5 November 1515[73] when the pope and the rest of the cardinals went to Bologna to meet Francis I. This meant that he was in control of Rome until the pope returned on 5 February, three months later.[74] It is striking that Rome was accorded a legate during the pope's absence, thus highlighting the multiplicity of Rome's roles in this period. Sometimes the city is seen as being synonymous with the papacy, and at others it is accorded similar status to other cities in the papal states.

One contemporary diarist, Cornelius de Fine, remarked what an excellent administrator Soderini was,[75] but there is some evidence of irregularity or, at least, partiality during his stewardship. On 26 December the pope wrote to Soderini[76] forbidding anyone from being ordained priest (*presbiter*) unless his claims had first been examined by Gabriele Fosco, the Augustinian archbishop of Durazzo. He also commanded that no one be raised to any dignity or status whatsoever except by Gianfrancesco Salvini, bishop of Viesti, the candidate's claims having first been examined by Fosco once again. Although a general prohibition against anyone else (except the bishop of Orange, Guglielmo Pelissier) being involved in conferring ecclesiastical status, on pain of excommunication and a fine, had already been stated, one person was singled out for particular, emphatic proscription – Geremia Contugi, then the bishop of Krania in Thessaly. Contugi was from Volterra and was a well-known satellite of Soderini.[77] His appearance here can only mean that Soderini was involved in a shady transaction of allowing unqualified candidates, presumably for a fee, to become priests. The other possibility, that Soderini was allowing the ordination of great numbers of priests in order to boost the ministry, is extremely unlikely. Unfortunately, no other letter from the pope to Soderini

---

[70] See Giustinian, *Dispacci*, III, p. 330 and Sanuto, *I diarii*, VI, 114.

[71] Sanuto, *I diarii*, VIII, 447, 23 June 1509.

[72] This was obvious even to contemporaries. See BV, Ottob. lat. 2137, f.23, and Paris, Bibliothèque Nationale, Fonds latins 12552, 97v, the diary of Cornelius de Fine, who states that Soderini was left behind because he was of a contrary faction to the Medici.   [73] AV, Fondo concist., Acta miscell. 54, 42r.

[74] Armellini, *Il diario*, p. 29

[75] BV, Ottob. lat. 2137, f.24 and Paris, Bibliothèque Nationale, Fonds latins 12552, 97v.

[76] The letter is in AV, Arm. XXXIX, 31, 167v–168v.

[77] For example, he was one of Soderini's bishop stand-ins in Vicenza. See G. Mantese, *Memorie storiche della chiesa vicentina*, III, II (Vicenza, 1964), p. 181.

issuing instructions like this has been found. While he was legate, Soderini lived in the Vatican and not in his own palace,[78] and in as much as anyone else could stand in for the pope, he was the pope's substitute

Finally, there was a suggestion that Adrian wanted to send Soderini as a legate to France in March 1523[79] but he never did. It is doubtful whether Soderini could have made the journey at his age. As an appendix to this list it should perhaps be added that in the interval between the election of Adrian and his arrival in Rome, a lottery was held and the cardinals were assigned cities to administer, and Soderini was assigned Ravenna,[80] but this was only a temporary measure.

Soderini was a canon of St Peter's for a short period from 20 January 1504 to 6 April 1505.[81] As such he counselled the pope about the government of the first church in christendom. In reality, however, although there were meetings in the basilica of SS. Apostoli,[82] the position was an important sinecure. Another task of his was that of protector of orders. This may have been a short-cut to the acquisition of certain abbeys and monasteries, and, in addition, it generated other rewards such as being the dedicatee of certain learned works. Julius II made Soderini protector of the Camaldolese order of Benedictine monks by a *motu proprio* on 20 November 1503. Pietro Delfino, the general of this order, wrote to Soderini that he could not think of anyone dearer or more pleasing who could have been appointed,[83] and the next day wrote to Julius in the same vein.[84] In theory, the cardinal was expected to facilitate matters for the order wherever possible and to present its case at the curia whenever necessary. The rationale behind the appointment of cardinals as protectors of orders, just as behind the nomination of others in the college as national protectors, was that the curia was the centre of power, and institutions and countries, however powerful themselves, needed officials within the inner sanctum to ensure that their interests were represented. Cardinals who were protectors of orders could also pull rank on local bishops and local rulers

---

[78] BV, Barb. lat. 3552, 25v.   [79] Sanuto, *I diarii*, XXXIV, 21.

[80] See BV, MSS Chigiani 1545, Tizio, 'Historiarum Senensium', IX, 91v, and C. Spreti, *Memorie intorno i domini e governi della città di Ravenna* (Faenza, 1822), pp. 49–50.

[81] BV, Arch. cap. S. P., Arm. 15, Decreti I, 142r and BV, Vat. lat. 6437 (part II), 298v.

[82] BV, Vat. lat. 6437 (part II), 298r.

[83] P. Delphino, *Petri Delphini generalis Camaldulensis epistolarum volumen* (Venice, 1524), VII, no. 80. It is also published by S. Fabbruccio, 'Elogia clarissimorum virorum qui ab anno primae solemnis instaurationis secundo usque ad MCCCCLXXVIII Pisanae Academiae lucem universae litterarie reipublicae decus addiderunt', in *Raccolta d'opuscoli scientifici e filologici*, ed. A. Calogera, XL (Venice, 1749), pp. 142–3.   [84] Delphino, *Petri Delphini*, VII, no. 82.

who tried to use their authority to intervene in disputes involving the orders. Soderini did, in fact, write to his brother Piero on two occasions in November 1504, interceding on behalf of the monks at Camaldoli, and he stressed that he was constrained to intercede because he was their protector.[85]

The situation was reversed in July 1508 when the Florentine government wrote to Soderini to enlist his help in stabilising the order and in the election of a new general who was either a Florentine citizen or subject, as Delfino was gravely ill and, they thought, about to die.[86] The workload imposed by this office must have been heavy.[87] Soderini's relationship with this order can be charted through Delfino's letters to him (Delfino lived on and last wrote to Soderini in 1523), but unfortunately there is no such easy way to observe his dealings (if any) with the Cistercians. The sole reference to his protectorship is provided by Ignazio Orsolini in a book of 1706 on Florentines who had become popes and cardinals, who wrote that after Pius III's death, Soderini was made protector of both the Camaldolese and the Cistercians by Julius.[88] On 29 November 1513 Leo appointed cardinal Bainbridge protector of the Cistercians for life,[89] so that if Soderini had ever held the office, he must have relinquished it by 1513. Although no official record survives, Soderini was also made protector of the Augustinians, as he revealed in August 1505 in a letter written to Isabella d'Este about some Augustinian nuns whom she had asked cardinals Soderini, Riario and Pallavicini to take under their wing. They were living in part of the church of S. Marco in Mantua, led exemplary lives and had been harassed by certain friars who had now been expelled from Mantua.[90] Soderini replied encouragingly; he had spoken to the pope about the nuns and had found him well-disposed towards them; he himself, as protector of their order, would not be found wanting in any scheme to promote their benefit and welfare.[91]

One of the most straightforward ways in which Soderini fulfilled his consiliar function as a cardinal was by attending the Fifth Lateran Council. He had been in serious trouble for his supposed involvement with the Council of Pisa in 1511, but this was at a political, not a

[85] BNF, GC 29 (109), 10 November (3422766) and 16 November (3422769).
[86] ASF, Sig., Miss. 1a Cancelleria 56, 88v, 16 July 1508.
[87] See BV, Vat. lat. 13698, 1r for one example of the level of involvement expected of Soderini by the pope.
[88] I. Ursulini, *Inclytae nationis Florentinae familiae suprema romani pontificatus ac sacra cardinalatus dignitate illustratae*, pp. 279–80.
[89] Chambers, *Cardinal Bainbridge*, p. 98.
[90] ASMa, AG, b.2994, lib. 18, 26v–27r, 12 August 1505.
[91] ASMa, AG, b.856, 31 August 1505.

doctrinal, level. The Lateran Council had been summoned to quash the authenticity of the Pisan Council but with little commitment, on the part of the pope, to the reform of the church which was supposed to be the main reason for its formation. The Lateran Council opened on 2 May 1512 but without Soderini, who was unwell.[92] He also missed the second session, but then attended sessions three to ten (two sessions were in 1512, five in 1513, one in 1514 and one in 1515).[93] There are only two pieces of information about Soderini and this council: the first that he celebrated mass at the opening of the sixth session on 27 April 1513,[94] and the second that he was deputed to sit on the commission to enquire into the restoration of peace and the healing of the breach with France mentioned above. Three such committees had been set up by the Lateran Council. This was the first, the second was concerned with curial reform and the third with the Pragmatic Sanction and questions of faith.[95] As Soderini did not return to Rome for this committee, someone else was drafted in his place. There is no clue to his views on any of the major issues nor is there any record of anything other than passive attendance.

Much of the rest of Soderini's time was taken up with liturgical and ceremonial occasions. The ritual practices of the pope and cardinals served to mark the passage of the christian year, to welcome new arrivals and to honour the departures of those with ecclesiastical weight. Additional tasks sometimes arose because of extraordinary events, such as the building of the new St Peter's. The foundation stone of this building was laid on 18 April 1506 by Julius II. Soderini, as all the diarists noted, celebrated the mass in old St Peter's which preceded the ceremony. The pope then descended to the foundations, the way strewn with planks and beams. On the way, there was a minor hitch when a water pipe burst, which the workmen tried to stem with pumps and buckets. After this moment of panic, when the threat of a landslide had passed, Julius continued down, accompanied only by three deacons who had been in attendance on the cardinals, buried twelve medals in a pot and laid the foundation stone over it.[96] This rather strange episode eventually ended without disaster. Ordinary events included the celebration of a great number of saints' feast days, with mass usually being conducted at the church of the saint. For example, on the feast of

[92] BL, Add. MSS 8442, 192v and 193r.
[93] N. Minnich, 'The participants at the Fifth Lateran Council', *Archivum historiae pontificiae*, 12 (1974), pp. 180, 194.   [94] BL, Add. MSS 8443, 36v.
[95] Pastor, *History of the popes*, VIII, p. 387.
[96] This is taken from accounts in Burchard, 'Liber notarum', II, p. 509 and de Grassis, BL, Add. MSS 8440, 336r–v. R. Lanciani, *Storia degli scavi di Roma* (Rome, 1902), I, pp. 142–3 based his version on de Grassis.

St Anthony, 17 January 1504, the pope and twenty-two cardinals rode to the church of S. Antonio; on the feast of St Gregory, 12 March 1504, the pope and twenty-five cardinals rode to the church of S. Gregorio; and on the feast of St Mark, 25 April 1504, the pope and twenty-five cardinals rode to the church of S. Marco.[97] Soderini was present on all these occasions and such examples could be multiplied many times. On 1 May 1509, the feast of St Philip and St James, the pope and sacred college went as usual to celebrate at SS. Apostoli, but Soderini, whose titular church it was, was ill and therefore not present although everything had been very satisfactorily prepared. The pope had been intending to visit Soderini after the meal in his palace next to the church, but changed his mind upon learning of the gravity of his illness.[98]

Soderini not only had to prepare and partake of mass, he had to say and sing it. He was good at this, at least in the opinion of Paris de Grassis, who was a hard taskmaster.[99] Only once did de Grassis criticise him either on his appearance or on his performance. On 8 May 1510, at vespers the night before Ascension Day, Soderini was suffering a little in the head, it was rumoured from venereal disease, and was wearing a black silk cap or bonnet under his red beret. De Grassis noticed this and was horrified, instructing him to keep his hood over his head in such a way that the bonnet could not be seen, and muttering that the least he could have done was to wear a red one. Finally, it was agreed both that he would keep his hood up and that he would not approach the pope.[100] Some masses carried more prestige than others and it is possible that the cardinals who were good performers were allowed to conduct these. Soderini applied for a licence to conduct mass at the high altar of SS. Apostoli two years running on Ascension Day 1514 and 1515[101] and, in fact, celebrated vespers on the eve of these days too.[102] It is not clear why he applied for this as he no longer had any connection with the church, having been promoted to a cardinal bishopric at another church, but it could be because he was still living in the palace next to the basilica.[103] Sometimes a pope specified which cardinal he wanted to give which

---

[97] See Burchard, 'Liber notarum', II, pp. 431–2, 439–40, 448.

[98] BL, Add. MSS 8441, 295v–296r.

[99] See Frati, Le due spedizioni, p. 219, 15 December 1510, mass was celebrated by Soderini 'bene solito suo more' and p. 270, 19 April 1511, the Saturday of Holy Week, 'Cardinalis Vulterranus, ut dicunt, laudabiliter celebravit suo consueto more' and BL, Add. MSS 8443, 206r, 31 December 1516, vespers on the eve of the circumcision, Soderini 'celebravit more solito'.

[100] BL, Add. MSS 8442, 44r and v.

[101] J. Hergenroether, Leonis X pontificis maximi regesta (Freiberg im Breisgau, 1884–1891), I, p. 565 and II, p. 92.   [102] BL, Add. MSS 8443, 115v and 133r.

[103] See below, pp. 212–13.

mass,[104] but mainly a kind of rota existed with variations for special services which had routines of their own. One instance of this was when Soderini, on 1 October 1523, having just been released from Castel Sant' Angelo, said the opening mass of the conclave, which was habitually celebrated by the second cardinal bishop, that is the bishop of Palestrina.[105]

As the average age in the college of cardinals was high, there were quite often funeral masses of cardinals to attend and funeral[106] and memorial masses for the dead popes to attend as well, not to mention those of lesser curia officials and other distinguished persons. For instance, on 26 February 1505 Soderini was one of twenty-five cardinals who attended a funeral mass for queen Isabella of Castile which took place in the chapel of the Spanish hospice. It was a grand affair with the Spanish ambassador and the household all dressed in black, many other ambassadors, the duke of Urbino, and the prince of Salerno present, and included a mass celebrated by the patriarch of Alexandria with singing by the papal singers.[107]

There was much ceremonial involved in the creation of new cardinals, and even in the consecration of new bishops. Soderini was the consecrator of Achille de Grassis, Paris's brother, on 19 April 1506, when he was made bishop of Città di Castello in the church of S. Lorenzo in Lucina. Two other cardinals, Giorgio de Costa, the cardinal of Portugal, and Robert Guibé, and many bishops were present.[108] Ceremony was used too on relatively minor occasions such as when Julius gave the papal master of ceremonies, Jacob Burchard, permission to use his coat-of-arms and to take the name of della Rovere, in the presence of Soderini in Castel Sant'Angelo on 3 December 1505.[109]

The translation of saints' bones also called forth great ceremonial. Soderini was involved in two ventures of this kind; one succeeded, the other was overtaken by political events. The successful one took place on 2 April 1511, when Soderini, as protector of the Camaldolese monks, presided over the translation of the bones of Sant'Apollinare from one site to another within the Camaldolese abbey of Classe[110] near Ravenna, which belonged to the congregation of S. Michele da Murano. It was he

104 For example, Julius insisted that Soderini celebrate the mass of the Virgin on 15 November 1506 in the church of S. Petronio in Bologna. See Frati, *Le due spedizioni*, p. 98, and the description by Francesco Pepi in ASF, Dieci, Resp. 87, 267r.

105 Sanuto, *I diarii*, XXXV, 55.

106 See, for example, Burchard, 'Liber notarum', II, pp. 394–7.

107 *Ibid.*, II, pp. 471–2.   108 BL, Add. MSS 8440, 338r.

109 Burchard, 'Liber notarum', II, p. 499.

110 G. Fabri, *Le sacre memorie di Ravenna antica* (Venice, 1664), I, p. 96 and G. Fabri, *Effemeride sagra et istorica di Ravenna antica* (Ravenna, 1675), pp. 81–2.

who had obtained the permission to do this at the behest of the abbot, Andrea Secchini. After a mass and a procession, the bones, found as in the previous translation of 1487 floating in water, were transferred to a restored Greek sarcophagus which then stayed in the crypt. The whole ceremony is minutely described by Paolo Orlandini in a letter written to Paolo da Lodi some five years later on 10 September 1516.[111] This translation was the occasion of a detailed description of the basilica of Sant'Apollinare by the Camaldolese monk, Vitale Acquedotti, who dedicated the work to Soderini on the same day, 2 April.[112] The piece was unusual for its time.[113] It was possibly as a result of this first success that Soderini may have had the idea of building a subterranean chapel for the body of S. Zanobi, the patron saint of Florence, whose relics had been moved to the cathedral of S. Maria del Fiore in April 1459;[114] unfortunately, Piero Soderini was deposed before anything could come of this.[115] Had Soderini thought of an underground chapel because of what he had seen at Rome?

Other than ceremonial there were also social duties, and sometimes the two became almost indistinguishable. For example, there were frequent marriages between the relatives of the popes and cardinals, and the Roman barons. A typically complicated marriage alliance was contracted on 9 November 1505 between Niccolò Franciotti della Rovere, a nephew of Julius through his sister who had been married to Gianfrancesco Franciotti, a brother of cardinal Galeotto Franciotti, on one side, and on the other Laura, the daughter of Orsino Orsini and his wife Giulia, who was a sister of cardinal Farnese. Soderini and six or seven other cardinals were present at this *sponsalia* as was the pope.[116] Such marriage arrangements amounted to political alliances, which were essential for the maintenance of some unity between the various power-hungry interests gathered in Rome; alliances were used to defuse potentially explosive situations and contain over-aggressive families by allying them with their potential rivals. Sometimes the marriage partners were of a wider Italian, rather than exclusively Roman, status.

---

[111] This is published in *Annales Camaldulenses ordinis Sancti Benedicti*, ed. J. Mittarelli and A. Costadoni, VII (Venice, 1762), pp. 407–11.

[112] The manuscript is in Ravenna, Biblioteca Classense. See M. Mazzotti, *La basilica di Sant'Apollinare in Classe* (Città del Vaticano, 1954), p. 241.

[113] R. Weiss, *The renaissance discovery of classical antiquity* (Oxford, 1969), pp. 123–4 places the work in a tradition of comparable detailed architectural descriptions.

[114] See F. Del Migliore, *Firenze città nobilissima illustrata* (Florence, 1684), p. 40 and A. Cocchi, *Les anciens reliquaires de Santa Maria del Fiore et de S. Giovanni de Florence* (Florence, 1903), p. 16.

[115] The only source for this is Richa, *Notizie*, VI, p. 139.

[116] BL, Add. MSS 8440, 282v and 283r.

On 2 March 1505 the marriage contract between Francesco Maria della Rovere, nephew of Julius II and prefect of the city, and Leonora, the daughter of the marquis of Mantua, was notarised by Camillo Benimbene, and almost all the resident Italian cardinals, including Soderini, were in attendance.[117]

The majority of these marriages were conducted with great pomp and splendour, from the signing of the contract to the wedding itself. Large sums of money were involved and the occasion prompted great festivities. Yet another della Rovere marriage illustrates this well. On 25 July 1506 marriage was contracted between Marcantonio Colonna, who was represented by his proxy, Prospero, and Lucrezia della Rovere, the daughter of Luchina, the sister of the pope, she herself being the sister of cardinal Galeotto Franciotti. The pope and fourteen or fifteen cardinals, including Soderini, were present.[118] The wedding proper took place on 2 January 1508 and many of the same people attended it.[119] Another half-ceremonial, half-social duty was to act as the executor of a fellow cardinal's will. For example, Soderini, Giorgio de Costa, Giovanni di S. Giorgio and Flisco were the executors of Antoniotto Pallavicino's will after his death on 10 September 1507,[120] and the executors of Soderini's will of 1524 were Flisco, Farnese and Scaramuccio Trivulzio.[121]

Meanwhile, Soderini's main social round consisted of dinners and parties with other cardinals, some members of the curia and some of the indigenous upper classes of Rome. A cardinal's life revolved around friends and colleagues who were also attendant at the papal court; other social contacts, such as political acquaintances or personal friends and relatives, were less in the public eye and on a different footing. The extensive nature of a cardinal's duties necessitated that nearly all a cardinal's public time was spent in company with other cardinals who thus became the most important single source of patronage and help of all sorts. However, Rome was not merely the centre of the ecclesiastical hierarchy but also the centre of an international political system. This meant that any ambitious cardinal had to seek links with foreign powers if he wished to rise to a position of ecclesiastical eminence. Such a position could only be sustained by pluralism on a grand scale, and sufficient bishoprics and benefices could normally only be accumulated through the influence of foreign powers or the pope. This involved something of a vicious circle, since the necessary links with these rulers

---

[117] Burchard, 'Liber notarum', II, p. 473.   [118] BL, Add. MSS 8440, 379v–38or.

[119] A. Ademollo, *Alessandro VI, Giulio II e Leone X nel carnevale di Roma* (Florence, 1886), pp. 30–1.   [120] BL, Add. MSS 8441, 157v.

[121] See Lowe, 'Francesco Soderini', appendix 4, p. 355.

were most easily established by cardinals who already enjoyed large numbers of benefices and who were, therefore, rich enough to be considered important. How Soderini used his multiple political connections both in and outside the college to augment and exploit his collection of bishoprics and benefices for financial and patronage purposes will be analysed next.

CHAPTER 15

SODERINI'S ECCLESIASTICAL CAREER: THE ACCUMULATION AND DEPLOYMENT OF BISHOPRICS AND BENEFICES

Soderini's ecclesiastical career followed the outline of his political career; at various stages Lorenzo de' Medici, Soderini's brother, Piero, and the king of France were all influential in his acquisition of bishoprics. Soderini's first preferment in the church was entirely the result of political patronage. There is no record of either Soderini or his family considering an ecclesiastical career for him before he was unexpectedly offered the bishopric of Volterra in early 1478. He had taken no orders and, indeed, was not to do so until 1486.[1] On the contrary, as has been seen, he had acquired a foothold on the bottom rung of the university ladder as a teacher of civil law and could have been expected to ascend it in the usual fashion. The promise of this bishopric for Soderini by Lorenzo de' Medici, probably as a reward for services rendered to him by Tommaso, Soderini's father, provided an alternative career. Antonio degli Agli, the former bishop, had died in the previous year of 1477 and by 5 February 1478 Lorenzo must have felt himself able to guarantee that Soderini would be given the bishopric; on that day Marco Strozzi, who worked for Soderini, was despatched to Pisa to find a substitute teacher,[2] and the change in career was set in motion. Marco Strozzi stated that the decision to switch from law to the church had been taken by Tommaso Soderini, Lorenzo[3] and 'other Mediceans', and that, on 19 January, he and Soderini had arrived in Florence to discuss these matters. Certainly, Lorenzo's support for the scheme was essential and is acknowledged both by the family and by outsiders. Tommaso Soderini wrote to Lorenzo on 19 February 1478 from Milan 'I have heard what you have done for my son both here and

---

[1] See above, p. 14.   [2] ASF, C. Strozz., CXXXVIII, 47r.
[3] On the crucial relationship between Tommaso and Lorenzo at this point, see Clarke, 'A biography', pp. 272–5.

171

at Rome in respect of Volterra',[4] and Filippo Strozzi wrote to his brother Lorenzo in Naples, on 16 February, that they had given the bishopric of Volterra to Francesco Soderini, and that through the intercession of Lorenzo it would be a fine acquisition for the whole Soderini family.[5]

Meanwhile, in the official letter written by the *Signoria* to the Florentine ambassador in Rome, Donato Acciaiuoli, on 9 February, it is quite clearly stated that when the opinions of the principal members of the government had been canvassed over the question of the next bishop, they had unanimously suggested Soderini.[6] The apparently low profile kept by Lorenzo on matters such as these was just an expression of his tactics and temperament, not a statement of affairs. Filippo Strozzi, in Florence on 16 February, wrote that Soderini had the bishopric, although it was not announced in Rome until 11 March, and in the intervening few weeks at least one setback occurred, to which the *Signoria* responded by declaring that they would accept no other candidate.[7] Lorenzo must have felt in control of the situation even though he was wrong to do so – Sixtus IV had already proved his unreliability by promoting Francesco Salviati to the archbishopric of Pisa in 1477, contrary to Medici wishes.[8] Perhaps on account of this, Lorenzo was prepared to make a special effort, even enlisting help from the Milanese, who were pro-Soderini because of their relationship with Tommaso, in order to obtain a tame bishop for the Florentine territories.[9] Affairs could be controlled fairly easily at the centre of the Medicean political system, that is, at Florence, but in the subject cities at the periphery, clerical clients were necessary to execute minor ecclesiastical manoeuvres essential for the maintenance of patronage networks.

Individual states had long felt that their own men should be preferred to their own bishoprics, and a sense of this is gained from the letter of 9 February to Acciaiuoli; the *Signoria* had written on previous occasions

---

[4] ASF, MAP, xxxiv, 56: 'I'o'nteso l'opere tue per 'l mio figliolo costì et a Roma per Volterra.'

[5] ASF, C. Strozz., ccxxx, 252r: 'Anno dato il vescovado di Volterra a messere Francesco di messere Tommaso Soderini, e per interciesione di Lorenzo fa messere e figliuoli bello acquisto.'   [6] ASF, Sig., Leg. e com. 19, 162r.

[7] *Ibid.*, 163r, letter to Donato Acciaiuoli of 5 March.

[8] Similar difficulties later dogged Piero Soderini in the struggle over the archbishopric of Florence in 1508, when he was able to block Guglielmo Capponi's application only to be forced to accept that of Cosimo Pazzi, another candidate backed by cardinal de' Medici. See below, p. 177 and Cooper, 'Piero Soderini', p. 304.

[9] D. Hay, *The church in Italy in the fifteenth century* (Cambridge, 1977), p. 16 wrote that 'both republican and later princely Florence was more anxious to secure obedient bishops in the *dominio* than in the capital itself'. See also Bizzocchi, *Chiesa e potere*, p. 217.

that because Volterra was of such importance, Acciaiuoli should prepare the pope and inform him that he was not to announce a successor to degli Agli who had not been proposed by the Florentines.[10] After the pope's compliance, they write to thank him in a similarly high-handed vein.[11] Lorenzo had successfully secured his objective and Soderini had acquired a benefice worth probably between 800 and 1,000 florins per annum (its tax was 500 florins per annum). As he was below the prescribed age of twenty-seven, he only held the administration of the bishopric until he reached the requisite age. Non-fulfilment of the technical requirements of the position would have been a drawback in cases of this nature, but could have been overridden or compensated for by backing from first-rate patrons. Soderini acknowledged his debt to his Medici kinsman in a letter written from Volterra on 20 June 1478, in which he addressed Lorenzo as his unique benefactor and claimed that nothing could give him more pleasure than the knowledge that he and his family were loved by Lorenzo.[12]

Although it seems certain that it was Lorenzo and the Milanese who had obtained the bishopric for Soderini, they had been forced to work through the usual channels. Soderini was related in consistory by cardinal Jacopo Ammannati and the pope reserved a pension of 100 florins from the bishopric.[13] The Milanese government had enlisted the help of Girolamo Riario and various cardinals (Ammannati, Stefano Nardini, the archbishop of Milan, and Giovanni Arcimboldi, the bishop of Novara),[14] while the Florentine government was indebted to an even larger group which included Girolamo Riario, Giovanni Tornabuoni (Soderini's uncle), and the cardinals Giuliano della Rovere, Giovanni Arcimboldi, Stefano Nardini, Antonio Jacopo Venier and Giovanbattista Zeno.[15]

Hard on the heels of this, there was an attempt to provide Soderini with another benefice, the archbishopric of Pisa (vacant after the death of Francesco Salviati in the Pazzi conspiracy), which also had an annual income of 800 florins a year. The suggestion was mooted by Tommaso Soderini and the Milanese government at the beginning of May,[16] but was stamped on by Lorenzo who had already proposed his own candidate, Gentile Becchi, the bishop of Arezzo, an older Medicean.

---

[10] ASF, Sig., Leg. e com. 19, 162r.
[11] *Ibid.*, 164r, letter to Acciaiuoli of 14 March 1478.
[12] ASF, MAP, xxxvi, 802.   [13] AV, Fondo camerale, Obl. et sol. 82, 110r.
[14] A. Natale, *Acta in consilio secreto*, I (Milan, 1963), p. 231, 9 March 1478.
[15] Del Piazzo, *Protocolli*, pp. 38, 41, 10 February and 7 March.
[16] Natale, *Acta in consilio secreto*, II, pp. 54, 76, 30 April and 9 May 1478.

Lorenzo was intent on recovering the face he had lost in the contest for the same bishopric four years earlier.[17] Another obstacle to Soderini's election was technical: Soderini's lack of qualifications. He was not the right age, and he had not taken minor or major orders. There had been difficulty enough in procuring a bishopric, and the procuring of an archbishopric was held to be even more doubtful and difficult.[18] The rulers of Milan then wrote directly to Lorenzo on 8 May, intimating that they understood that he was backing Becchi but still recommending Soderini. Becchi was 'a good man and one of Lorenzo's clients',[19] but Soderini was 'well-educated and virtually of the same blood as Lorenzo';[20] they felt that because he was a member of the Florentine ruling class, with a worthy father and related to Lorenzo, he would be a more popular choice among the people. He would also enable Lorenzo to gratify at one stroke private and public obligations, and would help to regain whatever honour Lorenzo may possibly have lost on the promotion of Salviati.[21]

The letter illustrates well the nature and extent of Lorenzo's patronage in these matters, but in this instance Lorenzo did not need to favour Soderini as he had already provided for him; nor was his own candidate successful. Sixtus was angry with Lorenzo over the repression of the Pazzi conspiracy, and was determined not to allow him to have his way with Pisa. In one sense, though, the Milanese were right, because Lorenzo would have been expected to recognise the claims of a blood-tie above that of adopted allegiance. His fear of the formation of an alternative power base can be measured in his ambiguity towards Tommaso Soderini and his increasingly distinguished family. Lorenzo had no wish to promote the interests of a nephew to the possible detriment of the interests of his son or sons. All this is made far more explicit in the run-up to the creation of cardinals in the late 1480s, when both Becchi and Soderini were candidates once again. Lorenzo initially preferred Becchi to Soderini, and then switched his support to his own son, Giovanni, whose candidature was successful. Later, another of

---

[17] This information is contained in a letter of 3 May from the Milanese ambassador in Florence, Filippo Sacromoro, in ASMi, SPE 294, 35r. See also Clarke, 'A biography', p. 275.

[18] ASMi, SPE 294, 35r: 'Per el vescho di Vulterra pareva da dubitare anco che non fusse reuscibile atteso la difficultà che se hebbe a farlo vesco, et non se pote obtenire ad pieno, nisi condictionaliter; molto più pareva de dubitare in farlo arcivescovo.'

[19] ASF, MAP, xlvii, 265: 'valenthomo et vostra creatura'.

[20] Ibid.: 'litterato et quasi del sangue vostro'.

[21] Ibid. A draft of this letter exists in ASMi, SPE 294, 53r.

Lorenzo's sons, Piero, was fearful lest Soderini's appointment as cardinal should create a rival Florentine cardinal to Giovanni.[22]

Volterra was the only bishopric that Soderini obtained before he was made a cardinal in 1503, and he continued to hold it until 1509 when he resigned it in favour of one of his nephews, Giuliano di Paolantonio, the ecclesiastical member of the family in the next generation. Giuliano became administrator of the bishopric (again because he was too young and had to wait until he was twenty-seven to obtain the title in full) on 23 May 1509. Marco Strozzi wrote to his uncle in Ferrara that Soderini had been ill, so Tommaso and messer Giuliano had gone to see him with the result that Giuliano had been made bishop and had been given other benefices, but with Soderini reserving their incomes.[23] This was a very common practice; Soderini, who was in no need of status, passed that part of the benefice on to Giuliano, but held on to the money.[24] Between 1503 and 1509 Soderini had, in fact, had the administration of two other bishoprics. As no one was supposed to have more than one bishopric, although many cardinals and high-ranking prelates did so, the subsequent bishoprics were held *in administrationem*, just as other abbeys could be held *in commendam*.[25] The reasoning was that a bishop could not be resident in more than one place, and that a grant of a bishopric *in administrationem* or an abbey *in commendam* carried with it a licence to be non-resident. However, since many bishops with only one bishopric were absentees and passed on their spiritual duties to others, this was at times an unnecessary distinction.

The first of the other bishoprics that he obtained (in 1504) was Cortona, also in Florentine territory, with a revenue of 400 florins per annum. The Florentine government, headed by Piero Soderini, had proposed their own candidate Antinori who, unfortunately, died before obtaining the benefice. As controversy then broke out at the papal court about it, the pope, not knowing whom else Florence would choose, thought that he would play safe and gave it to Francesco Soderini in a consistory of 6 March 1504.[26] However, Soderini soon ceased to be bishop[27] and Guglielmo Capponi was appointed on 25 May 1505. Soderini must have kept the right of regress because, on 15 November 1521, with the pope as proposer, Soderini resigned the church of

[22] See Picotti, *La giovinezza*, pp. 181–2, 213, 420–1, 488–9.
[23] ASF, C. Strozz., III, 134, 160r and v, undated.
[24] See A. Clergeac, *La curie et les bénéficiers consistoriaux* (Paris, 1911), pp. 49–50.
[25] *Ibid.*, p. 45 and Hay, *The church*, p. 18.
[26] ASF, Sig., Resp. 27, 44r, from Francesco Cappello in Rome.
[27] There are few traces of his episcopate. His arms in the *sala* of the palazzo del vescovo in Cortona are wrongly dated 1503. See also Rome, Arch. Sod., I, 323r.

Cortona (which was then given to Silvio Passerini, cardinal of S. Lorenzo in Lucina), reserving for himself a pension of 200 ducats and the continuation of the right of regress.[28] Regress was the facility kept by a prelate who ceded his benefice, to retake possession of it if his successor failed to pay the agreed pension or resigned the benefice or died.[29] It was an effective way of ensuring that a pension would be paid, and, as a side-effect, it meant that certain benefices remained in the hands of certain families. On Soderini's death all pensions and rights ceased, and, in theory, Passerini could have had the bishopric taken away from him.

The second bishopric that Soderini obtained during this period was that of Saintes in France. It was richer than many Italian bishoprics having an annual tax of 2,000 florins (the revenue is unknown but is likely to have been about 4,000 florins). This time it was not Florentine, but French, patronage that secured it for him. So close was the identification between the interests of the French and the interests of the Soderini, that Soderini came to be viewed in the curia almost as a French cardinal. On 26 June 1506 Julius II wrote to Louis XII thanking him for his recent letter on behalf of Soderini. Julius said that Soderini was dear to him and to the other cardinals, as well as to the king, and asked the king to help Soderini secure possession of Saintes.[30] A similar letter was despatched to Georges d'Amboise, cardinal of Rouen, one of the most powerful men in France and an old acquaintance of Soderini.[31]

Benefices like these were pawns in a political game between the larger powers, a point which is illustrated by the background to Soderini's acquisition of the bishopric of Saintes. Cardinal Ascanio Sforza held many benefices in France and after his death, on 27 May 1505, Louis XII informed Francesco Pandolfini, the Florentine ambassador at court, that he had written to the pope asking for a share of the spoils for Soderini.[32] The pope, too, wrote to Louis, announcing a forthcoming promotion of cardinals favourable to France, and demanding in return that he be allowed to propose candidates to benefices in France in general, and that he should have the say over what happened to Sforza's benefices in France in particular.[33] The result was that after this creation of cardinals, which took place on 1 December 1505, several French bishoprics were

[28] AV, Fondo concist., Acta vicecanc. 2, 203r. In between Capponi and Passerini there had been another bishop, Giovanni Sernino di Cucciati, but nothing is known about his transfer or his agreement with Soderini.   [29] Clergeac, *La curie*, p. 50.

[30] This brief from Paris, Archives Nationales, is published by L. Audiat, 'Évêché et chapitre de Saintes', *Archives historiques de la Saintonge et de l'Aunis*, 10 (1882), p. 81. There is a copy in AV, Arm. xxxix, 22, 526r.

[31] AV, Arm. xxxix, 22, 526r.

[32] See Cooper, 'Piero Soderini', p. 262 and ASF, Dieci, Resp. 83, 183r.

[33] P. Imbart de la Tour, *Les origines de la réforme* (Melun, 1946), II, p. 106.

given to Italians.[34] Soderini was an easy choice because he had the backing of the king of France and had not yet fallen from Julius's favour. Although it was not until the consistory of 27 January 1507 that he agreed to pay the common services on the bishopric,[35] he had been related to the bishopric before August 1506, as is shown by three briefs referring to it which were written by Julius during that month. On the 11th the pope had written to Soderini that he was free to elect whomever he wanted as vicars or other officials to collect the money from the benefices. Probably on the 16th or 17th[36] he wrote giving Soderini the faculty to dispose of benefices belonging to the church of Saintes.[37] On the 17th he wrote to the king of France asking him to ensure that Soderini took and kept possession of the church of Saintes.[38] So although the exact date of his preferment is not known, the time schedule fits in with the letters to and from the king of France. By early 1507 Mario Maffei was in Saintes, reporting back to Soderini on the affairs of his new bishopric.[39]

In late 1507 the question arose over who was to be the successor to Rinaldo Orsini as archbishop of Florence. Orsini wished to resign the archbishopric in an attempt to raise money. Francesco Guicciardini was convinced that Piero Soderini schemed to procure this strategically important archbishopric for his brother Francesco, but that he was foiled by the machinations of cardinal de' Medici.[40] The candidacy of the first aspirant found by Orsini, Guglielmo Capponi, was blocked by Piero Soderini, who managed to mobilise the requisite number of the *Signoria* to write a letter to Julius II opposing this appointment. As a result, Piero Soderini was accused of favouring the appointment of Francesco; to counter this, he maintained that any reform-minded Florentine from a good family would be acceptable to him. Cardinal de' Medici proposed Cosimo de' Pazzi, who was duly elected in February 1508.[41] Whatever Piero's and Francesco's designs (and Guicciardini is the only source for them), on this occasion the Soderini, as a family, were out-manoeuvred by the Medici, probably because of Piero's reluctance to be seen to be behaving in a straightforwardly dynastic fashion. Piero Soderini did not underestimate the importance of

[34] According to M. Edelstein, 'Les origines sociales de l'épiscopat sous Louis XII et François I', *Revue d'histoire moderne et contemporaine*, 24 (1977), p. 241, between 1498 and 1515 eighteen foreign bishops were elected, and held on, to bishoprics in France.

[35] AV, Fondo camerale, Obl. et sol. 88, 102r.

[36] The letter is undated but is preserved between others of these dates.

[37] AV, Arm. xxxix, 24, 412r–413r and 415 r and v.   [38] *Ibid.*, 379v.

[39] BV, Autografi Ferrajoli, Raccolta Visconti, 6630r, 6632r and 6632v.

[40] Guicciardini, *Storie fiorentine*, pp. 305–6 and 319–20.

[41] See Butters, *Governors and government*, pp. 127–9.

procuring this archbishopric for his brother, yet he felt constrained from appearing too publicly to be soliciting it.

Another episcopal appointment, to Assisi, has a chronology which is not altogether clear. There was no mention of Soderini in connection with it until 16 November 1509, when the pope, in a secret consistory, accepted the cession of the administration of the church of Assisi, offered spontaneously by Soderini, and gave it to Zaccaria Contugi of Volterra, reserving the fruits.[42] According to the episcopal historian, Eubel, the previous bishop had been Geremia Contugi, one of Soderini's entourage, so perhaps at some point Soderini had obtained the right of regress.

Soderini had a slack period in the episcopal lottery between 1509 and 1514 (probably because he was out of favour with Julius) but he then carried off a major prize. One of the characteristics of the Italian church system during this period was the practice of exchanging bishoprics: Soderini effected a threefold exchange. On 12 June 1514 Giuliano Soderini, bishop of Volterra, resigned his bishopric to the bishop of Vicenza, Francesco della Rovere; Francesco della Rovere resigned his bishopric of Vicenza to Francesco Soderini, and Francesco Soderini resigned the bishopric of Saintes to Giuliano Soderini. There was much minor reshuffling involved, too, in an attempt to even up the financial settlement because Vicenza had an annual income of 3,000 florins, Saintes probably about 4,000 and Volterra only 800–1,000. Baldassare da Pescia, Leo X's datary, writing of this to Lorenzo de' Medici, commented that the church of Vicenza was worth 4,000 ducats and that Soderini had agreed to give an annual pension of 2,000 ducats and certain other benefices to della Rovere in exchange.[43] Soderini kept a pension from the income of the church of Saintes although it is not known how much.[44]

It seems likely that Soderini initiated this exchange in an attempt to remove his family's concerns from Medicean Tuscany, and by placing a compliant nephew at Saintes, he kept control of his French possession. He was probably attracted to Vicenza because it was outside the Medici sphere of influence and close to friendly powers at, for example, Mantua and Ferrara. But its imperial connections may have caused embarrassment or difficulties later in his life when his French sympathies were perceived as obstacles to imperial favour. On 14 June the pope wrote

---

[42] ASF, C. Strozz., CCXXX, 190r.

[43] ASF, MAP, CVII, 39, Rome, 17 June 1514. He ended: 'Così hanno facto rinvolture et berlingozi cum regressu etc.' I would like to thank Nelson Minnich for this reference.

[44] Eubel, *Hierarchia*, III, 353. See also AV, Reg. vat. 1028, 37v and 1049, 262v.

four briefs about this exchange: to the emperor Maximilian I, to cardinal Matthew Lang, to the papal orator at the court of the emperor and to Raimondo Cardona.[45] He asked the emperor to tell his governor of Vicenza to intercede and help Soderini's procurators obtain the revenues from the church. The other letters were asking for assistance of the same sort.

On 16 June Alessandro Gabbionetta, the archdeacon of Mantua, an acquaintance of Soderini, wrote from Rome to Isabella d'Este asking that Mario Equicola, whom Soderini also knew quite well, be allowed to leave for fifteen days to take possession of the bishopric at Vicenza in Soderini's name.[46] Soderini was obviously worried about the bishopric and wanted to obtain immediate possession. Possibly there was some difficulty about the possession which is why della Rovere was prepared to renounce it in the first place. Soderini may have chosen Equicola because Cardona, whom he knew, was in the area and would have been in a position to offer help. Isabella replied from Pavia on 25 June and was oddly reluctant to release Equicola.[47] This bishopric was to cause Soderini some inconvenience and, finally, was to prove of no use, but the scheme must have seemed attractive at the time. It is perhaps worth remarking that the possibility of trading bishoprics enabled Soderini to convert an asset in France, gained through the favour of the French crown, into a more immediately useful piece of ecclesiastical property in Italy. This stands as a reminder of the opportunities open to the politically astute and well-connected cardinal for the maintenance of his political fortunes even in adverse circumstances.

Soderini was appointed administrator of the church of Narni at some date after 21 April 1515 when the previous bishop died. It was not a rich benefice, having a tax of only 200 florins. It is just possible that he was awarded it late in 1515 as a reward for being legate in Rome while Leo went to Bologna. On 18 May 1517 Soderini resigned Narni and it was given to Ugolino Martelli, but Soderini kept the right of regress and the money gleaned from the collation of benefices.[48] On 4 March 1523, as Martelli had died, Soderini exercised his right of regress and Narni was given to Carlo Soderini,[49] who was not a member of his immediate family but may have been a member of his household. He still held on to both the regress and the income. But when Soderini died on 17 May 1524, and his reign as patron ended, the bishopric was taken away from Carlo and, on 20 May, cardinal Cesi was promoted to it. One cardinal's

---

[45] AV, Arm. xl, 2, 186r-187r.

[46] ASMa, AG, b.862, and the comments on it by Kolsky, *Mario Equicola*, p. 143.

[47] ASMa, AG, b.2996, lib. 31, and Kolsky, *Mario Equicola*, p. 143.

[48] AV, Fondo concist., Acta vicecanc. 2, 30v.   [49] *Ibid.*, 223r and v.

secretary wrote that Soderini, by the time of his death, had resigned or vacated all his benefices except the bishopric of Narni, which he had renounced in favour of a nephew, possibly Giuliano or Francesco di Tommaso di Paolantonio, but the nephew had died during the period when Soderini was ill and the pope had given it instead to cardinal Cesi, who was a native of the city of Narni.[50] Some time in 1517, presumably before the 'conspiracy', Soderini was also given the administration of the church of Anagni, another relatively poor bishopric with an annual income of 500 florins. On 4 March 1523, in the same consistory as above, he vacated it and it was given to Luca da Volterra, a doctor in the service of Soderini, with Soderini, as usual, reserving the revenue and the right of regress.[51] This too must have ceased at his death but the next bishop, cardinal Alessandro Farnese, was not appointed until 3 April 1525.

Prior to the second 'conspiracy' of April 1523 and his exposure as a false friend of the emperor, Soderini was plotting to acquire a much more substantial benefice. By this stage in his life, he was an influential enough figure in Roman society to compel foreign powers, even those to whom he was known to be opposed, to consider buying his favour. The emperor Charles V could not afford to ignore, and was not foolish enough to underestimate, this elder-statesman cardinal. Before his election as pope on 9 January 1522, Adrian had held the bishopric of Tortosa in Spain which had an income variously estimated at between 4,000 and 10,000 florins. Adrian did not arrive in Rome until August and Soderini must already have had his eye on Tortosa. The duke of Sessa wrote to the emperor from Rome on 31 October that he had spoken with the cardinal of Volterra and had lavished a great many fair words on him. He reported that the cardinal was not, however, satisfied with words, but wished for deeds, asking for the bishopric of Tortosa free from all pensions. The duke considered that the emperor would do well to give the bishopric of Tortosa or the abbey of Monreale to the cardinal of Volterra, and he believed that the pope would also like it very much, although he was dissembling.[52] This indicates clearly that the bishopric was in the gift of the king of Spain, doubling in his role of emperor, and not the pope; the emperor made (for him) the right decision and gave it to Guglielmo Enkenvoirt, a familiar and fellow-countryman of the pope. The Tortosa incident illustrates the way in which the position of Rome as the capital of christendom enabled

---

[50] Sanuto, *I diarii*, XXXVI, 368, 21 May 1524, Marino da Pozzo, the secretary of cardinal Pisani, to Francesco Spinelli.

[51] AV, Fondo concist., Acta vicecanc. 2, 223v.

[52] *Calendar of letters ... between England and Spain*, II, pp. 501–2.

cardinals of weight such as Soderini to bargain with foreign powers for benefices and influence.

The see of Tortosa had not previously been held by an Italian, and the letter from the duke of Sessa shows how near Soderini came to victory in the acquisition of a Spanish bishopric of this size. In the late fifteenth and early sixteenth centuries there was no comparable process in Castile and Aragon to that in France whereby Italians were promoted to French bishoprics; in Spain, this did not happen until further into the sixteenth century. However, the essential point here may be less the nationality than the status of foreigner. Charles V may not have promoted Italian bishops to Spanish dioceses, but the case of Tortosa proves that he put forward foreigners who were subjects from his Burgundian inheritance. By contrast, the Italians nominated to French bishoprics were not subjects from another realm but quite simply foreigners, most of whom had, after 1516, been ambassadors, legates or nuncios in France; a French bishopric was seen by Francis I as a fitting reward for their work.[53]

After Soderini's rehabilitation under Clement VII, in September 1523, he lived quietly in Rome until his death in May 1524. In February he fell ill and took to his bed, and on the 22nd he made a new will. He also decided to dispose of his remaining benefices. Bernardo da Verrazzano was despatched to the Vatican to talk to cardinal Niccolò Ridolfi about certain conventions to do with the resignation by Soderini of the bishopric of Vicenza in favour of Ridolfi. He returned to confer with Soderini. They agreed upon a document of resignation to be drawn up by Domenico de Iuvenibus, a curial notary, and Bernardo and Domenico went back to cardinal Ridolfi's room in the palace where it was prepared.[54] News must have spread fast around Rome because, on 22 February, Filippo Strozzi wrote to Francesco del Nero informing him that Soderini had resigned the bishopric to Ridolfi, reserving a pension of 1,000 florins for a son of Tommaso.[55] Although this had been decided by the two parties, it was not announced in consistory until 14 March 1524 with the pope himself as proposer. The pensioner was Francesco di Tommaso di Paolantonio[56] and the pension was to be obtained thus: 500 florins from the Benedictine abbey of S. Genesio at

---

[53] See F. Baumgartner, *Changes and continuity in the French episcopate: the bishops and the wars of religion, 1547–1610* (Durham, 1986), p. 32 who cites M. Edelstein, 'The recruitment of the episcopacy under the concordat of Bologna in the reign of Francis I' (Ph.D. dissertation, Columbia University, 1972), chapters 3 and 4.

[54] This information comes from Bernardo's testimony of 10 February 1526 in the case to try the falsity of Soderini's 1524 will, Rome, Arch. Sod., III, 253v–254r.

[55] ASF, C. Strozz., III, 110, 204r. The letter is dated 22 February 1523 and although it is sent from Rome, it is in fact 1524.

[56] AV, Fondo concist., Acta vicecanc. 3, 30v.

Brescello in the diocese of Parma, and 500 from the abbey of S. Croce at Avellana or Fonte Avellana in the Marches.[57]

This outcome had not been secure from the start. On 20 February the Venetian orator, Foscari, wrote from Rome that Soderini's condition was worse and that he (the orator) had been to see the pope to ask him to give Soderini's bishopric of Vicenza to cardinal Pisani, a Venetian. The pope hedged by saying that his nephew, cardinal Ridolfi, had asked for it, but also that he would like to please the Venetian senate and he thought it a good thing that bishops should be natives of their cities.[58] Marino da Pozzo, the secretary of cardinal Pisani, wrote on the same day that cardinal Ridolfi had made an arrangement with the bishop of Volterra (he must have meant the cardinal of Volterra) to have the right of regress, although the pope had given hope to cardinal Pisani who da Pozzo thought might gain the bishopric but be compelled to pay a pension for it.[59] On the 25th Foscari reported that Ridolfi had been given the bishopric and that he (the orator) had lodged a complaint with the pope.[60] Letters of 5 and 6 March from Foscari showed that Pisani was still optimistic although the hoped-for renunciation had not taken place and the twenty-day time limit was almost up;[61] on the 18th Foscari had to pass on the bad news that finally Ridolfi had been given it in a public consistory but that he, Foscari, had again made a fuss about its going to an outsider.[62] In May the pope was still not being completely open because he said to cardinal Pisani's secretary that he wanted to give other benefices to Ridolfi and to give Vicenza to Pisani instead; obviously this did not work, so he promised to give Pisani the first free bishopric,[63] which chanced to be the much richer one (income 7,000 florins) of Padua, which he received either on 29 July or 8 August.[64] Here the claims of a papal nephew outweighed those of the Venetian senate pressing for an indigenous bishop.

Finally, there is a rather pathetic scene about a bishopric which occurred while Soderini lay dying. On 29 October 1522 he declared that he was in possession of jurisdiction over the church of Toul.[65] Toul was an anomalous and complicated entity. Together with Metz and Verdun, the so-called Trois-Evêchés, it formed a French-speaking part of the

[57] Rome, Arch. Sod., III, 157r, 22 February 1524. See L. Cottineau, Répertoire topo-bibliographique des abbayes et prieurés (Mâcon, 1935–70) for details of these two abbeys.   [58] Sanuto, I diarii, XXXV, 458.   [59] Ibid., XXXV, 466–7.
[60] Ibid., XXXVI, 6.   [61] Ibid., XXXVI, 41–2.   [62] Ibid., XXXVI, 91.
[63] Ibid., XXXVI, 368, 21 May 1524, Marino da Pozzo to Francesco Spinelli.
[64] Eubel, Hierarchia, III, 284.   [65] Ibid., III, 341.

empire but was enclaved within the independent duchy of Lorraine.[66] Toul had special juridical status as Nancy, the capital of Lorraine, lacked its own bishop and therefore belonged to the diocese of Toul. The administrator of the bishopric since 19 October 1517 had been cardinal Jean de Lorraine, a prince of the ruling house, and on 12 February 1524[67] he resigned it in favour of Hector d'Ailly de Rochefort, the bishop of Baonne. Soderini, although he was very ill, 'more dead than alive', insisted that he had the right of regress to this bishopric. In the meantime, Jean de Lorraine had resigned it and he went to see Soderini to request him not to give any trouble to the new French incumbent. Soderini refused and Lorraine became very angry, reminding him that he had no friend in the whole world but France and promising that he would make sure that France too became his enemy.[68] The most likely possibility is that Soderini acquired the right of regress to this bishopric through some exchange of benefices carried out with another cardinal or bishop. The history of the bishops of Toul is murky enough to conceal many such a transaction. Ulrich de Blamont was appointed in 1495 but from the start there were co-adjutors, among whom was cardinal Antoniotto Pallavicini, who had helped Soderini become a cardinal in 1503 and is the most likely donor of the right, and cardinal Raymond Peraud. Ulrich died on 3 May 1506 and Hugo de Hazards was not formally appointed bishop until 12 September 1507.[69] At some point during this period, Soderini must have come into possession of his claim.

Soderini's titulary appointments within Rome and her suburbs should also be brought into this discussion. He spent eight years as a

---

[66] For further information, see A. Girardot, 'Entre France, empire et Bourgogne (1275–1508)' and J. Coudert, 'Le siècle d'or de la Lorraine indépendente', in *Histoire de la Lorraine*, ed. M. Parisse (Toulouse, 1978).

[67] See Eubel, *Hierarchia*, III, p. 341 and A. Collignon, *Le mécénat du cardinal Jean de Lorraine (1498–1550)* (Paris/Nancy 1910), p. 12.

[68] ASMa, AG, b.868, 150r, B. Castiglione to marquis Federico, 9 April 1524: 'Mons.re del Lorena si parte molto malcontento del cardinale Soderini, il quale ancor che sia amalato, quasi più morto che vivo, presumendosi haver il regresso sopra un vescovato che teneva Mons.re de Lorena ne ne ha mai parlato finché sua S. R. ma non lo ha renuntiato ad un gentilhomo francese, e presentendo el prefato de Lorena che'l Soderino voleva vexare questo a chi lo havea renuntiato, è stato a casa sua in persona, e pregatolo a non volerla dar travaglio e non havendo potuto ottener questo, lo ha detto malissime parole, e raccordatoli che tutto il mondo gli è inimico excetto che Franza, e che li promette che farà che ancor Franza li serà inimica. El prefato R.mo Soderino non è restato per questo de far citar colui, di modo che la cosa è molto rotta.' There is another account with much the same information, written by Angelo Germanello to Giovanbattista Abbadino, secretary to the marquis, on the same day, ASMa, AG, b.868, 541r.

[69] See Eubel, *Hierarchia*, II, 283 and III, 341.

cardinal before he obtained a Roman bishopric, being first cardinal priest of S. Susanna from 31 May 1503 until 15 September 1508, and cardinal priest of SS. Apostoli from 1508 until 29 October 1511 when he was promoted to the cardinal bishopric of Sabina. This he also acquired for a straightforward political reason. Bernardo Carvajal, the previous bishop, was deprived by Julius II on 24 October for his involvement in the Council of Pisa and the bishopric was passed on to Soderini. When Carvajal was rehabilitated by Leo on 27 June 1513, the pope did not want to demote Soderini from cardinal bishop. There were no vacant cardinal bishoprics, so he elevated the see of Tivoli to this status as a special concession to Soderini and only for the duration of Soderini's incumbency. Presumably, having just made a truce with Soderini and his family, he could not allow the cardinal's position to be downgraded. He stressed that the bishop of Tivoli would enjoy all the privileges and prerogatives of the other cardinal bishops.[70] According to the consistorial records, Soderini became bishop of Albano on 6 August 1516,[71] but this notice appears to be a mistake.[72] On the other hand, Soderini was bishop of Palestrina from 18 July 1516 to 9 December 1523 and, in fact, fled first to Palestrina before going on to Fondi when he left Rome in 1517. When cardinal Grimani, the cardinal bishop of Porto died, following an old tradition that the cardinal bishops were allowed to choose their next Roman see,[73] Soderini chose Porto itself on 9 December 1523,[74] but after a few days, following the death of the incumbent, cardinal Carvajal, he was promoted to the bishopric of Ostia and Velletri.[75] This was the most prestigious one and the end of that particular road.

It will be evident from this that Soderini held more than one bishopric at a time, but his pluralism, although an abuse of the system, was not exceptional. Cardinal Jean de Lorraine's, for example, was on a much larger scale. Soderini only held six or possibly seven bishoprics whereas Lorraine, according to an estimate by Gams, held three archbishoprics and eleven bishoprics.[76] Soderini usually held only two at a time whereas Lorraine held many more concurrently. Of course, the cardinal of Lorraine came from a sovereign house and had the

---

[70] See Hergenroether, *Leonis X*, I, 1, p. 300. The document, dated 7 October 1513, is in AV, Reg. vat. 1076, 237v–238r.

[71] AV, Fondo concist., Acta miscell. 54, 42r.

[72] See Eubel, *Hierarchia*, III, 64, who is of the same opinion.

[73] For further information on this right of *jus optionis*, see *The catholic encyclopedia*, III, p. 340 and J. Sägmüller, *Die Thätigkeit und Stellung der Cardinäle* (Freiburg im Breisgau, 1896), pp. 179–80.

[74] AV, Fondo concist., Acta vicecanc. 3, 15v and 16r.   [75] *Ibid.*, 17v.

[76] P. Gams, *Series episcoporum ecclesiae catholicae* (Regensburg, 1873–86), 636.

backing of the king of France who, after the Concordat of Bologna in 1516, was able to dispose of French bishoprics to whomsoever he wished,[77] and all Lorraine's bishoprics were in France. Soderini had no such sustained support and had to find favour when and where he could. In many ways, the patronage networks in the curia (certainly for bishoprics) worked in favour of those not of Italian birth, because most Italian states had their own protégés in the college and the pope had his own favourites and relations, and there was often conflict between the two over candidates. There were far more Italian than non-Italian cardinals, and far more Italian than, say, French cardinals. Also, bishoprics in Italy were smaller, poorer and more numerous than those in France and Spain which tended to be larger and richer.

Whilst it is possible to provide a reasonably clear picture of Soderini's bishoprics, it is not possible to do the same for his other benefices, ranging from abbeys to churches to hospitals. It is notoriously difficult to make sense out of collections of information about individual benefices in the renaissance period for several reasons. First, provision to bishoprics and larger benefices provides evidence of patronage and patronage networks but, except in the most obvious of cases, the exact working of the patronage system for minor benefices remains obscure. In general, cardinals were responsible for finding and providing livings from benefices for a wide range of servants,[78] clients and friends, as well as for themselves,[79] in competition with other cardinals and their households and circles of dependents. Bishoprics may have had considerably larger incomes, but benefices of lesser value were in much greater number. Access to these smaller incomes lay with the faculty of the collation of benefices, which was attached to individual bishops, archbishops or abbots who controlled the allocation of benefices within their jurisdictions. Just as the cardinals accumulated bishoprics and benefices, so too they accumulated faculties of collation.[80] Thus the successful ones amongst them were able not only to provide additional incomes for themselves, but to secure incomes for their clients and

---

[77] During Francis I's reign, Lorraine was nominated to nine episcopal and archiepiscopal seats and was the richest prelate in France. See M. Edelstein, 'The social origins of the episcopacy in the reign of Francis I', *French historical studies*, 8 (1973–4), pp. 377, 380.

[78] The geographical range of diocese exhibited by members of Soderini's household may reflect in some measure not only the birthplaces of the clerks but also Soderini's ability to obtain benefices for them from diverse parts of the Italian peninsula.

[79] A. Prosperi, '"Dominus beneficiorum": il conferimento dei benefici ecclesiastici tra prassi curiale e ragioni politiche negli stati italiani tra '400 e '500', in *Strutture ecclesiastiche in Italia e Germania prima della riforma*, ed. P. Prodi and P. Johanek (Bologna, 1984), p. 77.

[80] See McClung Hallman, *Italian cardinals*, pp. 98 and 102–3.

dependents. However, mapping out from the extant documentation the patronage routes which led to the acquisition of a minor benefice is often impossible.

Second, lists of benefices are nearly always incomplete because of the limitations of source material available. Third, without the account books of the benefice in question, or the account books of the holder of the benefice, it is impossible to establish how much the benefice was worth in real terms. Fourth, the system of pensions and exchanges makes a nonsense of the figures even if the annual revenue of the benefice is known. Fifth, attempts to analyse the material in terms of geography seem doomed to failure, and certainly no significant pattern of distribution is visible in Soderini's case. This is tantamount to admitting that the intractable nature of the material on benefices means that at the moment few or minimal generalisations can be made, especially in the two crucial areas of financial gain and patronage. As a result of this, hardly any work has been done on these aspects of benefices whilst there have been many studies of individual abbeys or monasteries. Two articles on the benefices of two cardinals – Guglielmo Enckenvoirt[81] and Marco Barbo[82] – only serve to emphasise the very high number that they held, ninety-five known ones in the case of Enckenvoirt. No attempt to draw any conclusions has been made.

One of the most important points about benefices in this period is that the richer ones were viewed almost entirely either as pieces of property or as sources of income to be milked by the upper echelons of the clergy. No spiritual exertion was expected. Those of smaller income were used by the same grand members of the clergy, sometimes in collaboration with the heads of state, as rewards for faithful servants – crumbs from the rich man's table. Instances of this range from wholly clerical arrangements to transactions involving the influence of lay patrons. A purely 'clerical' case was that of Soderini's vicar-general in Vicenza, Teobaldo Ainardi who, on 14 January 1523, gave to Leonardo di Matteo da Panzano, a Florentine cleric, the archpriestship of SS. Prosdocimo and Donato of Cittadella in the diocese of Vicenza, in return for past work and loyalty.[83] A 'lay' case is illustrated by Soderini's letter to marquis Gianfrancesco Gonzaga on 31 December 1504 asking him to find a job or benefice for Guglielmo di Franco, a

---

[81] W. Munier, 'Willem van Enckenvoirt (1464–1534) und seine Benefizien', *Römische Quartalschrift für Christliche Altertumskunde und Kirchengeschichte*, 53 (1958), pp. 151–78.

[82] P. Paschini, 'I benefici ecclesiastici del cardinale Marco Barbo', *Rivista di storia della chiesa in Italia*, 13 (1959), pp. 335–54.

[83] Guasti, *I manoscritti*, p. 470, pergamene.

Mantuan citizen, because Soderini did not himself have anything with which to benefice him in the region of Mantua, where Guglielmo wanted to live out his days.[84] In essence, benefices were fragmented bonuses, portions of a cardinal's salary to be acquired and bartered with and invested. This attitude is exemplified in a letter written by Piero Soderini to Francesco on 12 March 1506, in which he says that he has heard of the death of the Baglioni bishop which is a sad loss, but as the benefices are all going to messer Gentile, the loss is more easily bearable.[85]

There were frequent disagreements over benefices and the ecclesiastical records are littered with instances of them. It was a point of honour as well as a canonical necessity to take possession of the benefice as soon as possible, and certainly within six months of being given it. The cardinals or bishops did not go in person but sent their procurators. Countless skirmishes resulted but the underlying political causes of these battles for supremacy sometimes remained hidden behind false façades. One such case unfolded around the taking possession of an abbey at Colle Val d'Elsa in 1516. Niccolò di Petro da Colle had already taken possession in the name of cardinal de' Medici, when Ser Eliseo da Colle, Soderini's secretary and a frequent procurator of his, Bolognino and some of Bolognino's sons came to take possession on behalf of Soderini. There was a fight in which three people were injured. The *podestà* wrote to the *Otto di guardia* who proceeded to summon Ser Eliseo to appear before them, to which Eliseo replied scoffingly that the *Otto* were not in a position to command him. In Rome, other negotiations were taking place. Antonio Zeno, another of Soderini's men, went to see Goro Gheri, the secretary of Lorenzo de' Medici and an ardent Medicean, but no progress was made. The *Otto* seized Eliseo who continued to be contemptuous so they subjected him to a whipping, to induce fear and as an example to others who were considering acting so presumptuously. They would have whipped Bolognino too had he not been so old.[86] The end of this story is unknown, but on 9 December 1518 Goro Gheri wrote that he had ordered Niccolò di Petro to relinquish the possession of a benefice in the diocese of Volterra to Soderini's procurators.[87] Soderini had scored a minor victory in his opposition to the Medici, and had scored it under their own noses.

In general, the Medici exhibited a suspicious amount of interest in Soderini's benefices. On another occasion, in 1518, they expended a

---

[84] ASMa, AG, b.856.   [85] ASF, Sig., Otto, Dieci, Miss. 6, 315r.

[86] This strange story unfolds in ASF in the pages of the minutario of Goro Gheri, I, 169v-171r. The letter to cardinal de' Medici is dated 7 December 1516.

[87] *Ibid.*, III, 245r.

great deal of effort finding out whether he had the right of regress over the Benedictine abbey of San Baronto in Pistoia.[88] Political enmity entered into every sphere of life. In December 1505 the Signoria had written to Soderini, asking him to intervene because Don Basilio, abbot of S. Felice in Piazza, a friend of the government and a person loved by the whole city, complained that cardinal de' Medici had molested his abbey without reason.[89] During the period of Piero Soderini's leadership in the city, the Medici were concerned to annoy not only the Soderini but also the Florentine government whom they associated with them. Hence this attack.

Placing impediments in the way of those taking possession was one possibility for political enemies, and impeding the collection of revenue was another. The lay rulers of the states in whose domain the benefices lay could either help or hinder in the expedition of such processes, as the enormous number of letters from the Vatican to these rulers, asking them for their help and informing them of events, testifies.[90] If the situation deteriorated, the pope could order an inquest and threaten reprisals, as he did in 1519 in response to a protest from Soderini about the occupation and dispersion of ecclesiastical goods in Vicenza.[91] Finally, as the death blow, secular rulers (especially those from outside Italy) could simply deprive their enemies of the benefices they held inside their dominions. In early 1522 the imperial ambassador, Juan Manuel, advised Charles V to take this course of action, adding that the king of France did it.[92] In fact, heads of state and governments played a crucial role in every aspect of the workings of the system.

The distinction between a consistorial benefice and a non-consistorial benefice was that the revenues of the former had to exceed a certain amount, set by the Council of Constance at 200 florins.[93] Supplicants desirous of obtaining consistorial benefices, who were, in the main, high-ranking prelates, had their cases referred for decision to consistories, where individual cardinals with their multifarious patronage networks fought over who should obtain what. The cardinal proposer for the bishopric or abbey to be conferred by papal provision received a gratuity (the *propina*). The procedure for non-consistorial benefices was different; supplicants were provided to the benefice once their

---

[88] See ASF, MAP, CXLIV, 90, and ASF, Il minutario di Goro Gheri, IV, 188r, 236v, III, 42v.   [89] ASF, Sig., Miss. 1a Cancelleria 55, 133v, 20 December 1505.

[90] See, for example, AV, Arm. XL, 4, 14r, a letter of 22 April 1514 to Ugone of Moncada, the prorex of Sicily, telling him that Soderini had resigned the monastery of S. Anastasia in the diocese of Messina which he had held *in commendam*.

[91] See Mantese, *Memorie*, III, II, p. 180.

[92] *Calendar of letters ... between England and Spain*, II, p. 404, 23 February 1522, Juan Manuel to the emperor.   [93] Clergeac, *La curie*, p. 44.

supplication had been agreed upon by the datary and signed by the pope or someone on his behalf. But after these basic divisions, there were still many ways of holding a consistorial benefice, ranging from provision proper (which was the most perfect form), administration, *in commendam*, reserving the fruits, regress and coadjutorship, to the union of one or more further benefices to the benefices whose title was already possessed.[94] Soderini was acquainted with all these types of involvement. His ecclesiastical possessions included many monastic houses as well as secular benefices. But of the almost random number of sixty or so benefices connected with Soderini which emerged in the course of this research, there is little that responds positively to analysis. They range across the whole of Italy, from Como[95] to Sicily,[96] and they include a substantial minority of French ones, especially in the dioceses of Tours, Le Mans, Fréjus and Lyons.[97] A rogue reference to Soderini's possession of the right of regress to the famous monastery of Montserrat near Barcelona in 1507,[98] an unlikely benefice for him as it was outside his normal sphere of influence, reinforces the point that little can be taken for granted in this matter. As it was prior to his fall from favour with Julius, perhaps the pope caused him to acquire it, or perhaps his international influence was even stronger than has previously been suspected. There are more Benedictine examples than anything else, but there is also a substantial number of Camaldolese,[99] a handful of Augustinian[100] and Cistercian[101] and one stray Cluniac.[102] Given the large number of Benedictine benefices, their predominance probably does not require further explanation.

It is not known exactly how the cardinals jostled and manipulated patrons and each other to obtain these benefices. It is possible that Soderini obtained extra Camaldolese benefices because he was protector

---

[94] *Ibid.*, p. 45.

[95] Hergenroether, *Leonis X*, I, p. 146. On 7 May 1513, the pope reserved benefices for Soderini in Cremona, Como and Bergamo.   [96] AV, Arm. XL, 4, 14r.

[97] See, for example, Hergenroether, *Leonis X*, I, p. 330, 7 November 1513 for mention of the Benedictine monastery of St Julien in the diocese of Tours.

[98] J. Manglano y Cucaló, *Politica en Italia del rey catolico, 1507–1516* (Madrid, 1963), II, p. 31.

[99] An example is the Camaldolese abbey of S. Savino at Cerasolo in the diocese of Pisa. See Rome, Arch. Sod., II, 262r, 31 January 1516.

[100] See, for example, Hergenroether, *Leonis X*, I, p. 103, 19 March 1503 when the pope confirmed Soderini in his benefice of the Augustinian priory of S. Elena in the diocese of Aosta.

[101] Both of these were in France. One of them was the monastery of Ste Marie de Clairmont (or Clermont) in the diocese of Le Mans. See Hergenroether, *Leonis X*, I, p. 331, 7 November 1513.

[102] The priory of S. Petri Signari in the diocese of Lyons. See AV, Arm. XXXIX, 25, 43r.

of their order, and possible that his governorship of Campagna and Marittima made it easier for him to acquire benefices in those areas, but neither of these explanations is certain. Lack of systematic data renders inadvisable attempts to calibrate a correlation between the range of sovereignties in which the benefices were held, and the ties between those sovereignties and Soderini.[103] Nor is there sufficiently consistent information to be able to decide whether he received more benefices during the reign of Julius II or that of Leo X, nor is it even known whether he ceased acquiring new benefices during his period out of papal favour in exile in Fondi.

Another question is the extent to which his bishoprics brought with them other benefices. For example, Soderini was being given money by S. Paolo Fuori le Mura, the greatest Benedictine convent in Rome, for the pension on the church of S. Saturnino de Monte Cavallo, from 1508 until his death.[104] This church was united with that of S. Susanna by Sixtus IV on 16 July 1483 and given to the Benedictine monks of S. Paolo by Julius II.[105] Soderini had made an agreement with S. Paolo about S. Saturnino on 11 October 1508, and had been moved from the church of S. Susanna to that of SS. Apostoli on 15 September 1508. It thus seems likely that this pension was a leftover from money received from S. Saturnino, due to him because of its association with S. Susanna and because he was cardinal priest of that church. When S. Paolo took over the church, they took on this obligation. On the other hand, Soderini had other financial arrangements with S. Paolo which involved payment of certain sums, so the connection with S. Susanna could prove to have been unimportant. There is no record of Soderini's having any other benefices within the city of Rome.

Soderini received incomes from at least two hospitals. One was the Ospedale della Scala for paupers in S. Gimignano, of which he was governor.[106] His long-standing relationship with the Benedictine monastery, later hospital, of SS. Nabore e Felice in Bologna, was rather stormy. He had a suit with them at the Roman *Rota* which was decided in Soderini's favour in 1514.[107] By 1517 Soderini, the administrator in

---

[103] A. V. Antonovics, 'The finances of the college of cardinals in the later middle ages' (D.Phil. dissertation, University of Oxford, 1971), p. 388, wrote that a long-standing source of cardinals' revenue was the pensions that they received from monarchs, ecclesiastics and cities to look after their interests at the curia, but that rewards were more likely to be revenues attached to benefices than cash.

[104] Rome, Arch. Sod., I, 404r–428r.

[105] C. Huelsen, *Le chiese di Roma nel medio evo* (Florence, 1927), pp. 457–8.

[106] Hergenroether, *Leonis X*, I, p. 103.

[107] The pope wrote telling the governor of Bologna about this on 9 May 1514, AV, Arm. XL, 2, 134r.

perpetuity of the fruits, income and produce of the ex-monastery of SS. Nabore e Felice, then a plague hospital, had rented this position out to Taddeo Frontani, a Bolognese citizen, for the annual sum of 350 gold ducats. If any quarrel arose out of this arrangement, cardinal de' Medici, the legate in Bologna, was to arbitrate and neither party was to be allowed to appeal against his decision on pain of a fine of 1,000 ducats.[108] This arbitration clause sounded ominous and by 10 December 1517 cardinal de' Medici had been brought in to effect a compromise, not between Soderini and the new plague hospital, but between Soderini and the *Quaranta* of Bologna (although they could have been running the hospital). Cardinal de' Medici decided that Soderini should be paid 1,200 ducats, which he was, and also that he should renounce his claim on a credit note for 2,000 ducats which he had been given previously and which he had to hand back within two months of his arrival in Rome (for he was at that point in exile and most of his personal papers would have remained in Rome).[109] It cannot have been a good time for Soderini to have had cardinal de' Medici as an arbitrator. In his 1524 will he leaves the pension from this hospital to his heirs, so he must have held on to it.[110]

Financial transactions such as the one outlined above make any attempt to work out Soderini's income from benefices a hopeless task in the absence of any full accounts. Litigation over revenues from a seemingly insignificant benefice could continue for years, but the revenues must have been sufficient to warrant this outlay of time and effort. These transactions reinforce the view that benefices were a cardinal's main source of income, the only real source over which he had any personal control, because by constant manoeuvring, and use of his influence and contacts, he would have been able to accumulate benefices. Those cardinals without a considerable number of benefices may, therefore, be assumed to have lacked financial assets too.

[108] ASR, Notari dell'AC 7156, 462r–463r, Francesco Vigorosi.
[109] *Ibid.*, 591r and v.   [110] See Lowe, 'Francesco Soderini', appendix 4, p. 355.

CHAPTER 16

PALACES AND OTHER PROPERTY

Late fifteenth-century Rome was a city with an expanding population and accommodation presented difficulties for every social group. These difficulties were compounded for the higher echelons of society who were obliged to show a certain ostentation in their style of living. From his arrival in Rome in 1480, Soderini, as a bishop and curia official, had a position to maintain which had to be reflected in the size and location of his residence. Elevation to the cardinalate would only exacerbate this problem. There were four obvious options open to the new arrival: he could rent or buy a palace of suitable magnificence, he could buy a property and alter it to his taste, or he could build a new palace. As David Chambers has demonstrated for the 1460s, cardinals who chose to rent often lost money.[1] Unlike cardinal Francesco Gonzaga, it appears that Soderini at no point rented his accommodation from someone else at a commercial rate. Rather, he employed a combination of the other three options. From the first he demonstrated his good business sense by his readiness to buy his own property and build and alter it if need be. Once, he made the mistake of investing in a property that was ultimately in the gift of the pope, and suffered for this when Leo X repossessed it; however, in general terms, it is likely that Soderini profited from his property dealings. Certainly, the very large costs involved can be taken as a guide to the strength of his enthusiasm.

Soderini had both an interest in building for its own sake and an acute sense of property development as a lucrative form of investment. On several occasions he involved himself in building projects which were not strictly necessary, and he seems to have been on close terms with

A version of this chapter appeared in K. Lowe, 'A Florentine prelate's real estate in Rome between 1480 and 1524: the residential and speculative property of cardinal Francesco Soderini', *Papers of the British School at Rome*, 59 (1991).

[1] D. Chambers, 'The housing problems of cardinal Francesco Gonzaga', *Journal of the Warburg and Courtauld Institutes*, 39 (1976), pp. 21–41.

Bramante.[2] That his interest was not purely aesthetic can be seen from his inclusion of shops in the façade of his new building in the Borgo, and the later employment of this building as a dowry for his niece. It is a telling comment on Soderini's view of his career in the church and its relation to his own affairs, that despite the fact that these buildings must have been financed to some extent from ecclesiastical revenues, Soderini seems never to have questioned that the resulting assets belonged to him and his family. In his extant wills of 10 February 1511 and 22 February 1524, he made elaborate provisions to ensure that these assets passed on to his nephews, thus proving once again that strategy was espoused at a family, as well as a personal, level.

When it had been decided by the *paterfamilias* of the Soderini clan and by Lorenzo de' Medici that Francesco was to pursue a career in the church rather than in law, his centre of attention switched from Tuscany to Rome. He was the first of many Soderini to make this transition, and also the first to acquire property there, so that when it became necessary for the whole branch of the family to leave Florence, they already possessed an impressive base in another city which could be turned into a second home. The earliest reference to Soderini's considering property in Rome is contained in a letter of 27 December 1479 from him to Lorenzo de' Medici, when he writes that he has heard that Lorenzo is going to Rome, where Soderini is to set up residence, and he would like to be there at the same time as Lorenzo whose presence would be useful to him in many ways.[3] This was an extraordinary moment to trouble Lorenzo, who was on his very delicate diplomatic mission to Naples.

The first indication of Soderini's interest in the Borgo dates from the early 1480s. His choice of the Borgo as a site for his house shows good taste and forethought. At the beginning of the 1480s it was not a fashionable district, although by 1510 Paolo Cortesi in De cardinalatu praised sites near to the Vatican for a cardinal, who would have to spend much of his time there, while also recommending proximity to the centre of Rome in order to facilitate business.[4] Soderini at this stage could not have known that he was to be promoted to the cardinalate, but his positions in the curia already gave him reason to be near the Vatican. Above all, the Borgo was convenient, as the Venetian

---

[2] See the letter from Soderini to Bramante of 1510 where he addressed him as 'prestantissime vir, amice noster carissime', in Rossi, 'Nuovi documenti', p. 136.

[3] ASF, MAP, xxxvii, 688.

[4] The chapter of Cortesi's work relating to the ideal palace for the cardinal is printed in both Latin and English, with a commentary, in K. Weil-Garris and J. D'Amico, *The renaissance cardinal's ideal palace*, Studies in Italian art history 1 (Rome, 1980), pp. 45–123; p. 71 discusses the siting of the palace.

1. Cardinal Francesco Soderini's building complex in the Borg
2. The complex at SS. Apostoli.
3. The complex at Torre Sanguigna.

2. Detail of a 1577 map of Rome by Stefano di Pérac, edited by
Antonio Lafréry, showing the location of Francesco Soderini's
properties.

ambassadors to the papacy recorded in May 1523.[5] By June 1483 Soderini had acquired three pieces of property in the Borgo on Via Saligata (later renamed Via Alessandrina and finally called Borgo Nuovo) from Filippo di Luigi Vigevano and his brothers,[6] the ground rent of which was due to the chapter of St Peter's.[7] He is also known to have leased other property in the Borgo from the chapter in 1484,[8] although he may possibly have done so the year before as well.[9] Soderini leased two separate pieces of property from the chapter in 1484, and these may have been the two leased by him in the Borgo which appear regularly in the rent books (censuali) from the 1490s onwards.[10] If this identification can be made, then the pair of leased properties can be linked to the three properties bought in 1483, by their common proximity to the house called the house of the queen of Cyprus,[11] also on Via Saligata.

On 24 August 1487 Soderini asked permission from the chapter to build on the property he had leased from them,[12] and this permission was granted with certain conditions.[13] The chapter stressed that the building was to be for private use by the Soderini family and that it was not connected with the bishopric of Volterra or any other of Soderini's benefices.[14] It would appear, therefore, that Soderini had been buying up small plots of land as they became available in the area around the queen of Cyprus's old house, with the intention of demolishing existing structures and building his own house. Rome at this time was full of very small dwellings, often temporary structures made of wood. The sites acquired by Soderini in the Borgo were probably pockmarked with such buildings, and in requesting permission to build Soderini remarked that the replacement of such ramshackle structures by a new building would redound to the credit, not only of St Peter's, but of the whole city.[15] However, not all the properties bought were to be levelled in this fashion. The rent book of the chapter for 1485 reveals that

---

[5] Sanuto, I diarii, XXXIV, 226.   [6] See Rome, Arch. Sod., I, 200r.
[7] The ground rents for the two properties were one ducat and one and a half ducats. See Rome, Arch. Sod., I, 200r and XLII, 28r.
[8] BV, Arch. cap. S. P., Arm. 41–2, Censuali 12 (1484), 20v.
[9] Rome, Arch. Sod., XLII, 29r.
[10] BV, Arch. cap. S. P., Arm. 41–2, Censuali 14 (1490), 11v, and, for example, ibid., Censuali 15 (1495), 8r. One of the entries for one of these properties is mentioned in C. Frommel, Der Römische Palastbau der Hochrenaissance (Tübingen, 1973), II, p. 213.
[11] In the censuali for 1490, the entries for Soderini's two standard properties are separated by the entry for the house which used to be leased to the queen of Cyprus.
[12] Rome, Arch. Sod., I, 201r.   [13] Ibid., 202r.   [14] Ibid., 201v.
[15] Ibid., 201r.

Soderini had already repaired one house in the area[16] which suggests that this house, at least, was not intended for demolition.

It is clear that building work had taken place on Soderini's site by 20 June 1488,[17] and in 1490 a house owned by Soderini displayed the sacred keys, the emblem of St Peter as well as of the pope, which were placed on buildings newly constructed on land belonging to the chapter.[18] From 1490 onwards, the chapter's rent books refer each year to one house owned by Soderini with a rent of four ducats.[19] References to the house of the bishop of Volterra crop up intermittently in other sources over the succeeding years. In September 1499, in a description of the confines of the house of Febo Brigotti, who was the doctor attached to S. Spirito, the property was located between the Via Alessandrina and the house of the bishop of Volterra.[20] In February of that year the limits of another property were defined in relation to the wall of Soderini's garden.[21] It would appear, therefore, that by 1490 Soderini had a house somewhere in between Borgo S. Angelo and the buildings that bordered on Via Saligata, and he was certainly living there in December 1502 when his brother was sent as Florentine ambassador to Rome.[22]

In 1499 one part of the Via Alessandrina was opened.[23] This was the old Via Saligata now straightened[24] and transformed into a more imposing approach road to St Peter's, and the area around it was designated for development by Alexander VI, ostensibly in honour of the impending jubilee of 1500. Soderini was included in a list of property owners in April 1500 whose land bordered on the new road and who were ordered to undertake building work to raise the tone of the neighbourhood.[25] Large-scale development along the road was almost certainly hindered by the numbers of people who owned small plots of land or buildings, but in May 1505 Soderini was given, by the hospital of S. Spirito, a number of properties between his house on Borgo S. Angelo and Via Alessandrina. Included among these was the

---

[16] BV, Arch. cap. S. P., Arm. 41–2, Censuali 13 (1485), 49v.

[17] Rome, Arch. Sod., I, 204r.

[18] BV, Arch. cap. S. P., Arm. 41–2, Censuali 14 (1490), 11v. For information about the sacred keys, see P. Pecchiai, 'I segni sulle case di Roma nel medio evo', Archivi, series II, 18 (1951), pp. 230 and 241.

[19] For example, BV, Arch. cap. S. P., Arm. 41–2, Censuali 20 (1503), 16v.

[20] ASR, Ospedale di S. Spirito 1444, 166v.   [21] Ibid., 153v.

[22] Burchard, 'Liber notarum', II, p. 340.   [23] Ibid., II, pp. 191–2.

[24] U. Gnoli, Topografia e toponomastica di Roma medioevale e moderna (Rome, 1939), p. 4.

[25] AV, Reg. vat. 874, 35v–37r. Some of this is published in Bullarium diplomatum et privilegiorum sanctorum romanorum pontificum Taurinensis editio, ed. A. Tomassetti, V (Turin, 1860), pp. 377–8. Compare this with the account given by de Roo, Alexander VI, IV, p. 483.

house of Febo Brigotti.[26] Now Soderini paid ground rent to the chapter of St Peter's and the hospital of S. Spirito. Shortly after this he embarked upon a major redevelopment of the site. What appears to have been happening, therefore, was that from the 1480s Soderini had been acquiring small pieces of property in the Borgo. From at least 1490 his own residence had been located on Borgo S. Angelo. He also owned properties in the block between Borgo S. Angelo and Via Alessandrina. The transaction of 1505 seems to have completed his control over a sufficient frontage on Via Alessandrina to enable him to start a major building project, and this coincided with his elevation to the cardinalate. The status of cardinal both necessitated greater display and provided greater resources with which to fund it. Maria Luisa Madonna sees the Via Alessandrina as 'the first classicising and neo-imperial street of modern Rome' ('la prima strada classicheggiante e neo-imperiale della Roma moderna'), and within this context she thinks that the Piazza Scossacavalli qualifies as the Forum of the Borgo.[27] Whether one agrees with this new image or not, there is no denying that Soderini had, with foresight and patience, acquired one of the prime sites in the whole of Rome.

What has not been realised before is just how great a financial asset this may have been. Via Alessandrina was the most important shopping street for pilgrims and tourists, and very high rents could be charged to shopkeepers or stallholders who worked on it. Not only were there stalls littered around the old and new St Peter's,[28] but other property owners on Via Alessandrina itself took advantage of the constant flow of visitors to fill their own pockets. Both palazzo Branconio and the palace of Jacopo da Brescia were constructed on Via Alessandrina in the early sixteenth century with shops on the ground floor of their façades,[29] which could have catered to the local population of Vatican courtiers and hangers-on as well as to the journeying faithful. Perhaps the jubilee year of 1500, with its vast crowds, persuaded Soderini of the wisdom of building shops on this street.

The development of Soderini's site in the Borgo may have represented a response to his new status but it also represented the

---

[26] ASR, Ospedale di S. Spirito 218, 37v and 38r.

[27] M. Madonna, 'Una operazione urbanistica di Alessandro VI: la Via Alessandrina in Borgo', in Le arti a Roma sotto Alessandro VI, ed. M. Calvesi (Rome, 1981), p. 6, and Roma, 1300–1875. La città degli anni santi. Atlante., ed. M. Fagiolo and M. Madonna (Milan, 1985), pp. 130–1.

[28] P. Pecchiai, 'Banchi e botteghe dinanzi alla Basilica Vaticana nei secoli XIV, XV e XVI', Archivi, series II, 18 (1951), pp. 81–123, especially pp. 106–11.

[29] C. Frommel, S. Ray and M. Tafuri, Raffaello architetto (Milan, 1984), pp. 157–64 and 197–216, especially p. 209.

culmination of a long-standing accumulation of property in the area. Nor was the development itself primarily a matter of show. Evidence both from Soderini's first will of 10 February 1511 and, in more detail, from a legal case of the 1560s involving the site, enables an accurate picture to be drawn up of the development. The will provides the first detailed breakdown of Soderini's complex of buildings in the Borgo. In it, he bequeathed to the church of St Peter's and the hospital of S. Spirito the ten old houses partly next to and partly near to the big house in which he lived himself, situated on Borgo S. Angelo.[30] In return, St Peter's and S. Spirito were to relinquish any rights over the land on which Soderini's big house stood, and the land on which his stables stood in Via Sacra,[31] so that his heirs and successors could hold them without payment of ground rent.[32] In addition, S. Spirito was to release the land and the rights over it on which the new shops and houses had been built in Via Alessandrina.[33] By this proposal, Soderini was seeking to complete the process of piecemeal accumulation which had started in the 1480s, and thus to transform the patchwork of small plots held by a variety of arrangements with both St Peter's and S. Spirito, into straightforward ownership of the land and the buildings constructed upon it.

In the will, Soderini was referring to the results of his development of the site which had taken place some time between his acquisition of the frontage on Via Alessandrina in 1505, and the composition of the will in 1511. A more precise date for the construction of the new shops, houses and their stables is provided by letters written by Jacopo Gherardi in Rome to Soderini in Tuscany in the autumn of 1509. Gherardi was Soderini's archdeacon and factotum and supervised Soderini's affairs while he was out of town. On 6 October Gherardi recorded that the entrances to the shops were completed.[34] In an undated letter written before 13 October, he reported that the shops were finished, that work on the stables was proceeding apace and that everything else had been done.[35] In both of these letters, Gherardi notes that reaction to the work has been favourable. From Gherardi's letters it is clear that the construction of

---

[30] ASBo, Notarile, Tommaso Grengoli, busta 18, filza 13 (1506–18), under date, and Lowe, 'Francesco Soderini', appendix 3, p. 331.

[31] The Via Sacra took the name of Borgo Vecchio in the early sixteenth century to distinguish it from the parallel Via Alessandrina or Borgo Nuovo. See Gnoli, *Topografia*, pp. 38, 40.

[32] ASBo, Notarile, Tommaso Grengoli, busta 18, filza 13 (1506–1518), under date, and Lowe, 'Francesco Soderini', appendix 3, p. 331.

[33] Lowe, 'Francesco Soderini', appendix 3, pp. 331–2.

[34] Volterra, Biblioteca Guarnacci MS 6204, 93v.   [35] *Ibid.*, 92v.

the shops and houses was a commercial enterprise, and he expressed the hope to Soderini that the stables and new buildings would be able to pay for themselves through their annual or monthly rent.[36] By 19 October Gherardi was speculating on the rents for both shops and houses – forty florins in *carlini* for a house and twenty for a shop – and he wrote that if those figures were correct, four had already found tenants.[37]

The whole question of shops in the ground floor of the façade of a palace (or in this case not the façade of a palace) is intriguing. Brenda Preyer in her article on Alberto di Zanobi Rinieri's palace, built in Florence between 1399 and 1402, shows that although the edifice looks as if it were built to accommodate shops on the ground floor, the spaces behind the façade arches did not function as rental shops.[38] She suggests that the arched design may have been connected with style rather than function. Richard Goldthwaite sees the emergence of the private patrician palace in Florence after 1400, which discarded the row of arched openings for entrances and shops common in the fourteenth century, in favour of a grand façade and one principal entrance or opening.[39] And Nicolai Rubinstein has explained the fiscal rationale for not building shops or houses to rent out in Florence after the *catasto* of 1427 which introduced taxation on income from rents.[40] The situation changed again on 26 April 1474 when tax incentives were introduced in Florence to encourage building by offering owners twenty years' tax relief on newly constructed houses which were rented out.[41] And while it is true that palaces constructed in the early sixteenth century in Florence do not have shops on the ground floor, and never could have done because of the presence of inbuilt benches (*panche* and *muricioli*), the idea must have lingered on. Thus, in the 1480s Filippo di Matteo Strozzi could suggest to his builders, albeit with tongue in cheek, that they design shops into the ground floor of his palace, which would bring in income for his sons. His idea was rebutted on the grounds that the arrangement would be ugly, degrading and in-

[36] *Ibid.*, 104r.   [37] *Ibid.*, 95r.

[38] B. Preyer, 'The "chasa overo palagio" of Alberti di Zanobi: a Florentine palace of about 1400 and its later remodeling', *Art bulletin*, 65 (1983), p. 392.

[39] R. Goldthwaite, *The building of renaissance Florence* (Baltimore, 1980), pp. 13–14 and Goldthwaite, 'The Florentine palace as domestic architecture', *American historical review*, 77 (1972), pp. 981, 983, 994.

[40] N. Rubinstein, 'Palazzi pubblici e palazzi privati al tempo di Brunelleschi', in *Filippo Brunelleschi: la sua opera e il suo tempo* (Florence, 1980), p. 29.

[41] A. Lillie, 'Florentine villas in the fifteenth century: a study of the Strozzi and Sassetti country properties', (Ph.D. dissertation, University of London, 1987), p. 329.

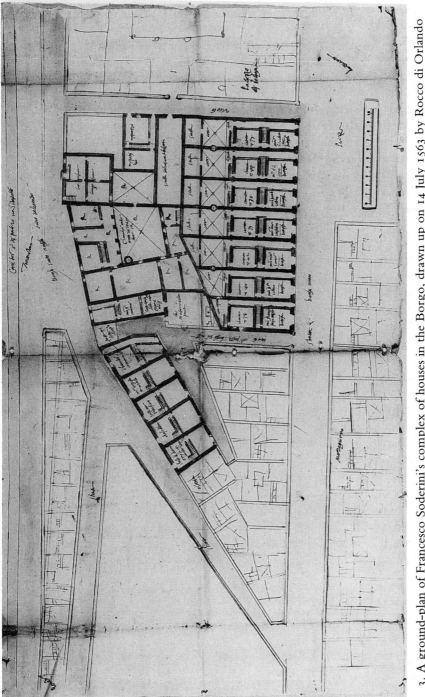

3. A ground-plan of Francesco Soderini's complex of houses in the Borgo, drawn up on 14 July 1563 by Rocco di Orlando and Nanni di Baccio Bigio (ASF, Mediceo 6409, cover for bundle of Soderini documents).

convenient ('di quanta brutezza, servitù et incommodo ciò saria alli abitatori').[42]

In Rome the genealogy of shops included in façades is slightly different. Christoph Frommel addresses the issue and links the form to ancient Roman and medieval Sienese practices. When he mentions Florence, it is to talk of the fifteenth-century palaces which, he claims, did not have shops because the outstanding wealth of their owners made it unnecessary. In fact, Frommel's hypothesis concerning the relationship between the wealth of the owner and the presence of shops in a palace seems misguided, for he sees it as the key to the problem, remarking that in the palace-building of the sixteenth century, shops played a larger role than before, because even the less financially solid builders could thus afford a palace. He believes that particularly for them the shops were an important aid in the financing of the new structure; the larger palaces rarely contained shops because they did not need them.[43] It seems likely, on the contrary, that Soderini chose to build his shops, knowing that they would be a sound investment, as is made clear in Gherardi's letters. He did not need to build them in any sense. What is also interesting is that Soderini may have conceived of the plan on account of his Florentine upbringing; for his brother, Piero, felt and acted in exactly the same way, utilising to the full shops he had expressly built next to his house at Ponte alla Carraia in Florence,[44] and ensuring that his descendants would enjoy the rents from shops in his palace block at Monte Citorio in Rome.[45]

However, in Rome there is an alternative genealogy arising from the idea of *case in serie*. These were identical or near identical houses, connected to each other structurally but otherwise independent, and they were the forerunners of the tenement block or terraced housing. Piero Tomei became interested in such houses in the 1930s and collected about one hundred examples of the type, their dates ranging from the end of the fifteenth century to the eighteenth century. These *case in serie* could be either composed of shops and attendant houses (as in Soderini's building), or houses by themselves, as in Tomei's example of the building in Via degli Amatriciani (now destroyed).[46] There is a definite

---

[42] *Vita di Filippo Strozzi il Vecchio*, ed. G. Bini and P. Bigazzi (Florence, 1851), p. 25 and G. Gaye, *Carteggio inedito d'artisti dei secoli XIV, XV, XVI*, I (Florence, 1839), p. 355.   [43] Frommel, *Römische Palastbau*, I, pp. 90–1.

[44] Razzi, *Vita*, p. 151.

[45] Rome, Arch. Sod., II, 18v. For more information on Piero Soderini's palace at Montecitorio, see F. Apolloni Ghetti, 'Nuovi appunti su Francesco Soderini cardinale Volterrano', *L'urbe*, 39 (May–August 1976), pp. 8–10.

[46] P. Tomei, 'Le case in serie nell'edilizia romana dal '400 al '700', *Palladio*, 2 (1938), pp. 83–6 and Tomei, *L'architettura a Roma nel quattrocento* (Rome, 1942), pp. 265–7.

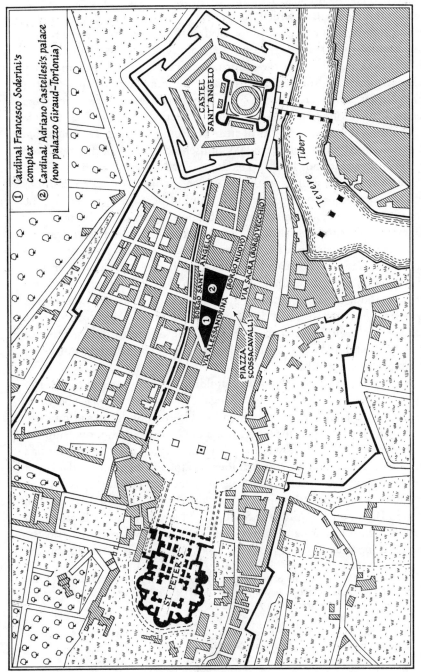

① Cardinal Francesco Soderini's complex
② Cardinal Adriano Castellesi's palace (now palazzo Giraud–Torlonia)

4. Schematic map of the Via Alessandrina and environs in the Borgo superimposed on a modern map of Rome.

difference between constructing a row of shops with attendant houses and designing a palace which incorporates shops into the façade on the ground floor. One reason why Soderini's shops and houses were consistently mistaken for a palace façade was undoubtedly their size – the block facing onto Via Alessandrina was very large by contemporary standards for unit housing, and the only buildings constructed on that scale at that time were palaces. Such a long and regular street frontage seemed to announce prestigious accommodation.[47]

On the subject of shops in or near palaces, Cortesi in *De cardinalatu* recommended that 'the cardinal's household should be far removed from those attractions likely to excite the evils of gluttony and of lust, but also from the sounds of things which invoke improper memories and which hinder the free play of the mind because of noise' and he condemned above all 'places in which both types of diversion occur together'. 'Gluttony and lust', he continued, 'are fostered by perfumers, venders of delicacies, poulterers, honey venders and cooks of sweet and savoury foods. On the other hand blacksmiths, carpenters, silversmiths, armorers and the like make noisy neighbors.'[48] Cortesi must have known about urban conditions in Rome at the time, and one reason why he went into so much detail was that he was aware how far from ideal were the living arrangements of some of the cardinals, most of whom would have been all too near these black-listed sources of temptation and trouble.

Further details about Soderini's building development in the Borgo can be found in the documents of a legal case which took place between 1561 and 1563. A dispute had arisen in 1518 over Soderini's attempt to discharge the dowry of his niece, Anna di Giovanvettorio, by using the Borgo complex. The dowry had been due since 1517 when she had married a papal nephew, Luigi di Piero Ridolfi. A large ground-plan of the complex (see figure 3) had been made by 14 July 1563 by the architects Rocco di Orlando, working for the Ridolfi, and Giovanni di Baccio Bigio, working for the Soderini.[49] Nanni di Baccio Bigio was a well-known Florentine architect and sculptor active in Rome and the surrounding area in the 1550s and 1560s.[50] Rocco di Orlando, on the

[47] S. Sinding-Larsen, 'A tale of two cities: Florentine and Roman visual context for fifteenth-century palaces', *Institutum Romanum Norvegiae: Acta ad archaeologiam et artium historiam pertinentia*, 6 (1975), p. 197.

[48] Weil-Garris and D'Amico, *Ideal palace*, p. 73.

[49] The ground-plan is folded in four and being used at present as a cover for the Soderini bundle of documents in ASF, Mediceo 6409.

[50] See the entry in the *Macmillan encyclopedia of architects*, ed. A. Placzek (New York, 1982), pp. 207–8 and A. Ronchini, 'Nanni di Baccio Bigio', *Atti e memorie delle RR. deputazioni di storia patria per le provincie modensi e parmensi*, 8 (1876).

other hand, has evaded attempts to trace him, and although he describes himself as an architect (*architetto*), he is described more bluntly by Bigio as a builder or mason (*muratore*). The ground-plan faithfully reflects the description and distinctions given in Soderini's will of 1511. There are seventeen houses, seven on Via Alessandrina, now called Borgo Nuovo, and ten on Borgo Sant'Angelo, 'all of them contiguous one to the other, bordered first by the street called Borgo Nuovo, second by the alley which runs along the palace of the cardinal of Bologna, third by Borgo Sant'Angelo, fourth by the alley which runs from Borgo Nuovo past Madonna della Purità[51] to Borgo Sant'Angelo, fifth by another alley which is opposite the door of Madonna della Purità, sixth by the inn[52] of ...'[53] All this is clearly shown in the drawing, as are the names of the tenants of each of the houses and the rents they were paying.

The first estimate of the value of the house for the court came from Battista di Raffaello Battaglioni, and with it he gave particulars of each property. However, as he wrote in the valuation that he did not have experience of Roman affairs, the accuracy of his estimates may be doubted. The eleventh house, the biggest, must have been Soderini's own, with a large number of rooms on four floors. It is the only house in which old and new structures are both mentioned, and this part of the complex probably included remnants of an older structure. It was valued at 2,150 *scudi*, which was by far the highest valuation.[54] According to Battaglioni, the first seven houses were worth 6,715 *scudi* and the next ten, 6,121 *scudi*,[55] whereas in fact the valuation of the ten came to a total of 7,221 *scudi* (his arithmetic being rather poor), making an overall total of 13,936 *scudi*.[56] The valuation produced by the Soderini's architect on 28 July 1563 was rather different. He estimated that the houses were worth 6,093 *scudi* 67 *soldi* as they stood but that they would be worth 9,973 *scudi* 67 *soldi* free from ground rents.[57] The Ridolfi's architect thought they would be worth 15,000 *scudi* if no

---

[51] According to both M. Armellini, *Le chiese di Roma*, ed. C. Cecchelli (Rome, 1942), II, p. 962 and Huelsen, *Le chiese*, p. 539, S. Maria della Purità was founded during the papacy of Clement VII between the years 1523 and 1530. It is clearly marked on the plan. It is possible that the tenth house from the 1511 will was in the place where the Madonna della Purità was later built. It seems certain that Soderini owned the whole block of land and the area would not have been left empty.

[52] U. Gnoli, *Alberghi ed osterie di Roma nella rinascenza* (Rome, 1942) offers a wealth of information but lists no *osteria* on Borgo Sant'Angelo. The majority of *osterie* in the Borgo are on Borgo Vecchio. P. Adinolfi, *La portica di S. Pietro* (Rome, 1859), p. 127, cited a pair near Piazza S. Pietro: one had the sign of a man with a carafe in his hand, the other the sign of a bishop.

[53] ASF, Medicep, 6409, Soderini bundle, second document, 1r. [54] *Ibid.*, 8v.

[55] *Ibid.*, 12v and 13r. [56] *Ibid.*, 12v and 13r.

[57] This part of the Soderini bundle is unpaginated.

ground rents were due. Although these estimates are not directly applicable to the earlier period, even the lowest of them represents a large sum of money, and the market value of the Borgo complex, especially taking into account the depredations of the sack of Rome,[58] testifies to the acuity of Soderini's business sense.

In short, the development represented an extremely successful investment for Soderini. The façade on Via Alessandrina was like that of a palace, although it concealed the upper storeys of the shops and houses which it had always been Soderini's intention to rent out. The whole complex, therefore, satisfied the demands of both ostentation and financial necessity. Soderini's own house or palace remained where it had always been, on Borgo Sant'Angelo, not on Via Alessandrina. Francesco Albertini in his *De mirabilibus* wrote of the *domus* or house in the Borgo constructed by Soderini[59] so he too must have fallen into the error of believing the façade concealed a palace. Just how valuable the site was became clear when Soderini found himself in need of cash after he had fled from Rome because of the so-called conspiracy of June 1517.[60] Ready money was of more use to him in exile than was property in Rome. On 17 November 1517 he informed the chapter of St Peter's and the hospital of S. Spirito that he intended to sell the houses in the Borgo, and that if they wished they could buy them for 10,000 gold ducats.[61] The chapter stalled by asking for a copy of the proposed deal so that they could scrutinise it at leisure,[62] but they must have decided against it, as by 20 January 1518 Soderini was using the houses as part of an exchange. By that date, he had paid only 4,415 ducats[63] of Anna di Giovanvettorio's dowry, and he and Luigi Ridolfi agreed that Ridolfi would pay back this money, and that Soderini would discharge his debt by giving Ridolfi the complex of houses in the Borgo,[64] which he formally did on 23 March 1518.[65] It was stressed again that the houses belonged to Soderini personally and were not connected with the fruits of his benefices.[66] From 1524 cardinal Ridolfi paid the ground rent for

---

[58] See ASF, Mediceo 6409, unpaginated part, articolo 6.

[59] F. Albertini, *De mirabilibus novae urbis Romae*, ed. A. Schmarsow (Heilbronn, 1886), p. 31: 'Domus de Sotherinis a Reveren. Francisco Florenti. card. Vulterrano constructa'.   [60] See above, pp. 114–120.

[61] This is recorded in Rome, Arch. Sod., II, 405r and XXII, 42r and v.

[62] Rome, Arch. Sod., II, 406v.

[63] There are two copies of the relevant document in Rome, Arch. Sod. The first, II, 439r, states that Soderini had paid 4,415 ducats; the second, II, 456r, that he had paid 4,600 ducats.   [64] Rome, Arch. Sod., II, 457r.   [65] *Ibid.*, 456v.

[66] *Ibid.*, 458r.

these properties and could have been living there in the big house at the end of 1526 and the beginning of 1527 when the census was taken.[67]

Not much can now be said with certainty of the appearance either of the building containing the seven shops or of Soderini's own residence. F. Ehrle described in 1927 how he had 'arrived in Rome in October 1880 and seen the palace [and by this he meant the Via Alessandrina block] still in its original form, in a conspicuously Florentine style,[68] modest but very elegant. A few months later workmen had moved in and the building took on its later vulgar physiognomy.' Ehrle commented that 'traces of the original were visible in the vaults of the seven shops on the ground floor and in the narrow, tall doorway in the middle of them, but that many more features were preserved in the façade facing onto Borgo Sant'Angelo'.[69] No one else even mentions Soderini's house on Borgo Sant'Angelo but instead attention is concentrated on the façade on Via Alessandrina. It is highly likely that Soderini's coat of arms was on the façade of this building to show that the whole block belonged to him, which may be one reason why people assumed that his palace was included in the structure. Ehrle also reproduced the schematic drawing of 'the palace of cardinal Soderini' (see figure 5) which first appeared in Rossi,[70] but again with no indication of its provenance. In it, there is no central door, merely seven shops and seven entrances for horses. There is no central door either in the ground-plan, but one does appear in the 1938 drawing by Lucilio Cartocci.[71] Many other differences exist between the two representations, notably that there are three floors besides the ground floor in the schematic drawing (as there were in 1563 according to the evidence in the legal case), whereas there are four in the Cartocci drawing. The windows and string courses have been altered, and the levels of the

---

[67] BV, Arch. cap. S. P., Arm. 41–2, Censuali 33 (1527), 137v and D. Gnoli, 'Censimento di Roma sotto Clemente VII', *Archivio della reale società romana di storia patria*, 17 (1894), p. 452.

[68] It is not known why Ehrle wrote this, for no obviously Florentine features are discernible or identifiable in or from any of the plans, schematic drawings, prints or records that have survived. One suggestion is that the building had rustication.

[69] F. Ehrle, *Dalle carte e dai disegni di Virgilio Spada*, Memorie II, Atti della pontificia accademia romana di archeologia, 3 (Rome, 1927), pp. 60–1: 'Arrivato a Roma nell'ottobre 1880 io l'ho veduto ancora nella sua forma primitiva, di gusto fiorentino spiccato, modesto ma elegantissimo. Però passarono pochi mesi ed i muratori alzarono i loro ponti e lo stabile ricevette la sua presente volgare fisionomia. La primitiva trasparisce ancor oggi nelle voltate delle sette botteghe del pianterreno e nell'unica porta stretta ed alta in mezzo fra esse. Molto più dell'antico si è conservato nella facciata verso Borgo Sant'Angelo.'

[70] Rossi, 'Nuovi documenti', p. 135.

[71] Cartocci did a series of drawings of the Borgo in a book entitled *La spina dei Borghi* (Rome, 1938), with a text by 'Ceccarius'.

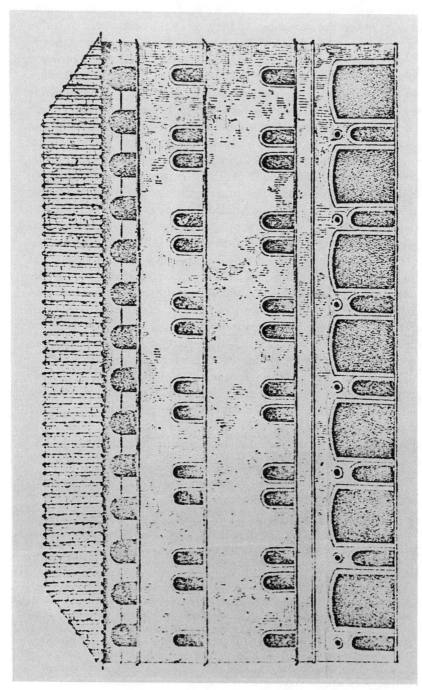

5. Schematic drawing of the façade of the Soderini complex of houses on Via Alessandrina, taken from A. Rossi, 'Nuovi documenti su Bramante', *Archivio storico dell'arte*, I (1888), p. 135.

floors changed, perhaps in the 1880s after Ehrle arrived in Rome. Another representation is in a print of the palazzo Torlonia in Borgo of 1838 which includes the end of the Soderini building in it.[72] This shows the palace still with three storeys, with the same string courses, and with the original rounded windows on the first and second floors. The third floor has been radically altered. The building was destroyed completely in 1937 to make way for the Via della Conciliazione.

Soderini's residence in the Borgo was not the only palace he possessed in Rome; he subsequently acquired two others. Of these, the first was the palace attached to the basilica of SS. Apostoli. Unlike the Borgo complex, Soderini's acquisition of SS. Apostoli owed nothing to the careful manipulation of the property market and everything to his ecclesiastical position, and this was to prove his undoing. He obtained the palace through his appointment as titular cardinal of SS. Apostoli, yet the claim of the titular cardinal to possession of the palace was open to doubt. The history of the ownership of the palace or palaces attached to the basilica is confused, not least because of their proximity to the Colonna precinct. Between 1471 and 1501 the buildings were owned by the cardinals Pietro Riario and Giuliano della Rovere, who were nephews of Sixtus IV and who held the basilica *in commendam*.[73] Essentially, there were two palaces attached to the basilica of SS. Apostoli, a larger one to the south and a smaller one, sometimes called 'del Vaso', to the north. The larger one has the more complicated and less accessible history,[74] and was reworked several times in the fifteenth century alone. Initially, a palace of Martin V stood on the site, which belonged to the Colonna, followed by the house of cardinal Bessarion, and then the initial Riario project which della Rovere took over and enlarged.[75] The palazzina della Rovere is also in this section.

The smaller palace to the north was built by della Rovere in the second half of the 1470s for his own personal use,[76] although he was compelled to give it to the Franciscans in June 1501. He may have been able to appropriate it for so long because he was the protector of the

[72] A. Nibby, *Roma nell'anno 1838*, II (Rome, 1841), p. 781.

[73] Eubel, *Hierarchia*, II, p. 71.

[74] See T. Magnuson, *Studies in Roman quattrocento architecture* (Rome, 1958), pp. 313–27. Magnuson relied heavily on Tomei, *L'architettura*.

[75] For information about della Rovere's building works at this palace, see D. T. Brown, 'Cardinal Giuliano della Rovere, patron of architecture, 1471–1503' (M.Phil. dissertation, University of London, 1988), chapter 4.

[76] See A. Vanegas Rizo, 'Il palazzo cardinalizio della Rovere ai SS. Apostoli a Roma', *Quaderni dell'istituto di storia dell'architettura*, 14 (1977–8), pp. 3–12 and I. Gatti, 'Il palazzo della Rovere ed il convento dei Santi Apostoli in Roma attraverso i secoli', *Miscellanea francescana*, 79 (1979), pp. 408–9.

Franciscan order.[77] The situation was further complicated by the presence of the Franciscans, who were busy in the 1470s and 1490s (and possibly from 1500–1) building conventual buildings and cloisters behind the small palace to the north of SS. Apostoli.[78] Thus, the larger palace to the south, which through usage came to be seen as the titular cardinal's residence, was, in fact, constructed on land belonging to the Colonna, and the smaller palace to the north, in fact, was the property of the friars. The *palazzina*, too, in all probability, was on land belonging to the Colonna. What is clear is that, in the final analysis, the titular cardinal was not in a winning position. All this is necessary background to what follows.

In 1506 della Rovere, now Julius II, rented 'the palace he had constructed as a cardinal' on the north side of SS. Apostoli to Marcantonio Colonna and his new wife, who was also Julius' niece, on condition that Colonna paid an annual rent of forty ducats to the titular cardinal,[79] and compensated the Franciscans with money and alternative accommodation. Deborah Brown identifies this palace with the *palazzina*,[80] but the compensation clause for the Franciscans, coupled with its position north of the basilica, show that this was the small palace. This is corroborated by a bull of Leo X which confirmed the transfer of the palace called 'del Vaso' with a tower, from the Franciscans to Marcantonio Colonna, with an agreement that Colonna would, in exchange, build a dormitory for the friars and pay them 150 *carlini* a year.[81] Therefore, by 1506 both the history of the ownership and the building history of the palaces attached to SS. Apostoli were in some disarray, and four parties – the Colonna, the titular cardinal, the della Rovere (backed by the papacy), and the Franciscans – all had claims on one or more parts of the buildings.

On 15 September 1508 Soderini became titular cardinal. Giuliano

---

[77] A parchment copy of the notarial document which was drawn up in Savona by Jacopo Giordano is in Rome, Archivio SS. Apostoli, pergamena B VIII, 359b. A note giving the salient facts about the transfer is in Rome, Archivio Colonna, Arch. III BB XX 114.

[78] See Brown, 'Cardinal Giuliano', pp. 94–100 and Gatti, 'Il palazzo della Rovere', pp. 416–23.

[79] A. Coppi, *Memorie Colonnesi* (Rome, 1855), p. 251. Unfortunately, his source for this, Rome, Archivio Colonna, VI, I, no. 114 is now missing from the archives, so that no more information can be gleaned.

[80] Brown, 'Cardinal Giuliano', p. 121.

[81] This is, at least, what it is stated should happen in a document of 19 March 1512 in Rome, Archivio Colonna, Arch. III BB VI 42, but this is a restatement of an earlier agreement (presumably the 1506 one). A bull of Leo X confirmed the transfer of the palace from the Franciscans to Marcantonio Colonna. See Rome, Archivio Colonna, Arch. III BB VI 43. It is noticeable that Julius has been expunged from this account.

della Rovere had been followed as titular cardinal by two other members of the della Rovere family: Clement and Leonardo Grosso. Then, in 1508, Leonardo and Soderini had exchanged cardinal priesthoods, and Soderini came to SS. Apostoli and Leonardo went to S. Susanna.[82] This may have been because Soderini wished to take over the building projects at SS. Apostoli. Prior to the discovery of the Gherardi correspondence, Soderini's contribution to SS. Apostoli had been dismissed as paltry, but it is now certain that he carried out major works there. That he had done something has always been known, thanks to the comments by Francesco Albertini who wrote, in the sixteenth century, about the palace at SS. Apostoli which cardinal Soderini 'wanted to perfect',[83] and stated that Soderini had initiated the work necessary for the completion of the sumptuous palace with its very beautiful garden.[84] Albertini's work was started in 1506, finished by 3 June 1509 and published on 4 February 1510.[85] By 1 May 1509 Soderini was living in the 'large buildings'[86] at SS. Apostoli, that is in the larger palace to the south, and when he left Rome that summer for a visit to Tuscany, building works must have been set in motion.

On 15 June of that year Soderini obtained a reduction in his ground rent of six ducats for his houses in the Borgo, from the hospital of S. Spirito, because of the nuisance he had suffered on account of the building works next door by cardinal Adriano Castellesi who was constructing what is now the palazzo Giraud-Torlonia.[87] In 1509, for the first time, Tommaso Soderini (son of either Giovanvettorio or Paolantonio) is mentioned as living in the house with Soderini.[88] So it could be that Soderini had moved to SS. Apostoli from the Borgo to escape the sounds and inconveniences of the building works of his neighbour, and that he scheduled his own building campaign at SS. Apostoli for a later date. If he hoped to avoid discomfort by doing this, he was over-optimistic, for on 13 October Gherardi wrote to Soderini, who was still in Tuscany, that work had restarted on Castellesi's palace, and would take in everything up to the roof.[89]

On 25 September Jacopo Gherardi had written from Rome about a

[82] Eubel, Hierarchia, III, p. 67.

[83] Albertini, De mirabilibus, p. 20: 'Palatium Sanctorum XII Apostolorum ... quod quidem Reverendissimus Franciscus Sotherinus Florentinus vult perficere.'

[84] Ibid., p. 54: 'Quid praeterea dicam de sumptuoso palatio Sanctorum XII Apostolorum cum viridario pulcherrimo quod quidem opus Reverendissimus Franciscus Sotherinus Florentinus vult perficere et iam incepit.'

[85] Codice topografico della città di Roma, ed. R. Valentini and G. Zucchetti, IV (Rome, 1953), p. 458.   [86] BL, Add MSS 8441, 294v–295r.

[87] ASR, Ospedale di Santo Spirito 218, 38r and Rome, Arch. Sod., I, 467r.

[88] Ibid., 39r.   [89] Volterra, Biblioteca Guarnacci MS 6204, 92r.

visit that morning to the buildings of Soderini's basilica, and he described the progress that had been made. The name SS. Apostoli is not used, only the word *basilica*.[90] He commented that he had seen and approved of the wooden *cubiculum* (panelled study) in position near the north window.[91] Two other salient facts emerged about the cubicle: that it was small and that it had been whitewashed.[92] Gherardi expressed regret that the first courtyard had not also been whitewashed, but said that the second courtyard was not so important as it was not so much in the public eye. He urged Soderini to spend the extra money as the amount involved was small, although the benefit to be gained was great.[93] In a second letter, which is undated but of October 1509, Gherardi wrote that work had begun at SS. Apostoli (therefore, previously the building was being redecorated and rearranged, rather than knocked down or built anew) and that the demolition of the old portico had commenced so that the stairs could begin to go up, starting at the foundations.[94]

These building works sound fairly significant and must have taken some time to complete. When Soderini wrote to Bramante from Vallombrosa, on 1 July 1510, that he wanted to return to Rome to press on with his building, about which he needed Bramante's advice,[95] it was probably the building at SS. Apostoli to which he was referring. The building works at the complex in the Borgo had been finished by the autumn of 1509 (though it is possible that Soderini may have wished to consult Bramante about the improvements for his *villa suburbana*[96] or about some other completely unknown building). On 24 December 1511 Bernardo Dovizi wrote to Giovanni de' Medici that Soderini was very well and was staying at SS. Apostoli.[97] The word used, *alloggia*, makes the stay sound temporary and it could be that building works were still continuing. It emerges from a later bull of 11 January 1517 that Soderini spent about 4,000 ducats on this palace,[98] so the building programme, as was indicated in Gherardi's letters, must have been extensive.

It is unfortunate that della Rovere's and Soderini's building work on this palace remain so elusive, but in the absence of documentation and

---

[90] Cf. P. Francesco Santini, *La basilica dei SS. Apostoli* (Rome, 1925), p. 32.

[91] Volterra, Biblioteca Guarnacci, MS 6204, 103v: 'Vidi cubiculum ligneum suo loco prope fenestram borealem locatum.'   [92] *Ibid.*   [93] *Ibid.*

[94] *Ibid.*, 92v: 'In aedibus basilice vostre etiam ceptum est opus. Vetus porticus demoliri cepta est ut detur principium scalis de novo a fundamento erigendis.'

[95] Rossi, 'Nuovi documenti', p. 136.   [96] See below, pp. 218–19.

[97] *Epistolario di Bernardo Dovizi*, I, p. 432.

[98] AV, Reg. vat. 1089, 163r–164r. I would like to thank Deborah Brown for bringing this document to my attention.

because of subsequent remodelling, it is impossible to know much more at present. Two points, however, deserve to be made; first, that Soderini obviously changed what was there as well as constructing new parts, and, second, that this kind of additional building and major and minor reworking was quite common at the time, and is probably typical of many cardinals' palaces. For an incorrigible fiddler in building matters such as Soderini, improvements were obviously irresistible. Only the palace of Torre Sanguigna, of the buildings we know he inhabited in Rome, was left by him in possibly the same state in which he found it. The alterations and additions, whatever they may have been, cannot have been strictly necessary, and as some cardinals never built or changed anything when they moved into other cardinals' ex-residences, they stand as proof of Soderini's intrinsic interest in building for its own sake.

Finally, by Leo's bull of 1517, the palace was returned to the Colonna of Genzano and Marino, which meant, in practice, to Prospero and possibly Fabrizio Colonna.[99] They were leased the property which they or their forebears had been forced, by apostolic decree, to give away to cardinal Riario. It appears that they had never been compensated for this appropriation. In return, they were to pay the titular cardinal an annual sum of forty ducats.[100] Thus, the ownership problem was resolved by a pope, just as it was started by a pope. Cardinals occupied houses adjacent to the titular churches as tenants by grace of the pope, if such houses were 'usable or improvable',[101] and Sixtus IV had allowed one of his nephews to do this without paying sufficient attention to the claims of the friars or of the Colonna to the land. When Julius II gave a palace back to Marcantonio Colonna, this was probably in partial compensation. By 1508–9, the palace went once again to the titular cardinal, Soderini. From the timing of the 1517 bull, it seems likely that the Medici pope was in some sense attacking Soderini, because there is no mention of any compensation to be paid to Soderini for his outlay, and 4,000 ducats is not a negligible sum. It is possible that Prospero Colonna, who was a particular friend of Soderini and in whose fief of Fondi Soderini stayed in exile from 1517 to 1521, would have come to some private agreement with Soderini whereby he compensated him for the loss of the palace or exchanged some appropriate piece of property. This could account for the statement in a letter of the Venetian orator, Gradenigo, in the autumn of 1520, that Soderini had sold his palace to

[99] See Litta, 'Colonna', in *Celebri famiglie italiane*, tables IV and VII and *Dizionario biografico degli italiani*, XXVII, pp. 288–93 and 418–26.
[100] AV, Reg. vat. 1089, 163r–164r.
[101] Chambers, 'The housing problems', p. 21.

the Colonna and that the Colonna arms had already gone up on it.[102] This account charts a classic pattern for cardinals' housing, in which a particular site or palace, having been used by one cardinal, was worked and reworked by a succession of others; the palace became marked so that only cardinals or very important Roman families could live in it.

Soderini also acquired the Torre Sanguigna, just north of Piazza Navona in the region of Ponte, from a fellow cardinal. It was, in fact, sold by Sebastiano Ferrero who had himself bought it from the heirs of Girolamo Riario, but it had been lived in and enlarged by Giovanstefano Ferrero, the cardinal of Bologna. Soderini bought the palace on 12 July 1511[103] for 9,500 ducats, 6,500 to be paid immediately in cash and the rest to be paid in two instalments of 1,500 each, one at Christmas 1512 and the other at Christmas 1513.[104] Included in the sale were houses other than the main palace,[105] and the boundaries were as follows: public roads on three sides, property belonging to Bartolomeo Saliceto on a fourth,[106] property belonging to the church of S. Apollinare on a fifth and property belonging to the convent of S. Agostino on a sixth.[107] These boundaries leave many questions to be answered. The extent of the property is not at all clear and has occasioned much subsequent confusion over the relationship between the palace of Torre Sanguigna and what became palazzo Altemps.

It has usually been assumed that the palace of Torre Sanguigna and palazzo Altemps are the same building (obviously with alterations) on the same site.[108] Although this may be the case, there are still a few areas of doubt. The first is that a palace attached to Torre Sanguigna appears on the Strozzi plan of 1474,[109] and this would provide a precedent for a building called the palace of Torre Sanguigna. Second, the document of 1483, in which Riario leaves a building to his heir Ottaviano, mentions the 'honorificentissimum palatium per ipsum constructum'.[110] It says that the palace is situated in Ponte near to the piazza of S. Apollinare, with buildings belonging to the heirs of Riccardo Sanguigni opposite and to one side (*in conspectu et latere*), and gives the boundaries

---

[102] Sanuto, *I diarii*, XXIX, 328. Why this should only have been recorded three years later is a mystery, but it could be that only at this point did Prospero take it over.

[103] A copy of part of this contract survives in ASF, C. Strozz., II, 134, 169r. A copy of the whole is in Rome, Arch. Sod., xxxix, 3r–17v.

[104] Rome, Arch. Sod., xxxix, 9r and v.   [105] *Ibid.*, 4r.

[106] He was Soderini's procurator for the sale.

[107] Rome, Arch. Sod., xxxix, 4r and v.

[108] See, for example, M. Festa Milone, 'Palazzo Riario-Altemps', *Quaderni dell'istituto di storia dell'architettura*, 24 (1977–8).

[109] A. Frutaz, *Le piante di Roma*, II (Rome, 1962), table 159.

[110] Festa Milone, 'Palazzo Riario-Altemps', p. 39.

as public roads on three sides and stables on a fourth. But nowhere is Torre Sanguigna, as an area, a tower or a palace, named. Third, in the lease of a palace in Ponte in 1566 by some Soderini, it is described as near to or next to the palace of S. Apollinare and public streets; the boundaries are never clearly stated.[111] Fourth, in the document of 1568 in which four of the Soderini sell a palace to cardinal Altemps, the palace is described as being de' Soderini, in the place called Torre Sanguigna, and Riario is not mentioned. Even Milone is forced to concede that there are discrepancies between the descriptions in the documents of 1483 and 1568, especially in the matter of the boundaries. In 1568 the building is surrounded by four streets, effectively occupying an isolated area separated from other habitation. Finally, it is perplexing to think that palazzo Altemps was previously referred to as palazzo di Torre Sanguigna when, in fact, it occupied a distinct and discrete block of buildings in an *isolato* away from that containing Torre Sanguigna itself. Of course, these difficulties could all be explained away, and it is unlikely that there were two separate palaces, both owned by Girolamo Riario[112] in the late fifteenth century and both owned by the Soderini by the mid-sixteenth century, but it is still an outside possibility, and one that has won a trickle of supporters over the years.[113] It is difficult to believe that the palace of Torre Sanguigna had its façade on Via dei Soldati, a considerable distance away from the tower itself.

The Sanguigni were an old-established Roman family with many active members living in the Ponte region in the fifteenth century.[114] The fourteenth-century tower and the houses attached to it had been converted into one dwelling early in the century by Cola dei Sanguigni (there is an inventory of Cola's belongings of 1424, presumably taken *in situ* from this house).[115] The tower is often mentioned[116] because it is a landmark, but it is sometimes difficult to establish whether it is just the tower, or the whole house including the tower, which is indicated, especially as the whole area was also known as Torre Sanguigna.

Although Soderini purchased the palace on 19 July 1511, he

---

[111] ASR, Notari dell'AC 6029, 207r.

[112] It is commonly accepted that the fifteenth-century palazzo Altemps was commissioned by him. See, for example, P. Tomei, 'Contributi d'archivio: un'elenco dei palazzi di Roma del tempo di Clemente VIII', *Palladio*, 3 (1939), p. 222.

[113] One example is U. Gnoli, 'Facciate graffite e dipinte in Roma', *Il Vasari*, 8 (1936–7), p. 103.

[114] P. Egidi, *Necrologi e libri affini della provincia romana*, II (Rome, 1914), e.g. pp. 479–81.

[115] P. Adinolfi, *La torre de Sanguigni* (Rome, 1863), p. 40. See also E. Amadei, *Le torri di Roma* (Rome, 1969), p. 56.

[116] See, for example, C. Cecchelli, *I Margani, i Capocci, i Sanguigni, i Mellini* (Rome, 1946), p. 28.

nominated Giovanvettorio and Tommaso di Paolantonio to take possession and rent it on his behalf,[117] and on 25 July they took possession.[118] As both the Paolantonio and the Giovanvettorio branches of the family were involved, the transaction would seem to have been the result of family discussion; the Soderini needed a further palace in Rome in which to concentrate their resources. The debt was finally paid off by Tommaso on 22 January 1515 when he was absolved of any further responsibility. There is no information on who was living there between 1511 and 1523. Giovanvettorio was teaching at the university of Pisa and would only have required an occasional Roman residence; Francesco Soderini, in 1511, had both the big house in the Borgo complex and the palace at SS. Apostoli, and he is known to have used both of them. However, circumstances were greatly altered on his return from exile in 1521. The Borgo complex had gone to Luigi Ridolfi in lieu of a dowry for Anna di Giovanvettorio and SS. Apostoli had been reclaimed for the Colonna, so it is extremely likely that Soderini was living at the palace of Torre Sanguigna from this time onwards. He was there when summoned to the Vatican by the pope in May 1523, because the Venetian orators reported that he and his household rode from his palace through Banchi and the Borgo,[119] and he died there in May 1524.[120]

According to the arrangement agreed by Piero and Francesco Soderini, and alluded to by Soderini in his final will of 1524,[121] the real estate of the two brothers was divided into two equal shares, one half going to the heirs of Paolantonio, and the other half going to Giovanvettorio and his heirs. As a consequence, an eighth share was owed to Giuliano, Tommaso, Giovanbattista and Piero di Paolantonio, and a quarter each to Giovanvettorio and his one son, Tommaso. In a list of Soderini's properties in Rome, drawn up in 1553, which were to form part of the inheritance of Piero di Paolantonio, the palace of Torre Sanguigna, the house next to it called 'del Saliceto', and 'several artisans' houses and shops underneath the palace', are valued at 23,600 scudi.[122] Once again, the shops appear to have been incorporated into the fabric of the building. This document also provides information on the interim tenants: cardinal Innocenzo Cibo lived there from 1524 until 1535, on 16 August 1535 it was rented to cardinal du Bellay,[123] and

---

[117] Rome, Arch. Sod., XXXIX, 25r.   [118] ASF, C. Strozz., II, 134, 169v–170r.
[119] Sanuto, I diarii, XXXIV, 221.
[120] Ibid., and Staglia de Actis's testimony of 5 February 1526 in Rome, Arch. Sod., III, 242r and v.   [121] Rome, Arch. Sod., III, 186r–189v.
[122] Rome, Arch. Sod., II, 148r. This information is subject to various interpretations.
[123] Rome, Biblioteca Nazionale Centrale, MSS Vittorio Emanuele 309, 105.

cardinal Giovanni de Tavera occupied it for a further, unspecified five years. In Bufalini's map of 1551 the palace was indicated as the 'domus oratoris Hispani'.[124] On 19 March 1566 the palace was rented out again by the Soderini (Giovanvettorio, Paolantonio di Tommaso di Paolantonio and his brother Alessandro) to Indico Avalos, the cardinal of Aragon, for a period of five years.[125] So the line of tenants between Girolamo Riario and cardinal Marco Sittico Altemps is now reasonably secure, and this palace can be seen to conform to the usual pattern of being a dwelling marked out for use by cardinals and the upper echelons of Roman court society. Assuming that the palace of Torre Sanguigna and palazzo Altemps are the same, nine individuals and their families owned or rented this palace in the ninety years between 1477 and 2 April 1568 when the Soderini finally relinquished their grasp and sold the palace to Sittico Altemps.[126]

It is unfortunate that so little is known about the palace at Torre Sanguigna, except that Vasari mentions that Polidoro da Caravaggio and Martino Fiorentino did *sgraffito* work in black and white on the façade of the house 'that belonged to the cardinal of Volterra at Torre Sanguigna', and inside the palace painted some coloured figures which turned out rather badly.[127] Another source claims that the tower itself was decorated with *sgraffito*.[128] It is impossible to match up the layout of the rooms provided by Milone, using information from documents in the Archivio Altemps, allegedly giving details of the rooms in the fifteenth-century palace of Riario, with indications given in an inventory of the palace of Torre Sanguigna written in May 1523.[129]

Another unknown factor is the length of time that Soderini managed to keep rooms in the Vatican. He certainly had rooms between 1504 and 1508[130] under Julius' pontificate, and possibly managed to keep them until the 'conspiracy' of 1517, because he is recorded as having them on 18 January of that year.[131] He must surely have forfeited them after this, may have regained them for a short period before Adrian VI arrived in Rome, when he was acting as cardinal governor, but was probably swept out in the general clear-up of the palace that took place under Adrian. Perhaps by 1524 he may once again have been a palatine

---

[124] Frutaz, *Le piante*, II, table 201.   [125] ASR, Notari dell'AC 6029, 207r.

[126] Adinolfi, *La torre*, p. 46.

[127] G. Vasari, *Le vite*, ed. G. Milanesi, 7 vols., v (Florence, 1880), p. 147.

[128] Amadei, *Le torri*, p. 56.

[129] Milone, 'Palazzo Riario-Altemps', pp. 14–18. For the inventory of 1523, see ASR, Notari dell'AC 410, 122r–128v and Lowe, 'Francesco Soderini', pp. 358–73.

[130] For references, see ASF, Dieci, Resp. 78, 21r (1504) and ASMa, AG, b.858, cardinal Sigismondo Gonzaga to marquis Francesco, Rome, 7 June 1508.

[131] Razzi, *Vita*, p. 161.

cardinal, with rooms in the Vatican, as a result of the election deal he made with Clement. The group of palatine cardinals at any one time was quite small but Soderini managed to have a rather special but different relationship with each pope, so he could always put forward a reason for having a room or rooms. Once they had been handed out, it must have been difficult to dismiss the occupants to make way for new ones, so the more senior Soderini became, the better the case he could put for having these prestigious lodgings.

In addition to the palaces and rooms listed above, Soderini acquired a *villa suburbana* in 1508. On 26 July of that year, Jacopo Gherardi wrote to a friend with the news that Soderini had bought a building in 'our suburb of St Peter' which used to belong to Girolamo Calagrano, the most important secret cubicular of Innocent VIII. It contained the 'Theodorine temple or building' and had above it the famous gardens 'next to the basilica of the blessed Michael'. He went on to report that it had a portico, an upper storey and bedrooms and was worthy of a great prince and spacious enough to accommodate comfortably a cardinal and his household.[132] Some of these references are problematical. Whilst Calagrano can be traced and his position evaluated – he had great authority and wealth during Innocent's pontificate and was made bishop of Mondovì in 1490[133] – neither Theodorina nor the gardens have been securely accounted for. The most likely person to have had an association with any building or buildings in this area is Theodorina, the daughter of pope Innocent VIII, but no association has yet been proven. The famous gardens referred to are most probably the gardens of Nero at the foot of the Vatican hill.[134] Finally, the basilica of the blessed Michael must refer to the church of SS. Michele and Magno in the Borgo. Although the church is mid-eighteenth-century in decoration, the core of the structure is still a Romanesque basilica,[135] and it is pleasantly sited on the lower reaches of the Gianicolo.[136] Soderini's *villa suburbana* must have been situated on this rather wild hill. Soderini

---

[132] Volterra, Biblioteca Guarnacci, MS 6204, not paginated but between 84v and 85r, i.e. 84 bis r: 'Cardinalis ... noster in suburbio nostro S.ti P. emit oedes, quae fuerunt Calagrani, Innocentii cubicularii, continentes Theodorine oedes. Habent supra se ortos celebres iminentes templo beati Michaelis in quibus sunt cenacula, porticus et cubicula quocumque magno principe digna, sedes vero ample admodum sunt, non tam ad habitandum magnifice quam idoneae, sed parvo sumptu cardinalis commode habitabat cum universa familia.'

[133] See R. Zapperi's entry on Calagrano in the *Dizionario biografico degli italiani*, XVI, pp. 403–5, Hofmann, *Forschungen*, II, p. 182 and Eubel, *Hierarchia*, II, p. 216.

[134] Machiavelli, *Lettere*, p. 298.

[135] R. Krautheimer, S. Corbett, W. Frankl, *Corpus basilicarum christianarum Romae*, III (Rome, 1967), p. 125; see also Huelsen, *Le chiese*, p. 388.

[136] Armellini, *Le chiese*, II, p. 1386.

appears to have had a predilection for this part of Rome, possibly because it was the area in which he first lived.

By 25 September 1509 Soderini had begun building at this villa, so he had three building projects running concurrently: the development in the Borgo with the stable, the palace at SS. Apostoli and the *villa suburbana*.[137] By 19 October he had reputedly made substantial changes.[138] Nothing further is known about this villa or what part it played in his life, except that he had disposed of it by the time he wrote his will of February 1511. David Coffin mentions papal bulls of 1516 and 1519 which encouraged 'suburban building by extending the building privileges granted by earlier popes for urban development to sites just outside the city "where many beautiful gardens, vineyards and other summer retreats and buildings, no less lovely than useful and necessary, have been rising in the last few years"'.[139] But Soderini's will of February 1524 does not mention any significant property by name other than Castelpulci outside Florence, and instead refers to the agreement reached between Piero Soderini and him whereby all their joint properties in Italy were to be left to their one remaining brother and their five nephews.[140] So it is not known whether he replaced his former suburban villa with another, still more splendidly constructed, to take advantage of the new building privileges (although the 'conspiracy' of 1517 could have interfered with his plans). One possibility is that he was involved in property speculation when he bought this villa, and that he was renovating and embellishing it in order to sell it for a higher price. Clearly, Soderini was interested in housing, at a residential and financial level. He was by no means unusual for a cardinal in embarking on these building schemes for palaces, but his speculative building of shops and smaller housing units, and his possible speculation in the property market, must have been considerably less typical.

Nor did Soderini confine his activity to Rome where it could be seen and appreciated, but continued to build even when exiled to the kingdom of Naples between 1517 and 1521. About a kilometre outside Fondi, towards Naples on the left of the Via Appia, near the sixtieth milestone, is a very long piece of reticulated Roman wall, broken at one point by a gate which bears two inscriptions.[141] On the north side is a

---

[137] Volterra, Biblioteca Guarnacci, MS 6204, 103v, where Gherardi writes to Soderini: 'de tertio tuarum edium habitaculo'. [138] *Ibid.*, 95r.

[139] D. Coffin, *The villa in the life of renaissance Rome* (Princeton, 1979), p. 245.

[140] Rome, Arch. Sod., III, 186r–189v.

[141] This site was the subject of F. Apolloni Ghetti's first article on Soderini, 'Il cardinale Francesco Soderini restauratore nel 1519 di un monumento classico', *Strenna dei romanisti*, 21 April 1976.

6. Francesco Soderini's coat of arms on the gate to his villa outside
Fondi.

Soderini coat of arms, displaying three pairs of antlers and the inscription
'Varronianum restitutum P. F. de Soderinis Car. Vulterranum an.
MDXIX' (see figure 6), and on the south side is the Colonna column
and the inscription 'Non inveni tantam fidem in Israel', with a little

7. The Colonna coat of arms on the other side of the gate at Francesco
Soderini's villa outside Fondi.

stag's head beneath (see figure 7).[142] The motto about faith is one of
Soderini's[143] and the stag's head must surely be another reference to the
Soderini family. Prospero Colonna had been given Fondi (and Itri and

[142] I am very grateful to Gino Paparello for giving me photographs of this gate.
[143] See C. Padiglione, *I motti delle famiglie italiane* (Naples, 1910), p. 99; J. Gelli, *Divisi,
motti, imprese di famiglie e personaggi italiani* (Milan, 1926), p. 452; and V. Spreti,
Enciclopedia storico-nobiliare italiana, VI (Milan, 1932), p. 341. Only Gelli singles the
motto out as belonging to Francesco Soderini in particular, not the Soderini family

Sperlunga and many other places) by king Ferdinand of Aragon on 15 November 1504 as a reward for his services in the war of Naples, which had been won by the Spanish.[144]

When Soderini left Rome in 1517 he went to Fondi and at some point acquired the villa and the land behind this wall. The wall has attracted much attention – its age and measurements are recorded with precision, $2\frac{1}{2}$ metres high and 120 metres long, built in the Augustan age between 55 BC and 50 AD[145] – and so have the large letters stuck into it (V. Varonianus P. I. F. C.). Arguments have raged over their material (were they of metal or green marble?)[146] and their meaning[147] and who removed them.[148] However, the villa itself has disappeared without arousing comment. In the sixteenth century, this Roman villa was lived in by Soderini but there is no indication of its condition. It is mentioned by two English travellers of the nineteenth century, Sir Richard Colt Hoare and Sir William Gell,[149] but only in passing, before or after a description of the wall. Gell even drew a sketch of the gate with the ruins of the house in the background.[150] It is also marked on a map of 1824 as the Villa Vatrone just outside Fondi on the Via Appia, but nothing is written about it in the text.[151] Occasionally, the gate and garden are said to be at Gegni, which comes from a corruption of *giovenca*, a heifer, the symbol of the goddess Isis to whom there had been a temple nearby,[152] and once the site is described as Monachelle.[153] The

in general. The line is from the Bible, Matthew 8:10 and Luke 7:9: 'I have not found so great faith, no, not in Israel' (King James version).

[144] Coppi, *Memorie*, p. 249.

[145] G. Lugli, *La tecnica edilizia romana* (Rome, 1957), I, p. 508 and II, CXLIII, 3.

[146] F. Notarjanni, 'Viaggio per l'Ausonia', in *Giornale enciclopedico di Napoli*, 7 (1913), IV (which I have unfortunately not been able to see) stated that they were bronze. Sir Richard Colt Hoare, *A classical tour through Italy and Sicily* (London, 1819), p. 82 thought that they must have been of *verde antiquo*. T. Mommsen, *Inscriptiones regni Neapolitani latinae* (Leipzig, 1852), p. 220 merely recorded both opinions. Modern writers all incline towards the metal.

[147] G. Sotis, *Cenno istorico della città di Fondi* (Naples, 1838), p. 56 suggested that they meant 'Valerius Varonianus Pontifex Isidis faciendum curavit'.

[148] See G. Conte-Colino, *Storia di Fondi* (Naples, 1901), p. 46.

[149] Sir Richard Colt Hoare, *A classical tour*, p. 82, and Sir William Gell, *The topography of Rome and its vicinity* (London, 1834), I, p. 237: 'Near Fondi is a Roman house, built upon a terrace of polygonal blocks, below which is a reticulated wall.'

[150] British School at Rome, William Gell notebook I, unpaginated, house of 'Varonianus P. I. F.' near Fondi. The date on the verso of the previous folio but one is 19 April 1826.

[151] Anon., *Voyage pittoresque, historique et géographique de Rome à Naples et ses environs* (Naples, 1823).

[152] Conte-Colino, *Storia*, p. 46 and M. Forte, *Fondi nei tempi* (Casamari, 1972), p. 620. Sir Richard Colt Hoare, *A classical tour*, p. 82 thought that it was a temple to Hercules.   [153] Lugli, *La tecnica*, II, CXLIII, 3.

garden passed to the estate of the bishop of Fondi, and after the diocese of Fondi was suppressed in 1818 and added to that of Gaeta, the garden became again private property.[154] It is now a modern housing estate and the inscription on the gate is the only record that Soderini restored a building in Fondi.

At some point, Soderini thought of building a monastery in the city of Fondi itself, and for this reason rented the Torre degli Stracciati[155] in the north-east corner of the walls at an annual fee of 25 *carlini*, but he later changed his mind. This would have been yet another building project;[156] it probably fell through because Soderini left Fondi. Possibly for this reason, the area of Fondi which includes this tower was known as 'cardinale' from the end of the seventeenth century.[157] In the list of Soderini's property drawn up to ascertain the inheritance of the nephews, the possessions at Fondi are valued at 1,200 *scudi*.[158] A final piece of building, this time at the episcopal palace in Vicenza, was due to the Soderini and probably to Francesco. They had built a new and very beautiful loggia, which, unfortunately, ruined the view from the bishop's apartments. Too hot in the summer and too cold in the winter, it was criticised in a letter from Vincenzo Duranti, the *maestro da casa* of both Soderini and the next incumbent, cardinal Niccolò Ridolfi, in 1529.[159] The use of the term 'the Soderini' indicates that the work may have been a collective effort, or perhaps the usage may indicate a slightly critical attitude. It should also be noted that before Soderini's elevation to the cardinalate, in his role as bishop of Volterra, he undertook, in 1498, the rebuilding of the castle of Berignone in the Val di Cecina which belonged to the bishopric.[160]

---

[154] Rome, Arch. Sod., II, 547v, and information from Rev. Geremia Iudicone of S. Pietro di Fondi, for which I am most grateful.

[155] The name is said to be derived from the old Fondi surname of Straczato or Stracciato (verbal communication from Rev. G. Iudicone).

[156] Fondi, Archivio di S. Pietro, manuscript entitled 'Sacro visitatio totius Fundanae diocesis ab Ill.mo et Rev.mo episcopo Joanne Baptista Comparino peracta anno 1599', 360r.

[157] Forte, *Fondi nei tempi*, p. 558. The other possibility is that the *rione* is named after the antipope Clement VII who had stayed in Fondi.

[158] Rome, Arch. Sod., II, 149r.

[159] ASF, Acquisti e doni 84, inserto 3, 3v, letter of Durante to cardinal Niccolò Ridolfi. I would like to thank Lucy Byatt for this reference. The whole garden was probably embellished by the Soderini, as Francesco Soderini's arms used to be over the entrance to the episcopal garden. See Mantese, *Memorie*, III, II, p. 183.

[160] ASF, Capitoli, Appendice 44, 22v: 'Hoc castellum tertio diritum per dominos Florentinos anno domini 1447. Ego F. Soderinus episcopus Vulterranus incepi reparare anno domini 1498 quod faustum felixque sit mihi et ecclesiae Vulterranae.' This is written in Soderini's own hand.

Thus far attention has been concentrated on property which Soderini acquired for his own use, comprising either existing structures in which he lived or sites on which he built new houses. Even in these instances he clearly regarded property and development as a form of investment which often yielded large returns. However, he owned other property in Rome and elsewhere which he had acquired purely for financial reasons. For example, he tried to effect an exchange of property with Cristoforo dal Poro, a papal servant with possessions in and around Bologna and Mantua, in May 1508. Soderini was offering land, vineyards and houses in Rome[161] which formed no part of the Borgo complex, and can, therefore, be taken as evidence of a wider holding in property.[162] He also accumulated other land and vineyards near the Borgo, situated just outside the Porta Viridaria[163] and seems to have been collecting property in the Fondi area, around Frosinone and Ferentino.[164]

In conclusion, Soderini's energetic interest in building ran in tandem with his career in the church. Soderini was happy to use his income from benefices and other ecclesiastical revenues to finance his building projects, but he acted upon the assumption that the palaces, houses and shops themselves, and the money they generated, belonged to him and his family. The importance for a cardinal of his family is also explicit in all Soderini's building acquisitions and enterprises. Soderini's Florentine background was equally crucial, even in his choice of property and his building activities in Rome. For example, all the major building in Rome with which Soderini was connected took place prior to Piero Soderini's downfall in 1512. It is legitimate to ask why was Soderini accumulating property in Rome before 1512? Did he foresee that the family might require an alternative power base? Policy may have changed after this date and, during Leo's pontificate, Soderini may have thought it more judicious to restrict his building activities in Rome to a minimum. Instead, he may have chosen to consolidate some country property outside Florence, for by that stage he owned Castelpulci,[165] a

---

[161] ASMa, AG, b.858, 19 May 1508, cardinal Sigismondo Gonzaga to marquis Francesco.

[162] For another example of this, see Lowe, 'Francesco Soderini', appendix 3, p. 339. In his will of 1511 Soderini leaves a house in the Borgo, which was not part of the complex, to Lucrezia, countess of Montagliana, the tenant of the house at the time.

[163] The Porta Viridaria was the third gate of the Leonine city. For Soderini's landholdings outside this gate, see Rome, Arch. Sod., xxii, 19v and 33r; Rome, Arch. Sod., ii, 286r; and ASR, Notari dell'AC 7155, 61r.

[164] Rome, Arch. Sod., iii, 6r and v, 12 October 1520.

[165] See Lowe, 'Francesco Soderini', appendix 4, p. 354 and G. Carocci, *I dintorni di Firenze*, ii (Florence, 1907), p. 431.

palace at Arcetri[166] and a palace inside the fortified compound at Empoli.[167] Emphasis upon these ties to his family and his *patria* should not be at the expense of motivation for building provided by his situation in Rome. Obviously, Soderini would have responded to demands for magnificence both because he was a cardinal and because he was the brother of the *gonfaloniere a vita* of Florence. Nor should personal inclination be downplayed; Soderini involved himself in building projects because he wanted to, and not because he was forced to do so. Other cardinals took different decisions.

[166] M. Menotti, *Documenti inediti sulla famiglia e la corte di Alessandro VI* (Rome, 1917), pp. 303–5 and Carocci, *I dintorni*, II, pp. 222 and 229.

[167] Rome, Arch. Sod., II, 148r.

CHAPTER 17

PRIVATE AND PERSONAL POSSESSIONS

The ostentation required of a curia cardinal was not limited to architectural display but also encompassed personal possessions. Between 30 April and 2 May 1523 an inventory was made of the contents of Soderini's palace by the criminal judge Rossello Rosselli, on behalf of Girolamo Ghinucci, the bishop of Ascoli Piceno (and Worcester), and ultimately on behalf of the pope, after Soderini had been imprisoned, on 27 April, by the pope for treasonable correspondence (through his nephew) with the king of France (see pages 132–4). It has been assumed that this inventory was of Soderini's palace in the Borgo, but it is now certain that it is an inventory of the palace of Torre Sanguigna. Parts of the inventory were listed by Rodocanachi[1] and parts treated very briefly by Frommel[2] but it has never been published nor analysed as a whole. There were many reasons why an inventory might be made of a person's belongings. Usually it was done immediately after someone's death, as such lists were necessary, for example, for divisions of property and goods after death, and for reckonings after the decease of a bankrupt.[3]

In Rome a cardinal's belongings, in theory, were supposed to revert to the pope on the death of the cardinal, unless the cardinal had papal permission to make a will with testamentary bequests, although in many cases they were handed on to the cardinal's family without any trouble. For example, an inventory exists of the belongings of cardinal Niccolò Flisco, dated 17 August 1524,[4] drawn up after his death from natural causes on 15 August, in order that his family might inherit his

[1] E. Rodocanachi, *La première renaissance, Rome au temps de Jules II et de Léon X* (Paris, 1912), pp. 37–45.

[2] Frommel, *Der Römische Palastbau*, I, for example, pp. 69 and 71.

[3] See the inventory of 11 March 1507 of the bankrupt Giovanni di Francesco Maringhi, who was the agent in Pera for several Florentine firms, published by G. Richards, *Florentine merchants in the age of the Medici* (Cambridge, Mass., 1932), pp. 185–201.   [4] This is in ASR, Notari dell'AC 411, 245r ff.

possessions. However, some popes intervened to seize the goods before the death of a cardinal. On 5 January 1503 Antonio Giustiniani reported that cardinal Battista Orsini had been taken to Castel Sant'Angelo, that his house had been emptied by the pope and that everything 'down to the straw' had been carried off to the Vatican.[5] Money, silver, tapestry and other moveable goods were picked out as being of especial interest. The diarist Tedallini wrote that after the consistory of 22 June 1517, when cardinals Riario, Sauli and Petrucci were accused of conspiring against Leo, the pope arranged that all Riario's silver and all Petrucci's belongings should be secretly collected and confiscated.[6] It was in actions of this nature that the pope showed his strength, because the cardinals could have no recourse to any law to retrieve what had been taken. On quick raids such as these, often no inventory was made.

It is interesting that the inventory of Soderini's palace is dated 30 April to 2 May, as there are reports of list-making and looting taking place earlier, and there would be no reason to delay for three days. The Mantuan ambassador wrote on 27 April that the sergeant went to the house with soldiers, and then the auditor of the *Camera* arrived, and they made a list of everything.[7] Filippo Strozzi wrote to his brother, on 28 April, that two chests had been taken away to the Vatican that morning, and rumours were circulating that they contained writing or more valuable objects.[8] On 2 May the ambassadors from three separate powers sent back reports. Foscari, the Venetian, reported that people were sent to Soderini's house and had found there about 50,000 ducats worth of money, silver and writings.[9] It may be that the writings referred to here were deeds or credit notes or bills of exchange which would have had a financial value. Galeotto de' Medici wrote to Florence that the auditor of the *Camera* had taken to the palace all the writings, notes, money, cash, silver and finely worked objects.[10] L'Abbadino sent a very full description back to Mantua. He wrote that the pope had requested that the locked chests, containing writings, money and silver, should be carried to his room in the Vatican and opened. According to cardinal de' Medici, the pope wished to touch with his own hands each

[5] Giustinian, *Dispacci*, I, pp. 309–10.
[6] Sebastiano Tedallini, *Diario romano*, ed. P. Piccolomini, in *Rerum italicarum scriptores*, ed. L. Muratori, XXIII, III, appendice (Città di Castello, 1907–11), p. 372.
[7] ASMa, AG, b.867, 56r, 27 March (a mistake for April).
[8] Bardi, 'Filippo Strozzi', p. 39.   [9] Sanuto, *I diarii*, XXXIV, 123.
[10] ASF, Otto di prat., Resp. 24, 225r.

individual piece of evidence. And day by day the writings were being read.[11]

On 4 May, Galeotto commented on the diligence with which all the writings taken from Soderini's house were being examined, on the basis that such words spoke for themselves.[12] Writing on 10 May, Galeotto related how several strong-boxes had been carried out of Soderini's house, and that the crowd and a member of Soderini's household had claimed that they contained money, silver, writings and other valuable objects. The pope, on the other hand, claimed that nothing but writings had been taken, and that whoever claimed otherwise was lying. In addition, he maintained that, in the course of compiling the inventory, very few ducats had been found.[13] Why the pope should lie quite so blatantly, when there was a public document setting out the truth, is not clear. The Venetian orator reported on 13 May that those things which (the pope denied) had been taken, had now been returned.[14]

This matter provides an opportunity to compare the news of the event with the event itself. The ambassadors did, at least, present both sides of the story and were not only reporting the pope's official news bulletins. It is possible that the official inventory also fudged the reckoning, but in that case it would have been easier not to take an inventory at all. Adrian was renowned for his fairness, and even if Ghinucci ordered trunks and cases to be sent to the Vatican without Adrian's prior permission, it is quite likely that Adrian would have returned those containing valuables which could have had no bearing on the case. The likelihood of this hypothesis is increased by the fact that Soderini, when he made his will of 22 February 1524, only mentioned some writings pertaining to Piero Soderini which the pope had taken away and not returned, and 2,300 ducats,[15] whereas he would surely have listed other valuables such as silver had they also been missing.

The inventory[16] lists nine chests and strong-boxes which are locked up and sealed by the auditor for the pope. Three are recorded as containing cloth, one *res minute*, two writings and one silver vases. The contents of the others are not mentioned. No attempt is made to list the objects in these trunks. This means that an analysis of the items in the inventory would in any case be incomplete. This basic difficulty is

[11] ASMa, AG, b.867, 77r: 'Et Sua S.tà con le mani sue, secundo me dice Mons. Ex.mo de' Medici, ha voluto toccare ogni cosa remoto, ogni testimonio. Et de dì in dì va legendo le scritture.'

[12] ASF, Otto di prat., Resp. 24, 221r, 4 April (a mistake for May) 1523.

[13] *Ibid.*, 231v.   [14] Sanuto, *I diarii*, XXXIV, 149.

[15] See Lowe, 'Francesco Soderini', appendix 4, p. 355.

[16] See ASR, Notari dell'AC 410, 122r-128v and Lowe, 'Francesco Soderini', appendix 5, pp. 358–73.

compounded because those doing the inventory only recorded ten rooms[17] – there was no kitchen for example, nor any offices – and there must have been many more rooms in the palace. Furthermore, in some rooms, such as Soderini's *anticamera*, hardly any objects at all are recorded and there must have been more, so that the inventory, even with complete lists of the items in the sealed chests and strong-boxes, would be far from exhaustive. However, it is possible to make some elementary observations, even if it is not possible at this stage to judge whether any of Soderini's possessions were distinctly Florentine in their design or provenance.

From the information in the inventory, it appears that the disposition of the rooms in the palace at Torre Sanguigna, and the dispersal of objects and furniture within those rooms, was quite standard for a person of Soderini's wealth and status. The rooms included a main hall (*sala magna*), a *guardaroba* (literally, a room where belongings were stored), Soderini's bedroom, his study (*studorio*) and a *cubiculo* or *cameretta*. It is not entirely clear but it is likely that the sequence of the rooms in the palace corresponded more or less to the normal pattern, with the main hall leading, possibly through other rooms, to the antechamber and the bedroom, which in turn led onto the study and the *cameretta*.[18] As far as the furniture was concerned, it too appears standard; for example, the bedroom furniture was exactly what one would have expected, even having the requisite number of mattresses on the bed.[19] The cardinal had a study full of books, and a separate little room full of his most precious possessions, including gold, silver, jewels, plates, glasses, forks and spoons. It was usual for such objects to be concentrated in the study or *cameretta*, and for fewer loose objects to be found elsewhere.[20] Interest in the inventory must therefore focus upon what information of a personal nature it can reveal about the owner of its contents.

Detailed comparisons between inventories are not yet feasible because very few partial or complete inventories of late fifteenth- or early sixteenth-century cardinals living in Rome have been published.[21]

[17] I am here assuming that there were not two *sale magne*, but one, which seems especially likely as the first time round some furniture is listed, and the second time only the contents of a wooden chest.

[18] P. Thornton, *The Italian renaissance interior* (London, 1991), p. 302.

[19] *Ibid.*, p. 167; ASR, Notari dell'AC 410, 126v and Lowe, 'Francesco Soderini', p. 367.   [20] Thornton, *Italian renaissance interior*, p. 13.

[21] E. Rodocanachi, 'Le luxe des cardinaux romains de la renaissance', *Revue des questions historiques*, 89 (1911), especially pp. 415 and 417. D. Chambers, *A renaissance cardinal and his worldly goods: the will and inventory of Francesco Gonzaga (1444–1483)* (London, 1992), pp. 144–88 publishes a post-mortem inventory of cardinal

Nevertheless, Soderini's inventory does appear, to a large extent, to reflect his cardinalitial tastes and lifestyle. The most obvious manifestation of this is the colour of the materials, clothes, hangings, furniture and fripperies which were nearly all between red and reddish-purple and pale red, either *rosso, rosato, rosino* or *pavonazzo*. These four shades could vary according to the quality and combination of the dyes. *Rosso* was likely to be a brilliant red, made either from kermes which was the most prestigious and most expensive dye, imported from the East (it is here in the inventory in *damasco carmesino*, for example), or from the less exotic European *grana*. In 1464 Paul II had decreed that kermes be 'the cardinals' purple, even though it was red'.[22] *Rosato* and *rosino* were lesser shades of red, and *pavonazzo* (peacock colour) is variously thought of as being the reddish-brown of a peahen or, more likely, a mulberry colour. From antiquity, it had been associated with majesty and senatorial dignity. There is little in the inventory that is not in one of these shades. Apart from one blue cape (*cappa di ciambellotto azuro*) and a heavy black coat (*giubbone di raso nero*) with detached sleeves (*maniche*), those items which are in other colours are not clothes but are nearly all pieces of cloth, blankets (*coperte*) and canopies (*speraveri*), and are exclusively in black, white, blue and green. Red predominates to an extraordinary degree: the clothes are all red, the gloves are red, the silk tassels (*fiocchi di cardinale di seta rossa*) are red, the shoes (*calzone*) and stockings (*calze*) are red, the nightclothes (4 *costume di lecto di taffeytate carmesino*) are red. To go with this, the harness for the mules (*fornimenti di mula*) are a similar colour. As a part of the furnishing, there are loose red cushions (*cussini di raso carmesino*) and whole red suites (1 *furnimento di lecto di panno rosato in 6 peciis*) and Soderini's bed is in different shades of red.[23] Even more solid pieces of furniture do not remain unaffected; for example, there is a chair covered in red velvet (*una sedes coperta veluto rubeo*). Although it was necessary for the clothes to be in these colours, the rest must have been a matter of choice and taste. Many specific details of clerical dress were determined only by post-Tridentine legislation,[24] but there were quite strict pre-Tridentine rules which the papal master of ceremonies, Paris de Grassis, always tried to enforce. Not only was the colour (*rosso* or *pavonazzo*) important, but possibly

---

Francesco Gonzaga, dated 27 October 1483, recording his possessions in Bologna and Mantua, but it is not known how many of his Roman effects were included.

22 J. Herald, *Renaissance dress in Italy, 1400–1500* (London, 1981), p. 91.

23 C. Mazzi, *La casa di maestro Bartalo di Tura* (Siena, 1900), pp. 28–9 wrote that red was the usual colour for *lettiere* (settles, day beds) and their drapes, and it could be that beds were often red too.

24 B. Ganter, *Clerical attire: a historical synopsis and a commentary* (Washington, 1955), p. 160.

also the material, and some liturgical days demanded one outfit, some days another.[25] Even the number of layers worn, and the presence or absence of capes at various times, probably conformed to some ancient code of unwritten rules which only became crystallised into permanent regulation after the Council of Trent.

If Soderini had become a devotee of the colour red as a result of being a cardinal, it appears that other aesthetic decisions had also been taken as a result of being an ecclesiastic. His palace was littered with the paraphernalia of ceremony and faith so that the distinction between the secular and the religious seems to have become blurred. Objects used in the celebration of mass are listed side by side with kitchen utensils and writing implements; they are no longer things apart. To some extent those taking the inventory may have been responsible for this impression, but it is very unlikely that they moved objects from one room to another to include them in the inventory, and it is the mixture of the religious and the everyday within the same space that is remarkable. Soderini's taste had been formed by expensive cloth and the fine craftsmanship of chalices and crucifixes, so that for his own pleasure he must have bought red silks, damasks and velvets and commissioned, bought or collected much fine silver and jewellery. It is obvious from the inventory that Soderini's interest in possessions lay predominantly in these expensive areas, but he may have accumulated them primarily for use, and only secondarily to form part of a collection to be displayed.

His career in the church meant that at home he kept not only ecclesiastical vestments, such as his cardinal's beret (*beretta*) and other hats (*capello*),[26] chasubles (*pianeta*), stoles (*stola*), albs (*camice*), maniples (*manipolo*) and amices (*amito*), but also altar cloths or palls (*palleo*), corporals (*corporale*), altar cushions (*cussanetto d'altare*), aspergilla (*asperge*) for sprinkling holy water, cruets (*phiole*), chalices, crosses, crucifixes, candlesticks (*candelleri*) and a number of *agnus dei* and *pace*.[27] All these last objects were made from extremely expensive materials such as gold and silver, and decorated with pearls and other precious gems. They combined with more secular goblets (*coppa*), tankards or jugs (*bochale*) and cups or glasses (*taccea*) to form one single collection of precious metal and jewel work, which may well have merged in

---

[25] M. Lonigo, *Delle vesti purpuree et d'altri colori con quali va adorna la dignità cardinalitia* (Venice, 1653) gives the post-Tridentine rules. Although the early ones will not have been as complicated, they will have had the same essential structure.

[26] On cardinals' hats, see H. Hynes, *The privileges of cardinals* (Washington, 1945), pp. 22–3.

[27] See *L'oreficeria nella Firenze del quattrocento*, ed. M. Ciardi Dupré Dal Poggetto (Florence, 1977) for examples of candlesticks, chalices and *pace*.

Soderini's mind so that the function of these objects lost any power to be a force of separation. These expensive items, whether designed for ecclesiastical or worldly purposes, had not only aesthetic and functional value, but must in addition have been appraised for their moveability and realisability; they were portable investments to be used in times of need. Soderini was, in this respect, perhaps representative of one type of a late fifteenth- and early sixteenth-century pre-Reformation, renaissance cardinal, the religious content of whose life was not a major differentiated facet of it, nor an overriding principle as such, but a completely integrated part which was accepted without question. Traditional christianity in the renaissance has been characterised as the 'matrix of experience',[28] but it was a matrix which was so universal that it did not excite comment. As far as Soderini was concerned, religious and spiritual considerations would always play second fiddle in his life to political and financial ones, but this does not mean that they too did not have their place.

The inventory does shed some light on Soderini's personality and tastes. Sometimes it even manages to do this in spite of omissions by those compiling the list. For example, it is obvious[29] that Soderini had a sizeable and wide-ranging library in his study, of both manuscripts and printed books, but the tabulator chose not to count or catalogue them; there is, however, supportive documentation in the entry of 'six printed and manuscript books by various authors' which were in another room.[30] It would be rather odd of Soderini to own both an organ (*organum*) and a harpsichord (*clavicimbulum*) were he not interested in music in some sense, but most probably not as a practitioner.[31] He had far more tapestries in his house than paintings, and some of them were old and valuable; unfortunately, their subjects (except that they were embellished *cum figuris* and *con l'arme a verdura*) are not recorded. Tapestries decorated with scenes, coats of arms (which meant they had been especially commissioned) or human figures were particularly expensive,[32] and Soderini seems to have had a predilection for them.

Only two paintings were recorded, both of which were in his bedroom, one a picture of the Virgin Mary which is so standard that

---

[28] T. Verdon, 'Environments of experience and imagination', in *Christianity and the renaissance: image and religious imagination in the quattrocento*, ed. T. Verdon and J. Henderson (Syracuse, 1990), p. 5.

[29] ASR, Notari dell'AC 410, 126v and Lowe, 'Francesco Soderini', appendix 5, p. 367: 'In studorio dicti domini cardinalis fuerunt plures libri diversarum facultatum et diversorum auturum, quorum numerum non notavi.'

[30] ASR, Notari dell'AC 410, 123v and Lowe, 'Francesco Soderini', appendix 5, p. 362: '6 libri impressi et scripti manu diversorum authorum.'

[31] See below, pp. 265–6.   [32] Thornton, *Italian renaissance interior*, p. 48.

nothing at all can be deduced from his ownership, and the other a representation of St Jerome. It is possible that Soderini would have commissioned this because it portrayed a saint with cardinals' attributes, most likely with a cardinal's hat, but equally it could have portrayed Jerome and a lion or Jerome alone in the desert or Jerome in his study. All these topics were common in fifteenth- and sixteenth-century depictions of Jerome.[33] As well as these, Soderini owned a statue (*imagine*) of St Catherine which was displayed in the same room. In the area of pictorial representation, Soderini's taste seems to have been remarkably conservative. Two maps of the world (*mappemundi*) adorned the walls of his bedroom, and he was also the owner of a portulan chart (*carta di navigaro con soi fornimenti*). For recreation, he seems to have relied upon a chess-set (*ioco di schiachi*),[34] a catapult or crossbow (*balestra*) and five masks (*mascare*). His writing utensils included fancy pens (*penne d'argento* or *penne laborate d'oro*), a tempera pen, marble inkwells (*calamari di marmore*) and a primitive blotter in the form of a silver sandbox (*pulverino d'argento*).

Numbered amongst useful everyday objects were two little silver bells (*campanelle*) to ring for servants, two pairs of gold-plated scissors (*para di fornice inorate*), two silver toothpicks (2 *scalpi denti*), a brass balance (*stattera d'ottone*) and a silver ball used to hold perfume to sweeten the smell of a room (*palla d'argento de tenere odore*). Expensive trappings for his stable of horses and mules also crept in – iron stirrups decorated with gold (*staffi di ferro fornito con oro*), and a bit and a pair of gold spurs (1 *morso et uno paro di speroni dorati*). He obviously enjoyed wearing furs, having clothes made of and lined with them, as for example a wolf's skin collar (*colletto di pelle di lupi*) and a red camlet robe lined with fox (*veste di ciambellotto rosso foderato di vulpe*), and he even had boots (*stivalletti*) and shoes (*calzone*) lined in fur. His arms appear, but only on blankets or covers (*coperte*), pieces of material that hung down over entrances (*portiere*) and cushions (*cussini*). A stray piece of elephant, either a tooth or a tusk (*dente di elefanto*), is recorded, which could conceivably have belonged to Hanno, the elephant presented to Leo X. Finally, it emerges that Soderini had a pair of spectacles (*paro di occhiali*),[35] perhaps necessary after a lifetime of study, which he must have left behind when summoned to the castle. There are some glaring

[33] E. Rice, *St Jerome in the renaissance* (Baltimore, 1985), pp. 65, 75–6, 104–6.

[34] Chess-sets seem to have been usual items for cardinals to own. See Chambers, *A renaissance cardinal*, p. 156.

[35] These were quite common at the time among the higher echelons of Roman society, and they are occasionally shown in paintings of scholars in their studies, and in particular, in representations of St Jerome. See, for example, Matteo di Giovanni, *St Jerome in his study*, in Thornton, *Italian renaissance interior*, p. 225.

omissions which are also of use. For example, there is only one pair of breeches (*bracche*) as cardinals spent most of their time in robes and gowns. Nor is there any underwear mentioned (perhaps it was in one of the chests), although it usually features in inventories. Nor was there a clock or timepiece of any description.

These objects are of interest for what they reveal about Soderini's domestic life and about his taste, but they also reflect his wealth. Even this incomplete inventory bears witness to his grand and stylish living. Both the number and quality of the items listed confirm this impression. The virtual absence of paintings is not a statement about the wealth of the cardinal; it is rather a reflection of his priorities. Normally, inventories represented the accumulation of a whole family but Soderini was a bachelor prince without a wife and children, and if one or more of his nephews lived with him – Giovanbattista was certainly there when Soderini was summoned to the palace – it was probably in separate apartments which are not inventoried here. It would be interesting to know which, if any, of Soderini's belongings had been handed on to him by his father or other members of his family, because it seems such a fitting collection for a cardinal whereas his father was not an ecclesiastic. The only indication about the overall value of all this moveable property comes from a later, unknown date when Soderini's estate is split up, mainly between his nephews and great-nephews. Both Piero and Giovanbattista di Paolantonio were allocated an eighth of the value of the jewels and furniture of Soderini. This was apparently about 1,500 *scudi*, so the collection can be estimated to have been worth 12,000 *scudi*.[36] As the date of this sale or estimate is not known (it could be any time between 1524 and 1553 but is much more likely to be around the latter date), this valuation is not as helpful as it might be, but certainly the sum was not inconsiderable.[37] But it does seem low if individual items are compared with apparently similar items which are valued in the inventory of the possessions of Lorenzo and the heirs of Giovanni di Pierfrancesco de' Medici in Florence,[38] proving for a final time that the Soderini were always hampered in their opposition to the Medici on account of their inferior wealth.

It is noticeable that Soderini, who was highly pragmatic in his political and ecclesiastical life, was attracted to objects that served a double function: they were practical as well as beautiful. He concen-

---

[36] Rome, Arch. Sod., II, 148r and v.
[37] Rodocanachi, *La première renaissance*, p. 38 offers in comparison the sale of the belongings of cardinal Agostino Trivulzio which took place on 11 July 1548.
[38] See J. Shearman, 'The collections of the younger branch of the Medici', *Burlington magazine*, 117 (1975), pp. 22–7.

trated upon buying and collecting possessions that could be used as well as displayed. This approach could account for his apparent lack of interest in paintings and sculpture which, in his eyes, had a purely decorative purpose, whereas tapestries, plate, fine linen and rich materials were all usable objects as well as indicators of status.

CHAPTER 18

HOUSEHOLD AND ENTOURAGE

Soderini's household is much more difficult to reconstruct although it is known that he took a close personal interest in its composition. In July 1503 he wrote to Jacopo Gherardi saying that until his own arrival in Rome, Gherardi should do nothing about setting up a household, as he wanted to supervise matters in person.[1] A list of cardinals' households was drawn up on 28 December 1509 for the purpose of regulating how much wine per household could be exempted from tax. The largest household out of the twenty-six enumerated was that of cardinal Riario, with 250 members, and the smallest was that of Soderini, with 101; cardinal Carafa had 200, Medici 180, the cardinal of Aragon 172 and Flisco 110. It is not stated whether these are estimates or actual figures.[2] It is hard to imagine how over 200 people could have been usefully employed unless entertainment was on a grand scale. Some cardinals offered superfluous employment in their households in order to boost the number of their followers and thus to enhance their reputation for magnificence and liberality. Judging from the size of his household, Soderini seems to have been immune to such considerations.

His failure to meet contemporary expectations about household size led to his becoming notorious for his meanness. In a contemporary epigram, 'On Soderini's avarice' by Piero Valeriani, one Catellacius, an emaciated member of Soderini's household, is pictured gorging himself during the prelude to a play performed in the presence of Leo and many cardinals. Everyone was amazed at the quantities of food he consumed except cardinal Adriano Castellesi (Soderini's neighbour in the Borgo),

---

[1] Volterra, Biblioteca Guarnacci, MS 6204, 35r, 5 July 1503.

[2] AV, Fondo concist., Acta miscell. 3, 28r and v. D. Chambers, 'The economic predicament of renaissance cardinals', *Studies in medieval and renaissance history*, 2 (1966), p. 293 first brought this document to the attention of scholars. He also pointed out that the census of 1526 yielded a similar average per household to that of the tax document of 1509, although the extremities were much further apart, household numbers then ranging from 456 to 16.

who quipped that he would be more surprised if anyone left Soderini's house full.[3] The sixteenth-century historian, Nardi, however, defended Soderini's behaviour and attributed his reputation for meanness to the envy of others who were less administratively capable: 'By the ignorant he was reputed miserly, I do not know why, if not because he was not prodigal nor a spendthrift but a good and careful administrator of his house and household.'[4]

The household appears to have been an entirely bachelor establishment and so far no women have been found connected with it. Quite a large proportion of the household were clerks who could not have married and had families, but for the others who ranged from scribe or secretary (*cancelliere*) to manservant (*cameriere*), there were no such formal restrictions although their position may have demanded a semblance of celibacy. There must have been a high crossover between Soderini's ecclesiastical appointees and a certain section of his household servants, whom he helped to obtain benefices. Vicars-general of his bishoprics, such as Bartolomeo Soderini in Volterra,[5] and others with appointments in the bishopric, such as Mario Maffei, an archpriest,[6] discharged ecclesiastical tasks, but it was not always clear where the line came between work for Soderini, the bishop and cardinal, and work for Soderini, the private individual. The Franciscan, Marco Strozzi, seems to have been employed in both capacities,[7] and this blurring of the private and the official was commonplace. Strictly speaking, members of the *familia* should only have been concerned with the running of Soderini's household, and should, therefore, be differentiated from ecclesiastical and political servants and employees, but in practice no such division is sustainable at this period. Many people doubled up in their roles, and job descriptions were fluid. Some of Soderini's most

---

[3] Piero Valeriani, *Hexametri odae et epigrammata* (Venice, 1550), 108r and v.

[4] Nardi, *Istorie*, II, 69: 'Dal volgo [era] reputato avaro, non so perché, se non perché egli non era prodigo né scialacquatore, ma buono e accurato amministratore della casa e famiglia sua.'

[5] See Bizzocchi, *Chiesa e potere*, p. 249 and S. Salvini, *Catalogo cronologico dei canonici della chiesa metropolitana fiorentina* (Florence, 1770), p. 57.

[6] BV, Autografi Ferrajoli, Raccolta Visconti, 6227v. Mario was also Soderini's *conclavista* in 1513, AV, Fondo concist., Acta miscell. 3, 46v, and a canon of St Peter's. For further information on him, see J. D'Amico, 'The Raffaele Maffei monument in Volterra: small town patronage in the renaissance', in *Supplementum festivum*, ed. J. Hankins, J. Monfasani and F. Purnell Jr. (Binghamton, 1987), pp. 471–4.

[7] See U. Cassuto, *Gli ebrei a Firenze nell'età del rinascimento* (Florence, 1918), p. 67, C. Bresnahan Menning, 'Loans and favors, kin and clients: Cosimo de' Medici and the *Monte di Pietà*', *Journal of modern history*, 61 (1989), pp. 487 and 491, and above, pp. 16 and 171.

important overseers of affairs, such as Jacopo Gherardi, have no recorded position in Soderini's household.

Clerical familiars, whose names have occurred in various sources, included: Mauro, abbot of S. Trinita in Alpibus,[8] Piero di Jacopo da Campiano,[9] Jacopo da Carpi,[10] Marcantonio Gabutio da Sinigaglia,[11] Innocenzo Bondinari,[12] Rainaldo de Balacchis, provost of Rimini,[13] Giovanpetro Passalacqua da Como,[14] Staglia de Actis da Todi,[15] Marinangelis de Alexis da Narni (who revealed in 1526 that in his youth he had been Soderini's barber, chamberlain and steward)[16] and David de Mercuriis da Bologna.[17] Soderini had only one known non-clerical familiar, Giovanni di Cristoforo da Empoli.[18] Three chaplains are mentioned: Bernardino Capra da Mantova in 1512,[19] and Nicolaus da Busseio[20] and Giovanni de Pilariis, a priest from the diocese of Ostia, in 1524,[21] and in 1523 a doctor of Soderini's, Luca Giovannini da Volterra, who was bishop of Anagni, is named.[22] The major-domo (*maestro da casa*) could obviously be either a clerk or a layman. Four holders of this office are known: Basilio da Bagno, a Camaldolese monk (1506),[23]

---

[8] See ASF, Not. antecos. F121 (Marco da Favilla), 278r, 24 July 1503.

[9] *Ibid.*, 278v.

[10] ASBo, Lettere di diversi da Roma e Firenze al Senato (1507–1530), 153r, Albergato de Albergati, Rome, 3 December 1513.

[11] AV, Arm. XXIX, 72, 128v, 2 April 1514.

[12] ASMo, Archivio Estense, Cancelleria ducale, Carteggi dei principi esteri (cardinali) b.1427/178, 16 May (lacuna in text), Soderini to cardinal d'Este.

[13] ASF, Dieci, Resp. 78, 21r, 4 April 1504.   [14] *Ibid.*, 21r, 4 April 1504.

[15] Rome, Arch. Sod., III 242r. In 1526 he stated that he was about fifty years old, and had been the 'familiaris continuus commensalis' of Soderini for approximately eighteen years, up to the time of his death. He was a witness to Soderini's 1524 will, Rome Arch. Sod., III, 189v.

[16] Rome, Arch. Sod., III, 245r. In 1526 he testified that he was about fifty-eight years old and had been the 'servitor et familiaris continuus' of Soderini for thirty years or so. He too witnessed Soderini's 1524 will, Rome, Arch. Sod., III, 189v.

[17] See Lowe, 'Francesco Soderini', appendix 3, pp. 340–1. This *frate* is rather elusive. See *Epistolario di Bernardo Dovizi*, I, p. 336 (1511), where he is described as being from the order of the Servites, whereas Burchard described him in October/November 1503, when he was one of Soderini's *conclaviste*, as 'prior domus Sancti Iohannis Novelli ordinis canonicorum regularium Sancti Augustini extra muros Urbis' ('Liber notarum', II, p. 405). I have not been able to trace him further.

[18] ASF, Not. antecos. F121, 278r.

[19] ASMa, AG, b.860, Soderini to marquis Francesco, Rome, 12 May 1512.

[20] ASR, Notari dell'AC 411, 14r, 20 January 1524. Busseio, who could possibly have been French, was also a canon of Tortona.

[21] See Rome, Arch. Sod., III, 189v and Lowe, 'Francesco Soderini', appendix 4, p. 356.

[22] AV, Fondo concist., Acta vicecanc. 2, 223v, 4 March 1523. He could have been one of Soderini's four young Volterrans. See below, p. 244.

[23] See Machiavelli, *Lettere*, p. 176, Agostino Vespucci to Machiavelli, 28 December 1506, and also Guicciardini, *Storie fiorentine*, pp. 167–8 and B. Varchi, *Storia*

Marcantonio Gabutio, a clerk from Sinigaglia (1517),[24] the clerk Giovanbattista Isola (1523)[25] and the lay Vincenzo Duranti (1524).[26] The secretaries, too, could be lay or clerical: they included Antonio Zeno, a clerk from Ferrara (1503 and 1512),[27] ser Raimondo Raimondi, a clerk from the diocese of Cremona (1504),[28] Niccolò di Giovanni da Milano (1509),[29] ser Eliseo da Colle (1517 onwards)[30] and Piero

fiorentina, ed. L. Arbib (Florence, 1838–41), I, pp. 109–10. He was a friend of Machiavelli which provides another link between Soderini and Machiavelli. He was still alive and in the news in February 1517 (ASF, Il minutario di Goro Gheri, II, 30v), but he may by then have been working for the other (Medicean) side.

24 Razzi, *Vita*, p. 161, 18 January 1517.

25 ASR, Notari dell'AC 410, 128v and Lowe, 'Francesco Soderini', appendix 5, p. 371.

26 Rome, Arch. Sod., III, 158v, 22 February 1524. He went on to be cardinal Niccolò Ridolfi's *maestro da casa*.

27 Zeno was originally an official *cancelliere* or secretary working for the *Dieci*, but it seems that he left Florentine government service when Soderini was promoted to the cardinalate and he accompanied him to Rome. See ASF, Dieci, Resp. 75 and 76 which contain letters composed by Soderini and written by Zeno from Rome during the final months of 1503, and BNF, GC 29 (109) which contains a series of letters from Soderini, from late 1504 and early 1505, some of which are in Zeno's hand. Zeno later benefited from Soderini's ecclesiastical position, and was particularly involved in Tuscan affairs. He became provost of the church of Volterra (see ASF, Diplomatico 37, Comune di Volterra, 433r, 24 May 1520), founded the chapel of saints Peter and Paul in the cathedral in Florence in 1512 (ASF, Manoscritti 178, p. 69), and left a large bequest to Soderini's monastery of S. Giuseppe in Florence (see Calzolai, *San Frediano*, p. 55).

28 Raimondi also wrote Soderini's letters for him when he was a newly appointed cardinal. See ASF, Dieci, Resp. 76 and ASF, Sig., Resp. 27 and BNF, GC 29 (109) for examples. There is a notarial document in his hand in ASF, Dieci, Resp. 76, 127r–128r, dated 13 October 1503. With Zeno, he was one of Soderini's *conclaviste* in September 1503, Burchard, 'Liber notarum', II, p. 378. In August 1508 Soderini wrote to Machiavelli: 'messer Ramondo sarà stato di costà; et ci sarà grato habiate parlato insieme' (Machiavelli, *Lettere*, p. 188), so Raimondi had become an accepted part of Soderini's political machinery. In March 1512 Piero Soderini wrote to Giovanni Ridolfi about Raimondi 'il quale è stato lungo tempo et è secretario del cardinale di Volterra' (ASF, Sig., Otto, Dieci, Miss. 7, 80r). See also *Epistolario di Bernardo Dovizi*, I, p. 411, Dovizi to Giovanni de' Medici: 'io ve accerto che lui è mal contento di Volterra'. It seems that Soderini and Raimondi had a ploy of pretending that Raimondi was willing to betray Soderini; it is extremely unlikely that he did betray him as he worked for him for so long. As early as November 1504, Raimondi had gone through the motions of selling information to the Venetians, Giustinian, *Dispacci*, III, p. 311. In 1513 Raimondi is recorded both as Soderini's secretary and Leo's familiar, AV, Arm. XXIX, 63, 262v. He was an important employee and it is unfortunate that his notarial records have not survived in more profusion.

29 See Guicciardini, *Cusona*, p. 115. In September 1509 Soderini and his entourage stayed with *frate* Niccolò da Milano, the *spedaliere* at the hospital of S. Maria della Scala in Poggibonsi. According to a now untraceable manuscript in the Biblioteca Comunale of S. Gimignano, Niccolò had been Soderini's secretary; in 1505 he had certainly been his *cameriere*. See ASSi, Archivio dell'Ospedale di S. Maria

Edouardo Giachinotti (1519).[31] Some of the secretaries were notaries and there were other notaries, such as ser Domenico de Iuvenibus (who was also an attendant at the conclave of 1513)[32] and ser Enrico Umbstat from Mainz,[33] who could well have been members of the household because they were so intimately connected with it. Finally, two manservants are named: Antonio del Magno (1504)[34] and messer Barone (1507),[35] and several attendants at conclaves who have not been identified in more specific household roles: Giovan Girolami[36] and

della Scala, Deliberazioni 25 (1488–1551), 89r, 9 June 1505; 'Nicolò di Giovanni da Milano, cameriere del R.mo M. lo cardinale da Volterra' was appointed 'in hospitaliere et pro hospitaliere de lo spedale di Poggibonzi per un anno et più ad bene placito di decto M. lo cardinale'. He was still there in 1512. See ASSi, Archivio dell'Ospedale di S. Maria della Scala, Usufrutti, depositi e preste 172 (1416–1603), ciiii.

[30] Eliseo had been a familiar since 1503, ASF, Not. antecos. F121, 278r. He was particularly close to Soderini, was implicated with him in the 'conspiracy' of 1517 and went to Fondi, and was still his secretary during Soderini's final years in Rome.

[31] ASF, Il minutario di Goro Gheri, IV, Gheri to Benedetto Buondelmonti, 2 May 1519.

[32] BL, Add. MSS 8443, 13r. He was the notary of Soderini's final will of 22 February 1524.

[33] Umbstat was active in Soderini's circles from at least 1517 onwards (see ASF, Manoscritti Torrigiani, pergamene, 28 July 1517 and Guasti, I manoscritti Torrigiani, p. 465), and he was a witness of Soderini's last will.

[34] BNF, GC 29 (109) 3422762, 3 November 1504, Francesco Soderini to Piero Soderini, Rome.

[35] ASMa, AG, b.857, 14 November 1507, letters from Soderini to marquis Francesco and Isabella d'Este.

[36] BV, MSS Chigiani 1545, Tizio, 'Historiarum Senensium', IX, 86v. This may be the same Giovan Girolami who lived in France and was, if not an agent of Soderini's, at least an important contact. However, in 1506 Soderini apparently did not know him because Piero Soderini wrote a letter to Francesco in recommendation of him, ASF, Sig., Minutari 19, 135r, 3 November 1506. On 30 March 1507 Soderini wrote from Rome to Mario Maffei in Saintes, telling him to make use of Giovanni Girolami, 'perchè è parente nostro, perchè è homo intendente et pratico' (BV, Autografi Ferrajoli, Raccolta Visconti, 6229v). When Machiavelli was in France in 1510, Soderini wrote to him on 28 June: 'Giovanni Girolami sarà omni dì cum voi' (Machiavelli, Lettere, p. 210) so by then Girolami was Soderini's main French contact. In 1514 Soderini accorded to him and others some ecclesiastical privileges concerned with indulgences, absolutions, burials etc., ASF, Diplomatico, Riformagioni, Atti pubblici, 2 June 1514. He executed commissions for Soderini during the latter's exile, and was still going between France and Rome dispatching tasks for him in November 1522, as Juan Manuel wrote to the emperor that the cardinal of Volterra had sent his servant, Giovanni Girolamo, to the king of France and that he was then on his return to Rome with a safe-conduct of Prospero Colonna, Calendar of letters ... between England and Spain, II, p. 510. Amongst those letters intercepted in 1523 which led to Soderini's imprisonment, was one from him to Girolami in France, ASF, Otto di prat., Resp. 24, 203r. Many members of the Girolami family were later naturalised in France, including two called Giovanni. In July 1525 three

Giuliano da Crapania (1521),[37] Alfonso Paragrano (1521 and 1523), Giovanbattista or Gaspar da Iesi (1523) and Domenico d'Ancona (1523).[38] Others such as Antonio Segni[39] were known to be working for Soderini but it is not known in what capacity. There are yet other names of persons who probably were his intimates or agents, such as Filippo (1517)[40] and Lorenzo (1523)[41] Gagliano; they may even have been rather distant relatives.[42]

It is also probable that those people named as witnesses to the taking of the inventory of Soderini's palace in April/May 1523, and as the witnesses to his will of February 1524, were members of his household. Those who have not already been mentioned who were present for the inventory were: Francesco di Giuliano de Norcia; Martino Alueldensi; Petro di Mona Maria from Florence; Francesco Aqua, a clerk from Taletana; Polidoro Alberico, a clerk from Verona; and Guglielmo Valerio, a clerk from Geneva.[43] In addition, Giovanni Cattero and

brothers – Giovanni, Alessandro and Zanobi – were naturalised (*Catalogue des actes de François I*, ed. P. Marichal, v (Paris, 1887), no. 18473), and in November 1525 a Giovanni Girolami and his nephew were naturalised (*Catalogue des actes de François I*, v, no. 18512). E. Picot, *Les Italiens en France au xvie siècle* (Bordeaux, 1902), p. 117 insists that these two Giovannis should not be confused but it is rather difficult to tell them apart.   [37] See BV, MSS Chigiani 1545, 86v.

[38] During the conclave of 1523, two of Soderini's servants became ill and had to leave (had they been poisoned?). On 13 October Alfonso Paragrano left, and Domenico d'Ancona was admitted in his stead, ASF, Otto di prat., Resp. 30, 260v, Rome, Galeotto de' Medici. The admission of Domenico seems to have caused a small stir. It was reported that the guards and Sessa opposed it at first, saying that it was not lawful for an apostate, and a man convicted of crime, to enter, but that he was allowed to do so by the votes of the cardinals, *Letters and papers*, III, II, p. 1476, 19 November 1523. Unfortunately, it is not known what crime Domenico had committed. On 23 October Giovanbattista (according to Galeotto de' Medici in ASF, Otto di prat., Resp. 30, 331r) or Gaspar (according to Gattico, *Acta selecta*, I, p. 332) da Iesi also fell ill, and one Polidorus entered in his place.

[39] *Carteggi di Francesco Guicciardini*, I, p. 122.

[40] Razzi, *Vita*, p. 123, Francesco Soderini to Giovanvettorio, Rome, 30 May 1517: 'verso Filippo da Gagliano facciate ogni amorevol dimostrazione perché lo merita quanto parente che abiamo'.

[41] Lorenzo da Gagliano was closely involved with Soderini when he was imprisoned in April 1523. It was acknowledged at the time that Lorenzo too would be apprehended were he to be found. See Bardi, 'Filippo Strozzi', p. 39, Filippo Strozzi to his brother Lorenzo in Florence, Rome, 28 April 1523: 'Lorenzo da Gagliano et Giovanbattista si sono fuggiti che sarieno stati ritenuti.' Galeotto de' Medici wrote home on 10 May that Lorenzo da Gagliano had left Rome on the Saturday before the capture, had returned briefly during Monday night, escaping detention by the guard, and had not been seen since, ASF, Otto di prat., Resp. 24, 231v.

[42] *Lettere di Giovanbattista Busini a Benedetto Varchi*, ed. G. Milanesi (Florence, 1860), p. 99: 'Erano questi Gagliani parenti strettissimi de' Soderini, e questo Lorenzo faceva tutti i fatti del cardinale.'   [43] ASR, Notari dell'AC 410, 122r–128v.

Giovanni de Ballapannibus, an archpriest from Castro Nuovo in the diocese of Porto, in the company of six other known members of the household and hangers-on, witnessed Soderini's will of February 1524.[44]

Although these names represent only a very small proportion of the whole of Soderini's household, they do indicate certain tendencies. For example, Soderini seems to have had only one Florentine in his household and very few Tuscans, amongst whom the most important was Eliseo da Colle. Nor did he have any native Romans. The members of the household in the main were ambitious young men from outside Rome and outside Florentine territory, who wanted to make a career away from home and were attracted by the possibilities of the papal court. At least one non-Italian, Umbstat, has been found; there may have been others. Another source for recruitment may have been the households of other cardinals. For instance, when one cardinal died, his household was normally absorbed by other cardinals and curia officials, and Soderini probably gained several servants in this fashion. As is shown by the examples of Staglia de Actis, who had been with Soderini eighteen years in 1524, and Marinangelo de Alexiis who had been with Soderini for thirty years, some of the members were long-term.

That service in the household was considered a fitting apprenticeship for a job as a public administrator in Florence, and vice versa, can be seen in the career of Antonio Zeno. He was first of all a scribe (*cancelliere*) for a Florentine embassy in France and then a member of Soderini's household. In 1506 he wanted to be one of the commissioners to raise the tax of the *decima* in Florence, and wrote to Piero Soderini asking that his name be put forward. Piero wrote back to Francesco that he thought that this was a good idea because he was not a native but had knowledge of Florence, that he was prudent and had served their family.[45] This particular route worked because of Piero Soderini's influence, but service in a cardinal's household could equip one for other walks of life and provided scope for accelerated promotion and steady rewards. It also allowed laymen and clerks to perform similar jobs, although in theory most of the members should have been in holy orders or have had professional expertise of some description.

More specific remarks about the different jobs in the household are not possible without household accounts, but there were quite obviously people employed, for example, to cook and to look after the horses, who are not mentioned at all, so it is still possible that women might have been employed in the household after all. As most of the information about the household comes, in the absence of the relevant accounts,

[44] Rome, Arch. Sod., III, 189v.
[45] ASF, Sig., Minutari 19, 130r, 27 October 1506.

from letters concerned with politics, most of the names are of men involved, in some sense, in political activities. They were people whom Soderini sent abroad to liaise with the king of France, or to talk to an Italian power, or to carry messages to his brother. Or they were the writers of his letters, or people who would have been supposed to know his secrets because they were *camerieri* and familiars, and would have known who had been to see and talk to him, or notaries who knew what deals he had been making, or former attendants at conclaves who knew with whom he had negotiated to elect a new pope. All these people were of interest to Soderini's political opponents, and, therefore, their movements and activities were tracked and reported in letters, which is why their names are known at all. Those who actually worked in the palace and provided for Soderini's domestic comfort have faded from sight. So too have the arrangements for feeding, clothing and cleaning this vast mass of people; only occasional glimpses remain, such as Soderini's request to marquis Francesco Gonzaga in January 1507 for permission to export from Mantuan territory 500 sacks of grain and 100 sacks of beans to be used in his house.[46]

Soderini made provision in both his extant wills for the members of his household. In the one of 1511, he left a separate bequest for *frate* David de Mercuriis da Bologna whom he declared had served him for a long time, promising him 50 ducats a year for life unless he (Soderini) should provide him, before his death, with a greater sum from benefices.[47] He also left to each of his chaplains and squires or knights a horse or a mule, the correct clothes to wear at his funeral and as much money as his executors judged that their service required. Ten ducats were left to each groom and five to every other familiar.[48] By 1524, his wishes had changed somewhat. There was no mention of *frate* David, but every member of his household at the time of his death was to have clothes of mourning to wear at his funeral. He also ordered that all his wardrobe, including the tapestried cloth and cloth used for carpets or wall hangings and table coverings, should be distributed amongst his familiars according to merit and length of service and he prohibited the sale of any of them.[49]

A distinction should perhaps be made between the servants, both political and domestic, and more noble and highly educated young men who might have been participating in Soderini's patronage by living under his wing in Rome. The four young men whom Soderini

[46] ASMa, AG, b.1146, 549r.
[47] ASBo, Notarile, Tommaso Grengoli, busta 18, filza 13 (1506–1518), under date, and Lowe, 'Francesco Soderini', appendix 3, p. 340.   [48] *Ibid.*
[49] See Lowe, 'Francesco Soderini', appendix 4, p. 346.

summoned from Volterra in 1506 fall into this category. On 17 December 1506 one of the topics raised in discussion by the council in Soderini's bishopric of Volterra was a letter received a few days before from the cardinal in Rome.[50] It asked that four well-born and well-behaved young men, who were also good scriptors, be sent to him in Rome. The proposal was passed by sixty-two votes to ten.[51] It has been suggested that three of these young men were Geremia and Zaccaria Contugi and Luca Giovannini, all of whom later became bishops.[52] But Geremia had been made bishop of Assisi on 8 February 1496, ten years before Soderini asked for the young men, and was succeeded on his resignation on 16 December 1509 by Zaccaria.[53] Luca di Girolamo Giovannini, on the other hand, profited directly from Soderini's resignation of the bishopric of Anagni on 4 March 1523, and could easily have been one of the original four as he died only in 1541.[54] He had presumably also profited from having been Soderini's doctor. One young Volterran who lived in Rome with Soderini was Francesco Persio,[55] and it is possible that members of the Gherardi and Maffei families were among the four. No famous humanist has been found associated with Soderini's household, except Battista Casali who claimed in the oration he wrote to deliver at Soderini's funeral that Soderini had offered to maintain him.[56] It does seem strange that Soderini, who was interested in intellectual life and encouraged writers such as Casali and Gherardi and read their works, should not have offered his house up as a haven for aspirant young scholars, but further evidence that he did so is, as yet, lacking.

---

[50] Volterra, Arch. com., Deliberazioni A68, 27r and v. Unfortunately, the letter has not survived.   [51] *Ibid.*, 27v.

[52] L. Falconcini, *Storia dell'antichissima città di Volterra*, in Latin with Italian translation by B. Berardi (Florence/Volterra, 1876), p. 412.

[53] Eubel, *Hierarchia*, II, p. 109; III, p. 134.

[54] The cardinal relator was Soderini. See AV, Fondo consist., Acta vicecanc. 2, 223v and *ibid.*, Acta miscell. 6, 405r.

[55] Volterra, Biblioteca Guarnacci, MS 6204, 84 bis v, 8 July 1508. See below, p. 263.

[56] Milan, Biblioteca Ambrosiana, G33 inf., II, 294r.

CHAPTER 19

FINANCIAL RESOURCES: WEALTH, INCOME, CREDIT, LOANS AND PAWN

It is necessary now to consider both the sources and extent of Soderini's wealth in more detail. In the absence of account books, it is not possible to arrive at accurate figures; however, it is possible to achieve some sense of relative magnitude. Similarly, while figures cannot be attached to Soderini's different sources of income, some sense of their relative importance can be obtained.

An impression of Soderini's wealth at various times as compared to that of other cardinals in the curia can be gained from the opinions of contemporaries. In 1523 the Venetian orator, Foscari, sent home a list of the incomes of the thirty-five cardinals entering the conclave on 1 October. Those with the highest incomes were Medici with 50,000 ducats; Cibo (described by Foscari as Genoese but in fact reared in Rome by a papal family which later took over Massa)[1] with 26,000; Cornaro (Venetian) with 24,000; Santa Croce (Spanish) 16,000; Farnese (Roman) 15,000; Colonna (Roman) and Gonzaga (Mantuan) 12,000; Passerini (from Cortona) and Soderini with 10,000.[2] Many others were in the perfectly respectable and probably adequate bracket of 6–9,000 ducats. Other less fortunate ones were estimated to have 4,000 ducats: Piccolomini and Giles of Viterbo, general of the Augustinian friars, and de Cupis, Jacobazzi, Orsini and Cesi who were all Roman. Three had only 3,000 ducats: Campeggio (Bolognese), Pisani (Venetian) and Ponzetti (Neapolitan); and one only 2,000: de Numai, the general of the Franciscans. There is no amount written in for Enckenvoirt, nor for the four cardinals who were on their way, nor for those who were not coming at all, a group which included two veritable plutocrats – Wolsey and the brother of the king of Portugal.

Of course, these figures could bear little or no relation to the cardinals' actual incomes, but they do provide a guide to their credit

[1] See the *Dizionario biografico degli italiani*, xxv, pp. 249–54.
[2] Sanuto, *I diarii*, xxxv, 61–2.

ratings. Soderini was only in eighth place in the league although he was one of the longest-serving cardinals, but because of his reputation for meanness and his efficient money-keeping, his income may perhaps have been seriously underestimated. It does seem likely that his income was higher than 10,000 ducats, because he seemed to have ready cash when he needed it – for example, for some of the dowry settled on Anna di Giovanvettorio in 1517, or to finance Renzo da Ceri's expedition in 1522 – but it is possible that he lost much by being imprisoned by Adrian. On the other hand, there is no positive evidence that Adrian appropriated anything, except that Soderini in his 1524 will, stated that one of the chests in his room carried off by Adrian's officials contained 2,300 ducats which were never returned, and he instructed his executors to recoup this loss.[3] At the time, one contemporary estimated that Soderini's possessions were worth the huge figure of 50,000 ducats, but he gave no estimate of the amount of cash in the house.[4] Certainly, in 1518 a Medicean supporter could cite Soderini's wealth as one of the factors that made him a dangerous opponent.[5]

That Soderini's wealth fluctuated in real terms, and that the relative position of the cardinals changed during Soderini's twenty years in the college, can be seen by comparing the 1523 list with one of 1505 which was intended for a different purpose. On the feast of Corpus Christi (22 May) 1505, the processional route in Rome was to be hung with tapestry. The length of both sides of the route calculated together was 665 *cannae*, and a scheme was devised whereby each cardinal paid for a certain number of these *cannae* according to his 'condition, quality and faculties', so that the poor ones were given a smaller portion and the rich ones a greater.[6] Inevitably, the cardinals manoeuvred to keep their assessments at the lowest possible level, and some of the wealthiest ones were also those with most influence. Several cardinals – Riario, Sforza, Cesarini, Carafa, Girolamo della Rovere, Antoniotto Pallavicini and Sanseverino – were assessed at thirty-five *cannae* which was the highest, and five – Grimani, Medici, the cardinal of Portugal, Giovanni de Castro (castellan of Castel Sant'Angelo) and Luigi d'Aragona, whose father was a legitimised son of king Ferrante I[7] – were assigned twenty *cannae* which was the lowest assessment. One – Castellesi, always the

---

[3] Lowe, 'Francesco Soderini', appendix 4, p. 355.

[4] Sanuto, *I diarii*, XXXIV, 123, 2 May 1523, from Marco Foscari in Rome: 'li mandò a caxa a tuor le scriture e danari e trovò zercha ducati 50 milia tra danari, arzenti e scriti.'

[5] See ASF, MAP, CXLIII, 154 and Lowe, 'Francesco Soderini', appendix 2, p. 327.

[6] BL, Add. MSS 8440, 203r and v, diary of Paris de Grassis.

[7] See A. Chastel, *Le cardinal Louis d'Aragon: un voyageur princier de la renaissance* (Paris, 1986), p. 9.

odd man out – was assigned twenty-eight and the rest were fairly evenly split between twenty-five and thirty. Soderini had twenty-five.

Most of the names have changed between 1505 and 1523 but Soderini, although he has moved up, has not done so strikingly. Also, in the interim the Medici cardinal had become pope and enriched the next Medici cardinal to such an extent that the latter had become the richest member of the college. Even if the figures are inaccurate, a contemporary's estimate has some value. As a cardinal's lifestyle depended either more or less on credit, ratings were of prime importance. Many cardinals, although boasting seemingly spectacular incomes, had even greater outgoings, and consequently the possibility of generating credit was undoubtedly an essential part of funding the entire system. Nor should it be forgotten that skills of assessment and accounting were a part of everyday life, so that observers of the happenings and personalities of the papal court, such as ambassadors and papal bureaucrats, would have been expected to be able to produce appraisals of credit-worthiness whenever necessary. The ability to elicit high credit ratings out of relatively low incomes was yet another skill required from a successful cardinal.

The style of life of a cardinal was, as has been seen, inherently a matter of conspicuous consumption and ceremonial magnificence. Cardinals were expected to maintain large households, to inhabit impressive palaces and to entertain on a grand scale as part of the social exchanges and rituals that were so important in the life of the papal court. All this cost money – in large quantities. How did Soderini finance this life of luxury and display? One obvious answer is from inherited wealth but this is a subject of considerable obscurity. His father, Tommaso, rose to be a relatively wealthy member of his generation in Florence, his brother Piero Soderini was reckoned to be the richest man in his *quartiere* of S. Spirito in Florence in 1498[8] and when he died in Rome in 1522, it was rumoured that he left 100,000 ducats[9] (but when important people died it was nearly always rumoured that they had left vast fortunes). It is not clear where this money, or even a fraction of it, came from. Piero's income can have come only from business ventures[10] and from property, of which he owned a considerable amount in Rome.[11]

[8] L. Marks, 'La crisi finanziaria a Firenze dal 1494–1502', *Archivio storico italiano*, 112 (1954), pp. 50–1.

[9] ASF, Otto di prat., Resp. 25, 261v, 16 June 1522, Galeotto de' Medici.

[10] Clarke, *The Soderini*, pp. 111 and 119, and *Catalogue of the Medici archives*, sold at auction by Messrs. Christie, Manson and Woods, 4 February 1918, p. 181, covering the years 1498–1502.

[11] See, for example, AV, Vat. lat. 11985, 7v and 23r, and ASR, Collegio dei notari capitolini 14 (Antonio de Alexis), 77r, 78v, 79r–80v, 161r.

Nor is it known whether he managed to take money out of Florence with him when he left, nor whether or not he had arranged for it to be smuggled out later. If Piero's fortune was founded on inherited wealth, Francesco would have had his share too. But straightforward business ventures, such as partnership in a wool or silk firm, were denied to cardinals. On the other hand, Soderini clearly continued to draw sizeable revenues from properties in Tuscany, some inherited from his father, others bought subsequently when a cardinal.[12] The total amounts involved are unknown but they cannot have been sufficient to pay for the demands of living in Rome. The lifestyle and expenditure of a member of the Florentine ruling class, unless one were a member of the dominant branch of the Medici, were less grand and expensive than those of a cardinal, which required greater funding than was possible from Soderini's Tuscan and Roman property alone.

The only alternative sources of wealth available to Soderini were directly related to his ecclesiastical position. Cardinals resident in Rome could receive their share of half of the common services, which were divided between those cardinals present in consistory. These varied according to the size of the college and according to attendance, but could be as much as 1,489 florins in 1517 or as little as 407 florins in 1518 after Leo's mass elevation; the average for the years 1504–20 was about 900 florins a year.[13] This, while useful, was nowhere near enough. Nor did the official tip a cardinal received for relating a candidate for provision in consistory, help matters much.

By far the most significant source of ecclesiastical income open to a cardinal came from benefices.[14] This was acknowledged by more austere contemporaries like Paolo Giustiniani and Piero Quirini, who in a reform programme suggested that, as a remedy for avarice (and financial abuses generally), cardinals should not hold benefices but instead enjoy pensions from the papacy which should be very carefully

---

[12] ASF, Capitani di Parte Guelfa, Numeri rossi 85, 126v and 127r.

[13] Some account sheets of cardinal Niccolò Flisco (also cited by Chambers, 'The economic predicament', p. 297) show the sums that he received from this source during this period. They are the only ones that have come to light and there is nothing to suggest that Flisco was either particularly assiduous or particularly lax in his attendance at consistory. They are in AV, Fondo sacro collegio dei cardinali, lib. cedularum et rotulorum 1.

[14] On cardinals' incomes in general, see Chambers, 'The economic predicament', pp. 289–313. Antonovics, 'The finances', p. 383 writes: 'Probably the major source of revenue for most cardinals was that drawn from the benefices that they accumulated.' Soderini certainly kept close watch over the revenues generated by his benefices and their landholdings. See a list of account books that he (and possibly other members of the Soderini family) had in one cupboard, probably circa 1517/1518, Rome, Arch. Sod., XXXIV, 7r and v.

reviewed each year.[15] However, in the period under discussion, avarice, or rather a developed sense of self-interest, was a crucial quality for any cardinal. The range of Soderini's bishoprics and benefices has been analysed in chapter 15 and they could be put to a variety of uses. They could either be milked directly for financial gain, or used as patronage with which to enrich relatives and reward servants and dependants. Soderini proved himself expert in translating his personal and political alliances into ecclesiastical rewards, and then in exploiting those positions for his own advantage and that of his friends and relatives.

Ecclesiastical influence was in itself a highly marketable commodity. As has been seen, Soderini could draw upon two varieties, direct and indirect. On account of the structure of benefice holding, he was able to guarantee petitioners a specific income; he could also count upon access to the pope and other cardinals, with its attendant opportunities for ecclesiastical dealing and advancement. The whole question of perquisites, gifts and backhanders at the papal court is of the first importance. Unfortunately, it is also difficult to find direct evidence with which to study it. Soderini's complaint to pope Adrian, on 3 February 1523, that the cardinals were used 'to having a great many commissions from their friends and protectors, who had looked to them and who were served in their turn, but at present they did not have anyone who sought them out',[16] shows how closely linked the interests of the cardinals were with the old patronage which Adrian's reforming efforts were disrupting. It seems likely that Soderini did more than dabble in this lucrative trade. The story that Geremia Contugi sold ordination during Leo's absence in 1515[17] points to an altogether more substantial involvement. Soderini, in all probability, never questioned this system and learnt how to use it while a curia official. In May 1490 Jacopo Gherardi wrote to Soderini from Milan that he had arranged for one Fontanino, whom Soderini had so lovingly recommended, the faculty of obtaining benefices in the duchy of Milan up to the sum of 80 *aureorum*.[18] It is most unlikely that this transaction would have taken place without one or more exchanges of money, for venality and obliquity permeated every level of ecclesiastical business. When Tommaso Soderini left Francesco 2,000 *fiorini larghi* in his will of 27 August 1485 for the expenses of the episcopate of Volterra,[19] this was in

---

[15] See N. Minnich, 'Concepts of reform proposed at the Fifth Lateran Council', *Archivum historiae pontificiae*, 7 (1969), p. 225.

[16] ASF, Otto di prat., Resp. 24, 20r: 'havere assai commissione di loro amici et protectore che ricorreano a loro et erano serviti, che di presente non hanno alcuno che li ricerchi'. See above, p. 158.   [17] See above, p. 162.

[18] Gherardi, *Dispacci*, p. 471.

[19] ASF, Capitani di Parte Guelfa, Numeri rossi 75, 15r.

recognition of the kind of amount that Soderini might need in order to use the resources of the bishopric and its attendant opportunities to the full. The money was seen not so much as a lump sum to discharge debts, but as an investment that would yield returns.

It was with the same sort of expectation that Soderini must have commenced dealing in loans and pawn. Again, unfortunately, the evidence is tangential and thin. In his 1524 will, he listed a ruby decorated with diamonds and other precious stones which Isabella, wife of king Federico of Naples, had pawned to him for 2,000 gold ducats.[20] When he died, it was reported that he was owed 80,000 ducats, including 17,000 in cash from other cardinals, and 30,000 for jewellery,[21] and it may be that he specialised in loans. Certainly, he was also owed money by various individuals in France (see the clause to set up the college at the university of Paris in his 1524 will)[22] and in a list of the inheritance received by Francesco's nephew, Giuliano, bishop of Saintes, at the death of his uncle, one item was a credit note for 20,000 *scudi*, and there were two other credit notes, amounting to over 21,000 and 11,000 *scudi* respectively, whose value was to be split between several of the Soderini nephews.[23] These credit notes may have been constituent parts of the valuable writings (*scripture*) sequestered by Adrian in 1523.

Loans of this size would account for his ability to find ready cash when necessary, and this kind of contract would appeal both to his political shrewdness and his financial acumen. But Soderini could provide large sums of credit only as a result of his ecclesiastical income, which he then manipulated in such a way that it brought in extra money which was put to private use. As has been seen, this process was also employed in Soderini's building developments and his investment in property. Revenues from the church paid for land and property which became personal, not institutional, assets, and which in their turn provided profits. Arguably, however, the tendency to create episcopal dynasties within a family, with dioceses and churches passing from uncle to illegitimate son or nephew, opened the possibility, at least, that some of the ecclesiastical accumulations were intended or destined to

---

[20] See Lowe, 'Francesco Soderini', appendix 4, p. 350. Soderini obviously expected the money to be returned because he willed it, when restored, to the daughters of Tommaso di Paolantonio. On Federico and Isabella, see L. Volpicella, *Federico d'Aragona e la fine del regno di Napoli nel MDI* (Naples, 1908).

[21] Sanuto, *I diarii*, XXXVI, 368, 21 May 1524, Marino da Pozzo, secretary of cardinal Pisani, from Rome, to Francesco Spinelli: 'Item, che al cardinal Voltera era stà trovado cardinali debitori per ducati 17 milia et zoglie per ducati 30 milia di altri su le qual havia prestado, et tanto che sumava ducati 80 milia.'

[22] Lowe, 'Francesco Soderini', appendix 4, pp. 346–7.

[23] Rome, Arch. Sod., II, 148r and v.

remain attached to the church in one form or another. Soderini's nephew, Giuliano, was groomed for the episcopal succession and followed his uncle to Volterra and to Saintes, but was forced to share the Soderini spoils with his brothers and cousin, so only a portion of Soderini's church wealth was to remain in the hands of a churchman.

It is clear that Soderini was regarded by contemporaries as a financial administrator of no mean skill. It was almost certainly his care in such matters that acquired for him his reputation for meanness, but one commentator, Nardi, did not interpret his behaviour in this light. Indeed, according to Nardi, Soderini took financial efficiency so far as to refuse to fob off his servants and familiars with promises of benefices, but rewarded them with large, regular salaries.[24] For Soderini, ecclesiastical office seems to have been a source of political and financial power above anything else. Certainly in the matter of wealth, he conforms to the stereotype of a 'corrupt', pre-Reformation churchman, adept at turning every opportunity to monetary advantage.

---

[24] Nardi, *Istorie*, II, p. 69: 'e li suoi familiari e servidori non pascesse con le speranze di ristorargli, o con la distribuzione futura de' beneficii ecclesiastichi, come fanno molti, ma li recompensasse con grossi e continui salarii.'

CHAPTER 20

INTELLECTUAL LIFE AND THE INFLUENCE
OF HUMANISM

Soderini's early intellectual training was essentially legal. He studied civil law at Bologna and Pisa and it would be reasonable to suppose, as his and his family's first choice of career for him was to be a lawyer, that the subject held some interest. When he changed course and went into the church, in 1478, as bishop of Volterra, civil law was no longer of any use to him, and instead he probably directed his attention towards canon law and theology. Sebastiano Salvini, Marsilio Ficino's nephew, wrote to him at some point between April 1480 and May 1481 urging him to continue his study in these two subjects.[1] It must have been during this period that he composed his (untraced) work on the *Decretals*, as he would have been in no position to do it before. The *Decretals* of Gregory IX formed a substantial part of the curriculum for canon law students, and they would necessarily have been studied by anyone wanting an acquaintance with the subject. In essence, the *Decretals* contain an account of controversial points in canonical doctrine; they cite allegations of the parties in a particular dispute, and then the solution of the case or the statement of the rule of conduct.[2] The texts were soon glossed by adding to the manuscript copies both textual explanations and explanations of the subject matter.

The exact purpose of Soderini's work is not known. It is not mentioned until 1589, when M. Pocciantio stated that Soderini had written on the *Decretals* and that the work had been circulated in manuscript.[3] G. Eggs followed Pocciantio in his affirmation that Soderini had written on the *Decretals*, but added that he had also written 'Artificium reipublicae bene gubernandae' and a commentary on

---

[1] BV, Vat. lat. 5140, 16r.

[2] See, for example, *The catholic encyclopedia*, IV, p. 672.

[3] M. Pocciantio, *Catologus scriptorum Florentinorum omnis generis* (Florence, 1589), p. 68.

Aristotle.[4] If this last item seems an unlikely choice for Soderini, it must be remembered that he was the recipient of a letter in 1504 from Mario Equicola praising the delights of Lefèvre d'Etaples' commentaries and paraphrases of Aristotle's work on natural philosophy.[5] In 1722 Negri proferred the information that the manuscript on the *Decretals* was still in the hands of the Soderini family,[6] but by 1861 Litta reported that the manuscript was in the Biblioteca Magliabechiana, having previously belonged to the Strozzi.[7] It sounds as though this work was not an interlinear or marginal gloss, but a self-contained manuscript. Soderini himself possessed at least two copies of the *Decretals*, as is shown by his wills of 1511 and 1524, in which he left all his books to his nephew, Giuliano, with the exception of the better copy of the *Decretals* 'written on good paper' which, on fulfilment of certain conditions, he bequeathed elsewhere.[8] If indeed Soderini did write such a work, it would be evidence that he was taking his new career seriously. A knowledge of canon law would have been of real value to him as a curia official. In any case, as a referendary and auditor of contradicted letters, Soderini must have gained a thorough working knowledge of canon law which would have been of use when he was a cardinal.

There are other indications of both his aptitude for and his interest in law more generally. Girolamo Balbi, a humanist who had also studied law, addressed a poem to him which contained the exhortation 'But if you wish to get to know Solon, then look upon the worshipful countenance of Soderini'.[9] But this presumably dated from before Soderini's promotion to the cardinalate, and so is not evidence of an interest for the period after 1503, when he was once again based in Rome. However, on 29 December 1504, he was one of a party of cardinals who attended a public disputation at S. Eustachio by

[4] G. Eggs, *Purpura docta* (Munich, 1714), II, p. 318. D. Manni wrote the texts in *Azioni gloriose degli uomini illustri fiorentini espresse co' loro ritratti nelle volte della real galleria di Toscana* (Florence, 1745) and under 'Legge', he commented on Soderini and Filippo Corsini: 'i quali due ... hanno lasciate a posteri della presente facoltà opere considerabili', but gave no further details.

[5] See Aristotle, *Totius philosophiae naturalis paraphrases a Francisco Vatablo recognitiae* (Paris, 1528) 356v and 357r, 11 December 1504, and a discussion and English translation of this by E. Rice Jr., 'Humanist Aristotelianism in France: Jacques Lefèvre d'Etaples and his circle', in *Humanism in France*, ed. A. Levi (Manchester, 1970), p. 132.

[6] P. Giulio Negri, *Istoria degli scrittori fiorentini* (Ferrara, 1722), p. 222.

[7] Passerini, 'Soderini di Firenze', table 4.

[8] See Lowe, 'Francesco Soderini', appendix 3, p. 333, and appendix 4, pp. 348–9.

[9] G. Balbi, *Opera*, ed. J. de Retzer (Vienna, 1791–2), I, p. 227. See the article by G. Rill in *Dizionario biografico degli italiani*, v, pp. 370–4.

Giovanbattista Ricci, a consistorial advocate from Casole in the Sienese *contado*.[10]

In Soderini's will of 22 February 1524, there appears a bequest to found a college in Paris for Italian students of canon law and theology.[11] This is certainly further evidence that Soderini deemed these subjects worthy of study, but as an ecclesiastic he would have been expected to patronise these two disciplines, and as a lawyer he would have been aware of the university of Paris's excellence in these two fields. Much more unusual was the idea of a foundation in Paris by a foreigner and, in fact, the choice of Paris was more an expression of Soderini's political tastes than of his educational zeal.[12] In Soderini's will of 1511, there is no mention of the bequest to found the college, but by 1524 the political circumstances of Soderini and his family had changed considerably. He might have been expected to endow the universities of Pisa or Rome, but by moving outside the Medicean sphere of influence, he attempted to provide an alternative base in Paris for disenchanted or outlawed members of his family and possibly other anti-Mediceans. The Soderini were to have first refusal in the matter of places. The only precedent for the foundation of a college in Paris by Italians is provided by the Collège de Lombards, founded in 1334 by a motley band of four Italians, who were probably all living in France.[13] Soderini's plan was thwarted, and his scholarships in canon law and theology came to nought.

Little else remains which is connected with this sphere of interest. Neither Pietro Delfino's correspondence nor the records of the Fifth Lateran Council contain opinions on Soderini's stance on theology or canon law. Delfino at one point described him as 'a porphyry column of reform',[14] but this description related to some business within the Camaldolese order and does not appear to have wider implications. Soderini and Antonio Zeno, acting in their capacities, respectively, as cardinal protector of the Camaldolese and vicar to the protector, paid the travelling expenses of Francesco da Meleto, a reform-minded Camaldolese writer who was summoned to Rome under Leo X, but Meleto did not lodge with Soderini and nothing further is known of

[10] Burchard, 'Liber notarum', II, pp. 466–7.

[11] See Lowe, 'Francesco Soderini', appendix 4, pp. 346–7.

[12] For a more detailed discussion of this issue, see K. Lowe, 'Proposal for an Italian college', pp. 167–78.

[13] See Lowe, 'Proposal for an Italian college', p. 168 and P. Denley, 'The collegiate movement in Italian universities in the late middle ages', *History of universities*, 10 (1991), pp. 34–5 and 64–5.

[14] Delfino, *Epistolarum volumen*, book X, number 72, Delfino to Raimondo Raimondi, 30 April 1512. See also J. Schnitzer, *Peter Delfin General des Camaldulenserordens (1444–1525)* (Munich, 1926), p. 218.

their relationship.[15] It seems certain that questions of church reform and doctrine were not uppermost in his mind, but once again it should be stressed that contemporary christian values informed much of his life and behaviour.

One final and rather interesting point is that there may be a significant shift in the pattern of charitable bequests in the two wills of 1511 and 1524. One of Soderini's familiars, Staglia de Actis, a clerk from Todi, said in 1526 that Soderini had made four wills, one a long time ago, one while he was living in Fondi (between 1517 and 1521), another while he was in prison in Castel Sant'Angelo during Adrian VI's pontificate (between April and September 1523), and still another during his last illness (between January and May 1524). The one written in Castel Sant'Angelo was reputed to have been written in Soderini's own hand.[16] Only the first and last of these wills are known, and they show marked differences in emphasis, most notably in the then topical area of providing for masses to be said for Soderini's soul. As the middle two wills have not been found, this change in sentiment could have occurred at any time between 1511 and 1524. In the 1511 will, Soderini allotted money for masses to be said for his soul daily in the Ospedale di S. Spirito, St Peter's, S. Frediano in Florence and the cathedral in Volterra,[17] and money for a mass to be said in the church of S. Salvatore in Bologna (which is where the will was drawn up) on the anniversary of his burial.[18] By 1520 he had founded a chapel with two attendant chaplains in the cathedral of Volterra, providing it with revenue from the leases upon some property he had bought, so that it was no longer necessary to insert a clause for masses in Volterra in his will. Nevertheless, it is noticeable that there are no clauses in the 1524 will relating to any of the other four sites for masses, and in their stead (possibly) is the bequest to found a college at the university of Paris. Soderini had severed his links with the Ospedale di S. Spirito in Rome, and the Medici presence in Florence would have been sufficient to deter any mention of masses at S. Frediano. However, the contrast between the two wills is stark enough to make mere practical explanations for it unlikely. It may be that Soderini's view of the best way to ensure a brief stay in purgatory had changed. How far this represents a purely personal development, and how far it reflects changing patterns of pious expression in the world at large, remains an open question.

[15] See D. Weinstein, *Savonarola and Florence* (Princeton, 1970), pp. 355–6.

[16] Rome, Arch. Sod., III, 242v and 243r. The document is a copy of part of a case dating from February 1526 to ascertain whether or not this final will was false.

[17] See Lowe, 'Francesco Soderini', appendix 3, pp. 332–3, 336.

[18] *Ibid.*, appendix 3, p. 340.

Any discussion of the intellectual life and interests of Soderini inevitably involves an analysis both of his relationship with the humanists and of what he thought about humanism. He and his brothers grew up in Florence in the 1450s and 1460s and were accustomed from an early age to the presence and influence of humanists. Indeed, two of his brothers are known to have been educated by a humanist which makes it likely that Soderini was as well. This was in marked contrast to the experience of their father, Tommaso, who was probably brought up as a merchant.[19] In part, this was a generational difference; the humanist influence on the education and training of the Florentine ruling class had grown throughout the fifteenth century. It may also have been a result of the spectacular success of their father's career, and his desire to turn that success into continuing status for his sons. It is difficult, in the absence of sources of a personal nature, to gauge whether Soderini's integration into humanist circles was the result of convention or inclination. For instance, Marsilio Ficino wrote to all four Soderini brothers,[20] but Ficino's letters were not private documents; rather they occupied an uneasy territory between the private and the public. Both the complexity of the Latin in which they were written, and the moral, philosophical and theological topics which they discussed, show them to be a means of public display rather than private communications. They were written by Ficino for publication and prepared by him for the press. This element of display almost certainly played a part in the choice of addressee, and since the humanistically educated Soderini brothers were the sons of the second most important man in Florence, they must have appeared ideal correspondents. As there are no extant replies from Soderini to Ficino, this 'correspondence' cannot be used as evidence that Soderini shared Ficino's particular interests. It can, however, be used to demonstrate that he was a member of that Florentine political and social élite which, at this period, was adding at least a veneer of humanist education to its defining characteristics. It is likely that Soderini's achievements in this field set him apart from his contemporaries and represented an asset of real value for the pursuit of a political and ecclesiastical career.

Soderini's career provides an interesting case-study of the reciprocal bonds which bound humanistically educated members of the ruling class and their humanist instructors and clients. While the humanist client could hail the learning and beneficence of his intended patron, the

[19] Clarke, 'A biography', pp. 16–17.
[20] See Ficino, *Opera*, I, pp. 917, 884, 945 for examples of letters to Paolantonio, Piero and Giovanvettorio, and I, pp. 833, 910, 930 for examples of letters to Francesco. Ficino addressed more letters to Francesco than to the others.

patron could bask in the praise of the humanist and display his own learning and munificence by patronising him. Thus, both Ficino and Salvini had anticipated Soderini's elevation to the cardinalate in the 1470s and 1480s.[21] Each significant advance in Soderini's career, and indeed in the fortunes of his family, elicited outpourings from the humanists. For example, Raffaele and Mario Maffei wrote to him from Rome on 1 October 1502 to congratulate him and the Soderini clan on Piero's gonfaloniership.[22] Bartolomeo Fonti similarly praised Soderini's attainment of the red hat.[23] Neri Nerli wrote a whole panegyric to Francesco Soderini in which he praised not only his achievements but also those of his father, brothers and even a sister, Maria.[24] Throughout his life, Soderini continued to be the object of intermittent bursts of humanist praise.[25]

Hard on the heels of the flattering letter came the begging letter. As John D'Amico has pointed out, cardinals and other major curial figures provided the intercession necessary for humanists to acquire benefices and minor papal posts, and thus earn their living.[26] Unsurprisingly, therefore, a good deal of Soderini's correspondence with humanists was taken up with affairs of this sort.[27] For example, the letters between Salvini and Soderini (but mainly going from the former to the latter) are split between philosophical and theological argument, and expressions of concern for ecclesiastical and other preferment, both for Salvini, the client, and Soderini, the patron.[28] This unequal relationship undoubtedly left its mark upon the writing of Paolo Cortesi's *De cardinalatu*,[29] in which the ideal attributes of a renaissance cardinal were

---

[21] Ficino, *Opera*, I, p. 798, post 10 December 1477, and BV, Vat. lat. 5140, 17r and v.

[22] BV, Barb. lat. 2517, 36r.   [23] Fonti, *Epistolarum libri* III, pp. 42–3.

[24] Florence, Biblioteca Riccardiana, MS 951, 11r–32v. Nerli also addressed panegyrics to other members of the Soderini family.

[25] For letters from Balac Italus and Jacopo Antiquari, and poems from Pacifico Massimi, see BV, Barb. lat. 1822, 25r, 14 February 1514, J. Antiquari, *Epistolae* (Perugia, 1519), unpaginated, and BV, Vat. lat. 2862, 55v–56r, 57r–58r, 93v–94v. For Massimi's poems, see also M. Graziosi, 'Pacifico Massimi maestro del Colocci?', *Atti del convegno di studi su Angelo Colocci, Jesi, 13–14 September 1969* (Jesi, 1972), pp. 157–68.   [26] D'Amico, *Renaissance humanism*, p. 52.

[27] For Ficino, see *Opera*, I, p. 931; for Cortesi, see Florence, Biblioteca Marucelliana, BI 10, Part 3, A. M. Bandini, 'Memorie concernenti l'illustre terra di S. Gimignano', 200r and v, 24 August 1501; for Salvini, see BV, Vat. lat. 5140, 108r, 27 May 1481.

[28] See P. Kristeller, 'Sebastiano Salvini, a Florentine humanist', *Didascaliae. Studies in honor of Anselm M. Albareda* (New York, 1961), especially pp. 213–14 and pp. 231–2. The letters are in BV, Vat. lat. 5140. Soderini sponsored Salvini for his degree of master of theology in 1481, BV, Vat. lat. 5140, 104v.

[29] P. Cortesi, *De cardinalatu* (In Castra Cortesio, 1510), especially the chapters 'De erogatione pecuniarum quae supersunt', N 10r–NN 7v, and 'De simonia', r 1v–r

set out. Amongst these, on a par with other expressions of magnificence, was an interest in and patronage of humanist scholarship. Cortesi's book contains references to and flattery of many contemporary cardinals and was part of an (unsuccessful) publicity campaign by Cortesi to win himself a red hat.[30]

It is clear that Soderini was prepared to respond to such blandishments with words and deeds. Thus, he replied to favourable remarks in *De cardinalatu* by telling Cortesi that the age was indeed fortunate in having produced so many clever people and such friends.[31] These compliments ranged from a commendation of Soderini's moderation in eating habits (it was said that he never spent more on a meal than was necessary for the maintenance of his studies or his business affairs), to approval because Soderini, in his role as a protector of religious orders, took human weaknesses into account and was willing to make exceptions.[32] A passage in a letter written by Soderini to Cortesi after Soderini's acquisition of the bishopric of Saintes in 1506 shows once again that their relationship was based not only on mutual esteem but also on patronage: 'I have always wanted to be able to promise you that participation in all of my good fortune which I was able to give. I understand your wishes relating to the benefices in the diocese and will bear them in mind each time I have something to share out.'[33] Thus, although the humanist Cortesi was not a member of Soderini's household, nor attached exclusively to one particular cardinal, he held a prominent position in Soderini's wider network of clientele. Certainly, too, Soderini was sufficiently convinced of the value of humanist culture to ensure that his nephew Giuliano's education was supervised by Michele Acciari, a pupil of Poliziano.[34]

Therefore, at one level Soderini was attached enough to humanist values to fulfil Cortesi's desired role of the cardinal as patron of letters,[35] but the interests and preoccupations of his clients should not automatically be imputed to him. In fact, it is noticeable that his concerns coincided rather more closely with Roman than Florentine humanism

---

6r. On *De cardinalatu*, see the article on Cortesi in the *Dizionario biografico degli italiani*, XXIX, pp. 769–70.

[30] See P. Cortesi, *De hominibus doctis dialogus*, ed. and translated into Italian by M. Graziosi (Rome, 1973), p. xii.

[31] Florence, Biblioteca Marucelliana, B1 10, Part 3, 229r, 12 July 1509.

[32] Cortesi, *De cardinalatu*, I 3r and R 4v.

[33] Florence, Biblioteca Marucelliana, B1 10, Part 3, 214r and v, 26 July 1506.

[34] See the letters of Acciari in BNF, Filza Rinuccini 17, fasc. 6, between 1505 and 1508, and Delcorno Branca, 'Un discepolo', especially pp. 467–9. Some of Acciari's letters are published in Verde, *Lo studio*, III, II, pp. 647–51.

[35] Cortesi, *De cardinalatu*, N 11r and v.

(at least as defined by John D'Amico), for he undoubtedly favoured history, archaeology and literary composition above philosophical speculation.[36] Evidence of Soderini's historical interests can be found in a remarkable exchange of letters between him and Marcello Virgilio, the chancellor of the Florentine republic, about an Etruscan find of 1508 near Castellina in Chianti.[37] Virgilio's original letter described the contents and layout of the newly discovered tomb. His interest in the objects was focused on the alabaster carvings on the lids of the urns, their gold decoration and, most importantly, on the inscriptions. Soderini was consulted as a likely connoisseur. In his reply, he took up in particular the question of the inscriptions, expressing a desire to help and attempting to work out when the Etruscan language disappeared. He betrayed a Florentine preoccupation with, and pride in, the antiquity of Tuscany and Florence, and an acquaintance with Alberti's *De re aedificatoria*,[38] which he used to demonstrate Alberti's views on the Etruscan language. Ten months later, in a second letter to Virgilio, Soderini wrote that he had done his best, had sent out the 'letters' all over Italy but no one had been able to decipher them. He again referred to Alberti, whom he said had written that Etruscan letters could not have come from Egyptian ones.

He also enclosed a gift, a copy of a small part of the manuscript of the first six books of the *Annals* of Tacitus, which he said had been brought to him from Germany. The passage was quoted by him on account of its historical relevance, as it mentioned the Florentines. This Tacitus manuscript is of special interest. The original extract sent by Soderini has not survived, but another copy of it, now in Florence, has a note appended to it which describes the six books as being newly found and says that they are in the hands (*in manibus*) of Soderini.[39] This could mean that Soderini's Latin phrase in his letter 'ex Germania nobis allatus fuit' was intended literally, and that the manuscript had indeed been sent from Germany to him. However, the first editor of Tacitus, Filippo Beroaldo the younger, stated in his dedication to Leo X in 1515, that the

---

[36] D'Amico, *Renaissance humanism*, p. 90. D'Amico's comparison is between Florentine humanism at the end of the fifteenth century (and particularly the circle around Ficino), and Roman early sixteenth-century humanism.

[37] For a more detailed discussion, see K. Lowe, 'An Etruscan find of 1508', forthcoming in *Journal of the Warburg and Courtauld Institutes*, where the letters will be published in full.

[38] The Latin text of *De re aedificatoria* was first printed in Florence in 1485 and first reprinted in 1512, so in 1508 Soderini must have been using the 1485 edition if he were not using a manuscript.

[39] This passage is edited in E. Rostagno, *Tacitus. Codex Laurentianus Mediceus 68 1*, IV (Leiden, 1902), n.3.

manuscript had been brought from Germany to Leo.[40] The manuscript could, therefore, have passed either from Soderini to Leo or vice versa. Whatever the truth of the matter, it is clear that Soderini was at some point in possession of the manuscript and this, combined with the exchange of letters over the Etruscan find, can be taken as evidence of a strong historical interest, as well as providing further evidence of Soderini's preoccupation with unusual manuscripts.

The only other manuscript from Soderini's library which has been found is a later fifteenth- or early sixteenth-century copy of the 'Notitia omnium dignitatum et administrationum tam civilium quam militarium'.[41] There are very few copies of the 'Notitia' of this date, all of which come from a now lost original which existed at Speir. The 'Notitia' itself was an early fifth-century compilation of information about the high offices of state in the eastern and western provinces of the Roman empire. The *ex libris* describes Soderini as the bishop of Ostia, a position he held only from 18 December 1523[42] to his death on 17 May 1524. It is not clear whether Soderini commissioned this manuscript copy or merely purchased it. Several of the four or five hands in which it is written look familiar and may be those of his scribes; but, equally, they may be representative late fifteenth- or early sixteenth-century hands. It is an indication of the strength of Soderini's involvement in serious historical study that he continued to procure rare and specialised manuscripts such as this up to the end of his life, even though he was bedridden from February 1524. A list of the books and manuscripts in Soderini's possession would allow a much fuller account of his legal, philosophical, historical and literary taste which would, undoubtedly, add flesh to the general outline which is all that can be sketched at the moment. But the quality and rarity of the two manuscripts known to have been in Soderini's possession indicate a manuscript library of outstanding value.

Nor is information about Soderini's literary interests much more plentiful. Some of his humanist clients and acquaintances (for example, Raffaele Maffei,[43] Jacopo Gherardi[44] and Paolo Cortesi)[45] wrote to him

---

[40] On this debate, see *Miscellanea filologica critica e antiquaria*, ed. C. Fea (Rome, 1790), pp. 27–9, J. von Stackelberg, *Tacitus in der Romania* (Tübingen, 1960), pp. 52–3, and the entry by E. Paratore on Filippo Beroaldo the younger in the *Dizionario biografico degli italiani*.

[41] This manuscript is now in Paris, Bibliothèque Nationale, Nouv. acq. lat. 1424. See also C. Jullian, 'Note sur un manuscrit de la "Notitia dignitatum"', *Mélanges d'archéologie et d'histoire*, 1 (1881), pp. 284–9.

[42] AV, Fondo concist., Acta vicecanc. 3, 17v.

[43] BV, Ottob. lat. 2377, 210r, and P. Paschini, 'Una famiglia di curiali : i Maffei di Volterra', *Rivista di storia della chiesa in Italia*, 7 (1953), p. 353.

[44] See Gherardi, 'Diario romano', p. lx.

about their work seeking encouragement which it can be assumed Soderini gave. He was wholeheartedly enthusiastic about Cortesi's work on the office of cardinals (in which he was presented in a thoroughly favourable light), and often praised it and its author in the highest terms.[46] On the other hand, only two works have been found which were dedicated to him, which is a very small number for a cardinal. Neither of the writers was a Florentine, and both books were written in special circumstances for specific reasons. One was the tract on S. Apollinare in Classe near Ravenna, written by a Camaldolese monk, Vitale Acquedotti, in 1511, which was mentioned above (p. 168) – Soderini was the dedicatee both because he was protector of the order and because he had recently arranged a translation of bones in the church.[47] The other was the *Lugdunense somnium* by Zaccaria Ferreri, which was published at Lyons on 13 September 1513. The presentation copy, however, was falsely dated 18 March, as Ferreri wanted to pretend that he had completed the poem within a week of Leo's election.[48] Ferreri was a Carthusian who became secretary to the Council of Pisa and therefore needed to gain the favour of the new pope, which he hoped to do by presenting him with the *Somnium*. A second dedication was made to Soderini in the form of an additional letter and poem.[49] Soderini, together with cardinals Grimani and Cornaro, was a recognised patron of Ferreri,[50] and the book pleased Leo sufficiently for him to allow Ferreri to go to Rome and become a member of his household.[51]

This paucity of dedications necessitates the conclusion that Soderini was not a flamboyant or influential patron who was willing to pay dearly for the services and attentions of humanists. But it does not contradict the assertion that Soderini was interested in their work. Cortesi in *De cardinalatu* painted a picture of Soderini as a man of serious intent, and one of his examples of Soderini's sayings in particular

[45] The extant letters go from Soderini to Cortesi, but it is obvious from these that Cortesi had been writing about his work.

[46] See BNF, II III 3, 128v, Rome, 4 January 1506, where Soderini wrote that Cortesi must have decided to make himself and his friends immortal by writing the book, and Florence, Biblioteca Marucelliana, BI 10, Part 3, 222v, Bologna, 30 December 1507: 'A noi qua pare che siate mirabile in questa vostra compositione.'

[47] See above, pp. 167–8.

[48] J. Shearman, *Raphael's cartoons in the collection of H.M. the Queen, and the tapestries for the Sistine chapel* (London, 1972), p. 1.

[49] The presentation copy is now in BNF, Banco rari 158. Copies of the *Somnium* include an illustration of Soderini sitting reading.

[50] B. Morsolin, *Zaccaria Ferreri* (Vicenza, 1877), p. 19.

[51] A. Ferrajoli, 'Il ruolo', 34 (1911), p. 369. For further information on Ferreri, see Ferrajoli, 'Il ruolo' (cont.), 41 (1918), pp. 91–104.

reinforces this impression. The comment was that 'Soderini, a man adorned with the use of things and dissemblingly learned in the science of great arts, often says that the daily conversations of men are accustomed to be consumed very rapidly without any conception of the learned disciplines'.[52]

Soderini certainly associated with learned men in Rome although the extent to which he did so is unknown. However, the glimpses afforded of his intellectual life point to an appreciation and understanding of humanist culture. On 19 October 1500 he wrote to Cortesi informing him of the impending arrival of one Demetrius (possibly Demetrius Calcondylas, the professor of Greek at the university of Milan),[53] whom he recommended that Cortesi should go to meet, because Cortesi's own interests had moved towards dialectic.[54] As has been noted, he had been friendly with Mario Equicola in Rome while still a bishop and diplomat, and he may have associated with him in France in 1502.[55] After Soderini's acquisition of a red hat, they remained in contact, and Equicola bragged that he was publicly favoured by Soderini during a stay in Rome in 1513.[56]

In a letter to Raffaello Maffei of 1507, Jacopo Gherardi mentioned Soderini side by side with a list of erudite men who had all been pleased by a passage from Dio Chrysostomos (AD 40 – after 112), the Greek Stoic-Cynic orator, which Maffei had annotated.[57] The list contained Filippo Beroaldo, Bartolomeo Saliceto, Domenico Crispo and Girolamo Massaino. It seems reasonable to conclude, from off-hand remarks like these, that Soderini was in constant contact with learned men, and took an active and informed interest in their studies. In addition, Cortesi described Domenico Crispo and Soderini as inseparable friends.[58] Crispo, who was from Pistoia, is an elusive figure who has escaped the attention of scholars, but both Gherardi and Cortesi obviously took his place in their circle for granted.[59] Not much is

[52] Cortesi, De cardinalatu, B 5v: 'Franciscus Soderinus senator homo rerum usu limatus et magnarum artium scientia dissimulanter doctus saepe dicti, celerrime hominum quotidiana colloquia solere sine disciplinarum cognitione consumi.'

[53] See the article by A. Petrucci on Calcondylas in Dizionario biografico degli italiani, XVI, pp. 542–7, especially p. 546.

[54] Florence, Biblioteca Marucelliana, BI 10, Part 3, 194r. See also BNF, II III 3, 128r.

[55] See Kolsky, Mario Equicola, p. 62, but the letter discussed by Kolsky from Soderini to Equicola was written from Paris in 1502, not 1501 (Soderini was using the Florentine form of date).

[56] Luzio, 'Isabella d'Este', p. 458, letter of 23 March 1513.

[57] Volterra, Biblioteca Guarnacci, MS 6204, 79r, 7 October 1507.

[58] Cortesi, De cardinalatu, H 6r.

[59] Confirmation of the constituency of the group comes from another letter of 1507, this time from Soderini to Mario Maffei, where mention is made of a proposed trip

known about him, other than that he gave Latin sermons and wrote Latin comedies,[60] and held a minor post in the curia (he was custodian of the porta del Popolo).[61] At some point he travelled to Hungary, but was already active in Roman humanist circles by the 1490s, when he knew Battista Casali, another of the humanists in Soderini's orbit.[62]

Of the others in the list, Beroaldo is well known as a translator and editor of Greek and Latin texts, and as a writer of Latin poems. As has been mentioned above, Beroaldo produced the *editio princeps* of the first six books of the *Annals* of Tacitus, the manuscript of which had been, at some point, in Soderini's possession. Another link between Soderini and Beroaldo is provided by Francesco Persio, one of the young Volterrans in Soderini's household, who died in Rome on 8 July 1508 aged nineteen. Proof of his unfulfilled talent, in the form of a poem he had written in praise of Beroaldo, was sent by Jacopo Gherardi to Paolo Riccobaldi.[63] Bartolomeo Saliceto is another mysterious figure who was associated with many humanists but of whom there are no extant works. He was Soderini's neighbour at Torre Sanguigna and acted as Soderini's procurator for the sale of that palace. Soderini must have known of him by March 1488 at the latest, because in that month Lorenzo de' Medici wrote to the pope, Soderini and the Florentine ambassador in Rome, Giovanni Lanfredini, about 'messer Bartolomeo Saliceto'.[64] The fourth of the learned men, Girolamo Massaino, wrote tracts on the government of the church and edited Alberti's *Opera nonnulla*.[65] It seems certain, therefore, that Soderini valued and encouraged humanist scholarship and spent time in the company of learned men, but it is not possible to say very much about Soderini's own scholarly activities.

Apart from his (possible) study of the *Decretals*, the one area of scholarship in which he took an active and personal interest was oratory;

to Cisterna with Jacopo Gherardi, Saliceto and Crispo, during which there will be much talk of the absent Mario. BV, Autografi Ferrajoli, Raccolta Visconti, 6633r.

[60] P. Kristeller, *Le Thomisme et la pensée italienne de la renaissance* (Montreal/Paris, 1967), p. 73. One of Crispo's sermons 'De ascensione', given in front of Wladislaus II, king of Hungary and Bohemia, is in the Bibliothèque du Serail in Istanbul, and a Latin comedy 'Sirus' is in the university library in Salamanca. See P. Kristeller, *Iter Italicum*, IV (London, 1989), p. 607.

[61] AV, Arm. XXIX, 56, 18v, 7 November 1503.

[62] Milan, Biblioteca Ambrosiana, G 33 Inf., I, 162v and 316v–317r, 318r–319r. The latter two are letters from Casali to Crispo of 1494.

[63] Volterra, Biblioteca Guarnacci, MS 6204, 84 bis v.

[64] Del Piazzo, *Protocolli*, p. 371.

[65] For the former, see Kristeller, *Iter Italicum*, I, pp. 295, 307; and for the latter L. Alberti, *Opera nonulla*, ed. G. Massaini (Florence, c. 1498–9), of which there are only ten extant copies.

hence, his curiosity about a passage from Dio Chrysostomos. He was famous as an orator during his lifetime, delivered many orations in his capacity as ambassador[66] and was especially remembered for his Latin speech delivered before Sixtus IV on behalf of the Florentines in November 1480.[67] He is known to have had an impressive speaking voice and manner[68] which gained him a reputation in diplomatic and ecclesiastical circles, and that is probably the reason why he was chosen to celebrate mass on important occasions. This concern for oratory must have led to a concern for rhetoric in other forms. Cortesi wrote that Soderini was asked what he thought about the rhetoric of the age, and replied that he thought it more learned in judgement than eloquent in utterance, comparing it to a woman who had the wherewithal to give birth to a child but having been made pregnant, instead miscarried.[69] Soderini's own oratorical skills may also explain his patronage of Battista Casali, who was an orator at the papal court. Casali, in his funeral oration for Soderini, declared that Soderini had offered to support him on many occasions.[70] Soderini may indeed have subsidised or maintained many humanists (although there is no evidence, except from Volterra, to justify this claim), but it would be more in keeping with his character were he to have considered bed and board for humanists too expensive a charitable act or hobby, and to have chosen instead to patronise them as friends or as members of a more loosely defined clientele. Finally, it is worth mentioning a quotation from an oration, supposedly addressed by Demosthenes to Alexander the Great, which Soderini included in his 1524 will.[71] The passage cited concerned fortune, but its significance here lies in the confirmation it lends to Soderini's interest in classical rhetoric. In this way oratory and rhetoric, ancient and contemporary, provided the common ground on which Soderini and his humanist friends and clients could meet.

In addition to being able to read and write Latin, it appears that

---

[66] Negri, *Istoria*, p. 222 stated that there were 'molte orazioni da lui recitate nelle sue ambasciarie MS'.   [67] See above, p. 20 and below, p. 276.

[68] See Florence, Biblioteca Riccardiana, MS 951, 13v, Neri Nerli's panegyric of Soderini.

[69] Cortesi, *De cardinalatu*, N 5v 'huius etatis seculum eruditum magis in iudicando, quam in eloquendo disertim sibi videri respondit, ad eiusque mulieris dixit similitudinem transferri posse, que quanquam facile concipiat ad gignendum semen, minus tamen edere partum possit, proptereaque in utero abortiri nature imbecillitate soleat.'   [70] See below, p. 276.

[71] See Lowe, 'Francesco Soderini', appendix 4, p. 345. This 'oration' had been translated into Latin by Leonardo Bruni (see H. Baron, *Leonardo Bruni Aretino humanistisch-philosophische Schriften* (Leipzig, 1928), p. 179), and Bruni's translation must have been the one used by Soderini.

Soderini could write at least a little (and, therefore, it may be presumed, read and possibly speak) French.[72] But because he had no Greek,[73] he would obviously have been delighted that the humanists, by their translations, were making so many more classical texts available to him. It is, therefore, doubly unfortunate that no inventory was made of his library, which could have contained books and manuscripts in Italian, French and Latin. That the library was not just for show is proved by Cortesi's comment that Soderini always held audience in his study, so that he could return to his books without further delay once the petitioner or guest had left.[74]

Among Soderini's other interests may possibly be numbered mathematics and music. Of these two, the evidence is weakest for mathematics since it consists of only one reference from Luca Pacioli who, in his dedication of the *Divina proportione* to Piero Soderini, commented that Francesco, whom he had known at the Sforza court in Milan in 1498–9, and whom he described as most wise and his especial patron, was skilled in the subject.[75] However, the compliment was limited because, according to Pacioli, the rest of the family was similarly accomplished. A much stronger case can be made for Soderini as a lover of music. The presence of an organ and a harpsichord in his palace is the best proof available, but in addition Salvini wrote to Soderini, probably some time in the early 1480s, suggesting music as a remedy for his bad health and low spirits. The tone of the letter implied that it was being sent to someone who was already attuned to listen. Salvini continued 'It may be said that music is light and not fitting for a serious man, least of all an ecclesiastic', but he enjoined Soderini to consider king David who had enjoyed it in a decent fashion, and to enjoy it in a like manner with Paolantonio.[76] In May 1488 the Florentine government wrote to him

---

[72] See Paris, Bibliothèque Nationale, Collection Dupuy 262, 14 (old 16), a letter from Soderini to Louis XII of 13 March 1513. Soderini has written in his own hand at the bottom of the letter 'très humble et obeyssant servitour le cardinal de Xainctes'. The rest of the letter is in French but not in Soderini's hand.

[73] He had not learnt Greek as a child and did not learn any (so it seems) as an adult. Nor, so far as one can tell, did he borrow anything in Greek from the Vatican. See *I due primi registri di prestito della Biblioteca Apostolica Vaticana*, ed. M. Bertola (Città del Vaticano, 1942).   [74] Cortesi, *De cardinalatu*, L 3r.

[75] See L. Pacioli, *Divina proportione* (Venice, 1509), A2, dedication to Piero Soderini. At the end of the dedication, Pacioli said that he owed his very life to Francesco, which could be a reference to an unknown episode after the fall of Milan in 1499. The work was also dedicated to Ludovico il Moro.

[76] BV, Vat. lat. 5140, 113r and v: 'Dixerit fortasse quispiam, venerande pater, modulationem esse levem, non decere hominem gravem, dedecere sacerdotem.' It is not clear whether Soderini was being encouraged to listen to someone else's music or to play a musical instrument himself.

on behalf of Janes, a singer.[77] This could be Johannes Baltazar, who joined the singers in the papal chapel in June 1488 and stayed there, on and off, until 1501.[78] On the other hand, it could be a stray singer who needed an introduction at the papal court and Soderini was asked to help because he was known to be musical. These three discrete pieces of information do imply, at the very least, that Soderini enjoyed music enough for his enthusiasm for it to be common knowledge.

Finally, Soderini's appreciation of visual and fine arts should be investigated. As has been seen, he was interested both practically and theoretically in architecture and building. In marked contrast to this, there is no evidence to suggest that he was in the least interested in paintings or sculpture;[79] those items mentioned in the inventory were totally conventional objects concealed in the privacy of his bedroom, not on show in one of the public rooms. At no point do the sources reveal any communication with any artist (except Michelangelo who was sent to him by Piero Soderini),[80] and it is likely that he valued his tapestries, which were more precious, far more highly than his paintings, as he singled some of them out for special bequests in his wills.[81] What is clear from the inventory and the two wills is that he was particularly attached to jewellery and silver. These must have been immeasurably more important to him than panel paintings. In De cardinalatu, Cortesi recommended that cardinals should have display cabinets for both of them,[82] and Soderini certainly would have had bulging cabinets had he chosen to exhibit his collections.

Yet again, his attachment to various objects can be measured by his desire to ensure that they went to the correct person after his death. In 1524 he left to his only remaining brother, Giovanvettorio, a turquoise set in a gold ring, and to Giovanbattista di Paolantonio, a sapphire set in a gold ring, both of which Soderini used to wear on his fingers. Similarly, he bequeathed to his nephew, Giuliano, the bishop of Saintes and the ecclesiastical family representative in the next generation, a large sapphire which had previously belonged to Julius II, and a gold cross containing a piece of the true cross with a small gold chain, with which

---

[77] Del Piazzo, Protocolli, p. 375, 11 May 1488.
[78] See Richard J. Sherr, 'The papal chapel ca. 1492–1513 and its polyphonic sources' (Ph.D. dissertation, Princeton University, 1975), pp. 30–7 and 49–50.
[79] See ASR, Notari dell'AC 410, 126v and Lowe, 'Francesco Soderini', appendix 5, p. 367. He did have sgraffito work on the outside of Torre Sanguigna but nothing more is known about it.
[80] See Gaye, Carteggio, II, pp. 91–2 and ASF, Sig., Minutari 19, 148r.
[81] See Lowe, 'Francesco Soderini', appendix 3, p. 340.
[82] Weil-Garris and D'Amico, Ideal palace, pp. 83, 85.

he used to celebrate mass.[83] These jewels and relics, with their myriad associations, were, in this sense, the precious objects by which he wished his relatives to remember him.

[83] Lowe, 'Francesco Soderini', appendix 4, p. 349.

CHAPTER 21

IN PRAISE OF FRANCESCO SODERINI:
BATTISTA CASALI'S FUNERAL ORATION
OF 1524

The funeral oration for Francesco Soderini[1] was given on 18 May 1524[2] by the Roman humanist Battista Casali (1473–1525) in S. Maria del Popolo. Soderini had died on 17 May and, because of the fear of plague, it had been decided to exclude from the funeral all those not cardinals or officiating prelates. It was customary, in any case, that the pope did not attend cardinals' funerals, except in very special circumstances.[3] On the morning of the 18th, the core of the papal court met at Soderini's house at Torre Sanguigna and from there accompanied his body to S. Maria del Popolo, where it was buried amid the usual ceremonies and solemnities.[4] It was at this point that the funeral oration must have been delivered. Had it not been, the fact would surely have been noted by Blasio di Martinelli, the papal master of ceremonies, who on the contrary declared that everything had progressed as usual. It is quite interesting to speculate upon the time of composition of such an oration. Soderini had been dead for only a day although he had been ailing for months. It is possible that Casali had been forewarned that he would be expected to deliver the funeral oration in the event of Soderini's death.

---

[1] Milan, Biblioteca Ambrosiana, G 33 inf., II, 291r–295r. I would like to thank David Marsh for this reference. This oration is published as appendix 6 in Lowe, 'Francesco Soderini', pp. 374–9.

[2] BV, Vat. lat. 12276, 43v, diary of Blasio Martinelli da Cesena.

[3] J. O'Malley, *Praise and blame in renaissance Rome* (Durham, North Carolina, 1979), p. 13 gives as an exception to this rule the example of Sixtus IV presiding over the funeral of cardinal Bessarion in 1472.

[4] BV, Vat. lat. 12276, 43v. He was buried next to Piero Soderini, although the place may have been marked by an inscription rather than a tomb. See V. Forcella, *Iscrizioni delle chiese e di altri edifici di Roma dal secolo XI fino ai giorni nostri* (Rome, 1869–84), XIII, p. 523, n. 1294. Soderini had left instructions in his 1524 will for a 'depositum sive tumulum', Lowe, 'Francesco Soderini', appendix 4, p. 344. For information on the 'tombs', see F. Apolloni Ghetti, 'Nuovi appunti su Francesco Soderini cardinale Volterrano (continuazione e fine)', *L'urbe*, 39 (September–October 1976), pp. 13–14.

Paris de Grassis, in his unpublished work on curial funerals, 'Tractatus de funeribus et exsequiis in romana curia peragendis', recommended that a well-spoken member of a cardinal's household be selected in advance to deliver the oration for his patron.[5] On the other hand, it is also possible that Casali was only delegated this task at twenty-four hours' notice, and that he was picked because he knew Soderini and had some idea of his lifestyle and life-history. The question is whether the oration was considered part of the ceremony of the papal court, in which case the master of ceremonies, for example, might choose the speaker, or whether it was incumbent upon the family of the deceased to apportion this 'small and final duty'.[6] The fee for delivering an oration at the funeral of a cardinal was between fifteen and twenty-five gold ducats.[7]

Battista Casali was born about 1473 in Rome, attended the Roman academy of Pomponio Leto and taught Latin at the *Sapienza* from 1496.[8] In 1508 he was made a canon of S. Giovanni in Laterano by Julius II, and in 1517 a canon of St Peter's by Leo X. In 1514 he was appointed the deacon whose job it was to read the gospel in Greek in the papal chapels. He continued his association with the Roman academy and gained great repute as an orator, writing several other funeral orations for cardinals, including those for Giovanni Colonna (died 26 September 1508), Gabriel de' Gabrielli (died 5 November 1511), Robert Guibé (died 9 November 1513), Francesco Remolino (died 5 February 1518), Luigi D'Aragona (died 21 January 1519)[9] and Domenico Grimani (died 27 August 1523).[10] But he did not restrict himself to funeral orations; he addressed two orations of a different sort to Adrian VI – one of congratulation upon his arrival and the other a plea to keep the revenues of the *Sapienza* out of the clutches of the conservators.[11] Earlier in his career he had preached a third type of oration more frequently, that of a sermon *inter missam solemnis*. In one preached before Julius II on the

---

[5] See J. McManamon, *Funeral oratory and the cultural ideals of Italian humanism* (Chapel Hill, 1989), p. 26.

[6] All English phrases or sentences in this section in inverted commas are translations from the oration.   [7] McManamon, *Funeral oratory*, p. 27.

[8] There is a manuscript life of Casali written by P. Bigolini at the front of the collection of his letters, orations etc. in Milan, Biblioteca Ambrosiana, G 33 inf., II. See also S. Seidel Menchi, 'Alcuni atteggiamenti della cultura italiana di fronte a Erasmo', in *Eresia e riforma nell'Italia del cinquecento* (Florence, 1974), pp. 91–3.

[9] Both these orations are in Milan, Biblioteca Ambrosiana, G 33 inf., II, 51r ff and 56r ff.

[10] Milan, Biblioteca Ambrosiana, G 33 inf., I, 297v–303r, 309r–315r, (renumbered) 29r–37r, 37v–45r, 45v–50v, 51r–56r, 56v–62r, 69r–75r. See also McManamon, *Funeral oratory*, pp. 262–3 for a list of funeral orations composed by Battista Casali.

[11] See Ballistreri on Casali in the *Dizionario biografico degli italiani*, XXI, p. 76.

Feast of the Circumcision, 1 January 1508, in the main a conventional congratulatory speech on Julius's efforts against the Turks, he spun off into a comparison between ancient Athens and contemporary Rome.[12] He certainly had a tendency to follow up his own enthusiasms whilst at the same time being one of the most humanistic of the orators at the papal court during his period, a combination which could have contributed to his popularity. In 1517 he was living, as were many other members of the Casali family, in the parish of S. Trifone centred on S. Agostino,[13] which was very near to Soderini's palace at Torre Sanguigna; he died in Rome on 13 April 1525.

The text of the oration is preserved in a single clear copy, but the scribe was not a good Latinist and there are many passages which present syntactical difficulties. The oration is written in the classical epideictic style and follows its precepts with an almost dogged faithfulness. Treatise II, now ascribed with some certainty to Menander, written in the late third or early fourth century AD, incorporates the ideas on epideictic propounded by Aristotle in his *Rhetoric*, the *Rhetorica ad Alexandrum*, Cicero's *De oratore* and Quintilian in *De laude ac vituperatione*, and quickly became the standard reference text on oratorical matters.[14] There are two sections of Treatise II which could have had a bearing on renaissance funeral orations – the Imperial Oration and the Funeral Speech – but in fact Casali's oration is far more in line with the former than the latter. Eight features of epideictic speeches in general have been isolated and admirably described by John McManamon[15] in a study of the funeral orations declaimed over renaissance popes.[16] If one compares this outline with the presentation of material on Soderini's life and character by Casali, the extent of this particular debt can be gauged.

First, there is the *prooemium* when the speaker customarily professes his inadequacy in the face of so vast and difficult a task, although great freedom was always allowed in this section of the speech. If one omits the opening part of Casali's oration which introduces the theme of

---

[12] J. O'Malley, 'The Vatican library and the schools of Athens: a text of Battista Casali, 1508', *Journal of medieval and renaissance studies*, 7 (1977), pp. 271–2.

[13] A. Esposito Aliano, 'La parocchia "Agostiniana" di S. Trifone nella Roma di Leone X', *Mélanges de l'Ecole Française de Rome, Moyen age, Temps modernes*, 93 (1981), p. 515, using a census of 18 December 1517, records that, at that date, Battista was living in the parish with his brother, Matteo.

[14] See *Menander Rhetor*, ed. and trans. by D. Russell and N. Wilson (Oxford, 1981), pp. xix–xxiii. A Greek Aldine edition of Menander was published in 1508–9.

[15] J. McManamon, 'The ideal renaissance pope: funeral oratory from the papal court', *Archivum historiae pontificiae*, 14 (1976), p. 21ff.

[16] The schema are adapted from essential features set out by T. Burgess, 'Epideictic literature', *University of Chicago studies in classical philology*, 3 (1902), pp. 122–6.

fortune, this sentiment follows immediately.[17] The second point to be covered, *genos* or ancestry, includes references to country or nation, city and relatives. In Casali's oration, there is an encomium on the Etruscans and on Florence and then reference to Soderini's famous family is made, while at the same time it is stressed that he does not require reflected glory from them as he has enough glory of his own.[18] The third section on *genesis* or birth, where the speaker is instructed to include any noteworthy event preceding or attending the individual's birth, is omitted in Casali's speech. This is probably because Casali did not know of any contemporary dreams or other legends, and chose not to fabricate any; instead, he included a long embellishment of some early facts in the fourth section on *anatrophe* or youth, where he spoke at some length of Soderini's miraculous knowledge of the law at the age of sixteen, and his skill in public debate at the university of Pisa with the famous civil lawyer, Filippo Decio.[19] This had been possible on account of his natural genius and his father's tender nurturing of his abilities. The oration passes without pause into the fifth section which normally describes the person's choice of career, and here the image of Soderini as bishop of Volterra, ambassador and cardinal under a series of popes is flashed in front of the audience. The 'outline and conspectus of his attainments' is really part of the sixth section on *praxeis* or deeds, which then turns to look at the 'principle of his life and character'. This is an extremely important section designed to illustrate to the full the manner of the man's virtue, and often particular attention is paid to the cardinal virtues of fortitude, justice, temperance and prudence. A parallel to the seventh section of *sunkrisis* or comparison could be found in the extended discussion on whether or not Soderini was closefisted and in what, essentially, consisted generosity, and how what was considered generous in a prince was not generous in others.[20] The *epilogos* or conclusion rounded off the whole, in this case very neatly, by returning to the theme of fortune with which Casali had opened the oration. McManamon states that, for obvious reasons, two further sections – the lamentory and the consolatory – may be included. Here they are not.

[17] Milan, Biblioteca Ambrosiana, G 33 inf., II, 291r and v and Lowe, 'Francesco Soderini', appendix 6, p. 374.

[18] Milan, Biblioteca Ambrosiana, G 33 inf., II, 292r and Lowe, 'Francesco Soderini', appendix 6, p. 375.

[19] Milan, Biblioteca Ambrosiana, G 33 inf., II, 292v and 293r and Lowe, 'Francesco Soderini', appendix 6, pp. 375–6.

[20] Milan, Biblioteca Ambrosiana, G 33 inf., II, 294v and Lowe, 'Francesco Soderini', appendix 6, p. 378.

Thus, Casali's oration slips very easily into this general mould.[21] There are points highlighted by Menander himself as being worthy of inclusion which seem clear forerunners of parts of Casali's oration on Soderini, although of course the source may have been later writers incorporating Menander, or later composers of funeral speeches adopting his suggestions, rather than the author of Treatise II himself. For example, Menander wrote at length on encomia of cities and, as has been seen, it was usual for encomia of individuals to include remarks on their native country or city. Casali's description of Florence is quite detailed and astute and it follows Menander's suggested plan.[22] As he was not a Florentine, Casali must have based this section[23] upon Florence's popular reputation and it is one of the passages where personal judgement has combined interestingly with rhetorical practice.

Another instance where Menander's principles appear to have been applied is in his inclusion of a discussion of fortune,[24] but fortune is very changed in Casali's oration. The extended metaphor of life as a play, both directed by Fortune, appears at the beginning and end of the oration, and is a remarkable feature. Casali writes in the opening section: 'I naturally judge that the life of man is clearly a play, so to speak, which Fortune puts on; at her own whim she assigns diverse roles – sometimes of principal parts, sometimes of supporting – to everyone.'[25] To Soderini she indeed gave a great many different roles. Casali then places Virtue and Fortune in apposition: 'For set as Soderini was in the very kingdom of Fortune he could neither be seduced by the enticements of Fortune's winds, nor did he become puffed up, nor broken and amazed by the whirlwinds and storms of her veering blasts but that he wanted Virtue as his guide rather than Fortune.'[26] Such a theme, without mention of God or of divine destiny, shows the extent of classical influence.

In the concluding section, the simile is returned to: 'To this point,

---

[21] As do, for example, later funeral orations in France. See R. Giesey, *The royal funeral ceremony in renaissance France* (Geneva, 1960), p. 171.

[22] *Menander Rhetor*, p. 79.

[23] Milan, Biblioteca Ambrosiana, G 33 inf., II, 292r and Lowe, 'Francesco Soderini', appendix 6, p. 375.   [24] *Menander Rhetor*, p. 93.

[25] Milan, Biblioteca Ambrosiana, G 33 inf., II, 291r and Lowe, 'Francesco Soderini', appendix 6, p. 374: 'ita nimirum statuo vitam hominum esse plane quasi fabulam quandam quam fortunam exhibeat imponatque diversas omnibus suo arbitratu nunc primarum nunc secundarum partium personas.'

[26] Milan, Biblioteca Ambrosiana, G 33 inf., II, 291r and Lowe, 'Francesco Soderini', appendix 6, p. 374: 'Nam in ipso fortune regnio constitutus neque flantis fortune illecebris capi atque insolescere neque reflantis turbine ac procella frangi consternariaque potuit quo minus virtutem sibi quam fortunam ducem maluerit.'

Fortune bore herself as a companion to the virtue of this man. But finally, in the last act of the play, she waxed so savage and, so to say, hostile, that she cast him down into the deepest and almost unconscionable misfortunes. For it is generally true that just as great good fortune accompanies great men, so also equal Furies pursue him.'[27] The terrible fortunes in Soderini's case were the so-called conspiracies, exile and old age. Soderini triumphed over Fortune because he proved that he could withstand either good or bad fortune whereas Cato and his followers could not. Finally, Casali commends Soderini's actions and acting: 'He was a man who completed the whole play of his life, as a play is enacted right to the final act, with the greatest dignity and verve. He always held Virtue to be the guide of the true life; the chances presented by Fortune he indeed acquiesced in as though they were a play; finally when he was forsaken by Fortune he scorned them as a play; and indeed the life itself which we live is plainly nothing other than a play. This is the nature of the human condition.'[28] Soderini realised this and had his reward. Then, almost at the point where one has ceased to expect it, there is a reference to faith and God; Soderini is represented as being in God's presence, and Casali ends: 'To God we now give merited applause for a life which, like an energetically acted play, was well lived.'[29] Only at the last moment does he make the connection between classical and christian virtue, and it appears that it is the topic of fortune that is important and, in this highly developed form, is peculiar to Casali. In Menander only favourable fortune is to be praised;[30] here, Casali develops the idea by emphasising Soderini's ability to deal with unfavourable fortune. In this way, Casali contributes to the debate on whether man can direct (his own) fortune and the question of the efficacy of resistance to her/it.

Other features of the oration can be picked out as belonging to other

[27] Milan, Biblioteca Ambrosiana, G 33 inf., II, 294v and Lowe, 'Francesco Soderini', appendix 6, p. 378: 'Hactenus, Patres amplissimi, fortuna huius virtuti comitem se gessit. In postremo vero fabule actu tam seva tamquam infesta in Franciscum insurrexit ut eum in maximas ac pene deploratas calamitates coniecerit. Solent enim plerumque magnos viros ut magne fortune ita etiam pares Erunne consectari.'

[28] Milan, Biblioteca Ambrosiana, G 33 inf., II, 295r and Lowe, 'Francesco Soderini', appendix 6, p. 379: 'Quippe qui totam etatis fabulam ut exercitatus histrio usque ad extremum actum summa cum dignitate ac spiritu peregit. Qui semper vere vite ducem virtutem habuit; que vero a fortuna ostentabantur uti fabulam accipiebat, postremo cum a fortuna destitueretur uti fabulam aspernabatur, vita enim ipsa quam vivimus nihil plane aliud quam fabula. Sic sese res humane habent, Patres amplissimi.'

[29] Milan, Biblioteca Ambrosiana, G 33 inf., II, 295r and Lowe, 'Francesco Soderini', appendix 6, p. 379: 'Cui nunc pro tam bene gesta tanquam strenue acta fabula merito plausum damus.'   [30] *Menander Rhetor*, p. 175.

traditions. For example, although there is very little direct recourse to godly sensibilities, some christian precepts are discernible. Greek and Roman convention demanded recognition for civic duties and acts performed for others which happily coincided with christian ideals of sharing and giving.[31] Perhaps to a greater degree than most, Casali was oddly uninterested in representing Soderini as a fount of christian piety. In the section where one would expect to find examples of this, that on 'the principle of his life and character', the picture drawn of Soderini is of a humanist cardinal of the pre-Reformation, not of a pious churchman: he had an extremely retentive memory which enabled him to remember books that he had read fifty years previously, he was serious, he had a sense of humour, he valued his friends. The only piece of evidence which could be advanced in support of either claim was that he gave money to friends in need.[32] Liberality and wisdom were the two virtues most likely to be added to the four cardinal virtues and to be praised in these orations, and Soderini was duly praised for both. The acquisition of learning and wisdom therefore becomes important. A very minor instance of this is visible in Casali's tale of Soderini's being businesslike in pleasure since 'he would at certain times daily weary two or three by reading aloud to them and he never even spent such a leisurely and vacuous meal but that it was charmingly seasoned with some reading or debating'.[33] The reading of learned works during a meal was a facet of godly feasts depicted by Erasmus in *Convivium religiosum* and sometimes too by the preachers in their sermons;[34] it was, therefore, included by Casali as part of this tradition of the depiction of godly mores.

Examples from mythology and from Greek and Roman history are often recalled in renaissance epideictic orations. In Casali's on Soderini, Tantalus and his stone are summoned in the opening sentence and the power of the mere names of Achilles and Diomede is invoked on the second page. Nerva's son puts in a brief appearance as a precocious lawyer. Later, Casali praises Soderini's actions in choosing to bear bad fortune, as opposed to Cato and Scipio who preferred to kill themselves lest they be forced 'to play abject slavery to Caesar' ('Which Catos,

---

[31] See O'Malley, *Praise and blame*, p. 169.

[32] Milan, Biblioteca Ambrosiana, G 33 inf., II, 294r and Lowe, 'Francesco Soderini', appendix 6, p. 377: 'qui amici paupertatem sepius dono levarit'.

[33] Milan, Biblioteca Ambrosiana, G 33 inf., II, 294r and Lowe, 'Francesco Soderini', appendix 6, pp. 377–8: 'in ocio negocius, utpote qui duos tresve interdum quotidie legendo fatigaret et qui ne ipsam quidem mensam tam ociosam tamquam fatuam unquam habuit quin esset aliquod vel lectionis vel disputationis lepidissimum condimentum.'   [34] O'Malley, *Praise and blame*, pp. 180–1.

which Scipios will anyone boast to me of now?'),[35] and, finally, he compares Fortune's unreliable play to being 'borne on the wings of Icarus to that final point where at last we take a fall'.[36] Often these classical exempla are matched in other orations by stories from the christian fathers or by scriptural references, but in this oration these are noticeable by their absence.

It will be seen, therefore, that the encomium of Soderini put forward in this oration differs substantially from both history and biography.[37] In contrast to an historical approach, only facts which further the glorification of Soderini are included (except for the repudiation of the charge of meanness levelled against him), and there is no attempt to present an even résumé of his life or his achievements and failures, no attempt at narration. Exact truth is not necessary, and invention in certain circumstances is positively de rigeur. The relationship between biography and encomium is closer but biography is under more of an obligation to portray a rounded picture of the individual. If one investigates the 'facts' that are presented in Casali's oration, a clearer understanding of the distinction will emerge. The most pronounced and extended piece of exaggeration and myth-making is to be found in the section on Soderini as a lawyer at the university of Pisa. Casali states that in Soderini's sixteenth year he had already passed through the university and was a fully fledged lawyer. The process of becoming a civil or canon lawyer took at least six years in this period, and most of Casali's audience would have known this, some would even have been lawyers themselves. Casali's tale is rhetoric unbound, but it did contain elements of truth. Soderini was at Pisa at the same time as Filippo Decio; there would, in some sense, have been competition between them as they were both students together during the academic years 1473–5, and teachers for some of the academic year 1477–8.[38] In this year, Soderini would have been twenty-four years old, a far cry from the precocious sixteen of the oration. No evidence of hugely popular public disputations between the two of them have come to light, although it is possible that they took place.[39] But the whole description has been so

---

[35] Milan, Biblioteca Ambrosiana, G 33 inf., II, 295r and Lowe, 'Francesco Soderini', appendix 6, pp. 378–9: 'Quos mihi nunc quispiam Catones Scipiones iactet? Illi, ne servitute servire Cesari cogerentur ... '

[36] Milan, Biblioteca Ambrosiana, G 33 inf., II, 295r and Lowe, 'Francesco Soderini', appendix 6, p. 379: 'et Icari alis vehimur ut tandem corruamus'.

[37] Burgess, 'Epideictic literature', pp. 116–17.

[38] See Verde, Lo studio, III, II, p. 831 and I, pp. 302–3 (from Decio's career at Pisa), and the life of Decio by Francesco Boeza at the beginning of F. Decio, Commentarii in Digestum vetus (Venice, 1589), 2r for proof that they were teaching the Institutes at the same time.   [39] See Pocciantio, Catalogus, p. 68.

orchestrated that the matter and manner of their contest is left imprecise, and the story passes unchallenged due to lack of specificity.

Casali writes: 'As a result of this reputation the Florentine senate decreed his appointment over the Volterran church.'[40] This statement is palpably incorrect: Soderini was not made bishop of Volterra on account of his standing at Pisa; he changed career in mid-stream because his father, Tommaso, and Lorenzo de' Medici decided that they could procure the bishopric for him by using Lorenzo's influence with the pope. But the truth is either not known or disregarded as it would break up the flow of Casali's argument. On the other hand, Casali is correct when he reports that Soderini's speech before Sixtus IV caused a stir and was noted by diarists (for example, Gherardi), and it could have been transcribed and a copy lodged in the papal archive. Something persuaded Adrian to treat Soderini with more leniency when he was incarcerated in Castel Sant'Angelo in 1523, and it may have been the sight of this elegant and once successful speech. Casali is correct, too, when he writes that Sixtus made Soderini a referendary, which he did in May 1481, and that Soderini was raised to the purple by Alexander VI, which he was in 1503, and that he was left in charge of Rome when Leo went to Bologna, which he was in 1515. But, after all, Casali lived in Rome and these were facts which would have been easy enough for him to establish by inquiry at the curia.

Several other points deserve to be made. In the oration Casali states that Soderini offered him as much money as he wanted,[41] and this can probably be taken at face value. The charge of ungenerous behaviour levelled at Soderini probably arose from two causes – first, a comparison between him and the Medici cardinals, who were noted for their ostentatious hospitality, and second, Soderini was an efficient administrator and a canny businessman, not obsessed with conspicuous consumption even if he was a natty dresser,[42] so that he aroused envy (this point is brought out quite clearly in the oration). The reference to his generosity to his native country and his relatives shows that, at worst, he was not merely mean. Another section on Soderini in prison in old age illustrates that this episode had won him a certain amount of

---

[40] Milan, Biblioteca Ambrosiana, G 33 inf., II, 293r and Lowe, 'Francesco Soderini', appendix 6, p. 376: 'Qua fama senatus florentinus per motus Volaterrane ecclesie preficiendum curavit.'

[41] Milan, Biblioteca Ambrosiana, G 33 inf., II, 294r and Lowe, 'Francesco Soderini', appendix 6, p. 377: 'inter quos unum esse me profiteor cui pecuniam quantam vellem iterum atque iterum obtulerit.'

[42] Milan, Biblioteca Ambrosiana, G 33 inf., II, 294r and Lowe, 'Francesco Soderini', appendix 6, p. 377 where Soderini is described as being 'nitidus sine fuco'.

notoriety and that the action and the acclaim had done him more good than harm. The reactions of some of the ambassadors and other cardinals also show this. Thus far encomium and biography have blended together.

Not many funeral orations for cardinals from this period have been published although there are many in manuscript, so it is difficult to assess the degree of uniformity outside the restrictions of the epideictic type. Two such orations by Poggio Bracciolini, for cardinal Francesco Zabarella[43] and cardinal Giuliano Cesarini,[44] have been published, but they date from the first half of the fifteenth century. They both, as one would expect, follow the general pattern. The oration of Niccolò Capranica for cardinal Bessarion in 1472[45] is more interesting as it lists his writings, talks about his Greek and Latin library and, as befits a cardinal important for doctrine and religious matters, ends on a christian note of uplift. The eclectic oration for cardinal Francesco Gonzaga was delivered in Mantua in 1483 by Giovanni Lucido Cattanei, and published ten years later. It stressed, amongst other things, his good looks and social skills, his proficiency in rhetoric and his profound piety;[46] christian behaviour was at least here distinguished as a component of the rounded individual. Fedro Inghirami's oration for Ludovico Podocataro, of 1504,[47] is again severely classical, and Lorenzo Grana's for Giles of Viterbo, of 1532,[48] is understandably imbued with religious sentiment. Casali's oration for Soderini belongs definitely to the more classical of these traditions. His language is rigidly classical, with all the resulting circumlocutions for post-classical words, situations and ideas. For example, councils are senates, and Soderini is not made a cardinal but 'enlisted into this very body and senate'; he does not attend the university at Pisa but the Pisan gymnasium. Casali's syntax is woven with classical balances, his grammar infused with classical devices such as asyndeton. There are also classical echoes from literary sources, such as the passage where a young boy is compared to a field and his future intelligence to the farmer's yield, which requires cultivation by the father/farmer in order to produce a proper harvest, not one consisting of burrs and caltrops, which owes a debt to Virgil's *Georgics*, I, 150.

In conclusion, this Roman funeral oration from the first quarter of the

[43] P. Bracciolini, *Oratio in funere Francesci Zabarellae* (Passau, 1655), pp. 3–18.

[44] *Spicilegium romanum*, ed. A. Mai, x (Rome, 1844), pp. 374–84.

[45] L. Mohler, *Kardinal Bessarion als Theologe, Humanist und Staatsmann*, III (Paderborn, 1942), pp. 405–14.

[46] Chambers, *A renaissance cardinal*, pp. 93, 30, 67 and 27.

[47] *Anecdota litteraria*, ed. G. Amaduzzi and G. Bianconi, I (Rome, 1773), pp. 289–332.

[48] *Ibid.*, IV (Rome, 1783), pp. 293–322.

sixteenth century has both classical and renaissance elements in profusion, but very few elements from the christian tradition. It betrays its date most clearly in the extended conceit on life as a play directed by Fortune, and in the passages which describe Soderini's lifestyle in concertedly non-religious terms.

EXCURSUS: THE PORTRAITS OF PIERO AND FRANCESCO SODERINI

Francesco Soderini's appearance cannot be easily or securely ascertained for portraits of him are both scarce and elusive. One difficulty is that there is considerable confusion over the identities of Francesco and his brother, the *gonfaloniere a vita*, Piero. The only contemporary portrait definitely said to be of Francesco[1] went on sale at Sotheby's on 3 July 1929. It was lot number 86 in a collection of pictures from Kinmel Park, Abergele, North Wales, formed by H. R. Hughes[2] between 1850 and 1880,[3] and was described as being panel, half-length, of a man in a red dress with a black cap against a dark background, and it was attributed to Pontormo. The purchaser was A. L. Nicholson and the price was £180.[4] It has not been traced since this date. The portrait was later attributed by Bernard Berenson to Lorenzo Lotto and a photograph of

---

[1] A much later portrait, number 42 of a series of bishops of Saintes, existed in a collection formed by Joseph-Désiré Briand, the author of *L'histoire de l'église santone et aunisienne* (La Rochelle, 1843). Its authenticity is more than doubtful. See L. Audiat, 'La collection de portraits des évêques de Saintes', *Bulletin de la société des archives historiques, Revue de la Saintonge et de l'Aunis*, 15 (1895), p. 183.

[2] On the Hughes family and Kinmel, see 'A schedule of the Kinmel manuscripts and documents deposited in the library of the University College of North Wales, Bangor, by Captain D. H. Fetherstonhaugh of Kinmel Manor, Abergele, 1953', compiled by E. Gwynne Jones, librarian (February 1955), especially pp. 12–13, and Appendix II 'Hughes of Kinmel', still by E. Gwynne Jones, and M. Girouard's first article on Kinmel in *Country life*, 146 (1969), pp. 542–5.

[3] How this picture entered this collection remains a mystery, but H. R. Hughes may have purchased it from Colnaghi's in the late 1860s. See the Kinmel papers, University of Bangor, number 1498, which contains H. R. Hughes' bank passbook for 1866–76. He paid sums of about £280–£300 to Colnaghi's on several occasions during 1867–9, and it is likely that these were for paintings.

[4] A. L. Nicholson bought two other paintings from the collection, a Mabuse portrait of Henry VIII for £400 and an Antonio Moro self-portrait for £800. See the auctioneers' copy of the sale catalogue, numbers 78 and 81.

8. Portrait, said to be of Francesco Soderini, ascribed by Bernard
Berenson to Lorenzo Lotto, formerly in the H. R. Hughes collection
at Kinmel, sold at Sotheby's on 3 July 1929.

the portrait was included in the last edition of his work on Lotto[5] (see figure 8).

A similar fate befell the most likely portrait of Piero. It was sold in the Henry Doetsch sale of 22 and 24–25 June 1895 which was conducted by Christie's. Number 102 in the catalogue, it was said to be a portrait of Nicola Vonica by Ridolfo del Ghirlandaio (1483–1560), because on the frame was a medal of this man by Fra Antonio da Brescia.[6] The last line of the entry read that some specialists had attributed the picture to Lorenzo Lotto.[7] Berenson did so in the second edition of his book on Lotto,[8] and in the 1950s two Italians, Anna Banti and Antonio Boschetto,[9] discussed the attribution at greater length and announced that the painting had reappeared in a sale at Sotheby's around 1935. The only possible portrait to which they could be referring is number 7 in the catalogue of Sotheby's for 27–29 May 1935, school of Bronzino, portrait of a man in a black dress with a black cap.[10] The present whereabouts of this portrait (or, if they are not the same, of both these portraits) are unknown. The photograph of it, reproduced by Banti and Boschetto, showed a painting in much better condition than that reproduced by Berenson in his 1956 edition of Lotto, where it was described as 'half ruined'.[11] Berenson believed that the portrait was of Piero, and stated that the original cartoon for it was in the Devonshire collection at Chatsworth, attributed to Raphael[12] (see figure 9).

The Chatsworth drawing is in black chalk with colour wash on the face.[13] Suggestions as to the identity of the sitter have included cardinal

[5] See B. Berenson, *Lorenzo Lotto* (London, 1956), p. 29 and plate 75. Research at I Tatti in Berenson's old photographic collection drew a blank, and there is nothing to indicate that Berenson ever saw the picture. He probably acquired the photograph from A. C. Cooper, Fine Art Photographer, 3 and 4 Rose and Crown Yard, St James, London SW1, as Cooper's address is included with other details on the photograph, which are not, however, written in Berenson's own hand. Unfortunately, all Cooper's pre-war negatives were destroyed by enemy action in the Second World War.

[6] This medal is described by G. Hill, *A corpus of Italian medals of the renaissance before Cellini* (London, 1930), I, p. 125 and depicted in II, plate 89, number 476.

[7] See F. Lugt, *Répertoire des catalogues de ventes publiques: troisième période, 1861–1900* (The Hague, 1964), p. 590 and the priced Doetsch sale catalogue at the Victoria and Albert Museum Library.

[8] B. Berenson, *Lorenzo Lotto* (London, 1901), pp. 108–9.

[9] A. Banti and A. Boschetto, *Lorenzo Lotto* (Florence, 1953), p. 70.

[10] This was sold to R. E. A. Wilson for the small sum of £58.

[11] Banti and Boschetto, *Lorenzo Lotto*, plate 57, and Berenson, *Lorenzo Lotto* (London, 1956), plate 74 and p. 28.

[12] Berenson, *Lorenzo Lotto* (London, 1956), p. 29. In the catalogue of the Doetsch sale, this was said to be a portrait of cardinal Bibbiena.

[13] It is now number 756 in the Courtauld inventory of the Chatsworth collection and its old number used to be 49.

9. Black chalk drawing with colour wash, possibly of Piero or Francesco Soderini, from the workshop of Raphael, now in the Devonshire collection at Chatsworth.

Bibbiena,[14] Agostino Beazzano,[15] Piero Soderini[16] and 'a cardinal'[17] (who because of the likeness to the Lotto portrait may be cardinal Soderini). The head has been cut out of the original drawing, and pasted onto another sheet, toned with a reddish-brown wash. Only the face (and the background, which is different) seem to be in colour wash; otherwise, the black chalk gives the probably misleading impression that the sitter wears a black hat and a black garment. The shape of the hat does resemble a cardinal's *biretta*. Nothing, therefore, can be safely concluded about the sitter from his dress. The drawing is now judged to be from the workshop of Raphael, according to the notes made by Christie's cataloguers in 1980, although one previous attribution had been to Franciabigio.[18]

All these portraits could well be of the same man. They have been assumed to be of two different people because the Kinmel portrait shows the sitter wearing red, although significantly the cap is black. However, the red cloak is not similar to those worn by cardinals of the period which were the same length all the way round, and therefore covered up most of the arms, and which often had a hood. It is the kind of red shift which was worn by office holders in Florence and, more particularly, by *gonfalonieri*. On the other hand, the hat does look like a *biretta* and is not the *gonfaloniere*'s more complicated headpiece. Without the portraits themselves, it is not possible to judge whether the faces are all of the same person, but they are similar enough to belong to brothers. Nor is enough known of the physical appearance of either Piero or Francesco for a decision to be made on this basis. Berenson's reconstruction of the circumstances under which these portraits were painted is erroneous. Were Piero to have had his portrait painted in official robes, it would have been during his period as *gonfaloniere a vita* (1502–12), during which time he was in his 50s. Having left the city, it is very unlikely that he would have commissioned a portrait and

[14] The mount of the drawing at Chatsworth is inscribed in Padre Sebastiano Resta's hand 'Ritratto del cardinale de Bibiena'. Resta was an Oratorian who had travelled around Lombardy at the end of the seventeenth century collecting paintings. See M. Jaffé, *Old master drawings from Chatsworth* (Alexandria, Virginia, 1987), pp. 13 and 18.

[15] J. Crowe and G. Cavalcaselle, *Raphael: his life and works*, II (London, 1885), p. 330. This suggestion originated because of a supposed likeness between the face in the drawing and the portrait of Beazzano in the Raphael 'Navagero and Beazzano', now in the Galleria Doria Pamphili in Rome. On this, see R. Jones and N. Penny, *Raphael* (New Haven/London, 1983), p. 162 and plate 173.

[16] David Coffin, some years ago, upon seeing this portrait, scribbled 'compare with Lotto portrait of Soderini' in one of the Chatsworth catalogues.

[17] See the typed 'Catalogue of drawings in the collection of the duke of Devonshire' (1929), p. 188.   [18] Crowe and Cavalcaselle, *Raphael*, II, p. 330.

certainly not in Florentine garb, and not when he was in fear of his life on his way to secret exile in Dubrovnik. Francesco lived in Rome once a cardinal, that is from 1503 onwards, only returning to Florence and Tuscany for the summer break, so he would have been far more likely to commission a portrait in Rome than in his native city.

It is conceivable that this sitter, or sitters, is not a member of the Soderini family at all but, as Berenson pointed out, Silvano Razzi used the Doetsch portrait (or something very similar) as the basis for the portrait of Piero at the front of his biography of him in the early eighteenth century,[19] and so a tradition that it was must have already been in force by then. Razzi's portrait of Francesco bears no resemblance to anything so far discussed, and may have been an invention. On the other hand, the Razzi representation of Francesco has something in common with a portrait of Piero bearing the inscription 'Piero Soderini' painted by an unknown hand and now in the Uffizi.[20] There is another portrait of Piero in the Uffizi in the series commissioned by Paolo Giovio,[21] and later executed by Cristofano dell'Altissimo around 1570.[22] In this picture he looks downcast but at least is sporting his *gonfaloniere's* hat. Finally, there appeared at a sale at the Hôtel Drouot in Paris, on 14 May 1973, yet another picture of him, inscribed 'Piero Soderini G', which was attributed to the school of Pontormo,[23] just as the Kinmel portrait of Francesco had been attributed to Pontormo in 1929, and the attributions had come full circle.

It would be fair to assume that if these were portraits of the Soderini, they would, initially at least, have remained in the family. Mariano Vasi described a visit in the mid-eighteenth century to palazzo Spada, one part of which was inhabited by a Monsignor Soderini, where he was shown an antechamber, adorned with Soderini family portraits, among which he singled out two by Marco Benefial (1684–1764), one by Pompeo Batoni (1708–87) and another which he described as surprising, by an unknown hand.[24] Although the portraits mentioned are all from the eighteenth century, it is probable that the family's more remote forebears also embellished the walls. Family portraits were only one part

---

[19] Razzi, *Vita*, frontispiece, unpaginated.

[20] Its number is P. 2a, number 738 (edizione Alinari).

[21] See E. Muntz, *Le musée de portraits de Paul Jove* (Paris, 1900), p. 71.

[22] *Gli Uffizi: catalogo generale* (Florence, 1979), p. 656.

[23] See the reproduction in the Witt Library, Courtauld Institute, under Jacopo da Pontormo. This could have come from the Panciatichi or Bartolommei collections in Florence which Berenson claimed contained replicas of the Lotto portrait of Piero Soderini. Cf. Berenson, *Lorenzo Lotto* (London, 1956), p. 29 and Passerini, 'Soderini', *Celebri famiglie italiane*, illustrations.

[24] M. Vasi, *Itinerario istruttivo di Roma* (Rome, 1744), I, p. 70.

10. Eighteenth-century Roman bust of Francesco Soderini, possibly by Filippo della Valle, exhibited at Heim's in London, May–August 1976.

of a large and choice collection. On 18–20 December 1783, count Ottavio Soderini sold in Paris, at the Hôtel de Bullion, the collection of paintings and drawings which he had brought from Rome.[25] No portraits of Piero or Francesco are listed but they could have been swamped amongst the paintings attributed to famous artists such as

[25] F. Lugt, *Répertoire des catalogues de ventes publiques: première période vers 1600–1825* (The Hague, 1938), numbers 3631 and 3651. The sale had been postponed from 24–26 November which is the date of the catalogue.

Raphael and Poussin, and the drawings attributed to Michelangelo, Raphael, Titian, Andrea del Sarto and others.[26] By whatever routes, the Soderini portraits had reached England and Wales by the mid-nineteenth century only to be lost to view again in the 1920s and 1930s.

Finally, mention should be made of a pair of eighteenth-century Roman marble portrait busts of Piero and Francesco Soderini (see figure 10), with gilt-bronze inscriptions, which were probably commissioned around mid-century for a member of the Soderini family.[27] The portraits appear to be imaginary; certainly, they are not based upon the paintings discussed above. It seems certain that they must have been commissioned by a later Soderini who was keen to commemorate illustrious forebears, perhaps by Antonfrancesco (1660–1743) or Tiberio (1736–1817).[28] Possible sculptors include Giuseppe Rusconi and Filippo della Valle, who is the most likely candidate. This eighteenth-century renaissance of interest in Piero and Francesco as appropriate subjects for historicising busts reflects their enduring fame and adaptability as political role models for different centuries.

[26] O. Soderini, *Catalogue raisonné des tableaux et dessins qui composoient la galerie du comte Suderini à Rome* (Paris, 1783).

[27] See *Italian paintings and sculptures of the seventeenth and eighteenth centuries* (London, 1976), Heim Gallery exhibition catalogue no. 25, Tenth summer exhibition, 26 May to 27 August 1976, nos 38 and 39.

[28] Passerini, 'Soderini', *Celebri famiglie italiane*, table VII.

BIBLIOGRAPHY

MANUSCRIPT SOURCES

Bangor
Kinmel papers, University archives, 1498

Bologna, AS
Lettere dell'ambasciatore al Senato 6 (1523)
Lettere di diversi da Roma e Firenze al Senato (1507–1530)
Notarile, Tommaso Grengoli, busta 18, filza 13

Dubrovnik
Biblioteca Male Brače, MS 68, MS 195
Historijski Archiv, Miscellanea, saec. XVI, F III, I

Florence, Archivio Arcivescovile
Libro II di collazione

Florence, AS
Acquisti e doni 84
Capitani di Parte Guelfa, Numeri rossi 75, 85
Capitoli, Appendice 44
Carte Strozziane I, 10
    I, 136
    II, 134
    III, 108
    III, 110
    III, 134
    CVI, 20
    CXXXVIII
    CCXXX
Catasto 655
Consulte e pratiche 67

Dieci di Balia, Carteggi, Responsive 38, 72, 73, 75, 76, 78, 79, 83, 84, 87, 98, 117, 118
Diplomatico, Riformagioni, Atti pubblici
    Comune di Volterra
Lettere varie 14
Manoscritti 178
Manoscritti Torrigiani, busta III, fasc. 20
Manoscritti Torrigiani, pergamene
Mediceo 6409
Mediceo avanti il principato XXXIV, 56
    XXXVI, 802
    XXXVIII, 688
    XLIII, 25
    XLVII, 265
    LXXXV, 421
    CVII, 39
    CXXV, 143
    CXLIII, 92, 141, 154, 155, 156
    CXLIV, 12, 25, 90
Il minutario di Goro Gheri
Miscellanea repubblicana, busta VI, 206
Notarile antecosimiano B726, F121, M239, M570
Otto di guardia (epoca repubblicana) 182
Otto di pratica, Carteggi, Responsive 19, 22, 24, 25, 27, 30, 32
Repubblica, Balie 43
Signori, Dieci, Otto, Legazioni e commissarie, Missive e responsive 35, 68
Signori, Carteggi, Legazioni e commissarie, Elezioni e istruzioni 19, 21, 23, 26
Signori, Carteggi, Minutari 11, 19, 20
Signori, Carteggi, Missive 1a Cancelleria 50, 55, 56
Signori, Otto, Dieci, Carteggi, Missive, Originali 6, 7, 9, 10, 11
Signori, Carteggi, Responsive 12, 26, 27, 29, 30, 37
Signori e collegi, Deliberazioni di speciale autorità 40
Tratte 443 bis
Urbino I, G, CXXXII
    CXXXIV
    CCXXXVI, II
    CCLXV

Florence, Biblioteca Marucelliana
B1 10, Part 3

Florence, Biblioteca Nazionale
Autografi Palatini V
Filza Rinuccini 17, fasc. 6
Ginori Conti 21, 29

Magliabechiana VII, 1057
  VIII, 80
  VIII, 1392
  XXI, 155
MSS II II 131
  II II 133
  II II 134
  II III 3
  II III 74
  II IV 171
  II IV 295
  II IV 309
MSS Palatini 153
MSS Passerini 44
Nuovi acquisti 987

Florence, Biblioteca Riccardiana
MS 951

Fondi, Archivio Di S. Pietro
Sacro visitatio totius Fundanae diocesis 1599

London, British Library
Additional MSS 8440–4

Mantua, AS
Archivio Gonzaga, b. 809, 855, 856, 857, 858, 860, 862, 865, 867, 868, 1146,
    2911, 2921, 2994, 2996

Milan, AS
Sforzesco, Potenze estere 294

Milan, Biblioteca Ambrosiana
G 33 inf., I and II

Modena, AS
Archivio Estense, Carteggio degli ambasciatori, Firenze II
  Cancelleria ducale, Carteggio dei principi esteri (cardinali), b. 1427/178
  Cancelleria estero, ambasciatori (Roma), b. 27, 28

Palermo, Archivio Comunale
Sala diplomatica, Atti, bandi e provviste (1516–1517), Ind. V (no. 39)

Palermo, AS
Tribunale del real patrimonio, Lettere viceregie e dispacci patrimoniali 256, 261

Palermo, Biblioteca Comunale
4Qq D. 47

Paris, Bibliothèque Nationale
Collection Dupuy 262, 14 (old 16)
Fonds français 2962
Fonds latins 12552
MSS italiens 2033
Nouv. acq. lat. 1424

Rome, Archivio Colonna
Arch. III BB VI 42, 43
Arch. III BB XX 114

Rome, AS
Collegio dei notari capitolini 14
Notari dell'AC 410, 411, 6029, 7155, 7156
Ospedale di S. Spirito 218, 1444

Rome, Archivio S. Giovanni dei Fiorentini
MS 431

Rome, Archivio SS. Apostoli
Pergamena B VIII, 359b

Rome, Archivio Soderini
I, II, III, XXII, XXXIV, XXXIX, XLII

Rome, Biblioteca Angelica
MS 2110

Rome, Biblioteca Nazionale Centrale
MSS Vittorio Emanuele 309

Rome, British School
William Gell notebook 1

Siena, AS
Archivio dell'Ospedale di S. Maria della Scala, Deliberazioni 25 (1488–1551)
Archivio dell'Ospedale di S. Maria della Scala, Usufrutti, depositi e preste 172
    (1416–1603)

Vatican, Archivio Segreto
AA. Arm. I–XVIII, 5042
Arm. XXIX, 56, 63, 72
Arm. XXXIV, 12

Arm. XXXIX, 22, 24, 25, 31
Arm. XL, 2, 4
Fondo camerale, Obligationes et solutiones 82, 88
Fondo concistoriale, Acta miscellanea 6, 54, 70
  Acta vicecancellarii 2, 3
Fondo sacro collegio dei cardinali, Liber cedularum et rotulorum 1
Regesta supplicationum 806
Regesta vaticana 870, 874, 1028, 1049, 1076, 1089

Vatican, Biblioteca Apostolica
Autografi Ferrajoli, Raccolta Visconti
Archivio capitolare di S. Pietro in Vaticano, Arm. 15, Decreti 1
Archivio capitolare di S. Pietro in Vaticano, Arm. 41–2, Censuali 12, 13, 14, 15,
  20, 33
MSS Barberini 1822, 2517, 2799, 3552
MSS Chigiani 1545
MSS Ottoboniani 2137, 2377, 2817
MSS Vaticani latini 2862, 3920, 5140, 6437 (part II), 10966, 11985, 12276, 13698

Volterra, Archivio Capitolare
Deliberationes A, B

Volterra, Archivio Comunale
Deliberazioni del magistrato A 58, A 68
G (nera) 33

Volterra, Archivio Episcopale
Collazioni, 1478–92

Volterra, Biblioteca Guarnacci
MSS 5376, 5706, 6204

PRINTED PRIMARY SOURCES

Alberti, L. B., *Opera nonnulla*, ed. G. Massaini (Florence, c. 1498–9)
Albertini, F., *De mirabilibus novae urbis Romae*, ed. A. Schmarsow (Heilbronn,
  1886)
Amaduzzi, G., and G. Bianconi (eds.), *Anecdota litteraria*, 4 vols. (Rome,
  1773–83)
Antiquari, J., *Epistolae* (Perugia, 1519)
Aristotle, *Totius philosophiae naturalis paraphrases a Francisco Vatablo recognitiae*
  (Paris, 1528)
Armellini, M. (ed.), *Il diario di Leone X di Paride de Grassi*, (Rome, 1884)
Balbi, G., *Opera*, ed. J. de Retzer (Vienna, 1791–2)
Bertola, M. (ed.), *I due primi registri di prestito della Biblioteca Apostolica Vaticana*
  (Città del Vaticano, 1942)
Bini, G. and P. Bigazzi (eds.), *Vita di Filippo Strozzi il vecchio* (Florence, 1851)

Bracciolini, P., *Oratio in funere Francisci Zabarellae* (Passau, 1655)

Burchard, J., 'Liber notarum', ed. E. Celani, in *Rerum italicarum scriptores*, 34 vols. (Città di Castello, 1900–17) XXXII, I, II

Lettere di Giovanbattista Busini a Benedetto Varchi, ed. G. Milanesi (Florence, 1860)

Calendar of letters, despatches, and state papers relating to the negotiations between England and Spain, ed. G. Bergenroth, 12 vols. (London, 1862–1916)

Calendar of state papers and manuscripts relating to English affairs existing in the archives and collections of Venice, ed. Rawdon Brown, 5 vols. (London, 1864–73)

Cambi, G., 'Istorie', in *Delizie degli eruditi toscani*, ed. Ildefonso di S. Luigi, 24 vols. (Florence, 1770–89), XX–XXIII

Canestrini G., and A. Desjardins, *Négociations diplomatiques de la France avec la Toscane*, 6 vols. (Paris, 1859–86)

Lettere di Baldassare Castiglione, ed. P. Serassi (Padua, 1769)

Catalogue des actes de François I, ed. P. Marichal, 10 vols. (Paris 1887–1908)

Cessi, R., *Dispacci degli ambasciatori veneziani alla corte di Roma presso Giulio II* (Venice, 1932)

Cortesi, P., *De cardinalatu* (In Castra Cortesio, 1510)
  De hominibus doctis dialogus, ed. and translated into Italian by M. Graziosi (Rome, 1973)

Decio, F., *Commentarii in Digestum vetus* (Venice, 1589)

de' Conti, S., *Le storie de' suoi tempi (1475–1510)* (Rome, 1883)

del Badia, I. (ed.), *Miscellanea fiorentina di erudizione e storia*, 2 vols. (Florence, 1902)

Delphino, P., *Petri Delphini generalis Camaldulensis epistolarum volumen* (Venice, 1524)

Dovizi, B., *Epistolario di Bernardo Dovizi da Bibbiena*, ed. G. Moncallero, 2 vols. (Florence, 1955–65)

Fea, C. (ed.), *Miscellanea filologica critica e antiquaria*, 2 vols. (Rome, 1790–1836)

Ficino, M., *Opera omnia*, 2 vols. (Basle, 1576)

Fonti, B., *Epistolarum libri III*, ed. L. Juhasz (Budapest, 1931)

Frati, L., *Le due spedizioni militari di Giulio II* (Bologna, 1886)

Gaye, G., *Carteggio inedito d'artisti dei secoli XIV, XV, XVI*, 3 vols. (Florence, 1839–40)

Gherardi, A., *Statuti dell'università e studio fiorentino dell'anno MCCCLXXXVII* (Florence, 1881)

Gherardi, G., *Dispacci e lettere di Giacomo Gherardi*, ed. E. Carusi (Rome, 1909)

Giovio, P., *Lettere*, ed. G. Ferrero (Rome, 1956–68)

Giustinian, A., *Dispacci di Antonio Giustinian ambasciatore veneto a Roma dal 1502 al 1505*, ed. P. Villari (Florence, 1876)

Guasti, C., 'Documenti della congiura fatta contro il cardinale Giulio de' Medici', *Giornale storico degli archivi toscani*, 3 (1859)

Guicciardini, F., *Storie fiorentine*, ed. R. Palmarocchi (Bari, 1931)
  Storia d'Italia, ed. S. Seidel Menchi (Turin, 1971)

Carteggi di Francesco Guicciardini, ed. R. Palmarocchi, 17 vols. (Bologna, 1938–1972)

Hergenroether, J., *Leonis X pontificis maximi regesta*, 2 vols. (Freiburg im Breisgau, 1884–91)

Landucci, L., *Diario fiorentino dal 1450 al 1516*, ed. I. del Badia (Florence, 1883)

Letters and papers, foreign and domestic, of the reign of Henry VIII, ed. J. Brewer, 34 vols. (London, 1862–1932)

Longolius, C., *Orationes duae pro defensione sua. Oratio una ad Luterianos. Eiusdem epistolarum libri quatuor, etc.* (Florence, 1524)

Machiavelli, N., *Le opere*, ed. P. Fanfani and L. Passerini, 6 vols. (Florence, 1873–7)

    Lettere, ed. F. Gaeta (Milan, 1961)

    'Decennale primo', in *Il teatro e gli scritti letterari*, ed. F. Gaeta (Milan, 1965)

    Le legazioni e commissarie di Niccolò Machiavelli, ed. L. Passerini and G. Milanesi (Florence/Rome, 1875)

Mai, A. (ed.), *Spicilegium romanum*, 10 vols. (Rome, 1839–44)

Fra Mariano da Firenze, *Itinerarium urbis Romae* (Rome, 1931)

Martène E., and U. Durand, *Veterum scriptorum et monumentorum historicorum dogmaticorum moralium amplissima collectio*, 9 vols. (Paris, 1724–33)

Marucci, V., A. Marzo and A. Romano (eds.), *Pasquinate romane del cinquecento*, 2 vols. (Rome, 1983)

Masi, B., *Ricordanze di Bartolomeo Masi*, ed. G. Odoardo Corazzini (Florence, 1906)

Menander Rhetor, ed. and translated by D. Russell and N. Wilson (Oxford, 1981)

Mittarelli, J., and A. Costadoni (eds.), *Annales Camaldulenses ordinis Sancti Benedicti*, 9 vols. (Venice, 1755–73)

Molini, G., *Documenti di storia italiana copiati su gli originali autentici e per lo più autografi esistenti in Parigi*, 2 vols. (Florence, 1836–7)

Nardi, J., *Istorie della città di Firenze*, ed. L. Arbib, 2 vols. (Florence, 1838–41)

Natale, A., *Acta in consilio secreto*, 3 vols. (Milan, 1963–9)

Nerli, F., *Commentari de' fatti civili occorsi dentro la città di Firenze dall'anno 1215 al 1537* (Augusta, 1728)

Pacioli, L., *Divina proportione* (Venice, 1509)

Pitti, J., 'Apologia de' Cappucci', *Archivio storico italiano*, series 1, 4, part 2 (1853)

Rossi, V., *Pasquinate di Pietro Aretino ed anonime per il conclave e l'elezione di Adriano VI* (Palermo/Turin, 1891)

Rostagno, E., *Tacitus. Codex Laurentianus Mediceus 68 1* (Leiden, 1902)

Salvo Cozzo, G., 'Transunto del processo contro i fratelli Imperatori', *Archivio storico siciliano*, N. S. 7 (1882)

Sanuto, M., *I diarii*, 58 vols. (Venice, 1879–1903)

Tedallini, S., *Diario romano*, ed. P. Piccolomini, in *Rerum italicarum scriptores*, ed. L. Muraton, 34 vols. (Città di Castello, 1900–17), XXIII, III, appendice (Città di Castello, 1907–11)

Tomassetti, A., (ed.), *Bullarium diplomatum et privilegiorum sanctorum romanorum pontificum Taurinensis editio*, 25 vols. (Turin, 1857–72)

Vaglienti, P., *Storia dei suoi tempi, 1492–1514*, ed. G. Berti, M. Luzzati and E. Tongiorgi (Pisa, 1982)

Valeriani, P., *Hexametri odae et epigrammata* (Venice, 1550)

Varchi, B., *Storia fiorentina*, ed. L. Arbib, 3 vols. (Florence, 1838–41)

Vasari, G., *Le vite*, ed. G. Milanesi, 7 vols. (Florence, 1878–81)

Vettori, F., *Sommario della storia d'Italia dal 1511 al 1527*, ed. A. Reumont, in *Archivio storico italiano*, appendice VI (1848)

Weil-Garris, K., and J. D'Amico, *The renaissance cardinal's ideal palace*, Studies in Italian art history I (Rome, 1980)

Ziegler, J., 'Clementis Septimi episcopi romani vita', in *Amoenitates historiae ecclesiasticae et literariae*, ed. J. Schellhorn, 2 vols. (Frankfurt/Leipzig, 1737–8)

SECONDARY SOURCES

Ademollo, A., *Alessandro VI, Giulio II e Leone X nel carnevale di Roma* (Florence, 1886)

Adinolfi, P., *La portica di S. Pietro* (Rome, 1859)
La torre de Sanguigni (Rome, 1863)

Amadei, E., *Le torri di Roma* (Rome, 1969)

Ammirato, S., *Delle famiglie nobili fiorentine* (Florence, 1615)

Anon, *Voyage pittoresque, historique et géographique de Rome à Naples et ses environs* (Naples, 1823)

Antonovics, A. V., 'The finances of the college of cardinals in the later middle ages' (D. Phil. dissertation, University of Oxford, 1971)

Anzilotti, A., *La crisi costituzionale della repubblica fiorentina* (Florence, 1912)

Apolloni Ghetti, A., 'Il cardinale Francesco Soderini restauratore nel 1519 di un monumento classico', *Strenna dei romanisti*, 21 April 1976
'Nuovi appunti su Francesco Soderini cardinale Volterrano', *L'urbe*, 39 (1976)
'Nuovi appunti su Francesco Soderini cardinale Volterrano (continuazione e fine)', *L'urbe*, 39 (1976)

Armellini, M., *Le chiese di Roma*, ed. C. Cecchelli, 2 vols. (Rome, 1942)

Audiat, L., 'Evêché et chapitre de Saintes', *Archives historiques de la Saintonge et de l'Aunis*, 10 (1882)
'La collection de portraits des évêques de Saintes', *Bulletin de la société des archives historiques, Revue de la Saintonge et de l'Aunis*, 15 (1895)

Bandini, A., *Il Bibbiena o sia il ministro di stato delineato nella vita del cardinale Bernardo Dovizi da Bibbiena* (Livorno, 1758)

Banti, A., and A. Boschetto, *Lorenzo Lotto* (Florence, 1953)

Bardi, A., 'Filippo Strozzi (da nuovi documenti)', *Archivio storico italiano*, series V, 14 (1894)

Baron, H., *Leonardo Bruni Aretino humanistisch-philosophische Schriften* (Leipzig, 1928)

Baumgartner, F., *Change and continuity in the French episcopate: the bishops and the wars of religion, 1547–1610* (Durham, 1986)

Bec, C., 'Les Florentins et la France ou la rupture d'un mythe (1494–1540)', *Il pensiero politico*, 14 (1981)

Berenson, B., *Lorenzo Lotto* (London, 1901)

Lorenzo Lotto (London, 1956)

Bertelli, S., '"Uno magistrato per a tempo lungho o uno dogie"', in *Studi di storia medievale e moderna per Ernesto Sestan*, 2 vols. (Florence, 1980)

'Di due profili mancati e di un bilancino con pesi truccati', *Archivio storico italiano*, 145 (1987)

Bizzocchi, R., 'Forme e techniche del potere nella città (secoli XIV–XVII)', *Annali della facoltà di scienze politiche, università di Perugia*, 16 (1979–80)

'La dissoluzione di un clan familiare: Buondelmonti di Firenze nei secoli XV e XVI', *Archivio storico italiano*, 140 (1982)

Chiesa e potere nella Toscana del quattrocento (Bologna, 1987)

Black, R., 'Machiavelli, servant of the Florentine republic', in *Machiavelli and republicanism*, ed. G. Bock, Q. Skinner and M. Viroli (Cambridge, 1990)

Bocci, M., 'La badia di Morrona e un prepotente vescovo di Volterra', *Volterra*, 3 (1964)

Breisach, E., *Caterina Sforza* (Chicago, 1967)

Bresnahan Menning, C., 'Loans and favors, kin and clients: Cosimo de' Medici and the *Monte di Pietà*', *Journal of modern history*, 61 (1989)

Briand, J.-D., *L'histoire de l'église santone et aunisienne* (La Rochelle, 1843)

Brown, A., 'The Guelph party in fifteenth-century Florence: the transition from communal to Medicean state', *Rinascimento*, 20 (1980)

Brown, D. T., 'Cardinal Giuliano della Rovere, patron of architecture, 1471–1503' (M. Phil. dissertation, University of London, 1988)

Bullard, M., '"Mercatores florentini romanum curiam sequentes" in the early sixteenth century', *Journal of medieval and renaissance studies*, 6 (1976)

Filippo Strozzi and the Medici: favor and finance in sixteenth-century Florence and Rome (Cambridge, 1980)

Burgess, T., 'Epideictic literature', *University of Chicago studies in classical philology*, 3 (Chicago, 1902)

Buser, B., *Die Beziehungen der Mediceer zu Frankreich wahrend der Jahre 1434–1494* (Leipzig, 1879)

Butters, H., *Governors and government in early sixteenth-century Florence, 1502–1519* (Oxford, 1985)

and J. Stephens, 'New light on Machiavelli', *English historical review*, 97 (1982)

Calzolai, C., *S. Frediano in Cestello* (Florence, 1972)

Carocci, G., *I dintorni di Firenze*, 2 vols. (Florence, 1906–7)

Cartocci, L., *La spina dei Borghi* (Rome, 1938)

Carusi, E., 'L'istrumento di assoluzione dei fiorentini dalle censure di Sisto IV', *Archivio Muratoriano*, 16 (1915)

Cassuto, U., *Gli ebrei a Firenze nell'età del rinascimento* (Florence, 1918)

Catalogue of the Medici archives, to be sold at auction by Messrs. Christie, Manson and Woods, 4 February 1918

The catholic encyclopedia, 16 vols. (New York, 1913)

Cavallini, M., 'I corali del museo della cattedrale', *Il Corazziere*, 16 July 1933

Cecchelli, C., *I Margani, i Capocci, i Sanguigni, i Mellini* (Rome, 1946)

Cecchi, E., 'Le scritte murali', in *Palazzo Davanzati*, ed. M. Fossi Todorow (Florence, 1979)

Cesareo, G., *Pasquino e pasquinate nella Roma di Leone X* (Rome, 1938)

Chambers, D., *Cardinal Bainbridge in the court of Rome* (Oxford, 1965)

'The economic predicament of renaissance cardinals', *Studies in medieval and renaissance history*, 2 (1966)

'The housing problems of cardinal Francesco Gonzaga', *Journal of the Warburg and Courtauld Institutes*, 39 (1976)

'Papal conclaves and prophetic mystery in the Sistine chapel', *Journal of the Warburg and Courtauld Institutes*, 41 (1978)

A renaissance cardinal and his worldly goods; the will and inventory of Francesco Gonzaga (1444–1483) (London, 1992)

Chastel, A., *Le cardinal Louis d'Aragon: un voyageur princier de la renaissance* (Paris, 1986)

Ciardi Dupré Dal Poggetto, M. (ed.), *L'oreficeria nella Firenze del quattrocento* (Florence, 1977)

Cimino, R., 'Un elefante alla corte dei papi', *Atti dell'accademia delle scienze di Torino*, 118 (1984)

Cinci, A., 'Il Monte di Pietà in Volterra', in A. Cinci, *Miscellanea storica volterrana* (Florence/Volterra, 1880)

Storia di Volterra (Volterra, 1885)

Clarke, P. C., 'A biography of Tommaso Soderini: a Florentine politician of the fifteenth century' (Ph.D. dissertation, University of London, 1982)

The Soderini and the Medici: power and patronage in fifteenth-century Florence (Oxford, 1991)

Clergeac, A., *La curie et les bénéficiers consistoriaux* (Paris, 1911)

Cocchi, A., *Les anciens reliquaires de Santa Maria del Fiore et de S. Giovanni de Florence* (Florence, 1903)

Coffin, D., *The villa in the life of renaissance Rome* (Princeton, 1979)

Collignon, A., *Le mécénat du cardinal Jean de Lorraine (1498–1550)* (Paris/Nancy, 1910)

Consorti, A., *Il cardinale Pompeo Colonna* (Rome, 1902)

Consortini, L., *Il castello antico di Volterra, il palazzo dei vescovi, l'iscrizione di Ranieri II degli Ubertini* (Lucca, 1922)

Conte-Colino, G., *Storia di Fondi* (Naples, 1901)

Cooper, R. L., 'Piero Soderini: *gonfaloniere a vita* of Florence, 1502–1512' (Ph.D. dissertation, University of London, 1965)

'Pier Soderini: aspiring prince or civic leader?', *Studies in medieval and renaissance history*, 1 (1978)

'Machiavelli, Francesco Soderini and Don Michelotto', *Nuova rivista storica*, 66 (1982)

Coppi, A., *Memorie Colonnesi* (Rome, 1855)

Cottineau, L., *Répertoire topo-bibiographique des abbayes et prieurés*, 3 vols. (Mâcon, 1935–70)

Crowe, J., and G. Cavalcaselle, *Raphael: his life and works*, 2 vols. (London, 1882–5)

Cruciani, F., *Teatro nel rinascimento: Roma, 1450–1550* (Rome, 1983)

D'Amico, J., *Renaissance humanism in papal Rome* (Baltimore, 1983)

'The Raffaele Maffei monument in Volterra: small town patronage in the renaissance,' in *Supplementum festivum*, ed. J. Hankins, J. Monfasani and F. Purnell Jr. (Binghamton, 1987)

de Angelis, P., *L'ospedale di Santo Spirito in Saxia*, 2 vols. (Rome, 1962)

Degert, A., 'Les origines de l'ambassade française permanente à Rome', *Bulletin de littérature ecclésiatique*, 22 (1921)

Delaborde, H. François, *L'expédition de Charles VIII en Italie* (Paris, 1888)

Delcorno Branca, D., 'Un discepolo del Poliziano: Michele Acciari', *Lettere italiane*, 28 (1976)

Del Migliore, F., *Firenze città nobilissima illustrata* (Florence, 1684)

Del Piazzo, M., *Protocolli del carteggio di Lorenzo il Magnifico per gli anni 1473–4, 1477–92* (Florence, 1956)

Delumeau, J., *Vie économique et sociale de Rome dans la seconde moitié du XVIe siècle*, 2 vols. (Paris, 1957–9)

Denley, P., 'The collegiate movement in Italian universities in the late middle ages', *History of universities*, 10 (1991)

de Roo, P., *Material for a history of pope Alexander VI*, 5 vols. (Bruges, 1924)

de Roover, R., *The rise and decline of the Medici bank, 1397–1494* (Cambridge, Mass., 1963)

Devonshire Jones, R., 'Some observations on the relations between Francesco Vettori and Niccolò Machiavelli during the embassy to Maximilian I', *Italian studies*, 23 (1968)

Francesco Vettori, Florentine citizen and Medici servant (London, 1972)

Dictionnaire du droit canonique (Paris, 1924–65)

Dizionario biografico degli italiani, 39 vols. (Rome, 1960–)

Edelstein, M., 'The recruitment of the episcopacy under the concordat of Bologna in the reign of Francis I' (Ph.D. dissertation, Columbia University, 1972)

'The social origins of the episcopacy in the reign of Francis I', *French historical studies*, 8 (1973–4)

'Les origines sociales de l'épiscopat sous Louis XII et François I', *Revue d'histoire moderne et contemporaine*, 24 (1977)

Edgerton, S., 'A little known "purpose of art" in the Italian renaissance', *Art history*, 2 (1979)

Eggs, G., *Purpura docta* (Munich, 1714)

Egidi, P., *Necrologi e libri affini della provincia romana*, 2 vols. (Rome, 1908–14)

Ehrle, F., *Dalle carte e dai disegni di Virgilio Spada*, Memorie II, Atti della pontificia accademia romana di archeologia, 3 (Rome, 1927)

Epifanio, V., 'Il cardinale Soderini e la congiura dei fratelli Imperatore', in *Atti del congresso internazionale di scienze storiche 1903*, 3 (Rome, 1906)

Esposito Aliano, A., 'La parocchia "Agostiniana" di S. Trifone nella Roma di Leone X', *Mélanges de l'Ecole Française de Rome, Moyen age, Temps modernes*, 93 (1981)

Eubel, C., *Hierarchia catholica medii aevi*, 4 vols. (Münster, 1901–10)

Fabbruccio, S., 'Elogia clarissimorum virorum qui ab anno primae solemnis instaurationis secundo usque ad MCCCCLXXVIII Pisanae Academiae lucem universae litterariae reipublicae decus addiderunt', in *Raccolta d'opuscoli scientifici e filologici*, ed. A. Calogera, 40 vols. (Venice, 1755–84) XL (Venice, 1749)

Fabri, G., *Le sacre memorie di Ravenna antica* (Venice, 1664)

Effemeride sagra et istorica di Ravenna antica (Ravenna, 1675)

Fabroni, A., *Historiae academiae Pisanae volumen I–III*, 3 vols. (Pisa, 1791–5)

Fagiolo, M. and M. Madonna (eds.), *Roma, 1300–1875. La città degli anni santi. Atlante.* (Milan, 1985)

Falconcini, B., *Vita del nobil'uomo Raffaello Maffei detto il Volterrano* (Rome, 1722)

Falconcini, L., *Storia dell'antichissima città di Volterra*, in Latin with Italian translation by B. Berardi (Florence/Volterra, 1876)

Felice, B., 'Donne Medicee avanti il principato', *Rassegna nazionale*, 146 (1905)

Ferrajoli, A., 'Il ruolo della corte di Leone X', *Archivio della reale società romana di storia patria*, 34 (1911), 36 (1913) and 41 (1918)

'Il matrimonio di Adriano Castellesi poi cardinale e il suo annullamento', *Archivio della reale società romana di storia patria*, 42 (1919)

La congiura dei cardinali contro Leone X, in *Miscellanea della reale società romana di storia patria*, 7 (Rome, 1920)

Festa Milone, M., 'Palazzo Riario-Altemps', *Quaderni dell'istituto di storia dell'architettura*, 24 (1977–8)

Forcella, V., *Iscrizioni delle chiese e di altri edifici di Roma dal secolo XI fino ai giorni nostri*, 14 vols. (Rome, 1869–84)

Forte, M., *Fondi nei tempi* (Casamari, 1972)

Frenz, T., *Die Kanzlei der Päpste der Hochrenaissance (1471–1527)* (Tübingen, 1986)

Frommel, C., *Der Römische Palastbau der Hochrenaissance* (Tübingen, 1973)

S. Ray and M. Tafuri, *Raffaello architetto* (Milan, 1984)

Frutaz, A., *Le piante di Roma*, 3 vols. (Rome, 1962)

Gams, P., *Series episcoporum ecclesiae catholicae*, 3 vols. (Regensburg, 1873–86)

Ganter, B., *Clerical attire: a historical synopsis and a commentary* (Washington, 1955)

Gatti, I., 'Il palazzo della Rovere ed il convento dei Santi Apostoli in Roma attraverso i secoli', *Miscellanea francescana*, 79 (1979)

Gattico, G., *Acta selecta caeremonialia S. R. E.* (Rome, 1753)

Gelcich, G., *Piero Soderini profugo a Ragusa: memorie e documenti* (Dubrovnik, 1894)

Gell, Sir William, *The topography of Rome and its vicinity* (London, 1834)

Gelli, J., *Divisi, motti, imprese di famiglie e personaggi italiani* (Milan, 1928)

Gherardi, A., 'Come si accogliesse in corte di Francia la nuova dell'elezione del gonfaloniere Soderini', *Archivio storico italiano*, series v, 1 (1888)

Giesey, R., *The royal funeral ceremony in renaissance France* (Geneva, 1960)

Gilbert, F., 'The Venetian constitution in Florentine political thought', in *Florentine studies*, ed. N. Rubinstein (London, 1968)

Ginori Lisci, L., *I palazzi di Firenze*, 2 vols. (Florence, 1972)

Girouard, M., 'Kinmel, Denbighshire – 1', *Country life*, 146, 4 September 1969

Gnoli, D., 'Le cacce di Leon X', *Nuova antologia*, 2 (1893)
'Censimento di Roma sotto Clemente VII', *Archivio della reale società romana di storia patria*, 17 (1894)

Gnoli, U., 'Facciate graffite e dipinte in Roma', *Il Vasari*, 8 (1936–7)
Topographia e toponomastica di Roma medioevale e moderna (Rome, 1939)
Alberghi ed osterie di Roma nella rinascenza (Rome, 1942)

Goldthwaite, R., 'The Florentine palace as domestic architecture', *American historical review*, 77 (1972)
The building of renaissance Florence (Baltimore, 1980)

Graziosi, M., 'Pacifico Massimi maestro del Colocci?', *Atti del convegno di studi su Angelo Colocci, Jesi, 13–14 September 1969* (Jesi, 1972)

Guasti, C., *I manoscritti Torrigiani* (Florence, 1878)

Guicciardini, P., *Cusona* (Florence, 1939)

Hankins, J., J. Monfasani and F. Purnell Jr. (eds.), *Supplementum festivum*, (Binghamton, 1987)

Hay, D., *The church in Italy in the fifteenth century* (Cambridge, 1977)

Herald, J., *Renaissance dress in Italy, 1400–1500* (London, 1981)

Herde, P., *Audientia litterarum contradictarum* (Tübingen, 1970)

Hill, G. *A corpus of Italian medals of the renaissance before Cellini*, 2 vols. (London, 1930)

Hirst, M., *Sebastiano del Piombo* (Oxford, 1981)

Hoare, Sir Richard Colt, *A classical tour through Italy and Sicily* (London, 1819)

Hofmann, W. von, *Forschungen zur Geschichte der Kurialen Behörden vom Schisma bis zur Reformation*, 2 vols. (Rome, 1914)

Huelsen, C., *Le chiese di Roma nel medio evo* (Florence, 1927)

Hynes, H., *The privileges of cardinals* (Washington, 1945)

Illardi, V., 'Crosses and carets: renaissance patronage and coded letters of recommendation', *American historical review*, 92 (1987)

Imbart de la Tour, P., *Les origines de la réforme* (Melun, 1946)

Ingersoll, R., *The ritual use of public space in renaissance Rome* (New York, 1986)

Italian paintings and sculptures of the seventeenth and eighteenth centuries (London, 1976), Heim gallery exhibition catalogue no. 25

Jaffé, M., *Old master drawings from Chatsworth* (Alexandria, Virginia, 1987)

Jones, R. and N. Penny, *Raphael* (New Haven/London, 1983)

Jullian, C., 'Note sur un manuscrit de la "Notitia dignitatum"', *Mélanges d'archéologie et d'histoire*, 1 (1881)

Katterbach, P. Bruno, *Specimina supplicationum*, 2 vols. (Rome, 1927)
Referendarii utriusque signaturae (Città del Vaticano, 1931)
Inventario dei registri delle suppliche (Città del Vaticano, 1932)

Klapisch-Zuber, C., 'Le nom "refait". La transmission des prénoms à Florence (xive–xvie siècles)', *L'homme*, 20 (1980)

Knecht, R., *Francis I* (Cambridge, 1982)

Kolsky, S., *Mario Equicola: the real courtier* (Geneva, 1991)

Krautheimer, R., S. Corbett and W. Frankl, *Corpus basilicarum christianarum Romae*, 5 vols. (Rome, 1937–77)

Kristeller, P., 'Sebastiano Salvini, a Florentine humanist', in *Didascaliae. Studies in honor of Anselm M. Albareda* (New York, 1961)
Iter Italicum, 6 vols. (London/Leiden, 1963–92)
Le Thomisme et la pensée italienne de la renaissance (Montreal/Paris, 1967)

Labande-Mailfert, Y., *Charles VIII et son milieu (1470–1498)* (Paris, 1975)

Lanciani, R., *Storia degli scavi di Roma*, 4 vols. (Rome, 1902–12)

Lee, E., *Sixtus IV and men of letters* (Rome, 1978)

Levantini-Pieroni, G., *Lucrezia Tornabuoni* (Florence, 1888)

Levati, P. Luigi, *Dogi perpetui di Genova an. 1339–1528* (Genoa, 1930)

Lierde, P. van, and A. Giraud, *What is a cardinal?* (London, 1964)

Lillie, A., 'Florentine villas in the fifteenth century: a study of the Strozzi and Sassetti country properties' (Ph.D. dissertation, University of London, 1987)

Litta, P., L. Passerini Orsini de Rilli, F. Oderici, F. Stefani, *Celebri famiglie italiane*, 11 vols. (Milan/Turin, 1819–99)

Loccatelli, E., *Vita del glorioso padre San Giovangualberto* (Florence, 1583)

Lonigo, M., *Delle vesti purpuree et d'altri colori con quali va adorna la dignità cardinalitia* (Venice, 1653)

Lowe, K., 'Cardinal Francesco Soderini's proposal for an Italian college at Paris in 1524', *History of universities*, 4 (1984)
'Francesco Soderini (1453–1524), Florentine patrician and cardinal' (Ph.D. dissertation, University of London, 1985)
'Questions of income and expenditure in renaissance Rome: a case study of cardinal Francesco Armellini', *Studies in church history*, 24 (1987)
'A Florentine prelate's real estate in Rome between 1480 and 1524: the residential and speculative property of Cardinal Francesco Soderini,' *Papers of the British School at Rome*, 59 (1991)
'An Etruscan find of 1508', forthcoming, *Journal of the Warburg and Courtauld Institutes*

Lugli, G., *La tecnica edilizia romana* (Rome, 1957)

Lugt, F., *Répertoire des catalogues de ventes publiques: première periode vers 1600–1825* (The Hague, 1938) and *troisième periode, 1861–1900* (The Hague, 1964)

Lupi, C., 'Delle relazioni fra la repubblica di Firenze e i conti e duchi di Savoia', *Giornale storico degli archivi toscani*, 7 (1863)

Luzio, A., 'Isabella d'Este ne' primordi del papato di Leone X e il suo viaggio a Roma nel 1514–1515', *Archivio storico lombardo*, 6 (1906)

McClung Hallman, B., *Italian cardinals, reform and the church as property* (Berkeley, 1985)

McManamon, J., 'The ideal renaissance pope: funeral oratory from the papal court', *Archivum historiae pontificiae*, 14 (1976)

  Funeral oratory and the cultural ideals of Italian humanism (Chapel Hill, 1989)

McNally, R., 'Pope Adrian VI (1522–1523) and church reform', *Archivum historiae pontificiae*, 7 (1969)

Madonna, M., 'Una operazione urbanistica di Alesssandro VI: la Via Alessandrina in Borgo', in *Le arti a Roma sotto Alessandro VI*, ed. M. Calvesi (Rome, 1981)

Magnuson, T., *Studies in Roman quattrocento architecture* (Rome, 1958)

Mallett, M., *The Borgias* (London, 1969)

Manglano y Cucaló, J., *Politica en Italia del rey catolico, 1507–1516* (Madrid, 1963)

Manni, D., *Azioni gloriose degli uomini illustri fiorentini espresse co' loro ritratti nelle volte dalla real galleria di Toscana* (Florence, 1745)

Mantese, G., *Memorie storiche della chiesa vicentina*, 5 vols. (Vicenza, 1952–74)

Marks, L., 'La crisi finanziaria a Firenze dal 1494–1502', *Archivio storico italiano*, 112 (1954)

Martines, L., *Lawyers and statecraft in renaissance Florence* (Princeton, 1968)

Mattingly, G., 'The first resident embassies: mediaeval Italian origins of modern diplomacy', *Speculum*, 12 (1937)

Maulde-la-Clavière, M. de, *La diplomatie au temps de Machiavel*, 3 vols. (Paris, 1892–3)

Mazzi, C., *La casa di maestro Bartalo di Tura* (Siena, 1900)

Mazzotti, M., *La basilica di Sant'Apollinare in Classe* (Città del Vaticano, 1954)

Menotti, M., *Documenti inediti sulla famiglia e la corte di Alessandro VI* (Rome, 1917)

Mercati, A., *Dall'Archivio Vaticano* (Città del Vaticano, 1951)

Mignet, M., *Rivalité de François I et de Charles-Quint* (Paris, 1875)

Minnich, N., 'Concepts of reform proposed at the Fifth Lateran Council', *Archivum historiae pontificiae*, 7 (1969)

  'The participants at the Fifth Lateran Council', *Archivum historiae pontificiae*, 12 (1974)

Mohler, L., *Kardinal Bessarion als Theologe, Humanist und Staatsmann*, 3 vols. (Paderborn, 1923–67)

Mommsen, T., *Inscriptiones regni Neapolitani latinae* (Leipzig, 1852)

Moroni, G., *Dizionario di erudizione storico-ecclesiastico da S. Pietro sino ai nostri giorni*, 103 vols. (Venice, 1840–61)

Morsolin, B., *Zaccaria Ferreri* (Vicenza, 1877)

Müntz, E., *Le musée de portraits de Paul Jove* (Paris, 1900)

Munier, W., 'Willem van Enckenvoirt (1464–1534) und seine Benefizien', *Römische Quartalschrift für Christliche Altertumskunde und Kirchengeschichte*, 53 (1958)

Najamy, J., 'The controversy surrounding Machiavelli's service to the republic', in *Machiavelli and republicanism* , ed. G. Bock, Q. Skinner and M. Viroli (Cambridge, 1990)

Negri, P. Giulio, *Istoria degli scrittori fiorentini* (Ferrara, 1722)

Nibby, A., *Roma nell'anno 1838*, 4 vols. (Rome, 1838–41)

Notarjanni, F., 'Viaggio per l'Ausonia', in *Giornale enciclopedico di Napoli*, 7 (1913)

Olitsky, R., 'San Giovanni dei Fiorentini: the sixteenth-century building history and plans' (M. A. dissertation, New York Institute of Fine Arts, 1951)

O'Malley, J., 'The Vatican library and the schools of Athens: a text of Battista Casali, 1508', *Journal of medieval and renaissance studies*, 7 (1977)

Praise and blame in renaissance Rome (Durham, North Carolina, 1979)

Padiglione, C., *I motti delle famiglie italiane* (Naples, 1910)

Pagliucchi, P., *I castellani del Castel Sant'Angelo*, 2 vols. (Rome, 1906–9)

Parisse, M., (ed.), *Histoire de la Lorraine*, (Toulouse, 1978)

Partner, P., *The lands of St Peter* (London, 1972)

Renaissance Rome, 1500–1559 (Berkeley, 1976)

The pope's men: the papal civil service in the renaissance (Oxford, 1990)

Paschini, P., *Domenico Grimani, cardinale di S. Marco (m. 1523)* (Rome, 1943)

'Una famiglia di curiali: i Maffei di Volterra', *Rivista di storia della chiesa in Italia*, 7 (1953)

'Tre illustri prelati del rinascimento', *Lateranum*, 23 (1957)

'I benefici ecclesiatici del cardinale Marco Barbo', *Rivista di storia della chiesa in Italia*, 13 (1959)

Passerini, L., 'Soderini di Firenze', in P. Litta *et al.*, *Celebri famiglie italiane* (Milan/Turin, 1819–99)

Pastor, L. von, *A history of the popes*, ed. F. Antrobus, vols. VI–IX (London, 1898–1908)

Pecchiai, P., 'Banchi e botteghe dinanzi alla Basilica Vaticana nei secoli XIV, XV e XVI', *Archivi*, series II, 18 (1951)

'I segni sulle case di Roma nel medio evo', *Archivi*, series II, 18 (1951)

Pellegrini, M., 'Ascanio Maria Sforza: la creazione di un cardinale "di famiglia"', in *Gli Sforza, la chiesa lombarda, la corte di Roma*, ed. G. Chittolini (Naples, 1989)

Pezzarossa, F., *I poemetti sacri di Lucrezia Tornabuoni* (Florence, 1978)

Picot, E., *Les italiens en France au XVIe siècle* (Bordeaux, 1902)

Picotti, G., *La giovinezza di Leone X* (Milan, 1928)

'Lo studio di Pisa dalle origini a Cosimo duca', in G. Picotti, *Scritti vari di storia pisana e toscana* (Pisa, 1968)

Pieraccini, G., *La stirpe de'Medici di Cafaggiolo* (Florence 1924)

Placzek, A. (ed.) *Macmillan encyclopedia of architects*, 4 vols (New York, 1982)

Pocciantio, M., *Catalogus scriptorum Florentinorum omnis generis* (Florence, 1589)

Preyer, B., 'The "chasa overo palagio" of Albert di Zanobi: a Florentine palace of about 1400 and its later remodeling', *Art bulletin*, 65 (1983)

Prodi, P., *The papal prince* (Cambridge, 1987)

Prosperi, A., '"Dominus beneficiorum": il conferimento dei benefici ecclesiastici tra prassi curiale e ragioni politiche negli stati italiani tra '400 e '500', in *Strutture ecclesiastiche in Italia e Germania prima della riforma*, ed. P. Prodi and P. Johanek (Bologna, 1984)

Razzi, D. Silvano, *Vita di Piero Soderini* (Padua, 1737)

Reinhard, W., 'Papa Pius: Prolegomena zu einer Sozialgeschichte des Papsttums', *Von Konstanz nach Trient: Festgabe für August Franzen*, ed. R. Bäumer (Paderborn, 1972)

'Nepotismus. Der Funktionswandel einer papstgeschichtlichen Konstante', *Zeitschrift für Kirchengeschichte*, 86 (1975)

Freunde und Kreaturen. "Verflechtung" als Konzept zur Erforschung historischer Führungsgruppen. Römische Oligarchie um 1600 (Munich, 1979)

'Struttura e significato del sacro collegio tra la fine del XV e la fine del XVI secolo', in *Città italiane del '500 tra riforma e controriforma* (Lucca, 1988)

Repetti, E., *Dizionario geografico, fisico, storico della Toscana*, 6 vols. (Florence, 1833–46)

Rice, E., 'Humanist Aristotelianism in France: Jacques Lefèvre d'Etaples and his circle', in *Humanism in France*, ed. A. Levi (Manchester, 1970)

St Jerome in the renaissance (Baltimore, 1985)

Richa, G., *Notizie istoriche delle chiese fiorentine*, 10 vols. (Florence, 1754–62)

Richards, G., *Florentine merchants in the age of the Medici* (Cambridge, Mass., 1932)

Ridolfi, R., *Vita di Niccolò Machiavelli* (Florence, 1972)

Rodocanachi, E., 'Le luxe des cardinaux romains de la renaissance', *Revue des questions historiques*, 89 (1911)

La première renaissance, Rome au temps de Jules II et de Léon X (Paris, 1912)

Les pontificats d'Adrien VI et Clément VII (Paris, 1933)

Ronchini, A., 'Nanni di Baccio Bigio', *Atti e memorie delle RR. deputazioni di storia patria per le provincie modensi e parmensi*, 8 (1876)

Rosmini, C., *Dell'istoria intorno alle militari imprese e alla vita di Gian Jacopo Trivulzio detti il Magno* (Milan, 1815)

Rossi, A., 'Nuovi documenti su Bramante', *Archivio storico dell'arte*, 1 (1888)

Rossi, V., 'Un elefante famoso', in *Scritti di critica letteraria (3). Dal rinascimento al risorgimento* (Florence, 1930)

Rubinstein, N., *The government of Florence under the Medici, 1434–1494* (Oxford, 1966)

'Machiavelli and the world of Florentine politics', in *Studies on Machiavelli*, ed. M. Gilmore (Florence, 1972)

'Palazzi pubblici e palazzi privati al tempo di Brunelleschi', in *Filippo Brunelleschi: la sua opera e il suo tempo* (Florence, 1980)

'"Reformation" und Ordensreform in italienischen Stadtrepubliken und

Signorien', *Reformbemühungen und Observanzbestrebungen im spätmittelalter-lichen Ordenswesen*, ed. K. Elm (Berlin, 1989)

Sägmüller, J., *Die Thätigkeit und Stellung der Cardinäle* (Freiburg im Breisgau, 1896)

Salvini, S., *Catalogo cronologico dei canonici della chiesa metropolitana fiorentina* (Florence, 1770)

Santini, P. Francesco, *La basilica dei SS. Apostoli* (Rome, 1925)

Sapori, A., 'Il "bilancio" della filiale di Roma del banco Medici del 1495', *Archivio storico italiano*, 131 (1973)

Sasso, G., 'Machiavelli, Cesare Borgia, Don Micheletto e la questione della milizia', in G. Sasso, *Machiavelli e gli antichi e altri saggi*, 3 vols. (Milan/Naples, 1987–8)

Schnitzer, J., *Peter Delfin General des Camaldulensordens (1444–1525)* (Munich, 1926)

Seidel Menchi, S., 'Alcuni atteggiamenti della cultura italiana di fronte a Erasmo', in *Eresia e riforma nell'Italia del cinquecento* (Florence, 1974)

Shearman, J., 'The Vatican *stanze*: functions and decorations', *Proceedings of the British Academy*, 57 (1971)

Raphael's cartoons in the collection of H.M. the Queen, and the tapestries for the Sistine chapel (London, 1972)

'The collections of the younger branch of the Medici', *Burlington magazine*, 117, (1975)

Sherr, R. J., 'The papal chapel ca. 1492–1513 and its polyphonic sources' (Ph.D. dissertation, Princeton University, 1975)

Sinding-Larsen, S., 'A tale of two cities: Florentine and Roman visual context for fifteenth-century palaces', *Institutum romanum Norvegiae: acta ad archaeologiam et artium historiam pertinentia*, 6 (1975)

Škunca, S., *Aelius Lampridius Cervinus poeta ragusinus (saec. XV)* (Rome, 1971)

Soderini, O., *Catalogue raisonné des tableaux et dessins qui composoient la galerie du comte Suderini à Rome* (Paris, 1783)

Solaini, A., *Guida di Volterra* (Volterra, 1901)

Sommario della storia e guida del museo della città di Volterra (Volterra, 1927)

Sotis, G., *Cenno istorico della città di Fondi* (Naples, 1838)

Spinelli, L., *La vacanza della sede apostolica dalle origini al concilio tridentino* (Milan, 1955)

Spreti, C., *Memorie intorno i domini e governi della città di Ravenna* (Faenza, 1822)

Spreti, V., *Enciclopedia storico-nobiliare italiana*, 8 vols. (Milan, 1928–35)

Stackelberg, J. von, *Tacitus in der Romania* (Tübingen, 1960)

Stephens, J., *The fall of the Florentine republic, 1512–1530* (Oxford, 1983)

Stinger, C., *The renaissance in Rome* (Bloomington, 1985)

Thomas, J., *Le concordat de 1516* (Paris, 1910)

Thornton, P., *The Italian renaissance interior* (London, 1991)

Tomei, P., 'Le case in serie nell'edilizia romana dal '400 al '700', *Palladio*, 2 (1938)

'Contributi d'archivio: un elenco dei palazzi di Roma del tempo di Clemente VIII', *Palladio*, 3 (1939)

L'architettura a Roma nel quattrocento (Rome, 1942)

Trexler, R., *Public life in renaissance Florence* (New York, 1980)

Gli Uffizi: catalogo generale (Florence, 1979)

Ullman, W., 'Julius II and the schismatic cardinals', in *Schism, heresy and religious protest*, ed. D. Baker, Studies in church history, 9 (Cambridge, 1972)

Ursolini, I., *Inclytae nationis Florentiae familiae suprema romani pontificatus ac sacra cardinalatus dignitate illustratae* (Rome, 1706)

Valentini, R., and G. Zucchetti (eds.), *Codice topografico della città di Roma*, 4 vols. (Rome, 1953)

Vanegas Rizo, A., 'Il palazzo cardinalizio della Rovere ai SS. Apostoli a Roma', *Quaderni dell'istituto di storia dell'architettura*, 14 (1977–8)

Vasi, M., *Itinerario istruttivo di Roma* (Rome, 1744)

Verde, A., *Lo studio fiorentino, 1473–1503*, 4 vols. (Florence/Pistoia, 1973–85)

Verdon, T., 'Environments of experience and imagination', in *Christianity and the renaissance: image and religious imagination in the quattrocento*, ed. T. Verdon and J. Henderson (Syracuse, 1990)

Vespucci, A., *Lettera a Piero Soderini* (Florence, 1957)

Volpe, G., *Volterra* (Florence, 1923)

Volpicella, L., *Federico d'Aragona e la fine del regno di Napoli nel MDI* (Naples, 1908)

Wedgewood Kennedy, R., *Alessio Baldovinetti* (New Haven, 1938)

Weinstein, D., *Savonarola and Florence* (Princeton, 1970)

Weiss, R., *The renaissance discovery of classical antiquity* (Oxford, 1969)

Winspeare, F., *La congiura dei cardinali contro Leone X* (Florence, 1957)

Wodka, J., 'Zur Geschichte der nationalen Protektorate der Kardinäle an der römischen Kurie', *Publikationen des Österreichischen Historischen Instituts in Rom*, VI, 1 (Innsbruck, 1938)

INDEX

307